HELEN MORGAN

HELEN MORGAN

THE ORIGINAL TORCH SINGER AND ZIEGFELD'S LAST STAR

Christopher S. Connelly

A note to the reader: This volume contains several instances of racially insensitive language. The author has chosen to document the original terminology to provide full historical context for the events under discussion. Discretion is advised.

Published by The University Press of Kentucky

Scholarly publisher for the Commonwealth, serving Bellarmine University, Berea College, Centre College of Kentucky, Eastern Kentucky University, The Filson Historical Society, Georgetown College, Kentucky Historical Society, Kentucky State University, Morehead State University, Murray State University, Northern Kentucky University, Spalding University, Transylvania University, University of Kentucky, University of Louisville, University of Pikeville, and Western Kentucky University.

Editorial and Sales Offices: The University Press of Kentucky
663 South Limestone Street, Lexington, Kentucky 40508-4008
www.kentuckypress.com

Library of Congress Cataloging-in-Publication Data

Names: Connelly, Christopher S., author.
Title: Helen Morgan : the original torch singer and Ziegfeld's last star / Christopher S. Connelly.
Description: Lexington : The University Press of Kentucky, 2024. | Series: Screen classics | Includes bibliographical references and index.
Identifiers: LCCN 2024010047 | ISBN 9781985900585 (hardcover) | ISBN 9781985900592 (paperback) | ISBN 9781985900615 (pdf) | ISBN 9781985900622 (epub)
Subjects: LCSH: Morgan, Helen, 1900-1941. | Ziegfeld, Flo, 1869-1932. | Kern, Jerome, 1885-1945. Show boat. | Hammerstein, Oscar, II, 1895-1960. Show boat. | Singers—United States—Biography. | Actors—United States—Biography. | Radio actors and actresses—United States—Biography. | Popular culture—United States—History—20th century. | Prohibition—United States—History—20th century. | LCGFT: Biographies.
Classification: LCC ML420.M617 C66 2024 | DDC 782.0092 [B]—dc23/eng/20240305
LC record available at https://lccn.loc.gov/2024010047

This book is printed on acid-free paper meeting the requirements of the American National Standard for Permanence in Paper for Printed Library Materials.

Manufactured in the United States of America.

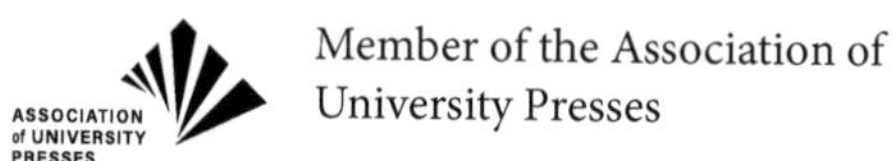

Member of the Association of University Presses

For my parents

Contents

Acknowledgments

More years ago than I care to admit, I told Miles Kreuger I was contemplating writing a Helen Morgan biography and asked him to talk me out of it. Instead, he mentored me through the process. For that, and for his friendship, my grateful thanks. Kreuger introduced me to Herbert G. Goldman, whose *Jolson: The Legend Comes to Life* remains the gold standard of show business biography. Goldman's tutelage, especially in regard to the science of compiling touring production playdates, proved invaluable.

I am humbled by the warm reception I received at the Margaret Herrick Library, Academy of Motion Picture Arts and Sciences; Billy Rose Theatre Division, New York Public Library; Oscar Hammerstein II Archive, Library of Congress; L. Tom Perry Special Collection, Brigham Young University; George Eastman House; UCLA Film & Television Archive; and the Fox, Warner Bros., and Universal Archives, School of Cinematic Arts, University of Southern California. The staff of all these institutions went above the call of duty in assisting this first-time author.

A special note of thanks to the Free Library of Philadelphia. Geraldine Duclow and Karen Suni of the Theatre Collection and everyone in the Rare Book Department graciously offered repeated access to Helen's scrapbooks, which served as my road map. This book could not have been written without them.

I would like to express my gratitude to David Pierce and everyone at the Media History Digital Library for making so many trade papers available to researchers online. Ditto to newspapers.com and all other entities that have and continue to digitize local newspapers.

The following archive employees graciously answered my questions, often by mailing packets filled with relevant photocopies: John Perriro (the Metropolitan Opera Archives), Barbara File (Metropolitan Museum of Art), Neil B. Todd (New England Historic Genealogical Society), Emily Clark

(Chicago Historical Society), Harold L. Miller (the State Historical Society of Wisconsin), Vincent Ancona (the Museum of San Diego History), Cynthia Murphy (Connecticut Valley Historical Museum), Mario Robert and Nicole Fontaine (Bibliothèque de Montreal), Sarah Montgomery (National Archives of Canada), Joan L. Clark (Cleveland Public Library), Jeff Korman (Enoch Pratt Free Library, Baltimore), Agatha P. Kalkanis (Music and Performing Arts Department, Detroit Public Library), James D'Arc (L. Tom Perry Special Collection, Brigham Young University), Steven Hallberg (Oregon Historical Society), S. J. Boldrick (Miami-Dade Public Library System), Jeanne T. Newlin (Harvard Theatre Collection), and Alice Lawlis (Ulster County Clerk's Office, New York).

Danville, Illinois, native Herb Depke offered invaluable assistance in organizing the Riggin, Coon/Morgan, and Lang family trees. Betty Morgan Asato and Gary Wilkins shared stories of the colorful histories of their families. Lois Cooper, Donna Gash, Lisa Imler, Donna Prather, Freda Gribbin, Ron Woodward, Kathy Burcher, Betty Gaff, Vivian Edwards, and Harold Long helped track down Helen's school records and other data concerning the Morgan and Lang families in and around Danville. Margie Yee and Kevin Cullen of the *Danville Commercial-News* were more than generous in providing access to old newspaper articles on Helen and her family.

Greg Plunges (National Archives and Records Administration) saw to it I obtained copies of the Morgan Prohibition case files.

In Chicago, Christina A. Reynen tracked down numerous legal and genealogical records for me. Others were equally helpful in visiting archives in my stead when traveling proved impractical: Bradd Bambo, Marion Bérubé, Robert M. Fells, Chuck Harter, David and Graceann Macleod, and Manivone Tangpraserth.

I wish to express my gratitude to those who spoke and/or corresponded with me concerning Morgan: Polly Bergen, Violet Carlson, Danny Dare, Elizabeth Collins, Kitty Carlisle Hart, Jean Howard, Art Horwitz, Mark Johnson, Allan Jones, John Latham, Arthur Loew Jr., Morgan Loew, Marian Seldes, and Walter Scharf.

Dr. Lokke Heiss and Dr. Kevin Connelly offered historical medical expertise. Josh Borden and Steven Capsuto translated French- and Spanish-language newspaper articles. Stephen Cole, Larry Moore, Alan Gomberg, and Rolando Salazar graciously provided their musical and musical theater expertise. In the days before DVD and TCM, David Bakish and Edith Klotz provided me with VHS copies of Helen's films.

Acknowledgments

My thanks to those who read various iterations of the manuscript and offered valuable feedback: Robin Gutkin, Jack Pelham, Joan Myers, and Dr. Daniel Helminiak.

The Daughters of Naldi, the sorority of vintage film scholars, offered friendship, advice, and long-distance research assistance. Key players were Joan Myers, Donna Hill, Mary Mallory, and Greta de Groat.

Eve Golden kindly introduced me to the good people of University Press of Kentucky. My thanks to Ashley S. Runyon, Margaret Kelly, and everyone at the press who guided me through the process and made this a better book.

I would like to thank Dr. Richard Koszarski, who replied to innumerable emails concerning *Applause* and East Coast film production with the patience of Job. Richard Barrios proved equally tolerant in guiding me through today's publishing landscape. Finally, I would like to thank my husband, James C. Goodwyne, who has lived with Helen almost as long as I have. He may not have considered proofreading, researching, and operating microfilm readers as part of the bargain, but he did it anyway.

Prologue

Songs from the Heart

In 1940, when reviewing Helen Morgan's act, Malcolm Johnson quipped, "Has any other performer within recent memory remained a celebrity so long on the basis of one role?"[1]

Johnson, and others, deemed Helen a one-trick pony: she could play Julie in *Show Boat*—and nothing else. Actually, she spent most of her career in revues, where she danced, sang in a variety of styles, and exhibited a flair for light comedy. Few performers of the Roaring Twenties and Sophisticated Thirties diversified as much as Helen: she was *everywhere*. She worked for Florenz Ziegfeld and was a popular radio and recording artist. She acted in silent films and weathered filmdom's transitions, first to the talkies in 1929 and later to the Production Code in 1934.

Helen Morgan did not invent the torch song, but it meshed perfectly with her unique vocal stylings. In an age when singers pushed out, she drew people in. Something special happened when she connected with a song of lost love. With little formal training, she turned "The Man I Love" and "Why Was I Born?" into one-act plays. Audiences had never experienced anything like her. Her torch songs caused a sensation that first pigeonholed and then eclipsed her.

She made headlines as a cabaret hostess. At her height, she was second only to Texas Guinan as the queen of New York's nightlife. These women beat the federal government in court and helped turn the tide against Prohibition. Helen continued to play the clubs though she preferred to work elsewhere, for while Repeal legalized liquor, gambling remained criminalized. The raids continued, and the mob still controlled the game.

For twenty years, she remained a study in contradiction: part "baby-talk" flapper in the Helen "Boop-Boop-a-Doop" Kane tradition, part Auntie

Publicity still for the 1927 production of *Show Boat*: the grand baby on a baby grand. (Author's collection)

Mame sophisticate. Onstage, she incorporated her debilitating stage fright into the act. Her wide-eyed terror made her weepy ballads all the more touching. However, it is important to remember that the image of the tragic torch singer was largely an act. Offstage, she was a delight, giggling through life with a sly glance and an outrageous pun. Ashton Stevens, dean of American critics, called her "the most untouched worldling" he ever met.[2]

Helen's addictive personality manifested itself not only in alcoholism but in acts of charity that exceeded human reason. As her fortunes increased and those of her country tanked, the child of poverty took it upon herself to spread her financial bounty everywhere. Friends feared that Helen had a pathological need to exit life as poor as she entered it.

To climax their 1957 biopic *The Helen Morgan Story*, Warner Brothers placed their Helen (Ann Blyth) in Bellevue, shaking from delirium tremens.

Yes, Helen drank. A lot. Like many Prohibition veterans, she paid for that rot-gut liquor later in life—but she remained a highly functioning alcoholic throughout most of her career. She never risked the employment of others with her bad behavior. Her reliance on brandy prematurely aged her and robbed her of her dancing ability, but she remained a safe bet long after *Show Boat* entered dry dock.

There was never a reason for Warners to up the melodrama. Enough drama and heartache existed in her life to plot a dozen films. She sang for royalty, worked for gangsters, beat the Feds in court, welcomed Charles Lindbergh to Paris, assisted victims of the Depression, campaigned for Franklin D. Roosevelt, and mothered everyone, from chorus girls to John F. Kennedy. She also created the role of Julie in *Show Boat*.

This is her story.

1

"Only Make Believe"

Helen Morgan's story begins and ends with Lulu Lang.

In 1877, Shadrach Lang set up a farm in Fountain County, Indiana, with Emma Scheckels Foreman and her son from a previous marriage. Shadrach and Emma's first child, Vida, arrived in 1878. The Langs moved to Bloomfield, Iowa, before Lulu's birth on February 4, 1882.[1] Returning to Indiana, the family welcomed two more boys and a girl—Grover, Elsie, and Ora Lee—before Emma died.

While grieving their mother, Vida moved to Chicago, and Lulu briefly ran the household—until twenty-nine-year-old Lillie Henry became the second Mrs. Shadrach Lang on July 16, 1899. Perhaps the seventeen-year-old clashed with her stepmother, or perhaps it was as simple as love, but Lulu Lang married Frank Allen Riggin on September 3, 1899, outside, at the side of the road, literally on the state line near Danville, Illinois.[2]

Frank Riggin, born in Attica, Indiana, on January 5, 1880, was the youngest of Lewis and Mary Ella May Riggin's four surviving offspring, and their only son.[3] Frank never escaped the shadow of his father, a Civil War veteran, cattle dealer, and township trustee who towered over his diminutive son by more than six inches.

Frank's own military career, during the Spanish-American War, proved as brief as it was undistinguished. While training at Camp Thomas, Georgia, Frank suffered from malaria and chronic diarrhea. He returned home ten weeks after he had left. He did not suffer alone. Overcrowding and unsanitary conditions served as an incubator for typhoid and malaria—and proved indicative of mismanagement and inhumane conditions throughout the country's military bases. Ultimately, 1,284 soldiers lost their lives without ever having seen action, with 343 from Camp Thomas alone.

~

Lewis Riggin provided the newlyweds with a Fountain County farm mortgage-free, but the marriage faltered. Frank remained weak from heart trouble and alternating bouts of diarrhea and constipation, which plagued him for the remainder of his life.[4] Then, on June 21, 1901, Lulu delivered, prematurely, a stillborn son.[5] Reeling from the loss, Frank sold the farm and joined his father's cattle business. In April 1902, he left Lulu, who was pregnant with their second child.

Lulu moved into a little house by the Danville railroad tracks. She worked in a hotel and kept her condition a secret until the night she called out sick and faced the trauma of childbirth, this time alone. At 12:15 a.m. on August 2, she gave birth, again prematurely, to a three-pound girl, whom she named Helen Emma.[6] The choice of the middle name was a valentine to Lulu's mother. Twelve days later, Lulu sheepishly returned to the hotel with an alibi for her unauthorized absence. Her boss took one look at the infant lying in a two-handed market basket, and Helen became the pet of both the hotel staff and its guests.[7]

The poor often rubbed liquor on a baby's gums to ease teething pains. Lulu did as well and also employed spirits as a pacifier whenever Helen fussed. Liquor became mother's milk to Helen. Polly Bergen believed that Lulu inadvertently triggered her daughter's biological propensity for alcoholism..[8]

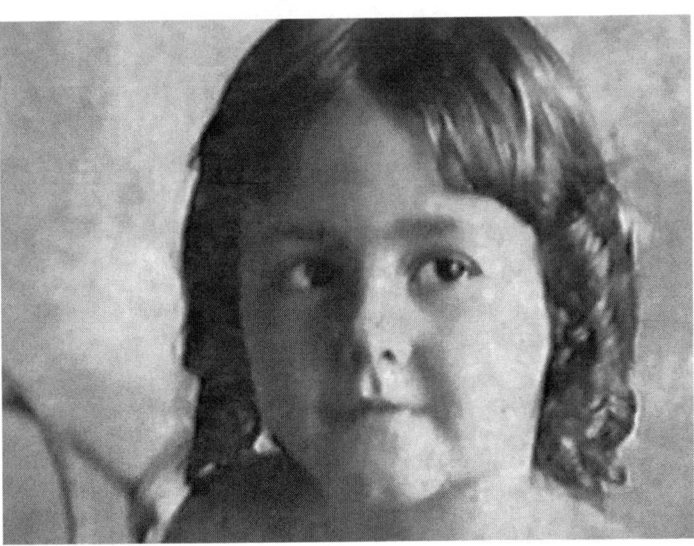

Helen, about age three. (Author's collection)

Frank sued for divorce, denying paternity and charging Lulu with habitual drunkenness and multiple accounts of adultery.[9] Lulu's first tryst, with John C. Purdy, ostensibly happened in September 1900, nine months before the birth of Lulu's premature, stillborn son (someone crossed out this event in the argument and did not introduce it as evidence). Another assignation purportedly took place in Danville's Brunswick Hotel with Charles Watts on November 4, 1901. Also born premature, Helen could not have been the issue of this act.[10]

The court granted Frank his divorce on January 29, 1903. Indiana law required a one-year waiting period before a divorcé could remarry, a fact that the local press reported when announcing Frank's marriage to Anna Watkins Goodwine on February 21 in Attica. Presumably, Lewis Riggin's political connections ensured that no one charged Frank with bigamy.[11]

Frank Riggin in 1938. The resemblance to his daughter is unmistakable. (Courtesy of the *Danville Commercial-News*)

A month later, Frank denounced the paternity of his daughter in his military pension.[12] In 1908, Anna gave birth to a son, Edgar Allan Riggin, a name later listed in Lewis Riggin's obituary as a surviving grandchild. Helen's was not.[13]

Lulu, in turn, wed William Wilkins, a widower and coal miner ten years her senior, on July 16, 1903, in Danville.[14]

Dan Beckworth founded Danville in 1827. The Vermilion River town prospered as a transportation center and, for a time, was bigger than Chicago. Abraham Lincoln practiced law there from 1841 to 1859. When rail displaced the river as the preferred means of transport, Danville, the state's largest coal producer, became a major rail town.

Also living in Danville was Lulu's father, who had abandoned farming for carpentry. Lillie gave Shadrach a son, Arthur Lewis, and two daughters, Bertha and Ruby. The girls became more like sisters than aunts to Helen.

Having remarried in haste, Lulu repented at leisure. Wilkins did not work steadily and drank his wages when he did. Arguments followed. In 1905, he walked out. Lulu and Helen left Danville and moved in with Vida and her husband, Webster O. Jones, on Chicago's South Side.[15] In 1908, with Vida's help on the witness stand, Lulu sued Wilkins for divorce.[16] Desertion was easy to prove, but Lulu, with no eyewitnesses, also charged her husband with domestic abuse: less than a month into their marriage, Wilkins, in a drunken rage, had threatened to kill her. A week after he left, the couple attempted reconciliation. When the meeting turned argumentative, Wilkins punched Lulu. A son from another Wilkins marriage later called Wilkins "the meanest son of a bitch to ever live,"[17] but one should not underestimate the lessons Lulu, and later Helen, learned from Frank Riggin: when obtaining a divorce, leave no character trait unassassinated.

During his brief tenure as her father, Wilkins had little effect on Helen's development, but the onus of being a poor relation compounded her growing body-shaming issues. The family considered Helen, with her dark hair and hazel eyes, homely in comparison to her blue-eyed, blonde mother and aunts. "Pretty is as pretty does," her mother would coo, but no words eased her daughter's pain.[18]

Genetically, Helen inherited the stamina of the Langs, but she was prone to sickness, like the Riggins. While decorating clay models during a kindergarten craft activity, Helen splashed paint in her eyes. By the time Lulu arrived at the school, her daughter could no longer see. For a year, mother and daughter tried multiple clinics and eye drops. One day, while Helen was walking past a man painting a building, a fire engine roared by. She turned her bandaged head toward the noise and took in the full glare from the wet red paint. Helen started to cry; she could see again. Gradually, her sight improved, but never to the point of 20/20 vision. She lived in constant terror that she would again lose her sight. Whenever makeup or other foreign matter got into her eyes, she became panic-stricken until the burning subsided.[19]

With the accident came two unintentional benefits. First was Helen's reliance on her hearing to compensate for the vision loss, which, in turn, only increased her interest in singing. As a toddler, Helen once mounted the ironing board while her mother starched the wash. In all seriousness, she announced, "I will now sing 'Three Blind Mice.'"

When Helen finished, Lulu applauded with gusto. "Marvelous! You will be a great star and make $1 million. What will you do with all that money, darling?"

"Spend it," Helen said, "or give it away."

The second benefit became apparent later in life. Helen suffered lifelong, debilitating stage fright, yet, in the glare of a spotlight, in even the smallest boîte, she could never make out the patrons in the first row. What she did not see, she did not fear.

One night, when she was seven, mother and daughter attended a picnic where Lulu, no athlete, played ball. Before going to bed, Helen removed her stockings and threw them aside. They fell behind her bed. The following morning, Helen could not reach them, and Lulu was too sore to move, let alone crawl under the bed to retrieve her daughter's hosiery. She told the girl to run out and play without them. Already suffering from hives, Helen unknowingly played in poisonous weeds. She scratched, infecting her hives so badly that she could not walk. Lulu pacified her devastated child by teaching her to sew. She also encouraged her to read to keep herself company. Even after the hives healed, Helen did not walk normally for several months.[20]

In late 1906, recently widowed Eli Jones asked his nephew, Webster, to take in his youngest daughters, Desylvia and Devida Mae. Childless, Webster and Vida agreed, and Helen found herself with two more "sisters."

While close, the girls did not always get along. One summer, Helen sold perfume door-to-door, not for cash but for toys. She worked until she earned a doll for each Jones girl as well as for herself. Despite being four years younger, Devida bullied Helen, who rarely endured the taunts and hairpulling for long before crying to Lulu. Her need for acceptance only made Helen try harder: her first gambit was always in the form of a gift.[21]

Not long after divorcing Wilkins, Lulu met thirty-one-year-old Tom Morgan. After a brief courtship, they ran off to St. Joseph, Michigan, where they tied the knot on August 12, 1909.[22] Both Lulu and Helen took Morgan's surname, but Tom never formally adopted his stepdaughter. Nor was he, technically, a Morgan himself. Born Thomas Coon in Louisville, Kentucky, on January 27, 1878, he was the second son of Louis Coon Jr. and Ellen Meehan.

The Coons were a rough lot. In 1882, baker Lambert Grunloh hit one of Louis Coon's sons, likely Thomas. The next day, as a streetcar passed the bakery, Louis jumped off and fired his gun three times. One shot missed. One hit Grunloh's son in the knee. The last struck the back of the baker, who, presumably, was running from the scene. Coon calmly resumed his post as the trolley's conductor.[23]

The Coons fled to the north, where they assumed the surname of Morgan, perhaps as a corruption of Ellen's maiden name. It did not take Louis "Morgan" long to find railroad work in Danville. When they came of age, his boys went into the business. Tom was working as a switchman in Chicago when he met Lulu.[24] The couple settled in Danville, first on Main, on the wrong side of the tracks, or in this case, the wrong bank of the Vermilion River. Cal Jamison operated a grocery store at the corner of Main and Third. Jamison's son Danny was Helen's first crush. She rode with him in his wagon as he made deliveries, while Disa, his younger sister, became her lifelong friend.[25] The two attended the Grant School together in the days when each of the six rooms sported its own stove for heat and kerosene lamps for light.[26]

Jamison was also a minister in the mission church that occupied the top floor of the building. Billy Sunday once preached there. It was there that Helen sang in public for the first time. Her soprano partner in their duet of "Don't You Know the World Is Dying for a Little Bit of Love" became so frightened that she never squeaked out a note. Helen, equally terrified, sang the alto harmony at the top of her voice, solo.[27]

With acts of charity ranging from small to profligate, Helen spent her life atoning for her perceived sins. She did not simply buy love, as she did with Devida Mae Jones; Helen could not stomach the sight of anyone as unloved as she believed herself to be. When some Grant School kids mocked a Mormon girl whose dark clothes and stockings made her stand out, Helen shamed her classmates into accepting her. As one friend put it, "The only way she found relief from her own pain was to share the sufferings of others."[28]

SCHOOLMATES—Helen Morgan, LeRoy Swisher and Spot, the Jameson's dog, play at old coal docks, South Gilbert and Catlin Road. Picture was taken during the time Helen lived in Danville and attended Grant School.

School days in Danville. (Courtesy of the *Danville Commercial-News*)

~

The Morgans moved to a rental property at 106 South Washington in Danville proper, but on the East Side, near the railroad where Tom worked.[29] Lulu took in boarders: specifically, her sister Elsie and her husband, Edgar Lopp. Helen had first assumed household chores back in Chicago, where she washed dishes. In Danville, she threw rocks at passing trains to spur engineers into throwing pieces of coal back at her, which she picked up and took home. She also cooked. Once, she rolled out noodles, dried them, and prepped the meat, but Lulu's instructions did not mention boiling the water before tossing in the noodles. They came out stuck together, like mutated octopuses. Nonetheless, Lulu served them. Helen later laughed: "They were almost dumplings!"[30]

Helen desperately wished she could buy every beautiful thing she saw for her mother. One Valentine's Day, she sighed over five-pound boxes of chocolates in a shop's window. Without the funds to purchase her prize, she spent what she had on penny candy, ran home, found a lodger's discarded shoebox, filled it with the sweets, and decorated it with what she found around the house. Lulu was thrilled, but Helen knew it paled in comparison to the box in the store window. She needed to work harder to validate her worth. She needed money.[31]

Around 1912, the family moved to the 1000 block of Kimber Street.[32] Helen continued her education at the Jackson School and, finally, the Washington School. She appeared in two plays at Washington, the second as Topsy in a skit marking Lincoln's birthday.

A preteen Helen Morgan. (Free Library of Philadelphia, Theater Collection)

While attending a nighttime class to improve her skills, Lulu, unable to afford a sitter, deposited Helen at the local library. She came back to pick her up just before closing time. Helen started at one end of the library and read everything in sight, "until [her] eyes got so bad the school teacher told [her] mother [she'd] have to stop. So she had to quit night school, poor darling."[33]

It lasted less than four years, but the closest thing Helen had to a normal childhood was her time as Tom Morgan's stepdaughter.

In early 1913, Morgan moved his family to Hamilton, Indiana, just across the border from Chicago. Whatever had brought Tom and Lulu together unraveled. Arguments turned violent. Lulu banned Tom from the house. He retaliated by breaking into their cottage and slicing a trunkful of her clothes into ribbons. The authorities arrested and fined him. Lulu obtained a legal separation on July 5 and a divorce eighteen months later.[34]

Bitter, Tom returned to his father's house in Danville.[35]

Just before noon on September 25, Tom Morgan and Edward Fowler got into a brawl at the William Haines Saloon. After the scuffle, Morgan went to another bar before returning home, where the police were waiting. His father advised him to turn himself in: Fowler had died of a fracture at the base of his skull, the result of six to ten blows to the head.

Morgan claimed that Fowler threw the first punch: Morgan had merely defended himself. The police, suspecting that the brawl had been a botched robbery, claimed that Morgan dealt the fatal blow with a blackjack. Because of the lack of evidence, the police later dropped the robbery charge.

In November, Tom Morgan stood trial for murder. The jury remained deadlocked, and a mistrial seemed imminent until they obtained permission to vote on manslaughter instead. On the lesser charge, they reached a consensus: guilty. Throughout it all, Morgan showed no emotion. His father and siblings stood by him in court. His estranged wife and daughter did not.[36]

In early 1916, weeks after his release, Tom Morgan, his father, and his siblings moved to Hammond.[37] Tom returned to his old job as a switchman on the Chicago and Eastern Illinois Railroad. In 1917, Hammond police accused him of a smash-and-grab jewelry store robbery.[38] He beat the rap and, on December 8, 1918, completed his parole.[39] Three years later, police charged him with complicity in an employee holdup aboard a Chicago-bound train. Morgan beat this rap too.[40]

Fifteen years would pass before Helen saw her father again, and she lived with the emotional scars from her daddies forever. If her beautiful mother

The Morgan boys—Michael, Henry, Dan, Louis, Tom, and John—at Edward's funeral in 1930. (Author's collection)

could not find and keep a man, what chance did Helen, who believed herself to be homely, have?

Lulu, having lost a son, and having three ex-husbands, invested all of her love and energy into the one constant around her. Simply put, Helen was the love of Lulu's life.

After leaving Tom Morgan, Lulu relocated to Gary, Indiana, where Helen worked outside the home for the first time, as a tea packer. Before long, mother and daughter returned to Chicago: "It was cheaper to move than be thrown out."[41] Lulu took in washing but worked primarily as a waitress. Helen cadged many a free meal where her mother worked.

While Tom Morgan stood trial in Danville, Helen contracted scarlet fever. She convalesced at the free Cook County Hospital until January 2, 1914. "There were twenty-six other kids in the contagion ward and their families used to send them ice cream, but mother was lucky to have money for carfare to the institution."[42]

Helen befriended Mike Fritzel, who opened his first great Chicago nightspot, the Arsonia Café, in 1904. That was where Bee Palmer invented the shimmy and, later, Gilda Gray perfected it. Other Arsonia veterans included bandleader Abe Lyman and singer Benny Fields. Florenz Ziegfeld picked Cliff "Ukulele Ike" Edwards out of Fritzel's joint.[43] Sometimes after school, while her mother was working, Helen hung out at Fritzel's, which was mere blocks east of home. Occasionally she sang songs like "Beautiful Isle D'Amour," copying the gestures she had seen others use onstage. Patrons gave her money. Fritzel kept a fatherly eye on the teen, even promising to marry her when she grew up.

Thanks to her love of books and need for validation, Helen was a good student despite multiple illnesses and as many school jumps. During the two years she attended Chicago's Brown School, Helen was a straight-A student, regardless, or perhaps because, of another change in the household.[44] In what was now a pattern, on February 10, 1916, Lulu wed Edward G. Kroeter, a bartender and a mean drunk.[45]

Helen did not cotton to her new daddy. She rebelled.

Over time, Helen rewrote her backstory, purging those awkward extra husbands from Lulu's *résumé*. Occasionally, she slipped. In 1930, Helen recalled her time under Edward Kroeter's roof: "I had a stepfather whose creed was—no work—no eats . . . so I worked."[46]

Within days of completing the eighth grade, Helen was working for the National Biscuit Company, presumably at the branch at the corner of Washington and North Morgan, about a mile east of the Kroeter digs. For twelve hours a day, she stood and lowered cracker boxes down a chute. Management believed that well-manicured women could maintain a faster work pace, and so Helen sat before the company's house manicurist, who marveled at the gawky teenager's beautiful hands. Helen resolved to cultivate her newfound asset.

Helen escaped the factory when a nurse in her boarding house suggested that Helen help alleviate the wartime shortage by becoming a practical nurse.

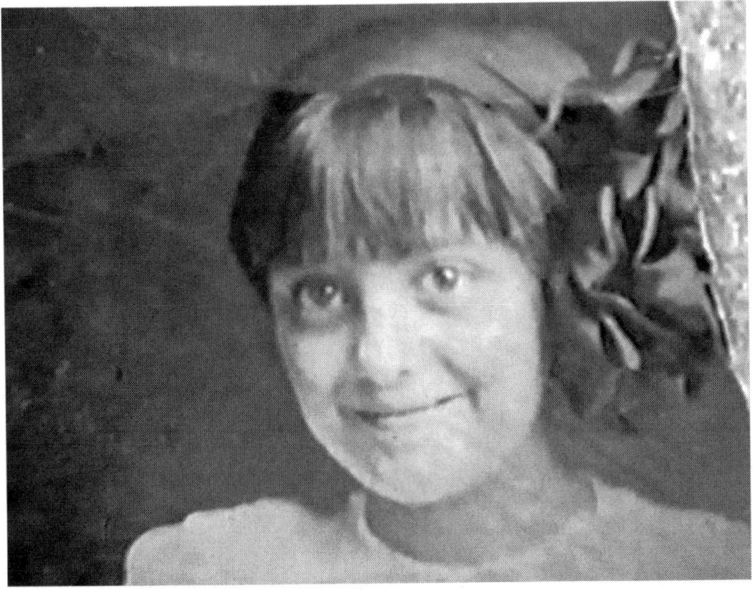

Helen, around the time she graduated from the eighth grade. (Author's collection)

Helen underwent cursory training, such as giving herself hypodermics filled with salt water. Satisfied with her pupil's progress, the nurse lent Helen a uniform and a pair of sensible shoes and sent the teen on her way. She was grateful for the work but lamented that her new wardrobe only added to what she considered her dowdy appearance.

Helen's first case was a girl with scarlet fever. Before long, Helen fell ill and administered half of the patient's medicine to herself. She also started smoking to keep awake while she worked nights. Her charge died, but Helen pursued her interest in health care by working a summer as a receptionist for Dr. James H. Williamson.[47] She lived with her aunt Elsie and her second husband, Robert Dillon.

Nurse Helen also worked during the 1918–1919 Spanish flu pandemic. When an elderly man died under her care, it fell to Helen to prepare the body. The ninety-dollar fee was welcome, "but it nearly made [her] a nervous wreck."[48] Her melancholy, fear of death, and that hated uniform factored into her decision, but in the end, she abandoned the profession because she could not afford the years of study required to become a registered nurse.

While in Danville, Helen also wrapped vegetables for a local grocer before her aunt Bertha secured her a job collecting delinquent payments for the local telephone company. Undone by the suffering of others, Helen quit after a few days.

In late 1918, Helen visited her father.[49] Twelve months before, drunk on whiskey, Frank Riggin attempted to kill his wife and son, but the shots he fired had gone wild. His aim was no better in his subsequent shootout with the police. They briefly committed Riggin to Indianapolis's Central Hospital for the Insane after he set fire to the mattress in his holding cell. Riggin later underwent the Keeley gold treatment for alcoholism in nearby Plainfield.[50]

The reunion went so well, Helen took the Riggin surname.

Returning to Chicago, she sorted buttons upstairs at Marshall Field's Department Store. When she found twelve that matched, she packaged them for sale. Confined within a cagelike metal cubicle, Helen sang to herself to break the overwhelming silence in the stifling heat. Management reprimanded her: she was not there to sing. Yet, in time, she escaped her prison to become chief mail-order clerk in the Trimmings Department.[51]

Weary of an endless parade of hand-me-downs from her extended family, Helen invested much of her five-dollar weekly salary on new clothes. Physical attributes she considered liabilities revealed themselves as assets. She had long despaired over her "wishy-washy" hazel eyes, but she eventually cherished their chameleon quality and employed elaborate eye shadow and mascara schemes to accentuate them.

Having completed the transition from ugly duckling to swan, Helen started dating.

On Sundays, she sang in the choir at the First Congregational Church. Depending on the version of the tale she spun, Helen took elocution—or voice—lessons from her church's choir director whose brother was a booking agent (or dance director).[52] Marveling at her legs, he offered to get her into the business. Helen agreed, but she harbored no dreams of artistic triumph. Stage work afforded a luxury unavailable to Lulu: Helen could wait to marry until she found a man to support her.

Quitting Marshall Field's, Helen debuted as a toe dancer in the chorus of the Marigold Gardens either in the March 1919 revue *Spring Joys* or, more likely, in May, when Bill Robinson broke the color barrier in *Starlight*.[53] Highlights of the later edition were "My Guiding Star," in which the girls came out on a darkened stage with illuminated stars in their hats, and "At the High Brown Babies' Ball," where the girls joined Muriel DeForrest in her celebrated shimmy. Specialty acts rotated in and out of *Starlight*; George Holland

and Rose Dockrill's Five Horses, which earned the odd distinction of being the first equestrian act in a Chicago cabaret, was among them.

The pride of German proprietors Karl, Emil, Robert, and Max Eitel, the Marigold began its storied existence as the Bismarck Gardens, the grandest of Chicago's sprawling belle époque wonderlands. The Bismarck featured a Dutch windmill, château, electric fountain, marble dance terrace, and, beginning in 1916, spectacular floorshows. Weather permitting, the revue played at the garden outdoors, which sat 4,000; then, at eleven, they moved inside to the Marigold Room, which comfortably sat 2,500 in one of the first public buildings to boast air-conditioning. Following Ziegfeld's lead, producer/director Edward Beck let the music take care of itself and concentrated on his girls. In an era where clubs used perhaps a dozen chorines, Beck employed up to forty. Helen, for a time, was among them.[54]

Throughout World War I, the Eitels committed to America's struggle overseas. They sold $100,000 of Liberty bonds on a single night and renamed the Bismarck the less Teutonic Marigold Gardens. When local bluenoses and the Brewery Association lobbied the Chicago Board of Aldermen to ban entertainment where intoxicants were sold, Chicago's club owners applied for special permits for the duration of the war as a morale booster. In turn, the army and navy came out publicly in favor of Prohibition as a means of shielding the military from the temptations of the cabarets, prompting the

Marigold Gardens, Chicago. (Author's collection)

city council to abolish all special permits. Prohibition came to Chicago on May 1, 1918, thirty-three months ahead of the rest of the country.[55]

Having sunk $600,000 into improvements in their establishment, the Eitel brothers kept their girls and obeyed the dry law—on paper. Alcohol still flowed. When a Marigold patron brought out a flask and placed it on a vacant chair, a diligent waiter placed it beneath the tablecloth. The use of the "Volstead hump" ensured that liquor remained convenient but out of view.

Helen left the Marigold Gardens on July 3, 1919, when Lulu and Edward Kroeter proudly gave their daughter, Helen Emma *Riggin*, to William Realino Zeh in marriage.[56] After a honeymoon in the nation's capital, the couple briefly lived with the groom's parents before taking up residence in the Edgewater Beach Hotel on Chicago's North Side.

On the surface, "Grumpy" Zeh was a made-to-order stage-door johnny. His father, William J. Zeh, was a Washington, DC, merchant. His mother, Mary Ann Varnell Zeh, was one of the most prominent Catholics in the District and, after the family's move west in 1909, in Chicago. The Zehs arranged an ostentatious wedding at Holy Name Cathedral. Mary Ann's charitable works, including her support for Saint Vincent's Infant Asylum, impressed her new daughter-in-law. Despite her Protestant upbringing, Roman Catholicism so fascinated Helen that, for a time, she dreamed of becoming a nun.[57]

In reality, Helen's husband was hardly affluent, and her in-laws were less than ideal. Papa Zeh made his reputation procuring coal for the Theodore Roosevelt administration during the strike of 1902, but six years later, bankruptcy and the accusation that he appropriated $25,000 of company funds forced the Zehs to move.[58] He made a quick enemy of Chicago mayor Carter Harrison Jr., who squashed Zeh's attempt to turn his grocery store in the dry Wilson Avenue neighborhood into a saloon.[59] Mary Ann Zeh considered herself principally an artist, although others considered her primarily a prude. In 1921, she headed a campaign to force artist Claude Buck to either rename his peasant *Madonna and Child* something secular or repaint the mother's skirt so that it came down past her knees.[60]

Having had enough, after eleven weeks of marriage, Helen packed up her belongings and many of her husband's and returned to the Marigold Gardens.[61]

Bill Robinson led the fall revue, *Spotlights*, which bowed on October 8. During the minstrel-show finale, the girls climbed upon wooden posts that supported a fence around the dance floor. After the show, the girls remained in position, strumming banjos, while patrons danced.

Around this time, Helen committed to using her Morgan surname professionally: it had more marquee appeal than Helen Riggin—or Zeh.

While she danced in the clubs, she supplemented her income by modeling. At five feet, six inches, she was considered tall—a born clotheshorse. The combination of dark hair and alabaster skin gave her a striking appearance. Sometimes she did print and runway work for clothiers, and sometimes she posed for commercial artists.

The Marigold staff took advantage of Helen's industry. One night, when the front office needed to fill a hole in the program, they pushed Helen onto the stage to sing and yelled, "You're on!"[62] She created no sensation but gained experience as a singer. She worked up a specialty to fill in when the orchestra tired of playing for the dancing public. While she sang soprano in the church choir, she mimicked the lower-voiced women who sang at the Marigold when she rendered ditties like "If I Can't Get the One I Want" in what she considered a hot style. Her church choir director advised Helen to sing in her own voice.

Fellow Marigold chorines Muriel De Forest and Betty Campbell graduated to solo spots, but no such promotion came Helen's way.

Snowflurries ushered in the new year. When Beck abandoned the Gardens to pursue other interests, Elmer Floyd assembled the subsequent production, with a brand-new chorus, in New York. Whether by Floyd's choice or hers, cutting bait was the best move for Helen. In October 1921, Chicago City Hall ordered all cabarets to cease entertainment by 1:00 a.m. Business plummeted. Even blockbuster events like Rudolph Valentino's Mineralava tour and Roscoe "Fatty" Arbuckle's post-scandal stage debut failed to help. The Marigold closed on December 9, 1923.

Six months after Helen abandoned William Zeh, Lulu put Edward Kroeter behind her.

Lulu wanted a home of her own, but, from the day they married, Kroeter insisted they reside in boarding houses. In July 1917, boardinghouse matron Mamie Ward saw Kroeter slap Lulu hard across the face. If Helen had not already moved out, she found her means of escape soon after this event—but Lulu stood by her man.

In December 1918, Lulu made a present for the mother of her husband's boss. Kroeter intended to wrap it in newspaper, but Lulu insisted on boxing it properly. They argued. When she refused to hand over the gift, he knocked her unconscious, placed her in their bed, and left. Later, while attending to her, Mamie noticed bruises on Lulu's arm and marks on her face.

The Kroeters moved to Minnie Page's boarding house, where, on January 2, 1920, he became quarrelsome. Refusing to argue, Lulu left their room for the kitchen three floors below to fetch his dinner. She stopped on the second-floor landing to light the gas lamp to illuminate the stairs. Kroeter ran after her and choked her. Lulu screamed. Mutual friend and tenant Joseph P. Monaghan heard her cries, ran to investigate, and commanded the man to stop. Kroeter replied, "That's all right; this is me." Whether Kroeter simply let go of his wife or deliberately pushed her down the stairs remains unclear. In any case, Lulu fell, and another man ran up the stairs and caught her before she hit the floor. A boarder helped Lulu into the parlor and, later, to the police station, where she filed a complaint. Accompanied by two plainclothes police, she set out to evict her husband, but on the way, she saw Kroeter coming around the corner from the boarding house, his suitcases packed. He promised not to bother his wife again, but later, when Monaghan reprimanded him, Kroeter spat, "Joe, I don't want you to have any sympathy for Lulu; I'm going to get her yet."[63]

By the spring of 1920, Helen and Lulu moved to 4807 Washington Boulevard, where they lived for the next eighteen months. Helen never regretted rescuing her mother from her toxic environment, and she later joked, "Have you heard why the three little mice left home? Because they found out their father was a rat."[64]

Helen received an offer for a touring show. The nightclubs, for now, were behind her.

G. M. "Bronco Billy" Anderson, the film pioneer who appeared in the seminal 1903 film *The Great Train Robbery* and who later, with George Kirke Spoor, formed Essanay Studios, also produced for the theater. In 1919, he jumped on the *Follies* bandwagon by mounting *Frivolities of 1920*. The more the critics, outraged by the underdressed women, panned it, the better the business—until an influenza scare, followed by a blizzard, forced the *Frivolities* to shutter on Broadway.

The production toured, playing the major eastern cities before heading west. As the company crossed the Mississippi, the Blake and Amber Agency put out a call for more girls. Production manager Frank Hill saw a trio in Chicago. The Morgan girl seemed too shy to be a successful chorine, but, in desperation, he hired her anyway.[65] The road apples likely debuted in Salt

Lake City on June 10. Among the "frivols" in which Helen participated were the two act finales: one, an Arab fantasia called "Omar the Wine Maker," the other, a celebration of the League of Nations leading to a number of military weddings. The seaside romp "On a Moonlight Night" came in handy while playing Los Angeles, when all 125 girls, in bathing suits, romped in front of the motion picture cameras for the Jimmy Aubrey and Oliver Hardy Vitagraph short *The Decorator*.[66]

San Francisco hosted the 1920 Democratic Convention. Anderson added an additional *Frivolities* performance to allow the delegates more time to ogle the women but did not pay his chorines for the extra work. They complained to Actors' Equity. After San Francisco, business was spotty. While in Oakland, the Gille Show Print Company attached a lien on the production, preventing sets or costumes from leaving the theater until Anderson paid the $700 bill. After Labor Day, the troupe endured three months of one- and two-night stands as they inched their way back to the Midwest.

In December, the exhausted company returned to full-week stands. The show received good notices in St. Louis, but attendance was so poor that the production traveled COD to Kansas City, where the advance was adequate, but the notices were terrible. Business dried up again. Claiming that they had not received a penny in two weeks, chorines Kittie Kelley and Marion Taylor appealed to a free legal aid society. An attachment placed on the box office receipts helped the two girls but blocked the payment of all other expenses, including company salaries, until after the settlement of all other legal issues. When others in the company learned of the attachment, they contacted the Equity office in Chicago, which sent J. Marcus Keyes down to investigate.

Keyes signed up performers who were not yet union members, while Equity's New York office wired $5,000 to pay hotel bills and return fares. He got the theater manager, Joseph Glick, to split the box office receipts so that the cast would receive some of its back salary. By intermission, Anderson instructed Frank Hill by wire to disband and sell the production but sent no money to pay off the company. Keyes authorized the company to strike. Glick offered the audience a refund for their tickets or passes for the following week's attraction.[67]

Equity made good on their promise to the company, many of whom had been subsisting on apples. Among the claims for back payment came one note for ninety-five dollars—from Helen Morgan.[68]

~

Back in Chicago, Helen picked up occasional movie-house vaudeville gigs. Sometimes she danced, but often, she led the audience in following the bouncing ball while singing old favorites like "When It's Harvest Time in Old New Hampshire" and "Down Where the Silvery Rio Grande Wends Its Way."[69] When those gigs dried up, she toiled as a waitress and a manicurist.

It was during those slow months in 1921 that Helen most likely worked at Mike Fritzel's Friar's Inn and the Rainbo Gardens. Initially, Rainbo proprietor Fred Mann obeyed Chicago's prohibition ordinance, but he later gave his customers what they wanted. Raids followed, most notably on August 9, 1920.[70] While agents removed contraband, the underground network warned the nearby Marigold and Green Mill. When the raiders showed up at the other cabarets, they found nothing. It was Mann who changed the format from floorshow to vaudeville. Acts changed weekly, sometimes nightly. Later, the club turned to contests and door prizes to lure trade. Between April and August 1921, the Rainbo hosted a series of Toddle contests.[71] The popular dance, half foxtrot and half shimmy, inspired Fred Fisher to dub the Windy City "that toddling town" in his 1922 standard, "Chicago." Helen likely played the Rainbo as part of a local vaudeville act—and not for a long stay.

Helen danced, briefly, in *Bubbles*. Frank Stammers wrote the forty-minute flash act, and C. B. Maddock produced. The premise: A maid (Marjorie Leach) in a sculptor's (Robert O'Connor) studio feeds an errand boy (initially Robert Woolsey, later William Kent, and then Jack Norton) soup accidentally made with soap. The boy sees "bubbles," in the form of sixteen female statues, come to life. Doubling as dancers and showgirls, the women, led by Queenie Smith, paraded in abbreviated, if vaguely Grecian, attire. In one number, they impersonated history's famous vamps. Likely replacing an exiting chorine, Helen bowed with the company at Chicago's Majestic Theater on August 15, 1921, at the start of the act's second season.[72]

The act caught the attention of the Shubert Organization, and on or about September 3, Helen joined *The Passing Show of 1921* as the annual revue ended the Chicago stand of its tour.[73] Her time as a Shubert girl, most likely as a firefly in the "Dream Fantasies Ballet," which opened the second act, was short-lived. A catastrophic fire in the company baggage car outside Montreal on October 23 destroyed the production's costumes, prompting the Shuberts to trim some of its cast, including Helen, to cut their losses.[74]

Columnist Dorothy Dey later confirmed that Helen went to Montreal as a chorine, although Dey's contention that it was in "a second-rate touring show" seems dismissive of a mighty Shubert production, even of an edition below par for the series.[75]

Having no other prospects, Helen stayed in Montreal. More to the point, she had no reason to return to Chicago. On September 5, eight weeks after divorcing Edward Kroeter, Lulu returned to St. Joseph, Michigan, and married Frank Payne, a widowed traveling salesman and semiprofessional minstrel from upstate New York.[76] In March 1922, husband number five acquired the Clyde Hotel in Clyde, New York. A few weeks later, the Paynes previewed their new venture, called the New Collier, by hosting the American Legion Fair and Bazaar, replete with a Payne minstrel show. Helen traveled from Montreal to meet her new stepfather. It is unlikely that she performed.[77]

For the grand opening, held May 6, Lulu prepared the seven-course banquet. Frank engaged an orchestra and other local artists for the entertainment. The press raved, but it soon became clear that, with Prohibition the law of the land, a sleepy hamlet close to the Canadian border could not support an upscale hotel and restaurant without the revenue of alcohol sales. Within months, the Paynes lost the New Collier, and their marriage was all but over.

2

"Insufficient Sweetie"

In Montreal, Helen found work as a comptometer operator for the phone company. With boundless enthusiasm and no budget, she decorated her flat with crepe-paper curtains and chairs repurposed from beer cartons. Lulu visited and thought it looked grand. Helen's one extravagant acquisition was a piano and lessons. She dutifully practiced her Bach and Massenet—at least the top lines.[1]

Helen returned to the modeling trade, working for everyone from the Greenburg-Smith cloak-and-suit house to Kayser Italian Silk Underwear.[2] On January 3, 1923, she stood out from a bevy of eight mannequins modeling 120 creations before 1,500 people during a Holt Renfrew and Company fashion parade at Windsor Hall. The *Star* adored "the audacious young 'flapper' who yawned in her peach colored negligee and blew butterfly kisses to the audience."[3]

Two nights later, atop Mont-Royal, which overlooks the city, Governor-General Lord Byng officiated the opening ceremony of the six-week Winter Carnival. In addition to the sports and parades, the festival included the first Miss Canada competition.

As a prelude, local businesses sponsored twenty-eight women who competed for the title of Miss Montreal. Local readership would choose fifteen semifinalists via a voting coupon published in a souvenir newspaper. The winner would join the Miss Canada hopefuls at the end of the carnival.

Helen competed as Miss Mount Royal, under the sponsorship of the eponymous inn. The hotel manager, Vernon G. Cardy, claimed that his $12 million Beaux-Arts wonder was the biggest hostel in the British Empire when it opened on December 20, 1922.

In those early days, contestants represented their hometowns as often as states or provinces. Therefore, the winner of the Miss Montreal contest would

Helen models for Kayser Italian Silk Underwear. (Free Library of Philadelphia, Theater Collection)

compete in both the Miss Canada *and* Miss America Pageants. Marcelle Gauthier, Montreal's 1922 entry, wanted another trip to Atlantic City. She competed under the banner of La Patrie Publishing Company. To even the playing field, sponsors vied to get their candidate into the papers and before the voters. On January 13, in Mount Royal's Salon Doree, the Elks used a tape measure to compare their nominee, Evelyn Cathro, with Miss Mount Royal. A week later, Cardy used the contest as a sales pitch to lure Americans parched by Prohibition to his colossal château. He sent Helen to New York to meet with the reigning (and only two-time) Miss America, Mary Katherine Campbell.[4]

Bedecked in $50,000 worth of Holt Renfrew furs, Helen entrained to Manhattan. Mayor John F. Hylan received the beauties at city hall. Each sat for the noted illustrator Harrison Fisher. On Sunday, they worshipped at Marble Collegiate Church before visiting the local parks and the zoo and attending a reception at the Automobile Club of America, sponsored by its Canadian counterpart. Later, the beauties were feted at a supper dance at the Waldorf-Astoria and visited the private Sixty Club, the Hotel McAlpin, and Elmer Floyd's Palais Royale. Helen best enjoyed New York shopping.[5]

Helen and Miss America Mary Katherine Campbell meet at New York's City Hall. (Author's collection)

As Miss Mount Royal, Helen rewrote her family history. Chaperoned by Mrs. Robert Harris, a very proper Helen described herself as the daughter of a Montreal businessman. While being interviewed, Campbell revealed her plans to attend college in the fall. Unable to afford such a luxury, Helen briefly dropped character, bluntly stating that she was finished with school.

Helen, Campbell, and Mrs. Harris attended the *Follies*, where the beauties stood in their box seats draped with the Canadian and American flags, receiving thunderous applause from the audience and the cast. Will Rogers announced from the stage that Ziegfeld's Glorified Girls had rivals. "And if they wish to join us they will be welcome."[6]

On Monday, General J. Leslie Kincaid, vice president of the United Hotels Company of America and director of the Mount Royal Hotel, feted the ladies with a dinner, again at the Waldorf. His guests included film star Richard Barthelmess; *Follies* beauties Helen Lee Worthing, Martha Lorber, and Mary Lewis; and many of New York's fabled Four Hundred. On Tuesday, artist George Maillard Kesslère threw an equally star-studded housewarming bash at his East Fiftieth Street studio.[7]

While boarding a special car supplied by General Kincaid and the United Hotels Company of America for the return trip, Helen made an announcement: she would soon return to New York to act in films.

Miss America joined the Miss Montreal candidates at a luncheon at the Mount Royal, which Pathé News filmed, taking close-ups of their sponsored contestant, Janet MacDuff, as well as Helen and Campbell. Previously, Hearst's International News covered the Misses America and Mount Royal's meeting with Hylan.[8]

Campbell, Helen, and the American visitors visited the Park Toboggan Club atop Mont-Royal. Cheesecake photos of the international pals, including shots of Helen, in a one-piece swimsuit, blithely throwing snowballs, found their way into the rotogravures of papers across North America. The cold held no terror for Helen. Back in Danville, she and her friends had subscribed to the legend claiming that one would not catch a cold during the winter if one ran barefoot around the house in the snow three times. The stunt may not have built up immunity against the common cold, but it did foster Helen's lifetime aversion to wearing shoes and, particularly, stockings.

On January 24, the entourage took in George Arliss in *The Green Goddess* at His Majesty's Theatre, then entertained the actor after his performance.

Mary Katherine Campbell and Helen clown atop Mont-Royal. (Free Library of Philadelphia, Theater Collection)

Helen was rarely starstruck, but the venerable stage and, later, Oscar-winning actor proved a notable exception. Even in the late 1930s, Helen's debilitating stage fright increased exponentially when she heard that Arliss was out front. During one nightclub appearance, his presence compelled her to leave the stage to compose herself.[9]

By January 25, more than one hundred thousand votes had arrived at the carnival headquarters. Of the semifinalists, the top five candidates each received over ten thousand votes, and the other ten received in excess of five thousand each. Not surprisingly, Mademoiselles Marcelle Gauthier and Gabrielle Rivest, sponsored by *La Patrie* and *La Presse*, the daily papers that distributed the voting chits to the public, advanced.

Helen Morgan's name was not among the semifinalists.

Robert Harris, the Mount Royal's publicity man and husband of the ladies' chaperone, explained Helen's failure to make it to the semifinal round: she was the victim of an organized effort to blackball her from the contest.[10] "We have . . . a letter written by one of the contestants to another party with regard to officially protesting against Miss Helen Morgan's inclusion among the winners in the voting competition, on account of her being an American."[11]

Regardless, the hands-across-the-border stunt continued as planned with a supper dance in the Grand Ball Room of the Mount Royal Hotel.[12] The following afternoon, Helen and Campbell joined the other Miss Montreal hopefuls at a tea dance at the Windsor Hotel. Afterward, Campbell quietly returned to America.[13]

Helen also left Montreal, but not before attempting damage control in the French press: "I hope that each one understands that, while born in the U.S., I consider myself Canadian and will always consider myself as a Canadian, wherever I may be."[14]

Returning to New York and the Waldorf-Astoria, Helen secured membership with the National Variety Artists.[15] Robert Harris arranged one day of work: a personal appearance at the Long Branch Ice Boat and Yacht Club, near Sandy Hook, New Jersey. Helen posed one last time as Queen of the Ice with the oldest active iceboat skipper, Captain Elisha Price.

Helen turned her attention to film.

Shot for Inspiration Pictures in Fort Lee, New Jersey, the Richard Barthelmess vehicle *The Fighting Blade* was a Cromwellian-era swashbuckler. Helen figured prominently, but unbilled, in one superfluous scene. While Barthelmess munches an apple in the town square, three women flirt with him. As they walk by, two maids push the third, mortified lass (Helen) into the arms of the bemused hero.

The American film industry was firmly entrenched in Hollywood by the mid-1910s, but New York's film colony refused to die. The erratic history of

Helen's last modeling job: posing with Captain Elisha Price. (Author's collection)

the Astoria studio, which opened under an unlucky star in October 1920, exemplifies the feast-or-famine existence of East Coast film production. One era of plenty began in the summer of 1922, when Paramount reopened the Astoria studio to reach its ambitious slate of forty-one feature films for the next six months. In January 1923, Paramount ordered another thirty-nine features for the first half of the year.[16]

Humphrey D. Howell tested Helen and placed her under contract with Paramount.[17] As with Inspiration, Paramount glorified but did not credit

Helen (*second from the left*) in her brief, extraneous film debut in *The Fighting Blade*. (UCLA Film & Television Archive)

Helen, relegating her to the sort of spotlighted cheesecake that Toby Wing provided in such 1930s fare as *42nd Street*.

Helen worked a few days on Paramount's latest speed-mad-driver extravaganza. Wallace Reid launched the series with *The Roaring Road* in 1919. An accident on the set of *Valley of the Giants* later that year, and the subsequent addiction he developed to the morphine shots a studio doctor administered to keep him going, prompted Paramount to adapt its formula to other contract players. Agnes Ayres, Reid's love interest in *Too Much Speed*, played the speed demon in *Racing Hearts*. Her follow-up, first titled *Contraband* and then *The Arms and the Girl*, eventually reached screens as *The Heart Raider*. While wearing only a swimsuit, speed gal Muriel Gray (Ayres) crashes her car into that of John Dennis (Mahlon Hamilton). Having met cute, she doubles down by betting her father (Frazer Coulter) that she will marry Dennis within three weeks. When she heads to Palm Beach in pursuit of her prey, Daddy takes out an insurance policy to protect himself financially from his daughter's antics. Also in Florida is Gaspard McMahon (Charlie Ruggles), a clerk sent by his employer, the selfsame insurance company, to marry Muriel

Helen (*far left*) in Paramount's *The Heart Raider*. (Courtesy of the George Eastman Museum)

Detail of Helen in *The Heart Raider*. (Free Library of Philadelphia, Theater Collection)

before her escapades result in a devastating policy payout. To make Dennis jealous, Muriel appears with McMahon in a charity pageant. Assisting the odd couple in the extended sequence are four beauties in pseudo-Asian garb. The first from the left is Helen Morgan.

While the production traveled to Florida to film exteriors, Helen stayed in New York, likely working a few days on the Pyramid feature *Wife in Name Only*. If she made the final cut of this (believed) lost film, she did so unbilled. Helen also earned newspaper copy by sitting on the opposite side of the table at a Brooklyn beauty contest.[18]

She later claimed to have worked with Nita Naldi, most likely as one of her maids in *Lawful Larceny*, shot at Astoria in April–May 1923. This film is also considered lost.[19]

It remains unclear how many films Helen made during her tenure at Astoria.[20] What *is* clear is that her visits to the lot decreased significantly during the summer, after the studio scaled back its quota from eighty to fifty-two features for the 1923–1924 season.[21]

Thanks to a kind word from supporter Helen Kiely, wife of director Elmer Clifton, Helen worked, sometime between late May and early July, on *Six Cylinder Love*, a comedy drama based on William Anthony McGuire's play of the same name. When the middle-aged Burtons sell their suburban house and return to the city, they offload their car to their neighbors, newlyweds Gilbert (Ernest Truex) and Marilyn (Florence Eldridge) Sterling. At Marilyn's urging, and like the Burtons before them, they live the high life. Ultimately, Gilbert loses both his job and their house. After Marilyn learns humility in their cold-water flat, this modern-day Job lands a new job *and* palms the car off on their janitor.[22]

With the acquisition of the car came a host of parasitic hangers-on. Among these was Helen, who received her first screen credit. Sadly, the film is lost, so it remains unclear how a "Gypsy Girl" joined the Sterlings' coterie, but the fact that screenwriter Carl Stearns Clancy worked *The Music Box Revue* into the mix may provide the explanation.

Her nest egg depleted and her film career stalled, Helen moved downtown to the Grosvenor Hotel. Economizing further, she fried eggs on an iron and fanned the smoke out the window. She also hung out at Gertner's, hoping to coerce the song pluggers who frequented the restaurant into buying her coffee and a meal and, hopefully, putting in a good word for her somewhere.

Florence Eldridge, Helen, Anne McKitterick, and Miss Lunney are more than Ernest Truex can handle in Fox's *Six Cylinder Love*. This was Helen's only credited appearance in a silent film. (Author's collection)

Helen studied voice. Not for musical comedy but for opera. One of her Miss Mount Royal contacts, Eduardo Petri, "offered to give [her] vocal lessons free. He said [she] could pay him back when [she] sang in grand opera. But the lessons didn't go so well."[23] Petri may have given Helen private lessons, but his primary endeavor at the time was the Free Choral School of the Metropolitan Opera Company. Heinrich Conried founded the school in 1903 to teach young singers choral repertoire to augment the Met chorus in its large-scale productions. Many parlayed their experience into full-time employment as Met choristers, but Helen never stepped foot on the Met stage.

Instead, on September 13, she teamed with pianist William Fairman for her first billed vaudeville appearance, playing a split week at Hagerstown's Maryland Theatre. The unnamed local critic paid little attention to her voice: "[If] there are any more beautiful there we would readily say there is some good good reason for that Canadian rush."[24] "Fairman and Morgan" completed the week in Trenton, where Helen performed a "pleasing song and pianologue specialty."[25]

She auditioned for Ziegfeld's new *Follies*. Unimpressed by her skimpy résumé, Ziegfeld deemed Helen not the showgirl type but placed her in the back row of *Sally*—at fifty dollars a week.

Before *Show Boat*, Ziegfeld's most successful production was *Sally*, wherein his *Follies* dancing star and former mistress, Marilyn Miller, became the biggest musical star of the 1920s. In a first from Ziegfeld, Miller earned a percentage of the gross in lieu of salary. Her contract stipulated that no one other than Miller was ever to play Sally.[26] The Jerome Kern–Guy Bolton Cinderella musical opened on December 21, 1920, and ran for sixteen months. Other productions ran longer, but thanks to the New Amsterdam's high

A studio portrait of Morgan while she played in *Sally*. (Free Library of Philadelphia, Theater Collection)

seating capacity, *Sally* played to over a million people in New York before going on tour—more than any American production up to that time.[27]

Helen joined the company in St. Louis on October 8, 1923, as *Sally* began its second season on tour, and the tempestuous Miller-Ziegfeld relationship unraveled. The year before, Miller defied Ziegfeld by marrying Jack Pickford. Ziegfeld blamed the younger brother of "America's Sweetheart," Mary Pickford for the tragic death of Ziegfeld's earlier mistress and Jack Pickford's first wife, Olive Thomas. Ziegfeld feared that history would repeat itself. Eight weeks into the new season, the expense of weekly hops forced Ziegfeld to cut corners. He reduced Miller's 10 percent of the gross to a still-phenomenal $3,500 weekly salary. When Miller realized that Ziegfeld would not honor their contract and star her in a new Broadway production by February 1, 1924, she missed a performance in Bridgeport. Miller claimed illness, but locals spotted the Pickfords in a local café while understudy Ethel Kelley went on before the hostile crowd. Ten days and many bad words later, Miller left *Sally*, severing ties with Ziegfeld for the next five years. Shirley Vernon came in from New York to head the cast but was no draw on the road. By the end of the year, lead comic Leon Errol's name appeared above the title.

While Ziegfeld and the Pickfords raged war, Helen occupied her time with a new beau. Possessing one of the finest names in New England, Lowell Fellner Almy was the stage-door johnny Helen had yearned for. His grandfather, banker Thomas Almy, cofounded the *Fall River Weekly News*. Their adopted son, Arthur Pickering Almy, married Lillian Beatrice Fellner, the daughter of a successful restaurateur.

When he came of age, Lowell Almy bypassed college and went into business, first as a confectioner's sales clerk and then as a wholesale jeweler. He first met Helen in a New York hotel—presumably the Grosvenor—while Helen pursued her film career. The two struck up a friendship until business prompted Almy's return to Boston. In early December, he caught a performance of *Sally* with his pal Edwin T. Hall, a shoe-machinery salesman.

Helen befriended Jean Gardner when she joined *Sally*, so it was only natural that when Almy and Hall haunted the stage door, the women divided and conquered. Throughout December, the men followed Helen, Jean, and *Sally* throughout New England. When Jean hung up her butterfly costume to dance in *Kid Boots*, the foursome planned a double wedding, on New Year's Eve, Jean's opening night on Broadway. Helen took the evening off, and the quartet raced upstate to Port Chester after the curtain fell. In the final minutes of 1923, each couple married.[28]

Helen played her final *Sally* performances on New Year's Day in Albany. At her farewell party, the cast presented the bride with a watch. Company manager Clarence Willetts announced that her retirement would be temporary; Helen would join a New York production the next season.[29]

"Doc" Almy, who returned to Boston to prepare for his bride's arrival, had other plans.

Almy abandoned his jewelry business to peddle pianos.[30] In March, when Helen expressed her desire to visit Jean Gardner in New York, he struck her. On April 1, while visiting his mother in Boston, he hit Helen again. It was a Kroeter redux.

Determined not to be the victim Lulu had been, Helen left Almy and returned to Chicago. Ensconced at 945 Central Park Avenue, Lulu now called herself Mrs. William Hess, perhaps to prevent her checkered matrimonial record from tainting her daughter's professional reputation. Whether Mr. Hess was real or imagined is unknown, but Lulu was still, legally, Mrs. Frank Payne.

When Almy begged for Lulu's assistance in getting his wife back, she arranged a country outing for the three. Almy produced papers for Helen's signature that would grant him permission to sell some communal property. When she hesitated, he tried to hit her again, ending all hope of reconciliation. On July 17, Helen sued for divorce. Employed, she waived her right to alimony. Almy did not appear in court. In his reply to the complaint, he denied the charges of physical and emotional abuse, countering that Helen had not "treated him kindly and affectionately" during their union.[31]

After divorcing Almy, Helen codified a backstory she told for the rest of her life. Gone was the fiction of Helen's comfortable upbringing. In court, Lulu perjured herself by declaring that Tom Morgan was not only Helen's father but also Lulu's first husband. Although he resided not thirty miles away, Lulu swore under oath that he was dead. Cast in Frank Riggin's role as a cattle dealer, Tom Morgan forever played all of Helen's fathers. She needed *a* father, but husbands proved expendable. Thus, in the world of Helen Morgan, William Zeh and Lowell F. Almy never existed. She later quipped that she departed *Sally* because "Marilyn Miller and everyone else was leaving and it was too comical. So I left, too."[32]

While erasing Lowell Almy, Helen signed with Albert Bouche for his Villa Venice roadhouse on Milwaukee Road by the Des Plaines River. Bouche spent $40,000 converting the former House That Jack Built into an eighteen-acre Venetian wonderland, complete with multicolored fountains, masks, and carnival grotesqueries. The extensive gardens included gondolas. When the renovation took longer than scheduled, Bouche utilized Helen and most of his Villa cast at his café on the Chicago Loop, the Moulin Rouge, which was then reopening after a one-year padlock for Prohibition offenses.[33] The revamped Moulin Rouge offered Chicago a ten-piece orchestra with continuous vaudeville and with dancing from seven to four nightly. Local interests strong-armed Bouche to abandon his in-town operation. He refused. On June 16, two days after Helen left to open the Villa show, someone rolled a bomb into the Moulin Rouge. The nearby Pathé Film Company shook to its very foundations. In the Hotel Richmond, directly above the club, the explosion shattered glassware and china. The blast seriously injured two men standing in the club's foyer, which the explosion obliterated.[34]

Within a month of the bombing of the Moulin Rouge, federal agents padlocked it again.

Meanwhile, north of town, Helen opened on June 14, playing three shows nightly, at 7:45 p.m., 11:30 p.m., and at 2:30 a.m. Helen was prone to epic stage fright before going on. On the night of her Villa debut, her jitters were evident *while* she sang. The sob in her voice panicked her audience and elicited their sympathy. By the end of her set, the crowd was hanging on to every note she sang. Wisely, she incorporated the sob into the act. "The first time was because I was scared. After that I gave it to the customers because they liked it."[35] Not used to giving three shows nightly, the novice chanteuse, billed as Miss Mount Royal, gave every encore the crowd requested and sang herself hoarse. Regardless, critics noticed that her "voice rival[ed] her looks and her gowns."[36] Within a few weeks, the club attracted two sets of patrons: those who came to hear Helen and those who paid for Tamiris and the other dancers.[37]

The Villa also offered gambling. During an August 28 raid, Bouche insisted the raiders remove their hats while indoors. The Reverend Elmer L. Williams did remove his, in addition to the roulette wheels and Bouche, who was later released on a $1,000 bond. On September 6, Williams revisited the Villa, but Bouche bested the "fighting preacher" by challenging the legality of the raids in superior court. On October 23, Bouche got back his wheels, chips, and tables, but by that time, Helen had moved on.[38]

For four decades, the Villa delighted Chicagoans, gamblers, and gangsters. The last time Dean Martin stepped onto the Villa stage, he cracked, in front of several unamused, fedora-wearing men, "This joint'll probably burn down over the week-end." Frank Sinatra pulled Martin aside and, in a stage whisper for all to hear, scolded him. "Sh, the fire's not until Tuesday."[39]

Actually, the Villa burned to the ground on Saturday, March 4, 1967, when the kitchen exploded and sent flames into the dining room. State fire marshal William Cowhey stated that he did not believe arson had caused the conflagration.

Lodging was included with her contract, so for nine weeks Helen stayed and played at the Villa Venice. Despite her success while singing "Lazy," "Poor Butterfly," and "Follow the Swallow," her sights remained set on opera. She spent her days learning Cio-Cio-San and other roles, but by September, she abandoned her operatic dream.

Helen moved on to the Montmartre and a sixty-dollar weekly salary. The club opened in 1907 as Pop Morris's Garden at Broadway and Lawrence. By 1910, the Chamales brothers gained control and renamed it the Green Mill Gardens, after the beer garden out back.[40] By the time it operated as the Montmartre Cafe, Al Capone, at least tangentially, controlled it.

It closed for remodeling during the summer of 1924, and bouncers turned away hundreds when the *New* Montmartre opened on September 17. Unimpressed, *Variety* suggested that the renovation consisted of little more than running a vacuum, but the writers enjoyed the floorshow, and Helen, immensely. The show business bible counted fewer than ten customers during the visit, but the fervor of opening night soon returned. For the first time in years, the Montmartre's balcony filled nightly.[41]

Heading the bill were Arnold Johnson's Melody Boys and emcee/comedian Frank Libuse. Playing in Johnson's band was a teenage Benny Goodman. The Montmartre billed Helen third, but not as a blues singer. Mirth Mack, fifth on the bill, was. Two months into the season, Johnson, Libuse, and Mack left the floorshow. Replacing them were Julia Gerity (the Queen of Syncopation) and her Windy City Blue Blowers and, already a staple of Chicago nightlife, singer Ruth Etting. Helen retained her higher billing over Etting, which irked Moe Snyder, Ruth's brutish manager and husband, but the triple play of Gerity, Morgan, and Etting proved a knockout. Throughout December, management billed the trio as "the Big Three." After the addition of singer Herbie Vogel, the tagline changed to "Four Aces (hard to beat)."[42] The quartet would be short-lived. Mismanaged, the Montmartre shuttered in late January.

With her hair in a flossed bob, there was more Lorelei Lee than Julie LaVerne in Helen's stage persona, as exhibited in the songs "Too Tired to Wash the Dishes" and "Insufficient Sweetie." The gold-digging flapper won the support of eminent Chicago critic Amy Leslie, who built up her protégée in print.[43] When the Montmartre shuttered, Leslie advised Helen to take another crack at New York and wrote letters of introduction to George Belasco, George White, and Ziegfeld.

Helen auditioned again for the Great Glorifier. "Good teeth," Ziegfeld said. "Walk over to the wall and back." Nonplussed, Helen followed orders. He did not remember her from *Sally*, but his judgment was the same: this exotic creature was not showgirl material. Yet he cast her, not in his *Follies of 1925* but in *Louie the 14th*. The Romberg operetta concerns an army cook (Leon Errol) who remains in France after the war. Paul Trapmann (J. W. Doyle) hosts a ritzy dinner party. Realizing he has only invited thirteen, he asks the rubber-legged comedian to complete the table. Hilarity ensues. Joining Helen, back in the chorus, were Louise Brooks and Peggy Fears.

Once Ziegfeld was out of earshot, Helen muttered, "I'm a singer, not a dancer. I'll make my mark singing or die in the attempt."[44]

3

Scandalized

Before the ink dried on the contract, Helen plotted her escape. She played the out-of-town break-in engagements but left *Louie the 14th* before its Broadway opening.

Back in Manhattan, Helen auditioned for the nightclub circuit. Lew Leslie expressed interest in having her open his Rue de la Paix but ultimately passed. Jimmy Durante and partners Eddie Johnson and Harry Harris offered Helen fifty dollars a week at their Club Durant. She pushed for seventy-five and lost the deal.[1] Harry Richman gave her a tryout at his Club Richman during this period, at her requested seventy-five-dollar salary.

Richman stated that he fired her after the first week, but his partner, Lou Schwartz, claimed that he farmed out the singer to Billy Rose.[2] But Helen steadfastly avowed that she owed "everything to Miss [Amy] Leslie. . . . She took me to New York, placed me in a cabaret there, and then brought the theatrical producers to see me."[3] Longtime friend Olga Swanson suggested that, with Leslie's capital, Helen bought her big chance in New York by becoming a partner at the Back Stage Club.

Not content to be merely a successful lyricist, Billy Rose first donned his producer's hat in 1924 with a revival of the 1893 Gussie Davis melodrama *The Fatal Wedding*, which he presented as a camp comedy. It failed on Broadway, but the audience reaction was positive, and Rose found his formula for success with the "Lost Generation": a mixture of nostalgia and comedy.

In 1925, he turned to the speakeasy cabaret. He rented a second-story loft over a garage at 110 W. Fifty-Sixth Street, the same block as the flourishing, and exclusive, Club Richman and Ciro's. Ziegfeld's set decorator, P. Dodd Ackerman, decked out the long, narrow room to resemble the backstage of a theater, complete with exposed brick walls, flats, sandbags, fire buckets, No Smoking signs, and the like. Rose bypassed a formal premiere and, at midnight, on or about March 12, 1925, quietly opened the doors.[4] Rose later joked about the cramped space, which sat, at best, 125: "[W]hen a busboy leaned over, we threw a tablecloth over him and put four chairs around him."[5] Cocktails cost $1.50. Scotch and champagne commanded $25 a bottle. A kitchen provided American and Chinese fare. The patronage of celebrities Buster Keaton, Sophie Tucker, Joe E. Brown, and others inspired civilians to step over Ackerman's row of footlights. Rose recouped his $4,000 investment in a week.[6]

Vaudevillian Sol Violinsky booked the entertainment, including singing waiters, a throwback from the days he and Irving Berlin sang at Mike Salter's saloon. Cigar-chomping comedian Joe Frisco emceed the floorshow, which included, as chanteuse, Helen Morgan.

Rose owned a macaw. Birds can be aggressive toward strangers, and Rose's once badly scratched the cheek of one visitor and nearly removed the finger from another. When Helen's benefactor introduced them, Rose started talking business only to notice that the singer was missing. Fearing the worst, he ran to the kitchen, where he found Helen putting grapes into her mouth and feeding them to the delighted bird.[7]

Helen learned her Club Durant lesson and accepted fifty dollars a week, less than she had earned in Chicago. She used no microphone, and even in the small room, one worked to hear her. She drew people to her and left them

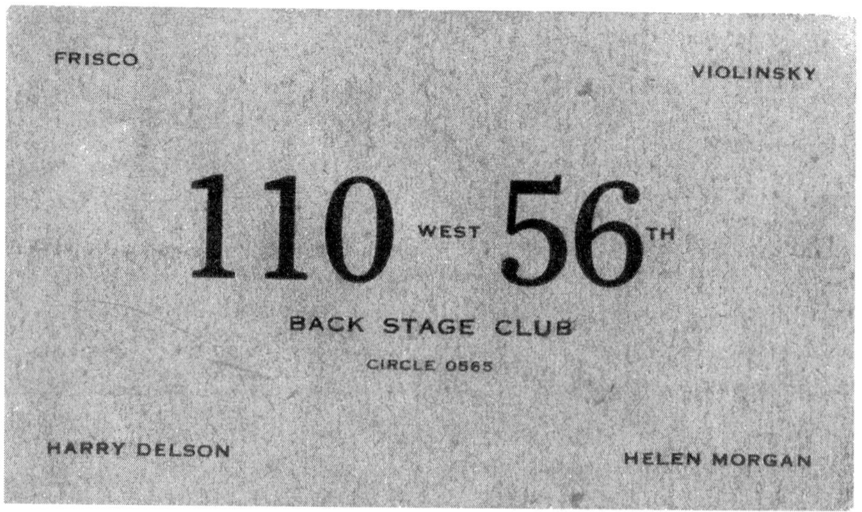

Entry to the Back Stage Club (note spelling). (Free Library of Philadelphia, Theater Collection)

hanging on to her every word. Helen never possessed a big voice, but she had presence and learned how to control an audience. Mining the comic gold-digger school of song at the Back Stage, she performed "the baby patter that gets the men," sounding more like the soon-to-be Helen Kane than Helen Morgan.[8] The lump in her throat was curiously at odds with the lightness of material like "You're the Only, Only One for Me" and instilled pathos in otherwise comic performances. To Manhattan sophisticates, she was different. Interesting. At the Back Stage Club, she earned a following that stayed loyal even after the repeal.

On March 21, George White honored Amy Leslie's request and visited the Back Stage. He agreed that Helen belonged in his *Scandals*. Al Green, of the *Greenwich Village Follies*, also stood at Helen's side with a contract in hand. She took in all this newfound attention, "big-eyed, innocent, calculating."[9] She signed a three-year contract with George White.

Beginning on April 7, Helen made multiple, often unbilled, appearances on WHN radio. With the cabaret so close to the studio, N. T. Granlund used Helen when he needed to fill airtime. Having dropped her Miss Mount Royal moniker, she billed herself as a "Chicago Prima Donna."[10] After New Yorkers claimed her as their own, she expunged the Chicago credits from her résumé.

On paper, Violinsky and agent Eddie Hitchcock were Rose's sole partners, but no one operated a New York speakeasy without the mob. The police raided, almost nightly, before gangster Max Arronsen "suggested" that he buy into the Back Stage. Rose declined. The raiders returned the following night. Violinsky and Hitchcock begged Rose to reconsider. With no recourse, he did. Arronsen dropped by the club regularly, taking his split to pay off the cops and city hall. Arronsen acted on the behest of Arnold Rothstein, a gangster who was already a Back Stage regular. "They were pals and Billy never knew," Arronsen noted years later.[11]

Rose ultimately won back every nickel he lost to the goons: "There's no bigger sucker. . . . Nobody ever taught a hood what to do with money."[12] Boys from all over the country came into town and blew their bankrolls trying to impress the more affluent, genteel clientele around them.

In May, Violinsky changed the floorshow. The new lineup: Eddie Cox, Gene Austin, Grace Chester, and Al Siegel's Orchestra. Helen went with George White. In November, Rose cashed out for $50,000 and opened the alcohol (and gangster)-free Fifth Avenue Club. After remodeling and reorganization, the Back Stage reopened in December with Tommy Lyman acting as emcee. It was about this time that Lyman coined a new term when he stepped up one night and announced to the crowd that he was going to sing "my famous torch song: 'Come to Me, My Melancholy Baby.'"[13]

The most significant event alleged to have occurred at the Back Stage involved Helen and a piano. The story goes that when so many people jammed together on the postage-stamp-sized dance floor on opening night, someone—Rose, or Ring Lardner, or a waiter, or just about anyone else—helped Helen atop the piano so patrons in the back of the long room could see her act.

Helen stated that her initial piano-sitting experience did not occur at the Back Stage but at her own Helen Morgan's 54th Street Club on November 20, 1926, the night Yale won its annual grudge football match over Harvard 12–7, "and the boys were whooping it up in deah old New York."[14] Perhaps the memory of her time sitting atop a fence post at the Marigold Gardens inspired Helen to jump atop the piano to avoid the drunken revelers and play to the back tables.

December 4, 1926: the first image of Helen atop a piano. (Free Library of Philadelphia, Theater Collection)

This telling of the tale rings truer than the standard version. No one covering the Back Stage cited Helen's novel stunt. They only hailed her voice and sunny disposition: "A cry for Helen Morgan to sing again. . . . Helen smiled and rose. The music started, Helen, a picture in tight fitting silver bodice and flowing skirts pranced onto the deserted floor. Quiet, while she sang."[15]

Helen never used the ploy in her first two Broadway appearances, and it did not become a standard part of her act until late 1926.

Another significant event first occurred when Helen made her Back Stage breakthrough: while working for Rose, she began to drink regularly. At Rose's directive, between sets, she mingled among her guests, many of whom offered her a drink. Most men of the era carried flasks filled with Scotch or gin, and so hostesses ordered something available only on the premises. For Helen, the choice was easy. Brandy carried a certain cachet: it was Ziegfeld's favorite drink.

Years later, in the film *Marie Galante*, Helen's character explained this system to Marie, who opted for a nonalcoholic cocktail. Unwilling to dupe her guests with soft drinks, Helen always chose the real McCoy: "If I can't drink a drink with my friends, they're not going to pay for it."[16]

Although the *when* of Helen's love for liquor is easy to pinpoint, the *why* is a trickier proposition. Two factors should not be underestimated: First, to many in the twenties, drinking was a political act, a rebellion against the status quo in general and the Volstead Act in particular. Second, at least at first, Helen enjoyed drinking. Assuming that Lulu did in fact use whiskey as a pacifier for her infant, Helen associated alcohol with comfort and home. In addition, the sickly girl with body-shaming issues who saw five fathers come and go before her twentieth birthday suffered from an inferiority complex that manifested itself in her epic stage fright. At one early audition, perhaps for Tommy Guinan's Playground, Helen's manager, Lou Irwin, saw her hurriedly down a couple of glasses of champagne to bolster her courage. The bubbles went to Helen's head. When she stood up, her legs gave way.[17]

Sitting on pianos kept Helen steady; it took a lot of alcohol to make her slur or forget lyrics. The Steinway stunt soon became a trademark, then a joke, and finally an ally. That football game was the reason Helen first hopped atop a piano. Brandy was the reason she stayed there.

Imitation is the sincerest form of flattery, except on the stage, where it is only a synonym for competition. After Ziegfeld created an institution with his *Follies*, the Shuberts countered with their first *Passing Show* in 1912. The proliferation of annual spectaculars continued. *The Greenwich Village Follies* debuted in 1919, *The Music Box Revue* in 1921, and *Artists and Models* and *Earl Carroll's Vanities* in 1923. Each revue provided beauties in varying stages of undress for tired businessmen to ogle, but Ziegfeld maintained an edge over his competition: his rare talent for making the whole thing intoxicating yet respectable.

Ziegfeld's chief rival was George White. The former hoofer produced thirteen dance-heavy *Scandals* between 1919 and 1939, more than any other series except the *Follies*. The upstart who brought the Charleston and the Black Bottom to white audiences infuriated both the critics and the theatrical establishment with his first production. Because he was not yet a member of the managers' guild, Actors' Equity did not picket him in 1919, and the only musical in town during that four-week strike cleaned up at the box office. White netted $400,000 on an investment of $50,000.

Helen played under White's multiyear contract system, at a $150 weekly salary the first year and $200 the second. She eschewed the double-booking performers of the era pursued among theater, vaudeville, cabarets, and film to concentrate on the stage. She also replaced her flapper's bob with the famous chrysanthemum cut, which helped brand her as a unique Broadway personality. While contemporaries like Ruth Etting spent hours before the mirror, Helen would often rush into her dressing room just before curtain, "dab on a little makeup, run her fingers through her hair, maybe cut off a lock or two and walk out looking like a million."[18]

On the first day of rehearsal for the seventh edition, May 15, 1925, Helen, in the newspaper parlance of the day, was first scandalized. Joining her was a new songwriting team. George Gershwin, who had provided the music for the previous five editions, departed after a contractual dispute. White hired the team of Lew Brown and Ray Henderson as a replacement but still held Gershwin's lyricist, Buddy DeSylva, under contract. He suggested that the three collaborate.[19]

During the out-of-town premiere in Atlantic City, Helen was so nervous that she nearly fell into the front row and into the laps of Al Jolson and Harry Richman.[20] She controlled her terror and, a week later, made her Broadway debut.

She played Kathryn, wife to Maxwell Zunzer (Harry Fox), in the skit "Drama Mixed with Revue." Under Tom Patricola's tutelage, the toe dancer learned to hoof and, in the second act, joined him in the dance sequence that concluded the "Cheap Guy" skit. In Helen's introductory number, "I Want a

Lovable Baby," her lonely-hearts-ad wish was answered with appearances by the Heavy Spending Baby (Fred Lyon), the Fickle Baby (Joe Sullivan), the Prehistoric Baby (Jim Carty), the Old-Fashioned Baby (Harry Morrissey), and finally, the longed-for Lovable Baby (Tom Patricola). Her duet with Harry Fox, "What a World This Would Be," provided a framing device for the blackout sketches that followed. While inauspicious, both songs were models of 1920s musical froth, the genre for which DeSylva, Brown, and Henderson would later provide the definitive examples in *Follow Thru* and *Good News*. As with the score, "embryonic" is an apt way to describe Helen's *Scandals* work. She brought a hint of pathos to lyrics like "All I want is one of them / but none of them want me" in "I Want a Lovable Baby" and "Though my life is sweet / joy is not complete / but what a world this would be / if you'd only agree to be happy with me."[21]

Helen's first Broadway appearance, in *George White's Scandals of 1925*. (Free Library of Philadelphia, Theater Collection)

In Chicago, Amy Leslie built up her protégée with her purple prose, but the New York critics assessed Helen as but a promising newcomer while they nominated "What a World This Would Be" as the show's sole potential song hit among little real competition.[22] One exception: Robert Coleman found Helen "a queenly beauty [with] a delightful voice" but wished that "White would allow her to sing just one real 'hot' 'blues' tune. We would walk a mile to hear her."[23]

Variety inadvertently snubbed Helen by crediting "What a World This Would Be" to the show's star, Helen Hudson. White capitalized on the confusion by having Helen Morgan understudy the other Helen throughout the Broadway run and subsequent tour.

The hit of the production was a show-stopping Charleston danced by Tom Patricola and sixty chorines. Sime Silverman charged that when dancing is the highlight in a "$4 Broadway musical show, it isn't a $4 show."[24] Outraged, White forbade his cast to advertise in *Variety*, which in turn chided White in print for his petulance.

Taking advantage of an unexpected upturn in post-summer business, White canceled an October booking in Chicago and brokered a deal with Paramount, which filmed the *Scandals* chorus performing "Beware of the Girl with a Fan" on the Apollo stage for the silent comedy *The Song and Dance Man*. Only after twenty-one weeks and revenue of over $500,000 did this version of the 1925 *Scandals* leave Broadway.[25] Eclipsed by the two best entries, which immediately preceded and followed it, the 1925 *Scandals* was nonetheless the fifth-longest-running edition of the series.

The careers of the two Helens, Hudson and Morgan, often intersected. Born at the dawn of the century, Hudson (née Tuttle) first trod the boards in the chorus of *The Pink Lady* when it played her native Philadelphia in 1914. She opted to stay home when the production moved on. On New Year's Eve in 1918, when the Eitel brothers renamed the Bismarck the Marigold Gardens, she made her Chicago debut in their *Frills and Thrills*. An eighteen-month run at the College Inn followed. She debuted in White's 1923 *Scandals* and signed on for three more years. Like Morgan, Hudson intended to cross over into grand opera, but her voice faltered in September 1925. She missed much of the post-Broadway *Scandals* tour as she sought medical treatment and vocal rest.

As the understudy, Morgan never went on for Hudson in New York, but in August, she sang Hudson's "Say It with a Sable" at a weeklong fur show at

Selbert's.[26] The number always killed, especially when fur-clad girls paraded about the stage and then dropped their wraps as they reached the footlights. Underneath, they wore little more than beaded net coverings.

The tour opened in Brooklyn and then played Boston, where, after the closing performance, Morgan overindulged and missed the train. She went to Brainard Field, pulled out a hundred-dollar bill, and was airborne for the first time in her life. She made it to Springfield, Massachusetts, in time and kept to the tour's timetable thereafter.

It was in Newark, New Jersey, that critics first weighed in on Morgan's performance of Hudson's material, which included "Fly Butterfly" and "Beware of the Girl with a Fan," as well as her own songs. They considered Morgan "a girl of considerable poise and charm, but lacking the vocal spell of her predecessor."[27] Morgan, and her notices, improved over time, but she remained one of many singing comediennes touring the country in big Ziegfeldian revues.

When the Baltimore stand was postponed a week, White picked up a booking in Washington, where Morgan "wouldn't have to croak a note, but she [could sing], and well."[28] Still, the change of venue and prima donna hurt the box office take in DC. Hudson opened in Baltimore but not in Pittsburgh, where the press not only deemed "What a World This Would Be" the hit of the night but also lauded Morgan's work in "Say It with a Sable."

After nine weeks of more performances missed than played, Hudson vowed to return for the Chicago premiere. However, on opening night, while standing in the wings, Morgan heard a commotion backstage and panicked, believing that the theater was afire. Stage manager Sammy Ledener cried, "For God's sake, Morgan, get ready right away. Helen Hudson, loosening up her voice just now, lost it completely. She can't sing a note."[29] The uproar exacerbated Morgan's stage fright. Somehow, she got through her first song before running offstage to vomit.

There was no impresario out front to sweep down and catapult young Morgan to stardom. But there *was* Amy Leslie. For weeks, Al Jolson and Eddie Cantor battled it out at the Chicago box office, although both stars were deathly ill. Cantor cracked first, closing *Kid Boots* on Monday, January 25. Relieved, Jolson shuttered *Big Boy* the following evening.[30] Amy Leslie insinuated that Jolson and Cantor quit, not to convalesce, but to avoid competition from a woman who "astonished by her willowy and sinuous dancing. . . . the loveliness of the Morgan voice matched her eyes and her dramatic talent is astonishing, both for comedy and travesty and serious effects."[31]

The *Tribune* critic never mentioned Helen Morgan at all.

Neither chorine nor star, Helen sadly watched her colleagues, swathed in furs, meet their beaux at the stage door while she braved the Chicago winter, alone, in her old cloth coat.

One day during this *Scandals* stand, Helen returned to Attica to visit Frank Riggin. Perhaps objecting to her profession, her failed marriages, or her choice of Tom Morgan's surname over his own, he refused to let her into the house, let alone speak to her. She never saw her father again.[32]

Hudson rejoined the show before it left for St. Louis, missed opening night in Detroit, but returned for Cleveland, where White disbanded the company after a forty-one-week season. As was his custom, he sold the production. For over a year, a reduced one-act tabloid, or "tab," version played film houses, three to five times daily. Leading a new, unknown cast, Sonia DeCalua shouldered the vocal assignments of the two Helens.

White enthused over Helen Morgan's singing, but he feared he would never mold her into another Winnie Lightner. Helen sighed, "No matter how hard I tried I couldn't be funny."[33] When the tour ended and White broke the news that he would not renew her contract, Helen confessed that she was worried. "I have enough money for coffee, but what about the cakes?"

"Don't worry, kid," said White. "I'll be the cakes."[34] The names stuck. She would forever call him "Cakes," and she would always be "Coffee" to George White.

Hudson's vocal troubles ended any hope for grand opera. She would not work for another five years, when she found radio work in Chicago. With her damaged soprano transformed into a husky contralto, Hudson's voice proved well suited to the torch songs her former understudy made so famous.

Leo Bernstein hired Helen Morgan when she limped back into town. The timing was perfect, for the marriage of Helen and the unimaginatively named 54th Street Club proved the turning point for a then marginally successful club—and for Helen. The cabaret occupied the top three floors of the four-story structure at 231 W. Fifty-Fourth Street. Al Raymo opened it in January 1926, and while the *Scandals* were folding in Cleveland, the Schwartz brothers (Arkie, Dave, and Lou) and Bernstein assumed control. With the change of ownership came a new floorshow, featuring Morgan.

On May 12, she introduced Irving Berlin's "At Peace with the World" with a rendition "so beautiful it held the entire roomful of guests so quiet you could hear a pin drop."[35] From here on, she made headlines whenever she sang her music of the night.

It was on Fifty-Fourth Street that Helen first obtained star billing and a healthy $250 weekly salary—days before her engagement prematurely ended. June 1 marked the first night of police commissioner George Vincent McLaughlin's curfew, which required all New York nightclubs to close at 2:00 a.m. The curfew came with little support from the office of Mayor Jimmy Walker. Texas Guinan's 300 Club and the Club Dover defied the edict, but most boîtes, including the 54th Street Club, complied. As a result, no one was in the building nine days later, when faulty wiring in the club's sign sparked an electrical fire shortly before 4:30 a.m. The fire department broke in through Standard Tire, which operated out of the ground floor, and a second-story window, while customers and employees from the neighboring clubs ran into the street to take in the excitement. By dawn, the fire was out, and $50,000 of finery was destroyed.[36] Arkie Schwartz vowed that the 54th Street Club would reopen in the fall, with Helen, as Gotham's most spectacular cabaret.

Unemployed, Helen assisted others. Two weeks after the fire, she played a benefit performance, in Harlem's Alhambra Theatre. The beneficiary was the mother of George W. Walker, the late partner of Bert Williams. With her Back Stage accompanist, Joe Santly, she scored with "Bye, Bye Blackbird" and "Tamiami Trail." She claimed that she started playing benefits as a way of keeping her name in the papers between jobs. Perhaps that was true, but her actions as the Queen of Benefits were right in line with the extravagant kindness she had exhibited as a child. Helen needed to be the most generous of all Broadway personalities.

Helen picked up a summer booking for Enoch "Nuckles" Johnson at Atlantic City's Silver Slipper. Business was off across the board during one of the wettest seasons in the city's history. Helen sang four shows a night, from ten until dawn, to mostly empty tables. More demoralizing than the empty houses was the mandate from management to romp conspicuously on the beach all day after a late night at the club, to drum up business. During her soggy week, Joe Santly came to Helen's rescue with an offer to sing "Breezin' Along with the Breeze" in a new revue. The song never made it into *Americana*, but Helen did.

Based upon the eponymous column in the *American Mercury* monthly, *Americana* was the brainchild of J. P. McEvoy. His "revue with ideas" differed from the Ziegfeldian model by being satirical in nature. Perhaps most revolutionary, in his desire for intimacy (and frugality), McEvoy eschewed the showgirls, reducing the then customary revue cast size of over a hundred to thirty-five. His women, most from the nightclubs, pulled double duty as both principals and chorines. Helen, an experienced singer and dancer, fit right in, but her $150 salary reflected her lack of stature on the stage. Only two people starred: William Collier (serving as both emcee and director) and Lew Brice (Fanny's younger brother). The physical design of the show was striking: a series of bold art deco pop-up paintings and caricatures by cartoonist John Held Jr.

Changes, including those to the cast and a move from its home at the Greenwich Village Theater to the tiny Belmont, forced back *Americana*'s opening night from June 21 to June 28, July 6, and beyond. Frustrated by

John Held's celebrated art deco set for *Americana*. (Billy Rose Theatre Division, the New York Library for the Performing Arts)

The diminutive Belmont Theatre, soon to be the home of *Americana*. (Billy Rose Theatre Division, the New York Library for the Performing Arts)

weeks of stops and starts, Collier quit the show. According to the Herndon office, he did so because of a fear that the writers saw him only as a straight man who could feed lines to Brice. Collier was more succinct: "I saw that the company was not good enough to open in New York at $5.50 a ticket."[37] Roy Atwell replaced him. Allan Dinehart received credit as director.

McEvoy, who first balked at the idea of an out-of-town tryout, conceded that opening cold in New York was no longer an option. He picked up split-week New Jersey shore bookings at Long Branch and Asbury Park. When the run completed on July 17, the production remained unprepared for its New York opening date du jour on the nineteenth, so it spent another week in rehearsal. If Helen joined the cast out of town, she did so unbilled.[38]

In the opening number, "American Revue Girls," women, garbed to reflect how various Broadway producers utilized showgirls, paraded down front. For example, Ziegfeld's girl (Isabelle Mason) glorified "the American goy." Helen lent support by dancing upstage. The "ugly child" remained uncomfortable with her body, especially her breasts, which were larger than fashionable during the flapper era. She was so self-conscious of the skimpy track pants she wore that she forbade Lulu from seeing her work in *Americana*.[39]

Helen, more undressed than usual, in *Americana*. (Free Library of Philadelphia, Theater Collection)

Americana distinguished itself with its stinging satire. In one number, a Jewish merchant supplied sheets to the Ku Klux Klan. One of Atwell's curtain speeches advocated a modest, Swiftian proposal for the Jazz Age. As federal Prohibition policy included the addition of toxins to wood alcohol, logically the government should poison lipstick to discourage flappers and their partners from pursuing their amorous endeavors. By rejecting the Ziegfeldian model, *Americana* paved the way for such topical revues of the thirties as *The Band Wagon* and *As Thousands Cheer*.

Still the soubrette, Helen shared vocals on "Blowing the Blues Away," "Why D'ya Roll Those Eyes?," and "Thanks Awful" with Lew Brice, Elizabeth Morgan, Lehman Byck, and Betty Compton, the mistress to Mayor Jimmy Walker. Several critics, including those writing for the *New York Times* and *Variety*, failed to mention Helen at all, but Robert Coleman again found her to be one of the few exceptional things in an ordinary show, particularly when she sang "Thanks Awful." Coleman said, "Morgan has the opportunity of her career, and she makes the most of it."[40]

Significantly, Helen was one of the few featured artists not to play any skits, presumably because of her failure as a comedienne in the 1925 *Scandals*. However, she was, in addition to Lew Brice and Harriette Burke, one of only three cast members to have a solo. Because it was a late addition, Helen's number, although planned, was never set. On opening night, she sang "For My Sweetheart."[41] Within a month, she was singing "The Two of Us."[42] While the trades touted both as successes, neither song remained in the production long enough to be listed in the playbill.

With her solo in limbo, so too was Helen's employment. She later claimed to have been hired, fired, hired, and fired again before finding salvation in her then boyfriend, composer Phillip Charig. One of many who contributed material, he was devastated at the prospect of cutting her from his show. Sensitive Helen was almost suicidal. Charig cornered producer Richard Herndon and pitched, "I've written a song just for her. Let her sing the song in the second act. Do this just for me and *I'll* pay her salary."[43] Herndon agreed. Henry Souvaine, another of the show's composers, taught Helen the number, but the effort involved in rehearsing new cast members and the other changes left no time to stage it. Souvaine and another contributing songwriter, Morris Ryskind, found a solution. One evening in early September, Helen walked down to the lip of the stage, sat, and announced, "I'm not in the program, but I would like to sing a song for you. It's called 'Nobody Wants Me.'"[44]

Without makeup or any other racist tropes, Helen convincingly played a light-skinned woman of color who lamented that she "never had a yaller boy to kiss me." The legend states that Jerome Kern heard the unusual singer that fateful night and immediately knew she was the woman to play Julie in *Show Boat*. Not quite. Kern and Oscar Hammerstein II would not begin writing until November. Still, months later, when the production team thought of white singers who could pass as a light-skinned woman of color who could pass as white, Helen's name headed the list, even if the role was not written for her.

As *Americana* continued its run, one by one, Helen lost her other vocal assignments. By mid-October, she was only singing "Nobody Wants Me." The suggestion to limit Helen's vocal chores may have originated from the Schwartz brothers or even Helen herself, in a desire to keep her fresh for her after-theater warbling on Fifty-Fourth Street.

After touring the subway circuit of New York's outer boroughs and subsequent five-week run in Boston, *Americana* shuttered in Philadelphia on April 16, despite good reviews.[45] Perhaps the intimate revue lost its charm when it left the cozy 515-seat Belmont for larger theaters out of town. Perhaps satire failed to play in Philadelphia.

Helen never endured the *Americana* tour. She chose to leave the production on Saturday, January 22, 1927, two weeks before the end of *Americana's* Broadway run. She remained in Manhattan and built upon her reputation as a nightclub attraction.

4

The Queen of Modern Song

During the restoration of her 54th Street Club, the "International Beauty and Personality Songbird" warbled at Tommy Guinan's Playground.[1] The sawdust cabaret had cheap furniture, rotgut liquor, and fast, loud, fun music. The sawdust on the floor made it easier to sweep up spilled liquor, vomit, and blood.

Tommy's name was above the door, but Nick Blair ran the club. Born Meyer Niklad in 1898 to Russian Jewish immigrants in the Bronx, Blair started out as a Broadway ticket broker. Short but tough, he was equally at home with gangsters and the moneyed class. He earned the trust of bootlegger Larry Fay who in turn hired him to run the El Fey when it opened in 1924. It was at the El Fey that Tommy's sister, Texas Guinan catapulted to the top tier of Broadway's hostesses. Thirty months later, Blair made Helen Morgan into Tex's main rival.[2]

When Broadway columnist Mark Hellinger visited the Playground, Blair asked his opinion of his new singer.

"Well, Nick," Hellinger started, "I'll tell you the truth. I think her voice is too weak."

Blair nodded. "That's all I wanted to know. When you say that, I know everybody else will like her. She's hired."[3]

Helen went over big at Tommy's, where she headed the payroll at $300 a week.[4] Morton Downey sang at $150 a pop. A Charleston dancer, George Raft, pulled double duty as emcee at the bargain price of $75. Like Helen, Raft was one of the softest touches on Broadway.[5] The two fell for each other despite Raft's Catholic wife, Grayce Mulrooney, who would not consent to a divorce. Raft and Helen dated openly but, in time, drifted apart.[6]

Under contract to Nick Blair, Helen played the Playground while Bernstein and Dave Schwartz reopened the 54th Street Club. Ben Bernie's brother Dave led the orchestra, and Helen Kane headed the bill. The boys closed in late October, completed the renovation, entered a partnership with Nick Blair, and set the opening for the party night of the year for the Lost Generation: Armistice Day.

The first major (and legal) headache: New York's building code required a fire escape. As designed, the club's escape needed to go through the rival Avalon Club, which also occupied the building.

Another headache: Lou Irwin's quest to procure Tommy Lyman as emcee fell through, perhaps because of salary, rumored to be the largest ever demanded for a solo cabaret act at that time. Al B. White, although not known as a master of ceremonies, was a capable mirth maker and proved a fine replacement. The remainder of the bill consisted of Wells and Brady, a blues/ukulele team from *Earl Carroll's Vanities*; Mary Lucas, a Texas Guinan dancing protégée; and Lawrence Murphy's dance band, here entitled Helen Morgan's Syncopating Six or Helen Morgan's Sextette. Another Chicago dancer, Loretta McDermott, came aboard as a last-minute replacement for Alice Bolden.

Suffering from a cold, Helen dropped a few *Americana* performances and ended her Playground stand a few days early to convalese. As a result, she did not return to 54th Street until November 16, when, accompanied again by Joe Santly, she sang "Hello, Bluebird." Her opening-night gown came directly from Paris. Vowing to be both a singer and fashion trendsetter, she always shopped with a man in tow to offer a second opinion but bought, at $350–$400 a throw, to impress women. "If the dowager wants to know what is down to the minute in Paris styles they can wander in any night," and see what Helen was sporting.[7] The former model bought, on average, four dresses weekly, as much to compensate for the wear, tear, and alcohol stains that came with the job as to inspire envious looks from her female clientele.[8]

The rechristening of the club incited debate over what to name it. Someone, probably Blair, wanting to differentiate the place from the 54th Street Club, vied for Helen Morgan's Merry-Go-Round. Simplicity won out, and the club opened as Helen Morgan's 54th Street Club, although some papers continued to list it as the Merry-Go-Round for months afterward.

Everybody went to Helen Morgan's during the 1926–1927 season. With a low two-dollar cover charge, it hailed itself as Broadway's "professional rendezvous."[9] As the hostess, it was Helen's privilege and duty to mingle with her guests. One such guest was publicist Billy Powell, whose client Herbert Fisk Johnson Sr. of Johnson's Wax paid homage whenever he was in New York.

Helen Morgan's 54th Street Club. (Author's collection)

Powell once convinced Helen to give the old man a thrill. Enjoying a laugh, Helen hopped upon her piano and cooed, "Oh, that's Johnson's Wax!"[10] Johnson was delighted. Powell's career was made.

At 54th Street, Helen divided her natural personality into two public personas: she was the bubbly hostess with a smile and a laugh for her patrons but also the sad singer of happy songs. And after that Yale-Harvard game, she became the fragile diva placed on her musical pedestal only to be abandoned there, dizzy from the height.

The jump from the Playground to 54th Street pushed Helen's salary to $400 a week. By January, it was $750. As her fortunes increased, so did her charity. On Thanksgiving night, she treated the entire cast of *Americana* to a postshow turkey dinner.

The childlike singer became prone to superstitious ritual. In addition to observing common theatrical customs, like avoiding whistling backstage or mentioning "the Scottish play" by name, Helen stepped into her gowns backward for good luck. Instead of storing shoes over her head, she kept them on low racks in her closets and dressing rooms. She did not allow any hat to lie on her bed.

Backstage, she locked herself in her dressing room while she battled her epic stage fright. Onstage, when the spotlight was on, Helen controlled her eclectic mob and never broke character. Safely perched on a piano, she used her perfect, expressive hands to focus her energy and control her terror, sometimes by twisting a finger on the piano lid or, more often, tugging and shredding a silk handkerchief. At the completion of her set, she distanced herself further from her public. She never bowed but climbed down from her perch and stood, rigidly, with a smile that was both happy and sad.

Audiences went wild over her.

With her name above the door, Helen became, after Harry Richman and the Guinans, New York's premier cabaret host. She began to travel in smarter social circles, such as the famed Algonquin Round Table, whose members were nightly visitors to the clubs that bore Helen's name. She entertained at the party Frances Wellman threw for Noël Coward and, subsequently, sang at the opening-night party for Coward's play *This Was a Man*.

She played private parties for the cream of New York society. When Schuyler Livingston Parsons opened his grand house, he invited fifty-five guests to a formal dinner. Mrs. Cornelius Vanderbilt sat on his right, and Mrs. Hamilton Rice on his left. Everything was perfect. After dinner, Helen entered, but before singing, she gave a ten-minute speech praising Parsons for his charitable works, especially for his kindness in offering her a spare room during those lean, early days. The more she spoke, the more she mortified her host, who recalled, "I saw horrified glances among the old girls and got some envious ones from the men. I had the strange impression that this new house had killed me and that Helen was delivering a eulogy over my dead body. Then she started to sing and was a sensation."[11]

Hungry for cash, Helen was not above taking the occasional stag party Joe Santly lined up for her. A friend remembered a time when Helen, drunk, sang between the sexually charged acts. All was fine until the host asked her for a vocal during the "acrobatic movements of the featured male and female performers of the night. Thinking she was a part of the other act, one of the drunker stags started to rip off her clothes. Helen . . . vomited all over him."[12]

Earlier in the year, when Police Commissioner McLaughlin pushed for a 2:00 a.m. curfew for all Rialto cabarets, Broadway pressured Mayor Jimmy Walker to back a more reasonable 3:00 a.m. closing time to accommodate the after-theater crowd. The matter remained in legal limbo for so long that the Main Stem believed city hall would never act at all. However, after a string of late-night crime, especially a $25,000 haul at the Club Biarritz, Walker's office pushed through the 3:00 a.m. closing time, with the teeth to enforce it, to go into effect on January 2, 1927.[13]

As a prelude, on December 21–23, the Feds raided fifty-eight New York cabarets, including Helen's, serving every owner with a padlock order. In addition to banning the manufacturing, selling, or bartering of liquor, the complaint enjoined those served from removing any property from the clubs while the temporary writs were in place. The Feds also served the owners with personal injunctions: anyone raided again would face contempt charges.

Meeting at the Club Alabam after the raids, cabaret owners formed the temporary Night Club Protective Association to combat the curfew. The association chose Alabam owner Sam Weiss to be its president. Helen's "angels," Lou Schwartz and Leo Bernstein, acted as vice president and treasurer, respectively. Joe George of the Hi-Hat served as secretary. Weiss proposed a $500 membership fee to secure a defense lawyer. Forty men and Helen attended the subsequent meeting, on December 29 at the 54th Street Club. When Weiss lowered the price to $100, eight paid their membership fee and an additional twenty-five pledged their support.

Further dispiriting New York's nightlife, the Curfew Act required each club to renew its cabaret license. A crackdown early in 1927 caught several operating without one. As a final means of intimidation, the city instituted a morality investigation for cabaret employers, entertainers, staff, and habitués to determine eligibility for club licensing. Enforcers of the decency clause harassed Helen, not because of her behavior but because of her loyal gay following.

When Mayor Jimmy Walker offered a special dispensation in the form of a final New Year's Eve revelry lasting until 8:00 a.m., the cabarets promised a blowout unheard of in Gotham. The Club Anatole charged forty dollars a person. Helen's charged a more reasonable fifteen-dollar cover. The remaining

Broadway nightspots fell somewhere in between. While prebookings were healthy, Larry Fay, the man who gave Texas Guinan her start, reopened his El Fey Club on New Year's Eve only to learn that his clientele preferred to eat and dance in a fancy hotel rather than risk going to a club. He closed the following night. The public stayed home after the curfew went into effect. Over the next six days, several clubs folded. Tommy Guinan limited his hours to just the weekend. The Night Club Protective Association disbanded.

Avoiding the nightclubs did the public no favors. Bellevue Hospital saw dozens of alcohol-poisoning cases. Throughout 1926, 750 New Yorkers died from bad booze. Thirty-eight died during Christmas week alone. An additional forty-one passed on New Year's Day, 1927. Hundreds more suffered blindness or paralysis. Much of the misery came courtesy of enterprising civilians who opened private clubs in their own homes. By driving Gotham's nightlife further underground, the curfew only increased the power of the bootleggers.

New Yorkers would always find a way to drink.

As Prohibition dragged on, incidences of poisoned alcohol increased, as did the health risk to those who imbibed. Major Chester P. Mills, who orchestrated the December 1926 raids, spent $8,000 over eight months collecting evidence. In 98 percent of the samples collected, New York's most fashionable watering holes cut their liquor, or adulterated it, often with wood alcohol.[14] Helen could not have drunk her way through Prohibition free of poisoned, industrial-grade alcohol.

Most of the Rialto clubs abided by the curfew despite the loss of revenue, but Nick Blair entered 1927 defiantly, openly enticing spillover traffic from nightspots that closed on time. Then on January 10, after Texas Guinan closed for the night, many of her patrons, including actor Lee Tracy and Ziegfeld beauty Peggy Fears, migrated to the 54th Street Club to hear Helen sing. At about 4:30 a.m., a buzzer sounded long and loud, ending the revelry and replacing the laughter with tense silence.

Two plainclothes police officers announced that it was well after closing time. The sullen clientele glared at the intruders and refused to move. After the cops threatened to bring the patrol wagon, the crowd exited in silence. By 5:00 a.m., the club was empty. Once on the street, the patrons heckled the cops, who dispersed them without incident.

Thereafter, Blair obeyed the curfew, dropping the late show and reducing the talent roster. Broadway nightspots struggled in early 1927, but the trio of Helen, emcee Al B. White, and dancer Loretta McDermott turned a profit while operating under a temporary padlock.

Helen's name, along with those of the owner of the building, Charles E. Miller; the Schwartz brothers; and the ubiquitous "John Doe" appeared on the December 1926 complaint. The temporary writ of injunction required a prominent display of the complaint within the club. When the case came before the Honorable William Bundy on February 17, only the John Does, identified as bartender Robert Kelly, manager on duty Herman Cohen, and Sidney Payne, faced Bundy's ire. He enjoined them from selling liquor at the 54th Street or anywhere else.

Thanks to the renovation after the June 1926 fire, Helen Morgan's had one advantage other Manhattan watering holes did not: multiple entrances. When Judge Bundy formally placed a six-month padlock on the second floor of 231 W. Fifty-Fourth Street, Blair moved the entrance to the third floor and kept right on pouring.[15]

In the early hours of February 17, federal agents raided the district's other profitable cabaret of note, Texas Guinan's. The following day, Tex answered to the December raids in court. Judge Bundy padlocked her 300 Club for six months. During the four weeks Tex scrambled to find a new location, Helen grew in stature from a popular hostess to a rival worthy of Guinan's crown as Queen of the Nightclubs. She also became just as big a Prohibition enforcement target.

Texas Guinan took to the legitimate stage in 1927. Backed by a full cabaret troupe, her *Padlocks of 1927* gave Broadway audiences a taste of a typical night in her club. By contrast, on January 24, Helen, as a solo act, broke the Keith-Albee circuit's ban on nightclub talent elbowing their way into vaudeville. She did it at their flagship house, the Palace, to boot. Helen entered wearing a three-tone blue street frock and sang two duets with her accompanist, Joseph Santly, who later filled time with a comedy solo while Helen changed into a black velvet evening gown with a large bow on the side. She ended with two solos from her stage shows and took three curtain calls. The industry publication *Zits* assessed Helen's merits, both artistic and practical: "There is not another singer like Helen Morgan in America, even though she was so nervous that she didn't do herself half justice. . . . (She) has a marvelous opportunity to develop into one of the country's greatest theatrical attractions. . . . The world is at her feet."[16]

By way of contrast, one Back Stage Club–era listener, dismayed by Helen's vocal production, issued a warning via a letter to *Variety*: "She better take care or it won't be long before she won't be warbling. It sounded so tired, not like the cooing voice I heard a few years ago."[17]

When covering Helen's Palace adventure, the press used the new moniker "the Queen of Modern Song."[18] She eschewed the popular Jolsonian trick of selling a song. She connected to the lyrics on a personal level and delivered them conversationally. With no formal training, she acted her songs, winning over audiences with simple, honest performances.

Ensconced as a full-fledged New York personality, Helen assembled her Manhattan home. In late 1926, she sent for Lulu.[19]

After Lulu, Helen had few female friends but many male ones. Offstage, she adopted their more casual dress and became one of the boys. In matters of the heart, she preferred the thrill of the hunt. If a man played hard to get, she wanted him even more. If a man pursued her with too much ardor, she cooled. Her actions, if emotionally unhealthy, fed her art. As her repertoire matured from lighthearted ditties sung with a catch in her throat to the dramatic torch songs she made famous, her behavior made it easy for Helen to lament the man that got away.

Not being assigned a single skit in *Americana* did not go unnoticed. Helen knew if she wanted to expand her career, she would have to prove she could act.

Beginning on January 12, a tiny Village theater at 22 Grove Street offered a changing bill of penny-dreadful one-acts under the title *American Grand Guignol Players*. A. Barton Hepburn Jr., a frustrated actor and the grandson of the head of New York's National City Bank, financed the enterprise in return for a prominent role onstage. Hepburn and the company opened with four playlets translated from, or based on, the Paris Grand Guignol repertoire. Heeding the negative response to the more gruesome aspects of the first bill, the company gravitated to sophisticated drama and melodrama. After six weeks and two programs, the production operated at a $5,000 loss, which Hepburn ate, but response to the second bill was better, bringing the weekly loss below $500. Believing the tide was turning, on March 4, Helen opened in the third bill of the series.

Penned in verse by Louis N. Parker, *A Minuet* featured the production's director, Georges Renavent, as a French marquis and Helen as a Marchionese, awaiting the guillotine in a Reign of Terror prison. To save her professional reputation should she flop in her dramatic debut, she spelled her name backward (Neleh Nagrom) in the program. The press enjoyed the ruse, but Helen left nothing to chance. One night, she bought out the house and invited friends and potential business associates to trek south of Fourteenth Street to judge her dramatic potential. Billed for *Divertissement* as Helen Morgan, she

Neleh Nagrom (Helen Morgan, spelled backward) in *A Minuet: American Grand Guignol Players*. (Free Library of Philadelphia, Theater Collection)

ditched the big white wig and fancy gown for simple black velvet to cover a lengthy set change between *A Minuet* and the third piece of the evening. Atop the piano, she sang three songs while "Banjo" Santly, again, assisted.

While her singing was the biggest hit of the evening, her acting also garnered praise. Percy Hammond called her a "raffish nightingale."[20] Walter Winchell lamented that it took two years for someone in New York to discover Helen's dramatic talent. "Her charm literally bowls you over. Her style, manner and refinement are exciting and . . . her dainty fingers contain as much if not more expression than all of the Little Theater groups in the town."[21]

Hepburn earned notices second only to Helen's for playing a disabled World War I doughboy poisoned by his unfaithful wife and her lover in *Casualties*. However, having inherited grief, and $5 million, from his conservative family, Hepburn abandoned the theater for Hollywood. His career as a film producer proved to be negligible, but he played small roles in several films over the next two decades.

With no replacement backers available, the *American Grand Guignol Players* ended with Hepburn's departure on Saturday, March 12, halfway through the bill's three-week run.

Helen earned only twenty-five dollars for her efforts and canceled vaudeville engagements to do it. Yet she earned publicity and experience that money could not buy. With no training, she proved herself as an actor. Years later, her most vivid memory of her visit to Grove Street was film producer Joseph Schenck giving her a lift in his Rolls-Royce after the performance.

The return of warmer weather, and Texas Guinan in her new digs, forced more cutbacks at 54th Street. By April, Helen was the only featured act in the floorshow. Then, on April 28, Blair threw a going-away party, replete with engraved invitations. The Queen of Modern Song abandoned her 54th Street Club before the end of the season for a vaudeville tour. In Europe.

In 1926, Algerian theater and casino impresario Edmond Sayag transformed a space on avenue Gabriel in Paris into the open-air fantasyland *Les Ambassadeurs Restaurante*.[22] His hook was presenting American headliners to the French and the tourist trade. Sayag's 1927 production, under the artistic direction of George Hale and in the tradition of the *Folies Bergère*, was *Broadway à Paris*. William Morris Jr. assembled the company in New York, and they shipped out on the *Rochambeau* on April 20. With a club to run, Helen boarded the *Suffern*, bedecked in a stylish snakeskin coat, two weeks later. She sailed into the messiest backstage battle of her career.[23]

The drama began in March when the Morris office booked Helen into London's Princess Club. A few weeks later, her 54th Street agent, Walter Batchelor, placed her in the City of Light at the Casino de Paris, followed by London's Café de Paris. Morris, in turn, booked her into *Broadway à Paris*, which promised a sixteen-week Paris run with a likely Berlin extension. Batchelor was livid. He could not afford for Helen to remain on the continent indefinitely. He also wanted her to debut in London, which offered additional bookings should she make a hit.

Unsure which agent would win out, Sayag omitted Helen's name from the large-print advertisements he ran in the Parisian press in the days leading to the premiere.[24] He then gave Paris its first taste of Helen in his basement restaurant below the *Theatre de la Micholodiere* on or about May 16.[25] Having scored at the *Micholodiere*, Helen debuted in earnest on the nineteenth before a premiere audience that boasted British princes George and Henry and the maharaja of Kapurthala. The slight in advertising prompted the press to misidentify her as a last-minute addition to the cast.

Helen, with accompanist Robert Sour, took the eighth spot in the first half.[26] French audiences, like their American counterparts, were stunned by this reserved woman who sang with hypnotic power and emotional depth while barely moving. She tailored her performance for non-English-speaking audiences by playing out the drama in the music. Because she approached her material like opera, the sob in her voice communicated more than a lyricist's clever rhyme. She also planned her gestures with such care that each lift of her hand contributed to the drama. The Paris engagement taught her to read varied audience responses for what they were: "Sometimes it would register approval by wild stamping and cheers while at other times it would only sit still and smile or weep."[27]

Offstage, Helen availed herself of the Parisian couturiers but only bought clothes for work. She wore the same simple dress during daylight hours, sprucing it up daily with a fresh flower, usually a camellia. Her Grand Guignol success inspired her to dream of, one day, playing *Camille.*

While Helen played *Les Ambassadeurs*, Charles Lindbergh made his historic flight across the Atlantic. On May 27, she sang at a gala in his honor to benefit the families of dead French fliers at the *Théâtre des Champs-Elysées.* The event attracted over 2,500 patrons and raised more than 325,000 francs. The auction of Lindbergh's autograph raised an additional $1,500 for the cause.

Besides Lulu, Helen's constant offstage Parisian companion was Dwight Fiske. Beginning in the late 1910s, the classically trained musician struggled to make it as a concert pianist. However, party guests loved his ribald *sprechgesang* to his own tinkling piano accompaniment. After Tallulah Bankhead took him under her extravagant wing, Fiske made his cabaret debut at London's Café Anglais. By 1930, he was the darling of New York's café society, and part of the so-called pansy craze. Because his material was more allegorical than out, he enjoyed a long career. He wrote, recorded, and played the best clubs until well after the war.

Night after night, Morgan and Fiske made the post-theater rounds, often at Chez Bricktop, the expatriate haunt run by red-haired woman of color Ada "Bricktop" Smith. While visiting, Fiske inevitably played his party pieces, and Helen wowed the crowd with song after song. Gratis. As they left, Smith fell over herself thanking the two for livening up her little boîte. One night, earlier than usual, Helen went in alone and asked Smith to see Bricktop.

Stunned, Smith blurted out, "*I'm* Brick."

"That's fine," Helen replied. "I'm Helen Morgan. I wanted to get a good look at you."

"But you've been looking at me all week."

"Yes, I know that. But I figured before I got started on the juice, I ought to come in and see what you really look like."[28]

Walter Batchelor won the battle of the agents.

Sayag fired Helen over her after-hours performances. It was one thing to moonlight for Sayag and another to give the show away in rival establishments. The show's attorney, Dudley Field Malone, convinced Sayag to rehire Helen until Batchelor found work for her in London. She opened at Leicester Square's Café Anglais a week before her legitimate British bow on June 20 at the London Coliseum. With her London accompanist, Bernard Grauer, Helen was big business at the Anglais, and her pay—$500 for the club and $750 for the Coliseum—reflected her increased drawing power.[29]

The night before her Coliseum debut, Helen and the Yacht Club Boys played a private party for the Prince of Wales. Although they had never met, Helen and the future Edward VIII shared a history. A newspaper story of the prince's 1923 trip to Canada used a Winter Carnival–era photo of Helen in a swimsuit, throwing snowballs.[30] The juxtaposition of images stuck in the public mind. Before long, some reporter or press agent claimed that the prince had attended the Miss Montreal contest.[31] Next came gossip of a love affair. Helen was loath to bring up the tabloid romance. Making a hit with the royals ensured bookings by more insular, socially ambitious London society matrons.

Aware of Helen's friendship with Fiske, a member of the royal household mistook this young American blues singer for a blue one and warned Helen not to sing any vulgar songs at the party. She replied, "If I did, you'd have to teach them to me."[32]

~

At the Coliseum, "despite apparent nervousness and a not too felicitous choice of numbers," Helen made a hit, especially when she sang "So Blue."[33] She held over another week.

Before sailing, and despite the potential of a protracted *Broadway à Paris* run, Helen signed for the intimate Broadway revue *A La Carte*, which promised sketches by George Kelly, who stayed with the project, and songs by Richard Rodgers and Lorenz Hart, who did not.[34]

Helen chose not to sail home after completing her chores at the Café Anglais and the Coliseum. Instead, on July 5, she abruptly quit *A La Carte* three weeks before its out-of-town tryout. Within the week, her strategy became clear: Walter Batchelor was deep in negotiations with Florenz Ziegfeld. Being cast in Ziegfeld's upcoming project, *Show Boat*, proved the better choice. *A La Carte* opened in New York on August 17 and ran for five weeks, but at a $114,000 loss.

With the change in booking, overnight, Batchelor found himself tasked with back booking his client to cover two additional months before Ziegfeld needed Helen home for rehearsals. And so Helen made her recording debut, waxing twelve sides for the English Brunswick label. Jazz pianist Leslie A. "Hutch" Hutchinson accompanied her on several cuts. One British critic liked her rhythmic style and upper vocal register but did not care for what he considered weak diction.[35] To modern ears, her diction is better than good, but her small voice disappears completely when the tiny jazz combo plays with gusto, especially on "Nothing But."

Two of the discs featured covers of numbers from American shows just opened in London: Rodgers and Hart's *Peggy-Ann* and George and Ira Gershwin's *Oh, Kay!* Curiously, Helen's *Oh, Kay!* cuts included "Do Do Do" and "Maybe" but not "Someone to Watch over Me." In the summer of 1927, the Queen of Modern Song sang a variety of popular songs with a hint of pathos in her voice. Torch songs would wait.

Helen's British invasion culminated in August with a week at the London Palladium. Fellow Batchelor client and Illinois native Maureen Englin also played London that summer. At Batchelor's suggestion, when Helen crossed the Channel, they met and bonded. Often, when Helen closed the Anglais for the night, she hopped over to the Florida Club to catch Maureen and have a nightcap. Sometimes Helen crashed at the Park Lane, Maureen's digs, as it was closer than her accommodations. When she was feeling mischievous, Helen swapped the shoes visitors had placed outside their rooms to be shined with those of a neighbor, giddy at the thought of the confusion that would ensue the next morning.

On Helen's opening night at the Palladium, Maureen went backstage and found the younger singer in a panic. Having eaten well that summer, the gown Helen had purchased in Paris no longer fit. Maureen let out the dress and pinned Helen back into it before she went onstage. When Helen hopped up on the piano, those pins dug into her sides. The slightest movement only increased her pain, but she got through her set.[36]

Lou Irwin cabled her to come home a few weeks ahead of Ziegfeld's schedule to a new club that would bear her name. Batchelor and the Myron S. Bentham office handled the cabaret contract as they had her European adventure. They would represent her for the next four seasons.

For the Morgans, high wages meant high living. On August 31, Helen and Lulu entrained to catch the *Ile de France*, with only four dollars on hand. Depending on which version of the story you believe, the ever-resourceful Morgans either stowed away in a friend's cabin or raised hell with the purser for not securing a reservation on the sold-out ship. In either case, Helen wrote a check for $1,150 for a first-class cabin. Only after the ship was too far out to turn back did Helen confess that the check was sure to bounce. Friends met the Morgans at the pier in New York with loans to cover the generous tips to the crew, but the French Line waited four months for payment from the singer, who had sailed to America in style. On credit.

5

The All-American Musical Comedy

In 1927, Ziegfeld presented *Show Boat* as "the all-American musical comedy."[1] It is. It celebrates America's optimism, its work ethic, its inventiveness, its tight-knit families and communities—and its music. Conversely, *Show Boat* exposes America's provincialism, intolerance, and, above all, racism. Ziegfeld's ultimate triumph boasts perhaps the greatest score ever written for the musical stage, Joseph Urban's unequaled physical production, and the indelible performances of the production's cast, particularly Helen Morgan and, later, Paul Robeson.

Jerome Kern read Edna Ferber's 1926 novel upon its publication. Captured by the romantic lure of the lovers who happily play out their lives on the river and unhappily away from it, he invited Oscar Hammerstein II to supply the book and lyrics for a stage musical adaptation. Working at a breakneck pace, the duo performed the first act for Ziegfeld just nine days after securing the musical theater rights. The impresario came aboard immediately.[2] His contract required that he have a working script by January 1, 1927, and that he open the production on or before April 1.[3]

Progress then slowed to a trickle. Ostensibly because he was readying *Rio Rita*, the opening attraction for his new Ziegfeld Theatre, Flo pushed *Show Boat* from spring to early summer—and beyond. In reality, he had cooled on the project, and on Hammerstein, who was tackling his first major writing assignment without his partner and mentor, Otto Harbach. Concerned that Hammerstein's script lacked comedy, in a March 3, 1927, telegram, Ziegfeld suggested hiring seasoned professional Dorothy Donnelly as a cowriter. Oscar Hammerstein balked at the idea and called in his uncle. Producer Arthur Hammerstein took out an option on the work that would last from April 2 until October 20. If it was not produced during that time, Oscar and Jerry could shop the property again. Convinced that Ziegfeld alone could handle his most ambitious project, Kern brokered a resolution. During the attempted coup, Arthur first announced Helen for *Show Boat*.[4] When Ziegfeld wrested back control, he did so with Helen Morgan, finally, on his radar.

Helen played Julie, the showboat's mixed-race leading lady. Her expulsion from the troupe upon the revelation of her (illegal) marriage to a white man affords the heroine, Magnolia, the chance to act onstage. Later, Julie abandons another stage job to benefit her spiritual sister.

With her acting experience comprising some negligible *Scandals* skits and ten days in the *American Grand Guignol*, Helen's ease in creating Julie was miraculous. She prepared using sides. These small booklets include only stage directions, cue lines, and one's own dialogue. On October 16, during the first read, inexperienced Helen read her cues along with her lines.[5] Oscar Hammerstein recalled, "She knew nothing of technique and yet she knew everything that really counted. God gave her an extraordinary instinct and she followed it." In the end, she required little direction "because everything she did seemed right."[6]

As the read-through occurred prior to the casting of Steve, Julie's husband, Oscar read opposite Helen.[7] She fell for the soft-spoken lug who resembled a linebacker more than a writer the moment she met him. Oscar Hammerstein endearingly said "Thank you" and "I beg your pardon" to everyone. Helen whispered to Kern, "Why don't you give him a break? He seems to understand the part."[8]

Hammerstein was enchanted, and possibly attracted, but it is unlikely that he ever dated Helen. With his marriage to Myra Finn failing, he was embroiled in an on-again, off-again affair with Dorothy Blanchard Jacobson, whom he would marry near the end of *Show Boat*'s Broadway run.[9] Still, Helen's infatuation with Oscar may have drawn her to his brother Reginald, who became a reliable arm ornament during her time on *Show Boat*.

Through Julie, Helen completed her metamorphosis from jazz baby to torchbearer. Helen did more than take the character home: she *became* Julie—wistful, tragic, exotic. She successfully relegated her torch singer character to the top of the piano, but after hours, Julie's tragic nihilism sometimes locked horns with her childlike gregariousness. Off stage, the combination was a disaster. On stage, it was magic.

On September 27, Helen returned to the world of the night at Chez Helen Morgan, the second club to bear her name. Among the opening-night guests was Roscoe Arbuckle, who agreed to emcee the festivities. Al Jolson, in town for the premiere of *The Jazz Singer*, sang "Me and My Shadow." Cliff Edwards sang "Let's Misbehave." Sid Grauman, comic J. C. Flippen, and United Artists president Joe Schenck were there as well. One wag reported, "The place was so full the tables were placed touching each other and it was necessary to give advance notice to clear the way before one could move."[10]

Helen again parlayed her cabaret success into radio exposure, but this time WHN came to her, broadcasting live from Chez Helen Morgan on Tuesdays and Fridays. While it is unclear whether Helen sang on any Chez Helen Morgan live feeds, it is telling that the transmissions ceased when she went on the road with *Show Boat*. The broadcasts promoted not just the existence but also the exclusivity of the club: black tie was de rigueur to gain admittance.

Anatole Friedman opened the room in 1925 as the Club Anatole. After two unprofitable seasons, he offered what he considered an unlucky room to Nick Blair. Helen's name made raising capital easier, but by opening night, Blair was reluctantly sharing Chez Helen Morgan with five other partners, chief among them being the silent one, mob boss Owney Madden.

In 1902, not long after immigrating to America with his Irish parents, the ten-year-old Madden joined the Gophers, the ruling Hell's Kitchen gang. Within seven years, he was the gang boss. At a dance hall on November 6, 1912, eleven gangsters from the rival Hudson Dusters shot Madden. He never fully recovered from his multiple wounds, but he got even: in time, the would-be assassins died, one by one. In 1923, he partnered with Larry Fay when the cabbie branched out into nightclubs. In time, Madden's Prohibition empire included the fabled Cotton Club.[11]

The Madden-Blair partnership began in mid-1927 when Madden invited Blair to Atlantic City. In the fall, Madden opened his own club on Fifty-Sixth Street. After Chez Helen Morgan, two blocks to the south, killed his business, the mobster walked up to Blair and demanded $1,700.

"What for?" asked the confused Blair.

"Your half of the trip to Atlantic City," Madden barked. "It cost me $3,400."[12]

Blair took cash out of the Chez Helen Morgan cash register and handed it to Madden, who stormed out. Realizing he should have partnered with Blair all along, Madden later muscled in for his cut.

After money, Madden's primary interest in Chez Helen Morgan was Helen. As her vocal repertoire became increasingly *tragique*, gangsters took her to their hearts. Aware that they might suffer premature death, she sang their requiem. Unlike her typical mobster fan, Madden wanted to know Helen intimately. One night he cornered her in her dressing room and revealed his feelings. One did not say no to Owney Madden, so Helen claimed to have just given the air to an upstart punk who threatened to get anyone who dated her. Madden was likely not fooled by the ruse, but, in an abundance of caution, he left Helen alone.[13]

Another Helen fan was a young Cockney actor, Archie Leach.[14] At Helen's 54th Street Club, Leach met Reggie Hammerstein, who introduced Archie (and Helen) to his uncle Arthur. Reggie's relationship with Helen aside, he took a special interest in Archie and landed him a bit part in *Golden Dawn*, the opening production at the new theater Arthur Hammerstein built in a bid to one-up Ziegfeld. After trouping through some Hammerstein and Shubert productions with little notice, Leach landed a film contract, went to Hollywood, and became Cary Grant.

Collegians remained loyal to Helen: a decidedly mixed blessing. The boys usually drank gin, which they brought in themselves. If they emptied their flasks, students usually left and procured gin elsewhere to avoid playing the club's prices. One Saturday, ten boys and their dates descended on Chez Helen Morgan to celebrate the day's gridiron victory. Even after the *couvert* was graciously waived, the boys could only pool enough cash to cover the twenty-dollar bill for ice, bottled water, and setups. The waiters received no tip. Having learned its lesson, Chez Helen Morgan preached its gospel to the other clubs on the Rialto: no one dressed like a college boy would get in on a Saturday night—especially during football season.

A more reliable admirer was Heywood Broun. The columnist had recently resigned from the *New York World* when they refused to run his pieces defending Nicola Sacco and Bartolomeo Vanzetti. In the *Boston Globe*, Gardner Jackson also unsuccessfully supported the Italian radicals. Weeks after the Sacco and Vanzetti execution, Broun and Jackson still mourned what they considered a travesty of justice. After several rounds at Chez Helen Morgan, Broun suggested that his friend climb up on the piano alongside Helen, which Jackson feared went against the house rules.

"Nonsense," Broun countered. "She loves it. I know Helen well. She'll probably even sing a song for you."[15]

Jackson maneuvered through the sea of tables and jumped onto the baby grand. Before Helen could react to her new neighbor, someone seized him from behind, carried him back to his table, and slammed him into his chair. He learned the hard way: boxer Jack Dempsey refused to allow anything to interfere with Helen's concert.

~

Helen rehearsed *Show Boat* from 11:00 a.m. until 11:00 p.m., sang at Chez Helen Morgan until 5:00 a.m., and repeated the process. "When I wasn't on stage I would sneak onto the top of a grand piano. No, I wouldn't sit on it—lie on it. And the kids in the chorus, bless their hearts, would cover me up with their coats. That's how I'd snooze until my cue came."[16] She had less than forty minutes of stage time, so the production team could have altered her calls to accommodate her schedule, but they resolved not to show her any leniency. While on the pre-Broadway tour, when Kern learned that Helen was picking up additional nightclub and benefit gigs, he insisted that she have a *10:00 a.m.* call time.

She never walked into rehearsal even a minute late.

When asked how she managed, Helen told orchestrator Robert Russell Bennett, "You take a stiff drink—I mean a very stiff drink—and it puts you right to sleep, then wakes you up full of energy in two or three hours."[17]

When Ziegfeld took his enormous production on its pre-Broadway tryout tour, Helen reluctantly abandoned her club, leaving soprano Yvette Rugel the unenviable task of pinch-hitting in her absence. Business in Gotham's nightspots was down across the board. One exception; Chez Helen Morgan raked in a record $18,000 weekly. Six weeks on the road with *Show Boat* would cost Chez Helen Morgan its momentum, a frightening prospect for those with a financial interest in the room.

When first fashioning the Julie subplot, Oscar Hammerstein deferred to Ferber's reluctance to have her work trivialized in a musical comedy. He included much of her dialogue in the miscegenation scene but improved on the novel by playing out the mixed-race melodrama on the showboat stage. The librettist employed similar faithfulness in dramatizing Julie's second-act appearance, which, in his initial draft, he copied virtually word for word from Ferber. In the novel, a bankrupted Ravenal borrows $1,000 from high-class madam Hetty Chilson and wins back double his loan. Forever proud, Magnolia visits Chilson to pay off her husband's debt. Bored with Magnolia's strength and virtue, Chilson commands her secretary to furnish a receipt. As she proffers the paper, the middle-aged retainer recognizes Magnolia and flees the room. Magnolia also makes the connection: the servant is Julie, fallen on hard times. The scene contained not a note of music.

Before Helen signed on to the project, Kern and Hammerstein eliminated the encounter and moved Julie's second-act appearance to the following scene, Magnolia's audition.

The new dramatic *and* musical moment finds Julie a cabaret singer. Bullied by Jake, the show's producer, the down-and-almost-out singer threatens to quit the show in retaliation but sings her sentimental, turn-of-the-century ballad before staggering off to her dressing room. In walks Magnolia, who auditions with "Can't Help Lovin' Dat Man" despite the fact that Julie has been cast as the show's sole chanteuse. Recognizing the voice, Julie reenters unnoticed and then sacrifices herself by leaving, thus starting her final descent into the gutter.

Although Ziegfeld, Kern, and Hammerstein were ultimately in charge, production stage manager Zeke Colvan performed much of the heavy lifting. The *Show Boat* rehearsal period and the first two weeks of out-of-town performances coincided with the pre-Broadway tour of *Golden Dawn*. While Oscar Hammerstein focused on his other production, Colvan staged the dialogue scenes, per Oscar's instructions. Colvan ultimately received sole credit as the show's director, but his billing during the pre-Broadway stand in Pittsburgh, "Dialogue Rehearsed by," may be more accurate.

One key scene Colvan staged was Helen's exit during Magnolia's audition. He choreographed Julie's pantomime down to the moment when her hand came up "to her mouth as though to stifle the words." Colvan later rehearsed Helen's understudy and helmed, by himself, multiple regional productions after the Broadway run, but he "was never able to get another actress to duplicate the move with the same precision."[18]

Helen's big number at Chez Helen Morgan was "The Man I Love." The Gershwins wrote it in 1924 for Adele Astaire to sing in *Lady, Be Good!* but cut it on the road. Thanks to Lady Edwina Mountbatten, who championed it, and her pet band, the Berkeley Square Orchestra, who plugged it, the tune became popular throughout England and France, where Helen heard it, and she brought it home.[19] By 1931, she had sung the song over three thousand times. Her heartfelt delivery caused such a sensation that, when reviewing *Show Boat*, Abel Green chided Kern and Hammerstein for interpolating a pale imitator of "The Man I Love" into that cabaret scene when Helen could have simply fit the original tune into a score laden with interpolations.[20] In his eyes, the weaker number was "Bill."[21]

According to P. G. Wodehouse, Kern wrote the melody to "Bill" as early as 1906, making it a product of the era it eventually evoked.[22] Wodehouse supplied a lyric to the tune, which Vivienne Segal sang during the 1918 out-of-town tryout of *Oh, Lady! Lady!!* In the song, Segal told the ladies of the ensemble how she loved Bill (Harry Fisher) in spite of his numerous faults. Although it was excised from the score prior to Broadway, Kern published the number and retained a fragment of the tune in the first-act finale. The following year, with a new lyric by Buddy DeSylva, Harry Fox sang to his dollar "bill" in *Zip, Goes a Million!* The show closed out of town, a singular occurrence in Kern's career. Marilyn Miller also sang it out of town, in *Sally*, but "Bill" proved as ill-suited to Miller as he was to Segal and Fox. For the next seven years, "Bill" collected dust in Kern's trunk.

Kern and Hammerstein wrote "Out There in an Orchard" for Julie's second-act appearance.[23] When Helen failed to put it over, an annoyed Ziegfeld called her into his office. She explained that she felt mismatched with the sentimental ballad. He suggested that she ask Kern for another. She did. Displeased, Kern dug out "Bill" and played it through with her. When Helen took it, he told her she was ridiculous to give up the other song. Days later, when she first sang the song within the context of the scene atop a piano, Kern cried.[24] Ziegfeld authorized the change but warned Helen that she was cutting her own throat.

The mawkish "Out There in an Orchard" gave Helen little to act, but, whereas others had failed, she made "Bill" work by playing a tragic subtext beneath an otherwise comic lyric.[25] "Bill" became code for the all too ordinary Steve Baker, who, unable to cope with the societal pressure of living in a mixed-race marriage, has deserted Julie. Without Steve and the security of the showboat, Julie has become an unreliable drunkard. A good Julie is barely able to sing "Bill."

"Bill" consistently stopped every performance for the remainder of Helen's life. She received countless requests in her nightclub and personal appearances to sing it for some William who felt a connection with Helen. One fan was cowboy star William S. Hart, who introduced himself to Helen after hearing her sing it. They became friends and corresponded regularly for years.

Musical comedy artists of the era *performed*, yet Helen, with little experience and no training, carried the dramatic miscegenation scene when Julie leaves the showboat and then *acted* "Bill." Composer Hugh Martin once asked director Joshua Logan about his most memorable moment in a theater. Logan answered that Helen Morgan singing "Bill" in *Show Boat* "was the greatest concentration of theater magic [he'd] ever seen in three minutes."[26]

~

Helen sings "Bill" in the original 1927 production of *Show Boat*. (Billy Rose Theatre Division, the New York Library for the Performing Arts)

P. G. Wodehouse wrote the original lyric to "Bill," but, to fit Kern's modification and to make the lyric not quite so comic, Oscar Hammerstein reshaped the words to the first seven bars of each chorus (or, as Kern preferred, "burthen"). Wodehouse consented to the changes, to the shared writing credit with Hammerstein, and to half of the lyricist's royalties.

However, librettist Guy Bolton had a long-standing alliance with Wodehouse wherein the two shared all book and lyric royalties equally. As Wodehouse's watchdog, Bolton threatened to bar "Bill" from *Show Boat* until Ziegfeld hammered out a new contract that benefited Kern, Hammerstein, Wodehouse, *and* Bolton. He later claimed that, for the 1936 Universal film, Hammerstein altered the lyric of "Bill" sufficiently to claim full authorship, thus denying Wodehouse and Bolton royalties. While the film tie-in sheet music was a direct reprint of the 1927 edition, the 1946 publication reflects Hammerstein's minimal lyric changes ("oh" replacing "and," "isn't" replacing "is not," etc.) from the 1936 film.

Because of Bolton's persistence, by the time of *Show Boat*'s 1946 Broadway revival, Hammerstein had relinquished all rights to "Bill" and paid Wodehouse and Bolton $5,000 in back royalty payments. He also wrote a disclaimer for the playbill: "I am particularly anxious to point out that the lyric to the song 'Bill' was written by P. G. Wodehouse. Although he has always been given credit in the program, it has frequently been assumed that since I wrote all the other lyrics for 'Show Boat,' I also wrote this one, and I have had praise for it which belongs to another man."[27]

The dispute did not end there. Later, Bolton accused Hammerstein's estate of pocketing all the lyricist royalties for "Bill" from the 1971 London stage revival.

Once in Washington, the *Show Boat* company spent two days loading in and teching the elephantine production. On November 15, 1927, Charles Winninger appeared before the curtain and warned the opening-night audience that they would witness every scene and song written for the show, even if they "didn't get out of the trenches until Septuagesima."[28] Exiting the theater at 12:50 a.m., many patrons believed that Winninger's prophecy had come true.

Exhausted but elated, the company went out on the town while Kern and Hammerstein pared the show down to a manageable length. Robert Russell Bennett found himself in a cabaret where Helen sang for the fun of it. A request went out for "My Heart Stood Still." Helen caught the song in *One Dam Thing After Another* in London. Rodgers and Hart recycled it in *A Connecticut Yankee*, which had just opened the week before, but the local band did not have the music. Bennett knew it but was in the club to relax, not to work. When she learned this, Helen marched over to him and pouted. "I'm mad at you."[29] Beaten, Bennett walked to the piano and asked what key she wanted. "I don't know," she answered. With her spotty musical training, this was something she had not yet learned, and, with her range, it had not yet been an issue. Bennett played the song in its original key.[30] It went over like gangbusters. For an encore, Helen sang, for the second time in public, "Bill."[31]

The cast, called at eleven the next day, found the National Theatre abuzz. Since nine o'clock, and unmindful of the chilling drizzle, the line for the box office had extended around the block and back again. Complementing the excitement outside, the company rehearsed the cuts they subsequently implemented during the four-hour matinee. The company rehearsed again and performed the evening show without dinner. Finally, *Show Boat* was in striking distance of a three-hour run time.[32] More pruning, additions, and rehearsals lay ahead, but the worst was over.

Helen suffered two major cuts in Washington. The first shortened the Pantry Scene (act 1, scene 2). Originally, Magnolia and Julie sang a reprise of "Make Believe" before "Can't Help Lovin' Dat Man." For the introductory verse of the former, Oscar Hammerstein fashioned a new lyric to "If We Were on Our Honeymoon" from Kern's 1913 effort *The Doll Girl*.[33] The sequence looks both forward and backward in Hammerstein's artistic development. On one hand, it evokes the through-composed operetta scenas he wrote with Otto Harbach. On the other, it foretells the restructured reprises he would write with Richard Rodgers (such as "Sixteen Going on Seventeen" from *The Sound of Music*) as well as the more natural transition between dialogue and song, such as *Carousel*'s bench scene. While deepening the bond between Magnolia and Julie, the number slowed the narrative.

The second deletion remains the most controversial. The miscegenation scene (act 1, scene 4) originally began with the brooding "Mis'ry's Comin' Aroun'" for Queenie, Julie, and the chorus. It added tension and emotional depth to the melodrama that followed, but six minutes of atmosphere was an unaffordable luxury for a show that always ran long. Ziegfeld cut it. The musical cornerstone of Kern's score, "Mis'ry" featured heavily in both the overture and the show's underscoring. Pained by the loss, Kern included the number in the first published edition of the score. Helen sang her verse as an introduction to both of her commercial recordings of "Can't Help Lovin' Dat Man."

Length may not have been the sole reason behind Ziegfeld's decision to cut "Mis'ry." It also made him nervous. It was one thing to confront social ills in a book scene or a satirical number, but a dark, gloomy chorale was something else entirely in a Ziegfeld spectacular. Then we have the original Queenie. Tess Gardella triumphed in her comic moments and sang her other, upbeat vocal assignments with verve. Not one critic found Gardella's performance lacking, but Ziegfeld, Kern, and Hammerstein may have feared that "Mis'ry" lay outside the acting range of this white woman playing the role in blackface. It may have been outside her vocal range too. The belter never sang above C above middle C in her other *Show Boat* numbers, but she sang sustained E's in "Mis'ry."[34] Perhaps the 1994 *Show Boat* revival, in which the song finally made its Broadway debut, provides the answer. Onstage, the song is overlong and static. Worse, at its climax, when Julie climbs onto the stage and "in spite of herself . . . start[s] rocking and swaying like the others," it takes on a cringeworthy trance/tribal feel.[35] Director Hal Prince trapped his Julie, Lonette McKee, on the showboat stage in her created persona. As the chorale built to its climax, McKee mimed her attempt to exit the glass house where she found herself imprisoned.

Show Boat prompted as large a developmental leap for Oscar Hammerstein in terms of race as in his skills as a librettist. A lifelong liberal, his penchant for race issues preceded Julie. Wanda, the mixed-race woman in *Rose-Marie*, and Azuri, the jealous Arab dancer in *The Desert Song*, are, in their way, Julie's sisters. The *Show Boat* difference is that, for the first time, Hammerstein wrote a mixed-raced character in a positive light—more so than Ferber created in her novel. The biracial Mooda in *Golden Dawn* (written during the *Show Boat* lull of February–July 1927) appears to be a transitional creation. On the one hand, she steals her lover's white baby and brings her up to believe that she is Black, but on the other, she kills the villain to save that child. Julie and Mooda are not only the precursors of the race issues Hammerstein would later examine with Richard Rodgers but also the first Hammersteinian Earth Mothers: the older, wiser, sympathetic female voices who advise ingenues that there's no use in wondering because your man may do something wonderful.

Show Boat did turn-away business in Pittsburgh, Cleveland, and, with the exception of the first two performances, Philadelphia. The announcement of a third week in Philly prompted lines to form around the block. Women tussled over standing-room tickets.

Out-of-town audiences cheered, but Ziegfeld's secretary, "Goldie" Stanton Clough, remembered Manhattan's flummoxed first-nighters being unsure if it was proper to applaud and break the continuity. Adding to the confusion was the decision not to include a curtain call. At the end of that performance on December 27, 1927, the spectators gave the production a little confused applause, then left in silence. Ziegfeld paced the lobby of his theater, second-guessing his decision to move *Rio Rita* from the Ziegfeld to the Lyric Theatre so he could tie down *Show Boat* in his own, larger house. He considered himself a fool to have strayed so far from his oeuvre. Afterward, Clough, Winninger, Tess Gardella, and Helen awaited the reviews at a local speakeasy.

They were raves.

Ziegfeld still mourned his folly, saying, "Maybe the critics did like it, but the public won't."[36] Arriving the following morning, he saw people mobbing his temple to the arts. Convinced that his theater was afire, he ran to see the carnage, only to find a throng buying tickets to the biggest hit of his career.

New York's critics reserved most of their praise for Ziegfeld and the writing team of Kern and Hammerstein. Note that no one in the original production was starred. All, including Norma Terris and Charles Winninger, were featured, which likely factored into often-perfunctory acting notices. Most simply noted that Helen sang two numbers in the style she had made famous in her club act. Robert Coleman declared that *Show Boat*'s success "shows that managers have not until now realized the tremendous possibilities of the musical comedy as an art form."[37]

The one contrarian was the *Billboard*'s Gordon M. Leland, who felt that the whole was less than the sum of its considerable parts. He placed the blame for this squarely on Ferber's second-rate source material and a few missteps in Ziegfeld's renowned genius for pacing. Leland also lamented that Helen "plays the part to perfection and is a loss to the production when her part is dropped out early in the second act."[38] If the notices were not all she might have wished, Helen led two hit numbers in the biggest show in town and had proved that she was a fine dramatic actor.

Then the bottom fell out.

Federal Prohibition administrator Major Maurice Campbell had a varied career before assuming the thankless task of enforcing Prohibition: veterinary surgeon, assistant city editor for the *New York Herald*, and a correspondent during the Spanish-American War. After his 1896 marriage to actor Henrietta Crosman, Campbell toiled as a theatrical press agent and later as a producer, notably of David Belasco's *Sweet Kitty Bellairs*. During the Great War, he attained the rank of major with the Fourth Division in the Argonne. After the Armistice, he directed movies, including Bebe Daniels in the 1920 silent version of *Oh, Lady! Lady!!* In 1926, he joined the dry forces. A year later, he replaced Chester P. Mills as head of the New York Bureau.

On December 28, he warned Broadway's watering holes to expect visits from undercover agents on New Year's Eve.[39] The club world, anticipating a $3 million boon from the three-day weekend, ignored the threat. The following evening, he assembled twenty-five federal agents at Grand Central Terminal. At 8:00 p.m., they boarded a train to Mount Vernon, and then they transferred to a bus. His ruse made everyone, including his agents, believe that the major would raid Westchester County, but at midnight, he gave the signal to drive back into the city.

A full house celebrated Helen's return to Chez Helen Morgan. The holiday spirits flowed freely. At about 1:20 a.m., while the orchestra played "My Blue Heaven," two men grabbed the club's doorman by both his arms and warned him to be quiet as other agents entered the cabaret. Still others guarded the exits. The major's chief lieutenant, Tom Shannon, walked onto the dance floor and announced the raid.

Prohibition-era clubs operated, openly and licensed, under the conceit that they provided only ice, mixers, and the like for patrons, who brought their own liquor. In a 1926 challenge to this loophole, federal agents raided several Chicago clubs and charged both management and patrons with selling and using setups. Helen's friend Mike Fritzel, owner of the Friar's Inn, and William R. Rothstein, then owner of the Moulin Rouge, challenged the new practice in court. Federal judge Adam C. Cliffe ruled that the Volstead Act outlawed not only places that sold liquor but also "places where people carrying liquor congregate."[40] In October 1927, Fritzel and Rothstein appealed to the US Supreme Court, which refused to hear the case.[41]

Two months later, at Chez Helen Morgan, patrons hissed when instructed to remain in their seats, and they continued their furor while the Feds searched upstairs for alcohol. Yet, when the boys returned to the dining room, they found the floor littered with empty flasks.

Campbell and Shannon grilled Helen, her staff, and the customers, the cheekier of whom identified themselves as Thomas Jefferson, Molly Pitcher, Jesse James, and the like. After more than two hours, Campbell released the patrons, who paid their tabs and collected their coats. By this point, only the women chose to jeer the Feds: their men had had enough of the ordeal. Even Helen accosted Campbell with unladylike language during her questioning.

In covering the raid, the *Daily News* described Helen—indeed, any woman—as a torch singer for the first time.[42] As late as November, the press still described torchbearers as reedy tenors. In time, the term would apply exclusively to women.[43]

Under the advice of assistant US attorney Robert B. Watts, Campbell did not charge Helen and her associates with supplying setups but, in a first in New York, with violating sections 3450 and 3452 of the Revised Statutes of 1878. He argued that the government received no duty for liquor it itself made illegal to import. A successful tool in almost four hundred cases in Chicago, and in twenty-five in Detroit, the Revenue Act declared "all tools, implements and personal property" subject to confiscation.[44] Chez Helen Morgan boasted a capacity of 350 guests and, on the mezzanine level, the rarest of the rare in upscale Prohibition nightclubs: a thirty-foot mahogany bar. Even so, the cabaret "defrauded" the government the import duty of $4.20 a gallon on just nineteen pints of champagne, eight quarts of Scotch, two quarts of both gin and rye, two and a half "bottles" of cognac, and one "bottle" each of Scotch, gin, rum, and Benedictine. Tax revenue was not the point. In addition to an estimated $75,000 loss in seized and damaged property and thousands of dollars in fines and legal fees, Campbell denied Nick Blair and his partners the New Year's weekend business, which included $10,000 in estimated cover charges alone. His goal was not to fine or imprison but to put the most popular club in town out of business. To achieve this goal, Campbell and his men did not raid Chez Helen Morgan; they destroyed it.

In under an hour, forty men emptied the club. Nothing, "not even a corkscrew was left on the premises."[45] Upstairs, the bar, back bar, tables, and chairs found their way into the six vans waiting outside. The main room lost music racks, a Christmas tree, tables, gilded chairs, silverware, linens, pictures, draperies, and a piano to the Knickerbocker Warehouse. Items not easily moved—booths and partitions attached to the walls—fell victim to the agents' axes. Viewing the carnage, one raider bragged, "It'll take 'em till Fourth of July to clean up the mess."[46] The only thing left intact was a huge mirror that, under ordinary circumstances, reflected the merriment of Helen's revelers. Perhaps it would not fit in the truck, or perhaps superstitious Feds erred on the side of caution and left the mirror intact. Cub reporter Sidney Skolsky arrived on the scene as the last of the fixtures were loaded onto the trucks, but he did witness a cop kicking the downed Christmas tree, expecting to discover a bottle of hooch but finding a rosary a patron had dropped while fleeing the raid instead.[47]

Campbell, who claimed that he had instructed his men to destroy nothing, nonetheless equipped his agents with hatchets and fire hooks. When newspaper photographers documented the carnage in exquisite detail, Campbell suggested that the club owners and their lawyers had staged the photos to elicit public sympathy. Whether he ordered the destruction, overzealous agents acted on their own while he stood by and did nothing, or the club's owners staged the event, the press still tried Campbell in print. He photographed all subsequent nightclub raids to prevent any further demonization.

Chez Helen Morgan in ruins. (Author's collection)

The chaos inside the club equaled the mayhem outside. A thousand onlookers assembled to heckle the agents. Even passing motorists loudly expressed their displeasure. After neighbors complained about the noise, police dispersed the crowd.

Every club on the Rialto heard the unhappy news before the Feds left Helen's club. Texas Guinan cracked, "I wonder if she'll get my room."[48] Every nightclub in the district closed that night at 3:00 a.m. on the dot and, thereafter, placed extra security on their doors.

Police transported eight waiters to the West Thirtieth Street station. Helen joined them, wearing an ermine wrap over an evening gown. When she sighed over the $2,000 fur while *Show Boat* was in rehearsal, Ziegfeld financed the purchase and deducted the price from her salary in easy installments. The prison matron took pity on Helen and the fur: "It was really funny; she was so worried about my white fur wrap and insisted on wrapping it up and giving me an old sweater."[49]

The interrogation angered Helen, but the two hours she spent behind bars, with a dope fiend and a woman accused of grand larceny, frightened her. After her lawyer, J. Arthur Adler, arranged bail, at 5:30 a.m., she limped

Helen never met a fur she didn't like. (Author's collection)

back to her suite at the Warwick Hotel, which was across the street from the Ziegfeld and steps away from Chez Helen Morgan.

A former assistant US district attorney, Adler had influential friends. Hearing about the destruction caused in the raid, US Representative Fiorello La Guardia vowed to investigate Campbell's vandalism, inspiring Adler to go on the offensive. He proclaimed that Helen was in no way connected with the running, let alone the owning, of Chez Helen Morgan. He decried the use of the revenue laws to seize assets as an abuse of the Constitution. He formally demanded the return of everything removed without a warrant, vowing to carry his case to the Supreme Court if necessary to win back the cabaret's furnishings. With hyperbole worthy of Barnum, Adler finished by pontificating,

"In my opinion, everyone who had a hand in this matter ought to go to jail. Before this case has gone far it will be the representatives of the Government who will be defendants."[50]

In addition to the fittings, Adler demanded the return of the club's books, which provided the agency with the names and addresses of dozens of Manhattan's elite who had made reservations, at twenty dollars a head, for New Year's Eve. After Adler threatened to explode a legal "bombshell" to combat the ham-fisted move, Campbell surrendered a copy of the reservation list and returned all money already collected.

On New Year's Eve, Campbell's men surveilled sixty restaurants and hotels, raiding four. On January 11, speaking before the Woman's Christian Temperance Union, Campbell called the Morgan raid, the only club dismantled, "the first gun fired" in his quest to mop up New York. Four hundred women cheered.[51] Conversely, while decrying the willful destruction on the Chez Helen Morgan raid, the Vatican publication *L'Osservatore Romano* mourned 65,000 deaths due to the noble experiment, more than the number of American causalities during the Great War. The Feds continued crunching numbers to indicate progress but fooled few into thinking that the situation was improving.

The day after the raid, Helen granted a lengthy newspaper interview. She publicly forgave the agents, noting that several raiders, unaware of the targeted club until they arrived, resented stripping the club and were consequently apologetic. Helen inadvertently torpedoed Adler's claim that she was merely an employee by stating that this was her first time as a nightclub owner. She also confessed, "My only worry today is about Mr. Ziegfeld's attitude. I'm desperately anxious to stay in my part in *Show Boat*." Ziegfeld was not about to lose his starlet to a prison, and his imprint is all over Helen's declaration: "I'm through with night clubs. If it was the purpose of the agents to discourage me by breaking up the club, they've succeeded. I'm through—forever."[52]

At the Casa Lopez, emcee Jack Osterman asked his patrons to offer a silent prayer for the safe return of the Chez Helen Morgan furnishings, a request the revelers greeted with laughter. A few days later, he made the same plea at the Sunday night Winter Garden concert, where the audience took his request to heart and prayed for Helen and Broadway's return to normalcy.

Adler proposed a compromise: if Campbell returned the seized property and dropped the charges against Helen, Adler would not press charges against

Campbell. The major refused, confident that he could convict Helen in court. On February 2, US attorney Charles H. Tuttle suggested that if the other defendants pleaded guilty, the government could afford to drop the charges against Helen and still claim victory. Campbell refused, which further alienated Tuttle, who was still insisting that his assistant, Robert B. Watts, had granted the major authorization to conduct *a* raid on December 29 but not the Morgan raid specifically. Furious, Tuttle exacted his revenge in print, opining that Campbell had no legal authority to destroy Chez Helen Morgan. On the fifteenth, after the third postponement of the case in federal court, Campbell and Tuttle met, this time in Washington, with the assistant attorney general and Prohibition czar Mrs. Mabel Walker Willebrandt. Considering that Campbell planned his raid with the knowledge and assistance of Washington, Willebrandt believed that he deserved support. She scolded Tuttle for bargaining over plea deals and authorized Campbell to prosecute whom he chose.

Realizing that a case reluctantly argued by Tuttle was a recipe for disaster, Campbell agreed to compromise. Emboldened, his foes chose not to bargain. Adler, through Tuttle, charged that on the night of the raid, $300 went missing from Blair's till. Adler also questioned the legitimacy of the major's office: With the results of his Civil Service Exam not yet verified, was Campbell, legally, a federal employee at the time of the raid? Then, emcee Arthur Gordoni refused to plead guilty. Beaten, Campbell abandoned the revenue statutes strategy to seize property. The next day, Watts dropped all charges against Helen, Gordoni, and headwaiter Louis Green. On March 14, the six remaining employees pleaded guilty. John Leonard, a cashier, paid a $150 fine; the other five waiters paid $100 each.[53]

Campbell's folly cost the American taxpayers $200,000. By late February, Rialto gossips were predicting that Willebrandt would transfer him away from New York, perhaps to the Midwest.

Adler then alleged that Campbell's men had further roughed up the furnishings while offloading the vans on the night of the raid. In response, on March 21, Campbell sent his own team of photographers to record the return of the confiscated furnishings—both to prevent any additional vandalism charges and to obtain proof in case any property made its way into another club. Newspaper photographers also congregated at the Knickerbocker Warehouse to obtain a visual record. Work halted for the day. On the following day, the cabaret's furnishings returned to their rightful owner. The remaining contraband was disposed of in accordance with the law.

Nick Blair did not wait on the courts. He had been vacationing in Havana at the time of the raid, and he refused to believe the news when he returned—until he saw the notice on the door of Chez Helen Morgan. Within days, he secured a new location. Despite her public declaration, Helen (and Arthur Gordoni) moved into Texas Guinan's old 300 Club, 151 West Fifty-Fourth Street, just a few doors down from Chez Helen Morgan. Ziegfeld, allegedly receiving a cut of the business, gave Helen his blessing. At the simply named Helen Morgan Club, Friedman's Orchestra provided music for the show and for dancing. These were no by-the-numbers dance arrangements. Some clocked in at over twenty minutes.

On March 13, Joseph A. Palma, chief of the New York branch of the Secret Service, was feted at the Hotel Commodore. Gordoni provided entertainment from the Helen Morgan Club, although Helen did not perform. Toastmaster that evening was US attorney Charles H. Tuttle.

New York was back to normal.

6

"I Want a Lovable Baby"

When 1928 dawned, Helen Morgan was an up-and-coming singer and actor. Within a year, she was the living embodiment of New York, as much a torchbearer of the city as Lady Liberty herself.

On Valentine's Day, she began a six-year association with Victor Records by waxing her two *Show Boat* hits. Leonard W. Joy, who conducted most of her Victor efforts, remembered that Helen "had an unusually high range; however, the warmth and richness of her tones gave the impression that her voice was much lower." The industry loved her. To Joy, Helen was "one who definitely transmitted to the people with whom she came in contact her immense vitality and joy of living."[1]

Helen's sides were, essentially, the *only* original New York cast recordings of *Show Boat*.[2] Despite their popularity, she hated hearing her own voice. Whenever someone played one of her records in her presence, she walked over to the phonograph, removed the needle, and broke the fragile shellac disc. *Variety*'s Abel Green shared Helen's dissatisfaction and suspected that her "shrill, raspy voice" was a result of not being "sufficiently rested from [her] previous night's work in show and nite club."[3] Perhaps, but seventy years later, this recording of "Bill" was inducted into the Grammy Hall of Fame.[4]

Within weeks of its reopening, Helen's was again one of the few profitable clubs in town. Helen's duties included encouraging her male clientele to drink and be friendly—but not too friendly. Having successfully rebuffed Owney Madden, she could shake off anybody, but sometimes she needed help. When "no" failed to deter a drunk offering to walk her home, Helen sighed and said, "I'd like to but I must go home with Mother."[5] Usually, bartender Robert Kelly, the man who took the rap in the December 1926 raid, escorted her home, and the "Mother" Kelly nickname stuck. Helen perpetuated the gag with a gift, usually a green tie, every Mother's Day.

Kelly offered protection when needed, but Helen still chose her escorts. In December 1927, George Jessel reprised his stage play *The Jazz Singer* for a six-week run of the subway circuit of the outer New York boroughs. One night, Jessel and playwright Samuel Shipman visited Helen's new club.

Jessel gushed, "You sing your songs as if Whistler had painted them." Enchanted, she invited him to stay after the club closed. At around 8:00 a.m., after much talking, laughing, and drinking, they went to breakfast. He was Helen's date on January 24, 1928, when Edna May Oliver wed broker David Welford Pratt at the Warwick, where Ms. Oliver also kept an apartment.

Once while lunching alone at Delmonico's, Jessel reconnected with screen actor Priscilla Dean, whom he took to a post-theater dinner before bringing her around to hear and meet Helen. He told Helen that he would escort Dean back to the Warwick, where the three of them lodged, but would join Helen once she closed up shop for the night. When he arrived at the hotel at about 5:00 a.m., the clerk informed him that Helen had already returned. Jessel ran to Helen's room without hearing the remainder of the message. He inserted his key, opened the door, and found Helen in bed with columnist Mark Hellinger.

Jessel was embarrassed.

Hellinger laughed hysterically.

Helen was furious.

Without covering herself, she charged. "How *dare* you bring another woman to my club!"

"Helen, my dear," Jessel began, inexplicably on the defensive, "you know who that lady is, and she knows how fond I am of you. That was just a little courtesy. Anyway, what right have you to squawk at my indiscretion? *You're* in *bed* with another man!"

Having none of it, Helen screamed, "Don't change the subject!"[6]

Perpetually generous, Helen never held a grudge, so long as the beneficiary of her largesse was appreciative. Jessel once turned up his nose at a Morgan gift. She huffed, "Well, perhaps if you paid me back what you owed me, I could get you what you might like!"[7]

Helen was never without a man for long. Eddie Cantor told the story about a friend who once approached Helen to inquire, "I know a fellow who's just crazy to meet you, but I don't know if he's your type."

Helen asked, "Is he a man?"

The fellow said, "Of course."

Helen said, "Well, that's my type."[8]

Midday on May 6, fire broke out at the Morgan Club. The damage was trifling. Besides, Nick Blair planned to relocate the Morgan Club in June. The former Band Box, at 134 West Fifty-Second Street, sported a retractable roof, where customers could escape the heat and dance under the stars. The move inspired a new name: Helen Morgan's Summer Home.

On June 28, 1928, at the Democratic convention in Houston, New York governor Al Smith, running on a platform of repeal, accepted his party's nomination for president. While Gotham celebrated his promise of emancipation, 160 federal agents raided eleven of Broadway's most fashionable cabarets. It was the largest raid in New York history. Five or six men in evening clothes visited each establishment. At the end of the first show, between 2:00 and 2:30 a.m., having proof of the selling of alcohol, an agent walked onto the dance floor and ordered the club to close. Helen Morgan's Summer Home, in operation for less than three weeks, earned the dubious honor of being the first raid of the night. While the Feds arrested the staff, the patrons paid their tabs. Then, while being ushered outside, many grabbed bottles for themselves, depriving the Feds of the opportunity to charge the Summer Home with possession of additional liquor.

A kindhearted agent permitted Helen to retrieve her belongings from her dressing room, where she swapped clothes with a hatcheck girl and slipped out unnoticed.[9] Also escaping capture was Texas Guinan. Her absence from her Salon Royale fueled rumors that someone had warned her ahead of the raid.[10]

On the morning of June 30, with Major Campbell threatening to issue warrants for their arrest, the queens of the night traveled to the Federal Building and surrendered, yet no one there could locate a warrant. Texas Guinan asked a clerk how he was. He replied, "Fine." She quipped, "How much fine?" The clerk suggested the women see Charles H. Tuttle. The politically ambitious US attorney dared not alienate New York society by charging the city's two most popular hostesses, and he was loath to aid Campbell. He unloaded Helen and Guinan on his second-in-command, Robert B. Watts, who, in turn, handed the women over to US commissioner Garrett W. Cotter. At one o'clock, minutes before Helen was due at the Ziegfeld for her matinee performance, Cotter charged them with violation of the Prohibition law. Entering her plea, Guinan declared her innocence in a loud, steady voice. Helen, in contrast, smoked Lucky Strikes, paced incessantly, and, when called upon, barely muttered, "Not guilty."[11] Cotter set bail for both at $1,000 and scheduled a hearing for July 19.

Campbell could not have pulled off such a huge operation without the assistance of Prohibition commissioner James M. Doran and his "mop-up squad" of federal agents. Doran averred that the raids were not politically motivated yet crowed that "the raids took place at what was regarded by Major Campbell as the psychological moment."[12]

Leading the operation was Mrs. Mabel Walker Willebrandt. She was no teetotaler, but when appointed assistant attorney general in 1921, she committed to upholding the law.[13] Early successes in the South aside, her frustration increased as the decade wore on, especially on the nightclub front. She firmly believed that "even a stupid nightclub hostess" could pick out a federal agent in the crowd, and she insisted that Manhattan's agents be inconspicuous.[14]

Major Chester P. Mills heeded Willebrandt's dictate. He used agents who looked and acted the part of upscale men-about-town, accompanied by glamorous female agent "dates," in his December 1926 sting at Helen's 54th Street Club. Arthur Gordoni claimed that Campbell hired exiled Russian countess Vera Mussina Pushkin in September 1927 to ingratiate herself among the Chez Helen Morgan staff.[15] The first agents to enter the Morgan Club in early 1928 were Mr. and Mrs. James L. White, whom the Campbell office set up as Denver tourists. The couple made the rounds, even appearing in the gossip columns, but the Morgan stronghold, wary of federal spies, proved a tough nut to crack. One night, Mrs. White stepped out of a cab in front of the cabaret and dropped a bottle of hooch, breaking it. The liquor flowed down the street. This damsel in Volstead distress aroused pity in the club's staff, who sold the Whites liquor.[16]

Willebrandt declared the practice perfected in Manhattan with the February 17, 1928, raid at New York's Jungle Club. Here, the men who wrecked Chez Helen Morgan all but apologized for disturbing their victims. These kinder, gentler agents *regretfully* gathered evidence. The major ensured that no one destroyed or removed the Jungle's furnishings. And minutes after the agents left, the dispersed patrons returned and resumed the party. Campbell settled the score by including the Jungle Club in the June 1928 sting, but Willebrandt herself added Helen's club to the list of targets. When Campbell announced his intention to visit the Summer Home at a pre-raid briefing, his agents, as delighted as he was by the chance to avenge the Chez Helen Morgan disaster, cheered.

Campbell obtained sufficient evidence to padlock twenty cabarets and to warrant future raids. Broadway shivered. There was only so much available real estate in the theater district.

Attorney Jack Adler vowed to get Helen and her club's staff off the hook. When asked why Guinan and Helen faced a court trial, the lawyer responded, "Publicity." He was right. Guinan and Helen's quest for arraignment marked the only time Helen Morgan appeared in the lead story on the front page of the *New York Times*.[17]

Cabarets continued operating. In the early hours of July 12, agents re-raided the Mimic Club, whose unfazed customers simply went next door, where Helen, in turn, dared the Feds to visit her establishment, bragging that they would not find an ounce of liquor on the premises. When reminded of the critics who called cabarets "dens of vice," she invited moral inspections at any time.[18]

Ten days later, agents padlocked the Mimic and seven other clubs in the district. Fear of additional federal activity, combined with the city's annual summer exodus, kept patrons away, even from the boîtes that escaped Campbell's wrath. By late July, only a few clubs, including Helen's, with its open-air dance floor, remained profitable.

On July 30, a federal grand jury indicted its first group of over one hundred raid defendants on two charges. The first, conspiracy, carried a maximum sentence of two years in prison and a $10,000 fine. The second, maintaining a nuisance, carried a maximum sentence of one year and a $100 fine. To save time, the grand jury bypassed individual arraignments, hearing new pleas and fixing bail en masse, in some cases in excess of the $1,000 bond set at the time of the arrest.

Presenting his evidence, US attorney Arthur H. Schwartz vowed to "use all of the teeth in the law."[19] The threat was the last straw for Helen and Ziegfeld. After she missed several nights at her club, on August 5, the Ziegfeld office stated that Helen had "notified her former employers in the cabaret that she has definitely withdrawn from after-theater singing."[20] From then on, Helen would "conserve all her energies for her work as a featured artist of the legitimate stage."[21] To ensure that the announcement was no publicity stunt, deputy US marshal Edward Runge served Helen with a personal injunction against any further Volstead violations. If caught with a drink containing as little as 0.5 percent alcohol, she could be held for contempt of court.

~

If the Summer Home offered a late show in July, Helen did not play in it. She left the club by 2:30 a.m. to catch the late train to Great Neck, a seaside community on Long Island's North Shore. Secluded by a grove of trees, the hundred-year-old cottage sat back from the road and provided the privacy she craved. Within weeks of renting the property, Helen and Lulu dubbed their street "Cat Alley." More than seventy-five feral felines cadged regular meals off the Morgans.

The beach was a novelty for the midwesterner. She swam a bit but spent most of her leisure time stretched out in an easy chair with a good book. Charles Ellis, her *Show Boat* scene partner and Eugene O'Neill specialist, inspired her to place the playwright's back catalog atop her reading pile.

She also enjoyed gardening. Corn, berries, and herbs did well there, but her watermelons got no bigger than baseballs. She puttered around the grounds in men's overalls, years before Katharine Hepburn and Marlene Dietrich made headlines by donning male drag. At night, she eschewed negligees for men's pajamas with bold colors and designs.

To Lulu's relief, on the North Shore, her daughter drank less and ate more. In the kitchen, Helen developed her own recipes. The presence of visitors—especially young Elizabeth Collins, whom Helen befriended at a benefit appearance—also curbed her alcohol intake. Not wanting the ten-year-old to pick up bad habits, Helen rarely drank around her. Whenever Lulu feared that Helen's imbibing was out of control, Elizabeth came to visit "Aunt Helen."[22]

Having produced four hit musicals (*Rio Rita*, *Show Boat*, *Rosalie*, and *The Three Musketeers*) in just over twelve months, Ziegfeld announced *six* musicals for the 1928–1929 season: *Whoopee*, a new *Follies*, a Kern and Hammerstein original, and musical versions of *Joan of Arc*, *Six Cylinder Love*, and *East Is West*.[23] He also placed Helen under an exclusive contract, which increased her salary from $600 to $700 weekly, and promised a leading role in one of those upcoming productions.[24] The most likely Morgan project, the Kern-Hammerstein vehicle, fell through Ziegfeld's fingers. Hammerstein spent the summer preparing *Good Boy*, *The New Moon*, and *Rainbow* for the new season. The earliest he could start on a new show was early 1929, beyond Ziegfeld's timetable. The writers also remained frustrated by how slowly the Ziegfeld office remitted their *Show Boat* royalties.[25]

When Oscar's uncle, Arthur Hammerstein, offered to produce the new work in the 1929–1930 season, Kern left Ziegfeld.[26] Arthur also got Helen. He claimed he lured Helen, not with Kern but with a revival of *Camille*, helmed by Arthur Hopkins, the producer-director behind *What Price Glory* and both of John Barrymore's productions of *Hamlet*. More likely, fearing that Helen's legal troubles would land her behind bars and that her "disposition sort of stifled her voice," Ziegfeld sold a damaged asset for $25,000.[27] The how of the Hammersteins acquiring Helen aside, Ziegfeld held a grudge. In December, he forbade Helen from accepting an invitation to sing at a Sunday night concert at Hammerstein's Theatre.

Ziegfeld resolved to fully utilize Helen for the remaining ten months of his contract. If she was going to moonlight, she would do so for him. In the *Frolic*. Within days of her arrest, Ziegfeld abandoned his new *Follies*. He would reopen the *Midnight Frolic*, again atop the New Amsterdam, to run in tandem with *Whoopee* downstairs. Ziegfeld's experience running a New York cabaret went back to 1914 when he opened a simple bar and dance hall atop the New Amsterdam Theater. When his *Danse de Follies* proved successful, he converted the space into a nightclub and opened his first *Midnight Frolic* in 1915. Ziegfeld shuttered the series in Prohibition-vexed 1922, and the space, after a $100,000 restoration, bowed as a conventional, but unsuccessful, theater.

On August 6, more than two hundred people appeared at the Federal Building for arraignment. Half were victims of the June raids; the rest were charged with other Prohibition offenses. It was only through newspaper coverage that Texas Guinan learned that the agency expected her presence. She made it a point to arrive early and reveled in the spotlight. One reporter admired her black ensemble. Guinan shot back, "How do you think I'll look in stripes?"[28] When asked if she, like Helen, would retire from the nightclub field, she replied, "Honey, I'm not a quitter."[29]

Helen was among sixty-five conspicuously absent defendants. After the forfeiture of her bail and the issuance of a warrant for her arrest, she appeared the following day, on Jack Adler's arm. In direct contrast with Guinan's boisterous performance the day before, Helen shook from nervousness and dabbed her eyes with a handkerchief.[30] With assistance from Adler, she averred that Agent Lon H. Tyson had perjured himself in a highly publicized affidavit that claimed that Helen said she had an "understanding" with the major that precluded the raid on her establishment.[31]

Most Prohibition-era offenders avoided prison and stiff fines by pleading no contest to lesser charges, saving the government court costs, but Campbell's threat to forgo the standard procedure of letting waiters off with a nominal fine, on top of recent severe judgments for possession, changed the minds of many caught in the June 1928 sting. Believing that there was no advantage in pleading guilty to anything, this time, 185 people chose to stand trial.

Within two weeks of Helen's retirement, the Summer Home resembled a morgue more than a nitery. Then the federal district court padlocked the Summer Home.

The pendulum began to swing in the opposite direction when Tuttle intervened and squashed the court's subpoenas of 125 club patrons, many from New York's finest families, to provide state's evidence in the cases springing from the June raids. Broadway received even better news in September, when Judge Thomas D. Thatcher declared all temporary padlocks, including the one on the Summer Home, illegal, stating, "To my mind, this practice of depriving persons of their property or the use of their property without a trial is shocking."[32]

Helen, preparing to return to the night shift, Ziegfeld style, left Lulu in Great Neck and moved back into the city, taking an unassuming apartment at 110 West Fifty-Fifth Street. To shuttle between two abodes, she purchased a handmade Isotta Fraschini, the same car in which Gloria Swanson, as Norma Desmond, terrorized Hollywood in *Sunset Boulevard*. Helen often raced to the theater via the Central Park bridle paths, wearing but a fur coat over those men's pajamas.

Meanwhile, Nick Blair vowed that Helen would fulfill their five-year contract, even if he had to force her out of *Show Boat* to do it. In the fall, he reopened the former Helen Morgan Club as the Casanova.[33] He engaged the services of another Helen—Kane—to put it over. Because the club, like the post-raid Summer Home, was strictly a setups affair, with no liquor sold, Morgan braved the injunction and christened the Casanova from the audience on opening night.

To commemorate the one-year anniversary of *Show Boat*, Ziegfeld rented an antique steam-powered calliope to play outside his theater. He also set up transatlantic telephone service between the New York and London *Show Boat* companies. His production remained popular, if eclipsed by the season's new offerings, especially his own *Whoopee*.

Backstage, Helen bounced from craze to craze with an all-consuming passion. In December, she spent over a hundred dollars on jigsaw puzzles, littering the dressing room she shared with Tess Gardella with stray pieces. In

March, she moved on to backgammon. Helen and Gardella, both perpetual dieters, played nightly. The prize: a piece of chocolate.

Helen's reading list evolved to James Stephens, Saki, and a copy of James Joyce's *Ulysses* with handwritten punctuation. When the Anderson Galleries auctioned off Jerome Kern's collection of first editions, Helen was there. She brought home no big-ticket items, but the sale inspired her to collect firsts on her own. She began with Hemingway's *The Sun Also Rises* and the works of D. H. Lawrence. A bookworm from childhood, she read her acquisitions "because it seems silly to collect something if you don't know what it's about."[34]

Helen avoided jewelry, even "grouch bags" of valuables worn about the neck for the inevitable rainy day. Earrings gave her headaches. Bracelets and necklaces annoyed her, although, while playing in *Show Boat*, she made an exception and regularly wore one-piece: a diamond "love altar." The gift came from an Englishman who wished to marry her. By early 1929, it was gone: friends suspected she had given it away. She also "lost" a $3,000 diamond brooch in a taxi.[35] In time, admirers gifted strategically. Flowers were appreciated, but 90 percent of the 264 Christmas gifts Helen received in 1928 were alcoholic. The choice was a sensible one. Each bottle of the "real McCoy" prevented Helen from downing the adulterated hooch prominent in even the most exclusive of New York niteries.

Helen always gave more than she received. On Christmas and New Year's Day, she set out special dinners for those stray cats back on Long Island. Every Christmas she was home, she gave a big dinner to show business "orphans" separated from their families during the holidays—complete with presents rarely as practical as the gifts she received. The parrot she gave Borrah Minevitch escaped, and the two spent three days desperately trying to catch it.[36]

Helen ended her brief retirement on December 29 when Ziegfeld's new *Midnight Frolic* bowed atop the New Amsterdam. Joseph Urban decked out the walls and the dome over the dance floor with a motif of yellow tulips, multicolored butterflies, and Ziegfeld's lucky mascot, elephants. Urban and Ziegfeld also closed off the balcony to configure the rooftop theater into a floor-show venue, which reduced the seating capacity from 760 to 340.

Reviews were positive, but some old-timers did not feel the old Ziegfeld magic in the new venture. Others carped that the premiere performance ran only fifty-one minutes. Still, the core material was strong: Ziegfeld's famous balloon girls, Eddie Cantor, Helen, and, headlining, Paul Whiteman and His

Orchestra. The centerpiece was a nostalgic reverie called "Reminiscing." *Whoopee* leading man Paul Gregory sang selections from hit shows from the pre-Volstead generation, while the showgirls paraded as the essence of *The Wizard of Oz* and *Mademoiselle Modiste* before being followed by their modern counterparts.

As the emcee, Eddie Cantor introduced Helen as "Fanny on the piano." In her preshow ritual, Helen visited him in his dressing room with lemon juice and honey, saying, "Eddie dear, your voice must be so tired. Try some of this. It's good for you."[37] During those first few nights, Cantor coerced impromptu performances from paying guests Fanny Brice, James Barton, and Odette Myrtil while Ziegfeld scrambled for additional acts, like Tess Gardella, to fill out the bill. After only ten days, Cantor stepped aside. Thereafter, Dan Healy, and then Charles Winninger, lifted Helen onto her piano.

Opening-night tickets went for $16.50. One table sold for $350. An agency reported offers of $1,000 for four chairs, and none could be had. After the premiere, prices were scaled at $6.69 per *couvert*.[38] Saturdays went for $7.70, although speculators charged as much as $80 for ringside tables. Cantor quipped, "It cost six dollars a ticket just to sit down. Oh, you couldn't afford to get up."[39]

Ziegfeld's lavish investment did not trickle down to Helen, whose $400 Roof salary was nothing compared to what she earned in her nightclubs. If the *Frolic* was Flo's stratagem to keep Helen sober, it failed. After finishing for the night at two, she habitually downed multiple nightcaps at another club, often Texas Guinan's, and then performed gratis.

Helen enjoyed watching showgirls work the *Frolics* patrons. She got off an outlandish pun at the expense of one unpopular young man, who, upon inheriting a fortune, experienced the new sensation of fighting women off. To Helen, "the undated [had] become the inundated."[40]

After more than a year, Helen's understudy, Eleanor Tierney, finally played Julie, from January 15 to 17, when Helen missed both her *Show Boat* and *Frolic* performances. Lulu explained that Helen had entered a private hospital to convalesce from influenza. Some wags suggested that the issue was emotional, not viral. Helen and Reggie Hammerstein had dated for so long that many expected them to marry, but the union frayed when Reggie left town in October for the protracted tryout of his Uncle Arthur's *Polly*. Helen focused on Arthur Loew, son of Marcus Loew, the founder of Loew's Inc. and the money behind MGM.

It is unclear when Helen and Arthur Loew began dating. It may have been during Helen's tenancy on Long Island's North Shore the previous summer, although it's likely that they met at an earlier date, as Marcus, if not his sons, frequented Helen Morgan's 54th Street Club.[41] In early 1929, the affair advanced to the point that Helen telegrammed Reggie, begging, "I want to be released." On January 14, Reggie confronted his rival. Loew denied any relationship with Helen. Upon her arrival, Helen learned of the row, left both of them, and "mysteriously disappeared."[42]

After his graduation from Hamilton, and his World War I naval service as a machinist's mate, Arthur Loew entered the family business.[43] In 1920, he wed Mildred, the only daughter of Paramount head Adolph Zukor. The power couple produced two children, Jane and Arthur Jr., but by 1925, their marriage existed in name only. Arthur Loew's career accelerated after his father's death in 1927. Not yet thirty and promoted to first vice president of Loew's, Arthur oversaw foreign sales. American silent films, at their artistic height, dominated the world market with a 40 percent share, compared to 12 percent in 1925.

His net worth exceeded $10 million.

Loew was as much a child of the 1920s as Helen. After Lindbergh flew to Paris, Loew obtained his pilot's license and installed a private landing field at Pembroke, the eighty-room mansion in Glen Cove he had purchased from Marcus Loew's estate. Joseph De Lamar built the North Shore compound in 1914. The forty-six-acre estate boasted a swimming pool, a home theater, an indoor shooting gallery, a private golf course, Tiffany glass, tennis courts, and greenhouses that provided fresh produce year-round. After Lamar's death by pneumonia in 1918, his heirs shuttered the estate rather than pay its hefty upkeep costs. One exception: in late 1923, Paramount rented Pembroke as a filming location for the Gloria Swanson vehicle *A Society Scandal*. A year later, Marcus Loew purchased Pembroke at public auction.

Arthur Loew also erected a dock for his yacht, which he used during the warmer months to commute to Manhattan. In 1927, he sailed to and from Canada along the Hudson and through Lakes George and Champlain. The round trip took two days. His globetrotting schedule often kept him away from Helen for weeks at a time, only for him to pop up, unannounced, to sweep her off her feet.

Helen fell for him hard.

~

On January 21, 1929, Helen returned to film in Universal's production of *Show Boat*. She appeared as Julie, but only in the film's prologue.

Thirty months before, Warner Brothers had debuted their Vitaphone sound-on-disc process with the intention of bringing the movie-palace experience of a full orchestra (and sound effects) accompanying a silent film to small-town America. Universal, having paid $65,000 in October 1926 to acquire the film rights to Edna Ferber's novel, planned to provide their audiences with a similar experience. Everything changed when Warners, unexpectedly, struck a nerve with the public when they used Vitaphone on a series of short subjects where artists sang, danced, and *talked* on-screen. Reaction to the addition of some "canned vaudeville" to the otherwise silent feature *The Jazz Singer* caused a greater sensation. When Universal announced that they would augment their *Show Boat* music track with spirituals and a singing actor as Magnolia, Ziegfeld, Oscar Hammerstein, and Edna Ferber engaged lawyers to ensure that not a note of Kern's stage score would be played on-screen. The pushback cost Mary Ellis, and then Zita Johann, the leading role but did not scuttle the production, in which Laura La Plante ultimately starred.[44]

Universal wrapped its silent treatment in October 1928, by which time the first two all-talking pictures, *Lights of New York* and *The Terror*, had taken the country by storm. In response, Universal hired A. B. Heath to re-film two reels in sound, not with Vitaphone but with Fox's Movietone sound-on-film method.[45] These attempts (and there were several) to turn late-era silents into the next *Jazz Singer* were called "goat glands," after the practice of implanting the gonads of goats, monkeys, and other purportedly oversexed mammals into aging men in hopes of restoring sexual virility. The studios believed their talkie implants would achieve similar box-office results.

Regardless, this *Show Boat* still proved wanting, so Universal struck a deal with Ziegfeld. For $100,000 and a percentage of the profits, Ziegfeld licensed some of Kern's music for the film, including La Plante's concert version of "Can't Help Lovin' Dat Man," but with the proviso that the film could not open in Manhattan until his stage production closed.[46] Aping the Vitaphone programs that preceded John Barrymore's *Don Juan* and *When a Man Loves*, Universal sent Heath to New York's Fox Movietone studio to film a sound prologue. To settle the question of salary, Ziegfeld summoned Helen to his office, where she met with Universal management. They offered her $7,000. She was overwhelmed, but Ziegfeld asked her to step out of the office. A revised contract awaited her upon her return. For $10,000. For three hours of work. It was the best wage she ever earned.[47]

Helen sings "Can't Help Lovin' Dat Man" in the prologue to Universal's 1929 filming of *Show Boat* (sequence is currently lost). (*Show Boat*, Warner Bros. Discovery, 1929)

Paul Whiteman's band began Heath's prologue by playing two pieces. Ziegfeld and Universal president Carl Laemmle followed in a mock-up of the Ziegfeld Theatre. The feature film's Cap'n Andy, Otis Harlan, appeared in character to introduce the acts that followed. Tess "Aunt Jemina" Gardella offered "C'mon Folks"; Helen and the Jubilee Singers (no quartet) sang "Can't Help Lovin' Dat Man"; Gardella and company returned for "Hey, Feller!"; and Helen and Jules Bledsoe topped everyone with "Bill" and "Ol' Man River."

Helen's contract included final approval over her footage, something she was loathe to give. Every frame horrified her. First, she complained that she could not understand herself. Ziegfeld and Universal applied pressure, assuring her that she sounded fine. And she does, but as Betty Comden and Adolph Green later spoofed in *Singin' in the Rain*, Helen overemphasized those round tones. It was one thing to sing "cahn't you see" in her contemporaneous commercial recording of "Mean to Me" and another thing for Julie, magnified on the silver screen, to sing about how her Bill "cahn't play golf or tennis or polo." She would affect more relaxed diction in her subsequent film work.

The greater shock, for a woman who suffered from body shame her entire life, was seeing her image magnified on the screen. She wore the costume she wore onstage for "Bill," but in medium close-up, a white blouse against a black gown accentuated her large bosom.[48] Worse, she had yet to learn to scale back her stage gestures for the camera.

In the end, she swallowed her pride, authorized the footage, and cashed the check. Delighted, Universal offered Helen $25,000 to star in a feature-length drama set, naturally, in a nightclub, and they would film in the East before she began rehearsals for her new stage show. She rejected the offer. Months later, she still wailed over that prologue footage, "You should see me. I look like nothing human." She claimed that Heath shot one song while she was trying to get a cinder out of her eye. "I wish they'd take the $10,000 back and destroy the film."[49]

Ziegfeld squashed Helen's wish to fly down to Florida the night before the premiere of Universal's *Show Boat*. She lamented the loss of two performances that Ziegfeld's insistence she travel by train—thirty-six hours earlier—had cost her, not to mention the early hour of departure. She exacted her revenge by flying home with Loew afterward.[50]

That Friday night, to cover a prescreening delay, Helen climbed atop a piano and sang before the capacity crowd at the Miami Capitol. After impromptu clowning by patrons Joe Frisco and W. C. Fields, the theater manager canceled the event and refunded the money. Earlier, union saboteurs had forced their way into the projection room, kidnapped the projectionist, and destroyed the sound equipment. The gala the following evening, March 16, at the Palm Beach Paramount marked the premiere of Universal's 1929 superproduction. Helen sang again, and Ziegfeld offered a few words.[51]

Early talkies favored lower voices. Sopranos, less so. The disastrous debuts of those who preceded Helen to the microphone—in particular opera's diva of the moment, Marion Talley—so haunted the collective memory that Robert Sherwood felt compelled to note, "I can't remember having heard any woman's voice come through the . . . loud speaker so successfully."[52] Only the *Billboard* vindicated Helen's misgivings by stating that she "photographed badly" and that her vocal performance suffered "from imperfect recording and reproduction."[53] Audiences disagreed. The prologue proved so popular, Universal cut and rereleased the Bledsoe and Helen footage as its own short, *Hits of Today*.[54]

The film itself did not please. When director Harry Pollard scored with the first of *The Cohens and The Kellys* comedies, Universal rewarded him with *Uncle Tom's Cabin*. Despite pacing issues with Harriet Beecher Stowe, Carl Laemmle gave him *Show Boat* on the rationale that directing one southern melodrama qualified him to helm another. In *Show Boat*, Pollard expertly provided period atmosphere, such as glimpses of nineteenth-century stagecraft, but his plodding tempo and aversion to film editing proved disastrous. With a 20-minute prologue, a 140-minute film, and an intermission, the evening was too long. Two weeks into its New York run, Universal trimmed over twenty minutes from the feature's running time. In this surviving general release form, the film still cries for scissors, but for the two static talking sequences, which Pollard did not film.

Excepting the shameless overacting of Joseph Schildkraut, the cast is marvelous—particularly Alma Rubens, whose Julie sidesteps race by remaining white throughout (a jealous Parthy kicks Julie off the showboat for being too close to the eight-year-old Magnolia). Later, when Maggie returns the borrowed money to the Chicago madam, Julie appears not as the servant but as Hetty Chilson herself. Silent film provided the ideal milieu to juxtapose the warhorses the showboaters perform and the melodrama the troupe endures off the stage. Few subsequent productions of the musical, on stage or screen, have proved as emotionally satisfying as Pollard's silent drama.

Despite the mixed critical reaction, this *Show Boat* proved the studio's highest-grossing film since *The Hunchback of Notre Dame* in 1923. However, Ziegfeld's fee for the music, coupled with the long and costly gestation period, absorbed most of the profit.

Helen shot her prologue numbers on Friday, January 25. After playing Julie that evening at the Ziegfeld, she performed her three-song *Frolic* set in the first act and then tried to beg off her second-act appearance so she could rest for her three scheduled performances the following day. The capacity crowd would not permit her to leave her perch. She sang three numbers before giving an impromptu curtain speech, in which she thanked those who had first supported her at the Back Stage Club and followed her in the ensuing years. Broadway gossip Alvin J. Kayton enthused, "It was the most informal, sentimental, and satisfactory evening the Frolic has had since New Year's Eve."[55]

After her Saturday marathon, Ziegfeld closed his *Frolic*, at a reported $65,000 loss. Deeming the nightclub setup too lowbrow, he spent an additional $10,000 to reopen the balcony and convert his *Frolic* into a conventional stage show. With increased seating capacity, the revamped *Frolic* bowed on February 6. Helen retained the third slot in the first act, singing a set of new numbers, most written by her accompanist, Martin Freed.[56] She returned, next to closing, with "My Man."[57] Freed's tenure, as for most of her accompanists, lasted about a year. Complicating their association was Freed's own alcoholism.

The new bill boasted Paul Whiteman, the Duncan Sisters, Helen, and Paul Gregory. Two weeks later, Maurice Chevalier made his American stage debut as the *Frolic*'s emcee and headliner. Also new to the Roof was a kindred spirit in the love of the grape, Lillian Roth. Helen warned, "Lillian darling, don't ever do to yourself what I'm doing."[58]

To follow Chevalier, Ziegfeld reached out to Will Rogers. When he declined, Helen headlined at the *Frolic* beginning Monday, April 8. She left the show the following week because of her trial, and Ruth Etting subbed for her. On April 27, Ziegfeld admitted defeat and closed the *Frolic* at a $75,000 loss. Scaled for a maximum weekly gross of only $12,000, which barely covered the salary for the cast, the *Frolic* could never turn a profit. The loss of alcohol revenue, as Lulu and Frank Payne learned, doomed the enterprise from the start.

The room stayed dark for a year before, benefiting from the theater setup, NBC utilized the Roof as a radio studio and for experimental television broadcasts. Later, it functioned as a rehearsal hall. Late one evening in 1959, after a rehearsal, on the stage of the former *Midnight Frolic*, Jerome Robbins and Stephen Sondheim mapped out "Rose's Turn," the classic final number of *Gypsy*.[59]

As she matured, Helen triumphed over many of her body-shaming issues, but one physical "inadequacy" haunted her throughout her life: for whatever reason, she was physically incapable of bearing children. When her career and finances jelled, the perpetually lonely child not only sent for Lulu but also adopted during the *Americana* run, only to have the baby die within a year.[60]

When Helen returned from London in 1927, she met Thelma Halloway. The vaudevillian's tale of impregnation and abandonment at the hands of her dancing partner, Joe Leonard, moved Helen to tears—and financial support.[61] Thelma gave birth to Dolores on March 11, 1928. A year later, the girl developed ear trouble, requiring great care and greater funds. Helen offered a novel solution: "Give her to me."

Baby Helen. (AP Photo)

As always, Helen went overboard in her new project until her legal woes returned. She accepted the risk that she might serve a five-year prison sentence but refused to gamble with the child's welfare. Days before she stood trial, she returned Baby Helen to Thelma, along with funds to care for the baby, just in case.

7

Trials

As her trial date loomed, Helen trembled: Mabel Willebrandt clearly had the upper hand.

By sacrificing the felony charge of conspiracy for the misdemeanor charge of maintaining a nuisance, Willebrandt won victories against the Yacht Club and the Owl Club. A jury required only two hours' deliberation to find Texas Guinan's brother, Tommy, guilty of maintaining a nuisance. Still, Willebrandt dreamed of winning felony convictions for Texas and Helen. On March 2, 1929, Congress fueled her desire by passing Senator Wesley L. Jones's "Five and Ten" Law, which permitted the agency to try all Prohibition violations as either a misdemeanor or a felony, with maximum penalties of five years in prison and a $10,000 fine.[1] Willebrandt's heart beat faster when the notoriously severe federal judge Edwin S. Thomas agreed to try Texas and Helen.

Willebrandt tried Tex's nuisance charge first, as only a misdemeanor. On April 11, Texas won her acquittal with a star performance on the witness stand that made fools of Willebrandt's star agents, the so-called Four Horsemen. After this blow, Washington predicted that Willebrandt would abandon her pursuit of Helen Morgan, N. T. Granlund, and the remainder of those indicted in the June raids. Willebrandt issued a statement to the contrary but abandoned the Jones Law.

Judge Thomas postponed Helen's trial an additional day to sentence thirty-five others, including the second hostess to stand before him. An alumna of Helen's 54th Street Club, Loretta McDermott, found her eponymous cabaret caught in the great 1928 mop-up. Although Texas testified—under oath—that she never drank and could not recognize alcoholic beverages by sight, McDermott, as her lawyer explained, could not "testify that she does not know liquor when she sees it and that she didn't see it sold in her club."[2] She pleaded guilty and received a $150 fine and a suspended sentence.

Adler persisted that Helen was innocent.

A persistent drizzle chilled the city on April 16, when six of Helen's codefendants pleaded guilty. When Nick Blair and Herman Brooks, the club's runner, failed to appear, Judge Thomas issued bench warrants for their arrests.

Special US attorney Leslie Salter replaced Major Campbell's nemesis, Charles H. Tuttle. A blond, slightly balding, clean-cut midwesterner, Salter fit Willebrandt's upscale image. By his side was Norman J. Morrison, the special assistant who failed to convict Texas.

Salter and Adler weeded down a pool of one hundred potential jurors, excusing many at odds with the noble experiment. One was a Morgan Club patron. Salter angled to impanel men he hoped were politically conservative. The average age of the twelve who served was fifty, ten years older than that of the jurors who acquitted Texas. Four were retirees. Still, one juror admitted his prejudice against Prohibition and its enforcement "but believed he could be fair about the thing."[3]

In his opening address, Salter charged Blair and "two associates whom the Agency had been unable to identify" of owning, operating, and maintaining a public nuisance at Helen Morgan's Summer Home. He charged that Helen's "duty was to draw crowds so that more liquor might be sold." He reminded the court of the Morgan name above the door of her previous haunts and said that "she told agents of how she often sat on the bar there and drank and sang."[4] Unlike at Chez Helen Morgan, there was no bar in the Summer Home, and Adler, taking umbrage at the distasteful way Salter used the word "bar," insisted that Salter stick to the case at hand. Thomas agreed, ordering that only evidence collected at the Summer Home be admissible.

John J. "Denver Johnnie" Mitchell, one of Willebrandt's Four Horsemen, took the stand. He testified that he visited the Summer Home on June 11, 14, 17, and 23, 1928. On that first visit, federal agent Lon H. Tyson and his wife accompanied Mitchell. They presented a business card from the Frivolity Club to gain entrance. Mitchell inquired, "With my card would it be necessary for me to tote my own liquor?"[5] The waiter asked what he wanted. Mitchell requested champagne and cocktails. After going into a huddle with some other waiters, the waiter fulfilled the order.

The agents did not meet Helen that first night, but during her show, Tyson shouted out a request for "Ol' Man River." Atop her piano, she replied, "All right, pie face. I'll sing your song."[6] Everyone in court, even Helen, laughed at the tale. Otherwise, Helen never uttered a sound, not even to make a suggestion to her counsel. Unlike Texas, Helen wore no jewelry to court, and she donned a businesslike navy blue suit. She did not play up to her all-male jury.

In need of a shave, Mitchell repeatedly glanced at the jury from the corner of his eye. Fidgeting in his chair, he reported how the trio spent $207.20 of taxpayer money at the Summer Home. Scotch and Rye cost ten dollars a pint, brandy went for fifteen dollars, and champagne for twenty-five dollars a quart. To ingratiate themselves, they tipped ten dollars to the headwaiters and seven dollars to their serving waiters. Despite the steep prices, none of the potables removed from the club for analysis were genuine. The rye and Scotch proved to be synthetic reproductions. The champagne, spiked sparkling white grape juice.[7]

During one visit, the headwaiter spied Mitchell and Tyson ogling the girls in the floor show. He took Mitchell aside and offered to "get [him] a blonde in three minutes if [he] wanted one."[8]

Agents Herrick and Hargrove and Hargrove's wife joined the trio for their second visit. This time, after asking and receiving an introduction, Helen sat with them. There was no Volstead hump at Helen Morgan's. The waitstaff served up rye in a ginger ale bottle placed on their table for all to see. Helen turned up her nose at the offer of Scotch. When Tyson offered to order champagne, Helen shrugged. Tyson suggested brandy, and Helen lit up: "Order brandy. That's my drink." When the waiter confirmed that they were out, Helen instructed Herman Brooks to "go over to the house and get six bottles of brandy. Tell mama to be sure not to give you the Napoleon." After Brooks left, Helen confided, "I love brandy. I've been drinking it all night with a friend in the rest room." Then she sent someone backstage to fetch her own bottle. Her guests consumed the remaining two ounces from that while they waited. Brooks reentered with a package the size of a suit box under his arm, took it to the kitchen, and returned with a ginger ale bottle, announcing, "Here's your brandy." The agents purchased two quarts. Helen admitted that the wholesale price for the Summer Home was $6.25. Retail was $15. "She said whenever they had a shipment sent to the club she had a couple of cases sent to her home. It was some of the stuff she had sent to her home we drank that night."[9] When Mitchell added ginger ale to his brandy, she warned that the blend would give him a hangover.

Mrs. Tyson sighed over her wish to open a club in Dallas. Helen replied, "Why don't you do like I do? There isn't any risk. Get a couple or three good fellows to go in with you and then, if there is any trouble, you are just an employee. They will take the blame."[10]

After closing for the night, Helen led her new companions across the street to the Furnace Club. Mitchell, with knowing glances to Adler and Salter, described how he lifted Helen onto the bar as if it were a piano as she pined, "Over at my club we used to have a bar. I used to sit on it a great deal of the time and sing and drink brandy."[11]

As the agents left, Helen, still on the bar, tossed dollar bills to the African American entertainers. Meeting up with the agents on June 23, she apologized for getting "tight on [them] Sunday."[12] Tyson scolded her extravagance, but she assured him that the cash had ended up with the Furnace's owner, to whom she owed money. However, when Tyson offered to buy the Summer Home, Helen spat, "My club is not for sale."[13]

Under cross-examination, Mitchell admitted that both he and Tyson had claimed the $92.60 tab from the third Summer Home visit on their expense reports. Mitchell brushed off the discrepancy as an oversight.

When Mitchell testified that he told Helen that he was in town on business and pleasure, Adler snapped, "Well, there was a great deal of pleasure in it, wasn't there, Mr. Mitchell?" When Adler suggested that the agents' objective was entrapment. Mitchell replied, "No, sir. We wanted to get her if she was guilty. We were after the higher-ups."

"Well, you had figured her as one, hadn't you?"

"We had."

"Then you were out to get her?"

"Yes, sir."[14]

Tyson went next. He corroborated Mitchell's testimony, adding "no one would take [his] money" for the champagne and Scotch he ordered before announcing the raid. As the courtroom emptied at the end of the first day, a wag asked if Helen felt that it was a good show. She replied, "No. It's the worst opening I've ever had."[15]

The prosecution continued on April 17 and into April 18. Adler asked how one could drink for hours without getting drunk. Tyson described some tricks of his trade: flicking cigar ashes into a drink and ordering a replacement, or bumping another agent's arm to spill the drink.

Tyson testified that Helen bragged that one could purchase anything in her club but gin, the result of Blair's continued ban on college boys from the Chez Helen Morgan days. On the seventeenth, as Adler began his cross-examination, Judge Thomas placed a hand to his right ear, shook his head, and called the lawyers to the bench. Thomas suffered from tinnitus, a side effect of a recent minor surgery. He recessed the court, visited his doctor, and resumed court at 2:00 p.m.

Adler hammered away at governmental waste in upholding the Volstead Act. Federal agents received a $5 per diem. This was sufficient when Tyson stayed at the Chesterfield and President hotels: rooms were $3.50 a day, and $1.50 covered meals. However, when Tyson and his wife stayed at the Astor, Uncle Sam picked up the $9 daily tab and still allotted Tyson his $5 allowance.[16] Adler then established that Tyson's wife also received regular Treasury Department per diem checks even though she had neither taken nor passed the Civil Service Exam.

On the eighteenth, Salter rested the case for the prosecution.

Before Adler began his defense, Nick Blair burst into the court and pleaded guilty. His attorney, R. F. Koenig, produced an affidavit, filed the day before, in which Blair explained that he believed that a death in Adler's family had forced a postponement in the trial. When he learned of the warrant for his arrest, he drove through the night in a blinding rainstorm to surrender.[17]

As a preamble to his defense, Adler motioned to have the charges dismissed, which Judge Thomas denied. Adler did not refute the testimony given by the federal agents but maintained that Helen sold the use of her name to the club's proprietors and, as a contracted employee, was not liable to the nuisance charge. "The papers and records of the club which were seized by the Federal agents at the time of the raid will conclusively show that she was paid a regular weekly salary."[18] He submitted Helen's checkbook, which documented her regular payment schedule, as evidence. Throughout the trial, Adler never referred to the club as Helen Morgan's Summer Home. Even when Salter tried to force him to call the club by the name above the door, Adler refused.

Adler called Helen's new manager, Myron S. Bentham, to the stand.

With thirty years of experience as an actors' representative, Bentham boasted a list of clients including Laurette Taylor, Leon Errol, W. C. Fields, and Mary Eaton. He also drew up Helen's contracts while she worked for Nick Blair. He initially rejected Blair's overtures until the restaurateur offered Helen $750 for performances, from one to three o'clock in the morning, six days a week. When Chez Helen Morgan began operating on Sunday nights as well, he secured $1,000 for his client. The move to the Summer Home upped Helen's salary to $1,250 a week. He testified, "She did not share in the profits and had no interest in the club other than her salary. She never worked in a night club after the June raid and said she would never play in one again at any price."[19]

Under cross-examination, Bentham affirmed that he visited the Summer Home multiple times but denied having purchased liquor there, as he "did not drink during the hot season." Metaphorically, Bentham thumbed his nose at the Feds when he admitted that he kept alcohol on his yacht: during the World War, he had lent his craft to the war effort. More than a decade later, he still used the honorary title of commodore with pride.

With Salter was the box of material seized from the Summer Home the night of the raid. From it, the prosecutor produced proof that Helen collected money directly from the club and that she had stopped paying Bentham his commissions on the rationale that her own contract with the Summer Home superseded her agreement with him. When asked for a copy of his most recent contract with Helen, Bentham confessed that it was not in the file he brought with him. Judge Thomas instructed him to return to his office, locate it, and return. When summoned during the afternoon session, Bentham was conspicuously absent.

Salter torpedoed Adler's claim that Helen was a hired hand. The papers likely corroborated Mark Hellinger's prior claim that, at Chez Helen Morgan at least, Helen received a percentage of the gross, netting as much as $3,500 a week.[20] Worse, he implied he had more embarrassing evidence in that box. In an abrupt about-face, Adler rested his case, denying Salter the opportunity to cross-examine Helen. She never took the stand.

In his summation, Adler attacked the methods used to entrap his client. He sneered at the lies government agents told to ingratiate themselves with their victims. He condemned the use of tax revenue to purchase and consume alcohol in order to make arrests. He accused the government of targeting a celebrity whose name would make the front page of the nation's newspapers. He denounced the suggestion that Lulu was a bootlegger and that the Morgans purchased liquor wholesale for themselves when the Summer Home received shipments. He decried the idea that Helen would advise strangers to set up a nightclub, with partners assuming the legal responsibility, while hiding behind the facade of being a paid employee. Finally, he railed against federal Prohibition enforcement policies: "You get men who shoot at women and fire on defenseless boats so they can justify themselves before certain hypocrites. A conviction in this case would be an approval of enforcement activities which have been condemned throughout the country."[21]

Addressing the jury, Salter freely admitted, "Of course the agents had to tell a lie! But the government approves of that."[22] He reminded the court that Adler failed to produce even one witness who denied the sale of alcohol at the Summer Home. While admiring Helen's decorum in the courtroom, he grieved for the youth of America, those who admired people like Helen. He warned that her conduct "would influence young girls to go slinking down the pathway of corruption and crime." In Salter's eyes, Helen "sold her birthright for a mess of pottage."[23]

Throughout the day, starting with Bentham's cross-examination, Helen's expressive hands trembled in abject terror. Her body shook from nervousness throughout the summation.

Thomas instructed the jury to, first, determine if the Summer Home had been a nuisance. The law considered "any place where liquor was manufactured and recurrently sold" a common nuisance. If the jury reached this conclusion, it was unnecessary to prove that Helen was an owner. A conviction required only satisfaction beyond a reasonable doubt that she had "aided, abetted, counseled or assisted the proprietors in maintaining a nuisance."[24]

When the jury retired at 4:35 p.m., Helen could no longer control her emotions. For the first time during the trial, the court saw her in tears.

On the first ballot, the jury voted eight to four in favor of acquittal. When they broke for dinner at seven o'clock, one lone juror held out for conviction. Deliberation resumed at 8:15. Twenty minutes later, the jury filed into the courtroom. Helen, missing her *Show Boat* performance, rose from her chair, pale and trembling. The jury announced its verdict: not guilty. Overwhelmed, Helen almost fainted. She began to cry softly, then, in relief, sobbed without restraint.

Puzzled, Judge Thomas raised a hand to his ear. Perhaps he did not believe what he had heard. Perhaps his tinnitus had returned. He then repeated the slight he made during the Texas Guinan trial the week before by stomping out of the court without even the courtesy of thanking the jury. Salter, accompanied by agents Mitchell and Tyson, exited the court just as quickly.

Adler, by contrast, grinned and stated that the "verdict had been expected and was just."[25]

After she composed herself, Helen turned to Adler and asked, "They can't change their minds, can they?"[26] On Adler's arm, Helen thanked and, impetuously, kissed each juror. Later, she wrote thank-you notes and offered each juror passes to *Show Boat*.

These men wore no rose-colored glasses. One juror remarked as he left the court, "There was no doubt . . . that Miss Morgan was guilty under the law. . . . The jury felt she was only earning her living and the law was wrong and that no conviction was possible under such circumstances."

Exiting the courthouse, Helen told the press, "I don't want to think any more about it."[27]

The law was less kind to Helen's codefendants.

Defending the Summer Home waiters, Adler reminded the court that they simply catered to the needs of New York's upper crust. Rising, Salter vehemently objected, opining that most Summer Home patrons were tourists, adding, "We cannot class the group patronizing the night clubs as representing the best people anywhere."[28] Thomas slapped the waiters with fines of $100 and two-month suspended sentences with a probation of one year.[29] Headwaiter Louis Zalud received a $300 fine and a suspended sentence of six months with a three-year probation.

Herman Brooks remained on the lam.[30] By the time the court lost interest in him, he was operating a mail-order narcotics business under the name Hyman Berger. Police arrested him in November 1932 in a hotel room filled with $25,000 worth of heroin, cocaine, opium, and morphine. For that, he served time.[31]

Adler, of course, prompted Nick Blair turn himself in and swear that he was the sole owner of the Summer Home as a means of exonerating Helen. For his trouble, Blair earned a $500 fine, six months in jail (suspended), and three years' probation. Undeterred, he announced that Helen would open the 1929 version of the Summer Home, atop 190 Columbus Circle. Helen begged to differ. Without Helen, Blair's new club never materialized, but he still had the Casanova. During the particularly difficult 1929–1930 season, he offered Helen $5,000 for a fortnight engagement to cover a gap between the end of Ruth Etting's engagement in December and the arrival of Jack Buchanan from London. "Nothing doing," she told the lawyer who presented the contract, uncharacteristically turning on the man who had sacrificed himself for her. "I will never work for that man again. I will never forget how mean he was to me during my trial."[32] Graciously, Etting remained.

The Feds visited the Casanova on September 21, 1931, and confiscated more than thirty gallons of contraband. Blair initially swore his innocence but later conceded his guilt in court. He paid a twenty-five-dollar fine.[33]

Alderman Murray Stand never stood trial.[34]

~

Helen's and Texas Guinan's cases, tried nine weeks after Chicago's Saint Valentine's Day Massacre, crystallized American opinion. Not only did Prohibition fuel shocking violence; it required hypocrisy to enforce. It was expensive. The US government recovered only $8,400 of its $75,000 investment in the June 1928 raids.

Jurors convicted only fifteen on charges that included jail time, and few served. In February 1930, Judge Thomas suspended the four-month prison term for Tommy, the biggest name sentenced in the June 1928 raids, although the $500 fine remained.[35]

N. T. Granlund, the biggest name after Texas and Helen, never stood trial.

Having declined to use the Jones Law on Helen, the Feds chose Anthony Sager as their New York guinea pig. The Brooklyn jury took only fifty minutes to find Sager not guilty. Defeated, Willebrandt threw the Jones Law on the rubbish heap along with the conspiracy charge. New Yorkers who violated the Volstead Act were never again charged with a felony.[36]

Prohibition was doomed.

In 1930, US district attorney Charles H. Tuttle ran for governor of New York. When local Republicans lobbied to grant New York breweries and distilleries alcohol permits to lubricate Tuttle's race, Major Campbell, announcing his support to repeal the Eighteenth Amendment, abdicated his office to Andrew McCampbell. In September, the major rocked the district by penning a series of tell-all articles chronicling his tenure for the *Washington Post*.[37] Later, he published the anti-Prohibition magazine *Repeal*.

Even with a dampened New York, Tuttle lost decisively to his Democratic challenger, Franklin D. Roosevelt.

A year after the opening, critic Felix Deyo revisited *Show Boat* to access it from a musical standard. After lauding Kern's score, he noted, "More than any other factor, the presence of Helen Morgan and her inimitable manner of singing lifts the show above most of its contemporaries."[38]

While the show remained profitable, by March 1929, the box office had fallen below a $35,000 weekly gross, the point where Ziegfeld could make more money with *Show Boat* on the road. However, until her legal troubles were behind her, Helen, appearing simultaneously in two Ziegfeld productions, could not tour. As winter turned to spring, many patrons visiting the

Ziegfeld inquired whether Helen was still in *Show Boat*. When informed that she was, tickets were purchased.

By April, the end was in sight. Ziegfeld permitted Universal to open their *Show Boat* film at New York's Globe Theatre on April 17, while Helen was on trial. After her acquittal, he posted a two-week closing notice for *Show Boat*. While the *Billboard* announced capacity audiences during that final fortnight, *Variety* observed only a slight uptick in business.[39]

The company traveled to Boston's Colonial Theatre for a capacity seven-week stay. June 1 marked the end of the theatrical season, and with it came the termination of Helen's contract.[40]

Two days after Helen's acquittal, Arthur Loew sailed, alone, to Europe. With the talking picture revolution in high gear, his mission was to ensure that American films continued to thrive overseas. He predicted, "It will be a long time before the talker pictures entirely supplant silents."[41] On May 22, as he began his return trip on the *Ile de France*, Mildred Zukor Loew announced that she and Arthur were separating, "to retain the respect of each other rather than remain together until domestic conditions became intolerable."[42]

At last, Helen and Loew could see each other openly.

In June, federal judge Alfred C. Coxe Jr. padlocked many of Broadway's 1928 mop-up victims. He closed the Summer Home for ten months and issued a permanent injunction against Nick Blair, Louis Zalud, and the club's operating company, Em-Mo Catering. He also ordered another court date for Texas and Helen, at which time he would decide whether to enjoin them "forever" from any Volstead violation.[43]

Assistant US attorney Maxwell Shapiro rounded up three of the famous Four Horsemen to testify on the government's behalf. Neither Texas nor Helen attended the hearing, but each sent J. Arthur Adler. Helen's case came up first, and Adler was ready. He need not have bothered. Shapiro rose and announced that the attorney general's office had advised him to drop the matter.[44] Judge Coxe immediately dropped all charges against Helen and Texas and cleared the court. A group from the Woman's Christian Temperance Union, present to enjoy the festivities, was dismayed by the decision. Several complained that the government's lack of resolve would never have occurred if Mrs. Willebrandt were in charge.

After receiving an offer to help regulate the fledgling aviation industry, Willebrandt resigned on May 28, 1929. When the aviation deal fell through,

Willebrandt found herself, at a $50,000 annual salary, representing Vino-Glo, a brand of syrup concentrate made from California grapes. At issue was that the concentrate easily fermented into a wine with 12 percent alcohol content. The Willebrandt-Vino-Glo marriage was a blessing for the California farmers. A competitor, Vino-San, found its warehouses raided, while Willebrandt's partners were untouched. Vino-San begged Willebrandt to provide them legal counsel as well, but she refused. The hypocrisy did not end there. Without preservatives, grape juice turns hard if it sits on the shelf for a couple of months. The phenomenon led to a St. Louis grocer's arrest in 1930 for selling a product "intended" for the unlawful manufacture of alcohol. With each passing outrage, it became clearer that Prohibition was unenforceable. Who do you prosecute for the natural process of fermentation? God?

8

Applause for and with Miss Helen Morgan

Summer 1929: the climax of the Jazz Age. Between Memorial Day and Labor Day, while the world put off all thoughts until tomorrow, unaware of how soon tomorrow would come, Helen Morgan completed her legal fight, rehearsed a new show, cared for her child, and made film history.

Beth Brown, a silent film editor and intertitle writer turned novelist, constructed her books with screen adaptations in mind. Her best-remembered work, and the only one to make it to the screen, *Applause*, is a heady mixture of romance novel and seedy melodrama wrapped in a show business setting: burlesque queen Kitty Darling (Helen) enrolls her daughter, April (Joan Peers), in a convent school to shield her from the wicked stage. Kitty's two-timing man, Hitch (Fuller Mellish Jr.), bullies her to take the teenager out of school and put her in the show. April falls for a sailor (Henry Wadsworth) but leaves him to remain on the stage and boost her mother's fading career.

Screenwriter Garrett Fort jettisoned Brown's more censorable episodes. Gone is frustrated classical actor Alto Birmingham, who, indisposed, snorts cocaine to get through a performance, snaps onstage, recites dialogue from *A Midsummer Night's Dream*, and gets the hook, ending his career. Gone is Kitty's botched shooting of Hitch during their relationship-ending argument. Gone is April's discovery that Kitty, also hooked on cocaine, sleeps with the company manager to keep her job. Fort combined April's two beaux for the screen. The first, Tony the sailor, returns to the sea and gives April a retired show poodle. Kitty works up an act with the dog while April romances Rodney Delacourt, a college boy and a doctor's son. In a final ironic twist, a producer catches her dog act. Had she lived, Kitty would have made the big time after all.[1]

When sound arrived, the film industry looked to the theater for talent. In May 1929, Helen signed on, at a $5,000 weekly salary, to play Kitty Darling in *Applause*.[2] She was not Paramount's first choice. In one of the more bizarre what-ifs of film history, the studio first reached out to Mae West, who sported the requisite blonde locks and Victorian curves for Kitty but was allergic to tragedy. She passed on the offer.[3]

Behind the camera, Paramount also offered stage director Rouben Mamoulian five years' employment—after serving a two-year apprenticeship coaching dialogue. He countered with the request to direct one film as his trial run. The Astoria studio, enjoying another renaissance, became his schoolroom. His curriculum? Watching Robert Florey shoot the Marx Brothers in *The Cocoanuts*, studying Jean de Limur's *Jealousy*, and "asking questions about lenses and things. After five weeks of that, I felt I had mastered it."[4]

Applause is the talkie that got movies moving again. Most early silents resemble the amateur videotaping of a play: the camera sits in Row E of the orchestra and records the action. By the mid-1920s, the industry had perfected the language of film: tracking shots, close-ups, fades, sweeps, and editing. The camera told the story. Talkies reversed the progress. The camera's mechanical hum forced the cinematographer, director, and assistant into soundproof booths, ironically called "iceboxes" by those who sweltered inside. Sound returned the camera to Row E. Mamoulian balked at confinement. "Talking pictures up to now have been . . . mirrors of acted plays—and that is not their purpose. . . . They should be motion pictures always using the old motion picture technique, but substituting dialogue for subtitles."[5]

With only a seven-week window between Helen's last *Show Boat* performance and her first day of rehearsals for her new stage show, Mamoulian's schedule afforded no margin for error. Paramount envisioned *Applause* as a splashy vehicle that would capitalize on Helen's image as a glamorous Ziegfeld girl. Director Rouben Mamoulian thought otherwise. He requested that the costumer make Helen dowdy and disheveled. Yet when she first walked onto the set, she was a vision. "What is this?" he demanded. The costumer replied, "She is a star, she must be beautiful."[6]

Louella Parsons sniped that the "pleasingly plump" singer should diet before appearing before the cameras.[7] Helen *was* dieting—gaining twenty pounds to bring Kitty Darling to the screen in all her faded glory. She gladly committed to a role far removed from her beauty-queen roots, but after *Applause*, shedding the pounds proved onerous. In 1930, her doctor warned that another intentional weight gain would prove disastrous to her career.

Helen Morgan in *Applause*. (Courtesy of Everett Collection)

"Suppose you were offered another role which required you to stouten up?" columnist Louis Sobol asked her. She replied, "I'd cut off a leg and shave my head if the role required it."[8]

Helen trusted her director completely and, under his guidance, turned in a powerhouse performance, one of a handful from that awkward, transitional period that remains compelling. Particularly in her climactic scenes, she is mesmerizing, an achievement almost as remarkable as what Mamoulian achieved behind the camera.

Having startled Broadway audiences with a dialogue-free opening sequence, the "symphony of noise" in the play *Porgy*, Mamoulian utilized ambient sound—as well as music and dialogue—dramatically throughout *Applause*. His actions may have been more self-preservation than artistic vision. Paramount economized by providing him only preexisting music—most notably, Dolly Morse and Joe Burke's 1928 hit, "Give Your Little Baby Lots of Lovin'." Even Jay Gorney and E. Y. Harburg's "What Wouldn't I Do for That Man?" was studio property.

On June 13, Mamoulian wished to shoot Helen singing "Give Your Little Baby Lots of Lovin'" as a lullaby while her teenage daughter (Peers) simultaneously says her prayers. The distance between the two made it impossible to record both voices on one microphone and on one channel. Mamoulian suggested that they use two mics and two channels and combine the tracks in printing. Cinematographer George Folsey and soundmen Cuyler Tuthill and Ernest Zatorksy swore that it could not be done. Mamoulian swore too and marched into Adolph Zukor's office. The studio head came down to the set and told the crew to follow the director. Taking on many of the duties of his resentful technicians, who called the project *Applesauce*, Mamoulian had two takes in the can by 5:30 p.m. After he left, the studio brass screened the rushes. The five-hundred-foot take, clocking in at almost five minutes, was a miracle. The camera movement drew the viewer into the scene. The sound recording was perfectly clear. Zukor sent the footage to the studio's sales conference. Grudgingly bowing to the fair-haired boy of the lot, Folsey asked for the camera placement for the next setup, Mamoulian ordered four cameras, with one shooting up from the two-foot-thick concrete floor. When the pneumatic drills arrived, he grinned, saying, "OK, that's enough. I've had my revenge."[9]

Applause filmed on Astoria's lower stages while Gertrude Lawrence's *The Gay Lady* took the larger, more comfortable space above. During that first week, Helen shot the sequence with young Mary Gertrude Haines. With little ventilation, the lights made the small set an oven. In a corset and a tatty blonde wig, Helen was drenched in sweat. "I'm melting away," she cried. "At the end of this picture, they'll be asking, 'Where's Morgan?'"[10]

Mamoulian wisely shot some sequences on location. He filmed the convent sequence at the H. H. Will estate in Rosslyn, Long Island. In Manhattan, he visited Pennsylvania Station and the observation deck of the AT&T Building. In the latter, while April and Tony look down on the harbor and the Statue of Liberty, a plane flies by and the camera tilts up to catch the sight. The spectacular footage was not unplanned. Mamoulian hired pilot Francis Brady to make the dangerous circular flight between the AT&T and Woolworth Buildings, bringing street traffic to a halt as locals gawked. For the Chambers Street subway station sequence, he employed a crew of forty-five and two hundred extras. The realism extended to the Wrigley's vending machine Tony uses. If you want to see how New York looked in 1929, see *Applause*.

Upon completion, 85 percent of *Applause* moved. Even the most fluid American silent films never moved more than 25 percent of the time. Mamoulian explained, "In the silent picture, movement of the camera was limited by the necessity of printed titles. The action was forced to a halt whenever a title was needed. But with present sound-recording methods, the dialog and sound can be continuous and the camera can move as it pleases."[11]

Kitty, like Julie, was a natural fit for Helen. When playing a scene opposite Fuller Mellish Jr., she recalled her stepfather, Edward Kroeter. It was not playacting for Helen. It was life.

Helen also made a guest appearance in *Glorifying the American Girl*. Paramount first sought to bring Ziegfeldian excess to the screen in 1925. Directors (Erich Von Stroheim, Dorothy Arzner) came and went, as did actors (Ruth Taylor, Louise Brooks, Clara Bow).[12] The one constant on the rolls was Ziegfeld himself, as nominal producer. While planning his six-production blitz of 1928–1929, Ziegfeld briefly considered capturing a pictorial record of his new *Follies*, which would have made *Glorifying the American Girl* the first all-talking musical film, but when his *Follies* morphed into the *Frolic*, Paramount shut down the production. Six months later, after MGM released *The Broadway Melody*, any all-talking, all-singing, all-dancing project was worth filming, and *Glorifying the American Girl* commenced principal photography at Astoria on April 22.

Mary Eaton played (ahem) Gloria, a department-store songplugger with dreams of *Follies* stardom. Encouraged by her monster mother (Sarah Edwards), Gloria leaves her beau (Edward Crandall) for some on-the-road seasoning with a song and dance man (Dan Healy). Ziegfeld's business manager, Stanley Sharpe, catches the act and offers (only) her a spot in Ziegfeld's new revue. Earlier drafts by Townsend Martin and James Ashmore Creelman ended Gloria's adventure by having her leave the *Follies* to marry her beau. Perhaps the success of weepy backstage melodramas, such as Al Jolson's *The Singing Fool*, convinced its final, credited writer, *Follies* alum J. P. McEvoy, to mix heartache with splendor: Gloria's beau marries her best friend (Gloria Shea). The couple sits in the audience applauding the glorified but heartbroken Eaton, who sings "There Must Be Someone Waiting for Me in Loveland."

The production wrapped in early June, but the initial cut underwhelmed studio brass. Director Millard Webb expanded the *Follies* section at the end of the film, much of it in early two-tone Technicolor. In one Ziegfeldian tableau, Olympic medalist and future Tarzan Johnny Weissmuller poses as Adonis in little more than a teal G-string. Giddy executives considered reshooting all of *Glorifying the American Girl* in two-tone, but reason soon returned to Astoria.

Paramount may have culled its three guest performances for *Glorifying the American Girl* from existing footage. On June 18, Rudy Vallée sang "Vagabond Lover" for a short feature that never materialized. Cavalierly, the crooner reported at eight in the morning, worked for a few hours, ran to the Brooklyn Paramount for a live stage performance, and returned at four in the afternoon to finish the shoot. He then gave the infuriated grips autographed portraits of himself, which, for weeks afterward, were prominently, if inappropriately, displayed in Astoria's restrooms.[13]

The two other *Follies* sequences received the best notices for the film. In one, Eddie Cantor performed the "Joe's Blue Front" skit from his 1920 Shubert revue *Midnight Rounders*. Although not credited, director Robert Florey claimed to have been behind the camera on some of the five shorts Cantor made between late 1928 and early 1930. Perhaps "Joe's Blue Front" was an intended Florey short that Paramount edited into *Girl*.

Florey also claimed that he filmed Helen singing "What Wouldn't I Do for That Man?" although it remains unclear whether Paramount ordered it as part of a feature, as a short, or as a screen test the studio chose to recycle. A look at the footage supports Florey's claim that Helen filmed it before tackling *Applause*.[14] Here she weighs less than she does as Kitty Darling, while the extra pounds she carried are evident in her follow-up film.[15] Whenever and by whomever it was shot, the sequence is startling, offering rare footage of Helen crooning from atop a Steinway. On the plus side, she easily traverses the difficult vocal line, and the white-draped piano setting dazzles. However, the gown she wears is less than becoming. As in the earlier footage of "Bill," Helen had not yet scaled back her nervous tics for the camera. She projects terror more than pathos.

After several rejected attempts, Helen commercially recorded the song on October 8—the day after *Applause*'s premiere. Victor credited the song's origin only to *Applause;* Remick credited its origin to both *Applause* and *Glorifying the American Girl* when it published the sheet music.

Local censors gave *Glorifying the American Girl*, peppered with multiple uses of "damn," a pass. One exception: local bluenoses successfully killed the racy advertising graphics in Minneapolis.[16]

Paramount blundered by scuttling a scheduled September release for a Christmas one. By that time, better films had beaten *Glorifying the American Girl* to the punch. The holdup also influenced Ziegfeld's feelings toward the project. In a telegram to Zukor dated August 9, 1929, Ziegfeld enthused: I HAVE SEEN PART OF THE PARAMOUNT TALKING PICTURE *GLORIFYING THE AMERICAN GIRL* . . . AND IN MY OPINION IT IS A PRODUCTION ESPECIALLY IN THE COLOR PARTS OF THE PICTURE THAT LIVES UP IN EVERY WAY TO THE MEANING AND SIGNIFICANCE OF ITS TITLE YOU ARE TO BE CONGRATULATED.[17]

Two months later, he objected to the studio's advertising campaign via letter, "which reads 'presented under the personal supervision of Florenz Ziegfeld.' Now you know, I had nothing whatever to do with the picture. In fact, I haven't even seen it."[18]

Helen wrapped on *Applause* on Friday, July 19, and began rehearsing her new stage show the following Monday.

Enamored by the idea of musicalizing Ferber's *So Big*, Jerome Kern began writing a score for it, but the Hammersteins, and Ferber, knew better than to attempt to outdo *Show Boat*.[19] Instead, drawing inspiration from a Kern dream of an old-time vaudeville set depicting New York's Riverside Drive, where girls rode bicycles and carried Japanese lanterns, Oscar and Jerry wrote *Just the Other Day*, a Valentine to the Gay Nineties. Oscar Hammerstein's tale of self-sacrifice concerned Josie Schmidt (Helen), who sings in her father's Hoboken beer garden and pines for sailor Tom Martin (Max Hoffman Jr.). Realizing that he loves her younger sister Nellie (Caryl Bergman), Josie tearfully steps aside. While serving in the Spanish-American War, Tom befriends brothers and New York socialites Rupert (Charles Butterworth) and James (Robert Chisholm) Day. Milquetoast Rupert falls for Dot (Violet Carlson), the piccolo player in Schmidt's beer-garden orchestra. An hour in, the show eschews Spain and war to become a standard Cinderella backstager. Josie triumphs in the Broadway show Rupert and James finance. She bounces back from her sailor by romancing the rich but too-respectable James before finding happiness with her composer, Sid Barnett (John D. Seymour), at the final curtain.

Oscar constructed a star vehicle that hewed close to biography. He included Helen's humble beginnings singing for pennies at Mike Fritzel's.[20] He nodded to her father by including the Spanish-American War as background and, as an in-joke, named Irene Franklin's Bowery diva Lulu after Ma Morgan. Addie's romance with James Day paralleled Helen's affair with

Arthur Loew. Oscar even translated the confrontation between Loew and Reggie Hammerstein into a fistfight between James Day and Tom Martin, replete with Addie/Helen heading into seclusion afterward. Curiously, he paired Addie with the fictitious show's songwriter, as whatever feelings Helen may have held for him during *Show Boat*'s birth remained forever frustrated. Tellingly, Oscar included a drunk scene, and not as a comic episode: Addie wants to forget that the man she loves has announced his engagement to her sister.

Kern provided Helen with the lion's share of the score, including three big torch numbers. As with "Bill," Kern and Hammerstein wrote conventional love ballads that only took on a tragic spin within the storyline. "Here Am I" stems from an anonymous love letter Josie writes to Tom Martin. She first sings her poem to Dot in a quest for feedback. Assuming that the note he received is from Nellie, Tom sings the song to Nellie, who, believing that Tom wrote the missive for her, shows it to Josie. Heartbroken, Josie sings it again. In the second act, Hammerstein introduced "Don't Ever Leave Me!" as a duet for Josie and James Day to express their ardor. Only later, when Helen reprised the number, did she give the lyric its tragic spin. Six weeks after the Broadway opening, she preserved the more somber version on record.

Oscar even set up the most straightforward torch song of the evening, "Why Was I Born?," to allow Helen to act in layers. She first sang "Why Was I Born?" atop an upright in the orchestra pit in her audition scene late in the first act. The composer, Sid, uncaringly reminds Josie of her failed attraction to the sailor, which prompts a more heart-wrenching performance.

Kern's greatest accomplishment was "Some Girl Is on Your Mind." Old-timer vaudevillian Jim Thornton, the composer of "When We Were Sweet Sixteen," appeared as himself in the Hoffman House bar scene in the second act. Completing Thornton's lachrymose barbershop quartet were Addie's three suitors and the male chorus. Haunting them, Helen offered counterpoint snippets from "Why Was I Born?" and "Here Am I."

Sadly, Helen never recorded "Here Am I," the rousing waltz production number "The Sun About to Rise," or the German folk song "'Twas Not So Long Ago." The last, like "Edelweiss" in *The Sound of Music* thirty years later, remains misattributed as an old German lied. Kern did interpolate vintage music for his overture, effectively establishing the era without pre-plugging his own tunes. The creation of the overture *Fin de Siècle* inspired a new era-appropriate title: in early August, Josie became Addie Schmidt and *Just the Other Day* became *Sweet Adeline*.

~

Helen exercised her star power by securing a place in the chorus for Gloria Le Bow, a roommate from her early New York days. She triumphed over costume designer Charles Le Maire, who designed a frilly concoction akin to the St. Pauli Girl's ensemble for her first entrance, carrying six mugs of beer in her father's beer hall. Helen wanted something simple and comfortable and in denim. She got denim. Her instincts were spot on. Playing a Cinderella role, she needed a strong visual contrast for her rags-to-riches journey. Later in the evening, when she wore a burnt-orange gown in front of a black velvet drop, the effect was stunning. Equally impressive was a creation in tight-fitting black taffeta married to a picture hat loaded with drooping ostrich plumes.

Compared to rehearsing *Show Boat* while doubling at Chez Helen Morgan, working on *Sweet Adeline* was a breeze for Helen, but Violet Carlson remembered Kern and Hammerstein as being extraordinarily demanding. With an increasingly matronly air, Helen (actually two years younger) took Carlson aside and cooed, "That's OK, honey. They were the same way with me in *Show Boat*. When they're tough on you like that, it means they like you."[21]

According to Carlson, brandy and champagne were never far from Helen's lips during *Sweet Adeline*'s run. She never slurred or went up on her words, but alcohol made her wobbly, especially while singing "Here Am I," during which she stood next to Violet. The soubrette, charged with keeping Helen steady, sometimes went as far as to hold the letter herself so it did not shake in Helen's nervous hands.

Violet confirmed that although Reginald Hammerstein received credit as having staged *Sweet Adeline*, Oscar directed and came up with a startling idea. Thirty years before Ethel Merman bulldozed her way down the aisle in *Gypsy*, Helen interrupted the rehearsal scene in *Sweet Adeline* in similar, delightful fashion.

Kern gushed that *Sweet Adeline* was the "easiest and pleasantest musical show in whose production he has ever been associated,"[22] but backstage, he butted heads with Arthur Hammerstein, who intended to use prerecorded music, played by the Philadelphia Orchestra, no less, for the production. The firestorm was quick and intense. The musicians' union squawked, and Ziegfeld publicly berated his rival, sneering, "No real artist would think of singing with a mechanical instrument."[23] Arthur rescinded the order and hired a full pit orchestra.

However, Hammerstein's *was* the first Broadway house wired for sound. The plot consisted of microphones in the orchestra pit connected to four speakers: two at the rear of the balcony and two at the rear downstairs. Helen used the technology to her advantage. The mics made her faintest, most plaintive pianissimo heard throughout the large theater. She drew her audiences to her and achieved the intimate one-on-one ambience that made her so successful in the clubs.

Premiering on August 19, *Sweet Adeline* conquered Atlantic City—its period flavor and Helen's performance chief among its assets. The *Times* touted "Here Am I" as the most likely song hit but also lauded the book, crediting Oscar Hammerstein with "a musical comedy plot that, of all things for a musical comedy plot to do, hangs together."[24]

Before rehearsals began, Oscar relaxed off the Connecticut coast aboard Kern's yacht, *Show Boat*, penning the lyric to "Don't Ever Leave Me!" as a gift to his bride, Dorothy, to whom he dedicated the libretto.[25] The boys recreated the romantic setting onstage for Addie and James.[26] Initially, another duet, "I'm Dreaming," preceded "Don't Ever Leave Me!," with both songs forming an integrated musical scena, akin to the "Twin Soliloquys" / "Some Enchanted Evening" duo in *South Pacific*. Axed out of town, presumably because of length, "I'm Dreaming" is lost to history.[27]

After a stop in Newark, *Sweet Adeline* made its triumphant Broadway bow at Hammerstein's on September 3, 1929, two weeks ahead of schedule. In honor of the premiere, Helen's Aunt Vida McTigue came for a lengthy visit. Vida, like so many others, marveled that Helen shed real tears when she sang.

The critical reaction was even better than the out-of-town notices. Regarding Helen, *Variety* enthused that she "captured the entire house, not by her singing, but by her acting. . . . [She is] set for a long stellar stage future if she wants it."[28]

Modern audiences lucky enough to see *Sweet Adeline* onstage still connect emotionally with Addie, but the stakes are not as high as they are in Oscar Hammerstein's best work. He grew as a librettist while fashioning Helen's material but remained content to rely on stock characters and vaudeville antics throughout the rest of his libretto. That said, as Robert Littell declared, "American musical comedy does not come any better than this."[29] Thanks to two star clowns in Irene Franklin and Charles Butterworth, laugh for laugh, it might be the funniest musical Hammerstein ever wrote, but it remains a lightweight *Pajama Game* in a sea of *South Pacific*s.

Robert Benchley cheekily summed up the enterprise by writing that it was "not without its dull stretches, and when they are dull they are *good* and dull."[30] In response to Benchley, fellow *New Yorker* contributor Gilbert Seldes took a closer look and marveled at how Helen arrived "just as surely at emotions far too profound for the setting, almost too intense to be borne." He fretted that impresarios would forever struggle to present her effectively. "For long minutes after she leaves the stage, her shadow rests on it, so that no change of scene or light, no entrance of stars or chorus is at all effective." Not one to bandy about the term "genius" lightly, Seldes applied it to Helen, whom he considered a worthwhile theatrical liability. "Until a proper medium is found for Miss Morgan, her presence in any show will only prove that the world is well lost for a few moments of exquisite beauty."[31]

The

By Benj

"S WEET
the c
"The
want
Adeline" once
Because there
be there and
nudity that w
A Hoboken
McGowan's P
Square roof-ga
de luxe to the
who knows th
And—Heler
the price alone
shuffling, the
country today,
honorable her
Franklin, cyni
C. Fischer in
of you, and l
yes, thirsty Ji
parched!

Helen Morgan's beauty and voice enhance the charms of "Sweet Adeline," a great musical comedy.

Helen Morgan in *Sweet Adeline*. (Free Library of Philadelphia, Theater Collection)

Helen took his encouragement to heart but feared that formal education would stymie her natural ability. She wrote to Seldes, "I don't believe in Dramatic schools. All I can do in the acting end is wait for a chance to work for a good director like Mamoulian."[32] Still, embarrassment about her humble beginnings and humbler education prompted Helen to improve her mind. During *Sweet Adeline*, she took up French and Italian and committed to memory the first act of *Manon Lescaut*, which she later sang for Otto Kahn. He offered a contract, but Helen balked at the last minute, a decision she later regarded as the biggest mistake of her career.

She befriended Sally Bates, who played the gorgon, Hester Van Doren Day, in *Sweet Adeline*. The fellow literature buff lent her *Zuleika Dobson*. Helen hunkered down with a work that she understood would be "good" for her. Halfway through Max Beerbohm's satire of Oxford life, she saw Bates backstage and, with some consternation, charged, "Why, Sally, this book is funny!"[33]

When Helen drank, the feelings of worthlessness grew exponentially, as indicated in her letter to Seldes: "Oh! Well, now please don't laugh at this silly note. Just want you to know I did see 'The New Yorker' and have been trying to improve myself and maybe be some day a really worth while [sic] person. Please be kind enough to destroy this letter and forget its contents."[34]

Armed with glorious reviews and the largest advance sale of its era, Arthur Hammerstein signed Jerry and Oscar to write a follow-up. He also planned a second company, to open in Chicago in an open-ended engagement and tour thereafter, similar to the way productions tour today. Blanche Ring would play Lulu. For the lead, he approached Grace Hayes, then Mary Charles, relative unknowns both, before realizing that Addie was a star role, not a star-making one. When Frank Craven, the once and future Stage Manager in *Our Town*, balked at filling Butterworth's shoes, Arthur chose to wait until his Broadway cast was ready to tour.

Dramatist Guild rules at the time reverted foreign production rights to the authors if the New York producer failed to exercise the option within sixty days of the Broadway opening. Ziegfeld failed to do so with *Show Boat* and lost his chance to participate in the 1928 Drury Lane production. In mid-September, Oscar pitched a London *Sweet Adeline* but brokered no deal that was satisfactory for the Hammersteins. *Sweet Adeline* has yet to receive an overseas production.

~

In the heady days following *Sweet Adeline*'s debut, Helen and Lulu left the North Shore and took up residence at 277 West End Avenue. Uncle Arthur, following Ziegfeld's lead, decreed that if Helen doubled while in his show, he would provide the work. He turned to his initial plan, the revival of *Camille* staged by Arthur Hopkins. The twist was that now Helen would play the doomed courtesan matinees only, daily, and then play Addie at night. It is unlikely that even the indefatigable Helen could have played twelve stage performances a week.[35]

In 1929, Helen earned as much as $8,000 weekly between the stage, screen, radio, and records. Stag nights were behind her, but she occasionally played private parties for $500 a tune.[36] Even then, cash rolled out faster than it rolled in. While playing in Atlantic City, Lulu sent a telegram informing Helen of a $776.06 overdraft in their checking account—and hoped she was well.[37]

One contributor to the Morgan red ink was a fellow midwesterner who received a letter from home saying her ailing father had but weeks to live. Jostled while battling through a Broadway crowd, she dropped her purse. Two newspapermen found it and the twenty-nine dollars she managed to save for her return fare but no identification. While spending their windfall in a midtown speak, one found the letter from home in the ripped lining of the handbag. In possession of the name and address of the owner of the purse, the guilt-ridden men haunted the Rialto, raising money to send the woman home. When asked for a donation, Helen took out her checkbook and underwrote the entire trip.

Over Labor Day, the Paramount suits privately screened *Applause*. If the footage from the studio's sales conference had impressed, the final product proved a revelation. Chief among the surprises was Helen's dramatic intensity as Kitty. Mindful of her disdain for that *Show Boat* film prologue, Mamoulian barred Helen from viewing the rushes but promised to show her a rough cut before *Sweet Adeline*'s pre-Broadway tour. Scheduling conflicts prohibited them from meeting. Her stage schedule forced Helen to miss the October 7 premiere of *Applause*, but the following evening, at a special midnight screening for the *Sweet Adeline* cast, she saw what the hubbub was about.

The lobby at New York's Criterion Theatre sported one retrospective display commemorating the theater's thirty-fifth anniversary and another celebrating Helen Morgan's film "debut." Three shorts preceded the feature. The first, *On the High C's*, featured Frances Williams and the Yacht Club Boys. The second, the Tom Howard comedy *The Spy*, featured Helen's *Applause* acting partner Jack Cameron. The third presented composer Charles K. Harris

When He Comes Home to Me—the lost Paramount short (note the Asian good-luck pendant). (Courtesy of Everett Collection)

singing his classic "After the Ball."[38] There was to have been a fourth short. In perhaps another Florey exercise, Helen sang Sam Coslow and Leo Robin's "When He Comes Home to Me."[39] Paramount never released it, but they subsequently sent out Helen's "What Wouldn't I Do for That Man?" from *Glorifying the American Girl* as its own short.[40]

Critics disagreed over *Applause*. Some found the director's innovations thrilling. Others believed he went wildly overboard and, with the camera's swooping and swerving, gave audiences a case of cinematic vertigo. Most concurred that by concentrating on the squalor of burlesque life, Mamoulian delivered too unpleasant an evening. Also problematic was the presentation of production numbers, which Astoria's primitive recording technology caused to echo and become mushy—in the parlance of the day, "tubby."[41] The garbled audio of "Oceana Roll" is particularly disappointing as the number offers rare footage of Helen the dancer.

Helen's honesty and commitment floored the critics. The *Billboard* gushed: "She has stamped herself as an actress of the first water . . . for never once in the entire picture does she make an effort to leave any other impression than that the woman is a coarse, blowsy creature. In less competent hands the role might have been nauseating."[42] Helen is mesmerizing in the climactic scenes. However, her inexperience derails her in the character's lighter moments. Often, she resembles a child playing dress-up in that ill-fitting wig. She jumps her scene partner's line in that groundbreaking five-minute shot, but Mamoulian retained the gaff because of her commitment to the scene. Helen does not merely stroke Joan's locks; without direction, she brushes the hair off her face, ensuring that Joan Peers is the focus of the shot. Mamoulian was gobsmacked. "That was Helen Morgan for you."[43]

Paramount ballyhooed *Applause* as the exemplification of its marketing slogan, "The New Show World": "New personalities, new treatment, new technique, startling departures from old film traditions—all of these elements of a new era in motion picture-making are combined in this elemental love story."[44] Before the premiere, Zukor and Jesse Lasky expressed their gratitude to Mamoulian for directing what Zukor called "the greatest film Paramount ever made."[45]

Director Rouben Mamoulian clowns with Joan Peers and Helen on the set of *Applause*. (Courtesy of Everett Collection)

Zukor and Lasky promised to turn Mamoulian's one-picture deal into the best contract in the business, but, after ending its successful run at the Criterion, *Applause* moved on in November to the Paramount and sank like a stone, the first of a string of lowest-grossing-film-of-the-month distinctions it garnered in most houses where it played. Its initial enthusiasm giving way to panic, Paramount held back on the film's wide release until January, hoping that by then the market would improve. It did not. Then, *Applause* cinematographer George Folsey developed the blimp, which encased the camera but not its operators and made Mamoulian's innovations appear antique.

A year would pass before Mamoulian megaphoned another production.

Exacerbating the beating that *Applause* took at the box office were the numerous and powerful local censor boards.

Paramount did what it could during production to stave off the bluenoses. Wardrobe altered some costumes to make them less revealing.[46] The poison Kitty takes was intentionally unnamed to prevent suicidal viewers from taking their cue from Helen Morgan.

Because his long fluid takes required no editing, Mamoulian achieved what veterans took years to master: editing in the camera. Sink or swim, Paramount was stuck with Mamoulian's vision. During postproduction, the studio's options to edit were limited. In one instance, someone came up with a genius solution. On-screen, Kitty originally comforted April by telling her two of the burlesque dancers were "as good *Catholics* as anybody, even if they do shake for a living." At the risk of offending the Catholic church, Paramount erased the word "Catholics" from the soundtrack. For a second, Helen moves her lips and we get no sound: *Applause* has literally become a silent movie.

Colonel Jason S. Joy, head of the Motion Pictures Producers and Distributors of America (MPPDA), requested that Paramount producer Walter Wanger keep Kitty and Hitch's marital status unmentioned throughout the film.[47] Mamoulian won this fight—up to a point. When Hitch enters the story, he is not married to Kitty. Later, he agrees to wed if April joins the company. However, Joy, or the New York State Censors, succeeded in clipping a pivotal scene wherein Hitch forces himself onto April, saying "You been holdin' out on your daddy all day . . . no room for icebergs in this family . . . can't father kiss his own daugh'er?"[48] Subsequent scenes of Hitch sexually accosting April remain in the film, but the audience is never reminded that Hitch is April's stepfather while he harasses her.

In the end, Mamoulian and/or the studio deleted eleven minutes of footage from the time they submitted *Applause* to the New York State Censorship Board, and the premiere run at the Criterion. Most cuts were benign, and consisted of fading in or out of scenes that were running long. Perhaps the most painful deletion was a solo dance by Helen.

Outside of New York, the cuts proved more painful. The MPPDA, and many local Censorship Boards, objected to the use of offensive language in the film, especially "dirty double crossin' broads," "everybody in the whole damn house," and "some God-forsaken farm."[49] Yes, the line that draws gasps from modern audiences also fell prey to *some* local censors' scissors: When asked his name, April's sailor boyfriend, clearly uncomfortable, admits that it's "Tony. I never liked it. It sounds like a Wop bootblack."

Pennsylvania and British Columbia banned the film entirely.[50] South Dakota prohibited children under sixteen from seeing it.[51] *Applause* played Cleveland, but the Ohio censors prevented it from screening downstate until additional cuts mollified their objections, which it did to no business.[52] Heavily trimmed, it fared poorly in Chicago, which both Helen and Joan Peers called home.

The downbeat story, censorship woes, and the stock market crash are not the only reasons for *Applause*'s financial failure. At this point in her career, Helen was largely unknown outside of New York and could not carry a film as did Jolson and Cantor, who had built up a loyal fan base by years of trouping throughout the country before their talkie debuts. Nevertheless, Paramount advertised the film using images of Helen the glamorous star. The tactic might have worked had they paired *Applause* with *When He Comes Home to Me*, but audiences were nonplussed to see such a dowdy creature onscreen after being promised a Ziegfeld beauty.

Applause and *Glorifying the American Girl* may have enjoyed better business as silent films. Paramount reedited both for theaters that had not yet converted to sound. Sadly, neither comparable financial reports nor silent prints exist for comparison with the sound issues.[53]

Despite its poor box office performance, all involved savored the satisfaction of the National Board of Review's assessment of *Applause* as "an exceptional picture."[54] Because of the protracted release strategy, the *Billboard* refrained from listing *Applause* on its "10 Best" list for 1929 but did give it an honorable mention.

In 1939, Paramount tapped Sidney Kingsley and Henry Hathaway to shoulder the screenwriting and directorial duties of an *Applause* remake to serve as a vehicle for Marlene Dietrich. The working titles waffled between *Portrait of a Mother* and *Every Day Is Sunday*. In the end, studio executives, still smarting over Dietrich's misbehavior on the aborted *Hotel Imperial*, passed on its temperamental star.[55] Gladys George briefly headed the cast list, with Betty Field tapped for the daughter, but in the end, Paramount scrapped the project.[56]

In the early 1960s, Hugh Martin contemplated adapting the story as a stage musical for Judy Garland and Liza Minnelli. His flirtation with the property coincided with the rediscovery of the film within the vintage film community.[57] *Applause* has since earned respect as a sui generis artifact of the early talking period, if not a classic. But what an artifact! Here is New York at the height of the 1920s madness. Here are the first, tentative steps out of the technical limitations that kept pioneering sound cameras immobile. Here is the full spectrum of Helen's untapped, untrained talent, giving a performance of such intensity that it is often painful to watch.

9

America's Greatest Star

Impressed by the Labor Day screening of *Applause*, Paramount signed Helen for *The River Inn*, also at $5,000 a week. Ben Hecht (*The Front Page*) *very* freely adapted Dashiell Hammett's novel *Red Harvest* for the screen.[1] *Red Harvest* contains roadhouses, bootleggers, and a mug, sent in to mop up vice and corruption, who gets romantically embroiled with a dame who is involved with a local mob boss. Any similarity between Hecht's story and Hammett's novel ends at this point: Garrett Fort took Hecht's story treatment and created a screenplay, retitled *Roadhouse Nights*, wherein Willie Bindbugel (Charles Ruggles) investigates the disappearance of a fellow reporter at a Michigan roadhouse, where he finds his old flame Lola Fagan (Helen Morgan) singing. Lola must choose between the reporter and her brutish manager and lover Sam Horner (Fred Kohler). Held over from *Applause* was Fuller Mellish Jr., who played Hogan, one of Kohler's goons. He died of a cerebral hemorrhage on February 3, 1930, days before the release of *Roadhouse Nights*.

From October 7 to November 20, Helen filmed by day and played Addie onstage by night.[2] "Of course, the bad part of this is getting up in the middle of the night. I mean, we're here at 9 a.m. half asleep." Still, the leisurely pace of film work was preferable to the cabarets: "The bunk. . . . Do you think it's fun going around glad-handing people and asking Mr. Scriffus how he is and asking Mr. Scroffus how *he* is? Who cares? Being the big-hearted hostess winds up a big headache."[3]

Fort found a spot in *The River Inn* for producer Walter Wanger's latest find: the comedy trio of Lou Clayton, Eddie Jackson, and Jimmy Durante. The Schnozzola featured heavily in the role of Helen's accompanist. Clayton, Jackson, and Durante were even busier than Helen. In addition to headlining the cabaret show at Les Ambassadeurs, during the week of November 9–15, they *tripled* into the Palace.

~

Helen did not appear in *Sweet Adeline* on December 11–15. The Hammerstein office blamed her absence on laryngitis, but the singer's illness conveniently occurred when Paramount, facing the financial loss on *Applause*, dropped her from their roster.[4]

Roadhouse Nights premiered on February 21 in two simultaneous New York engagements. Rudy Vallée headed the stage show at the Brooklyn Paramount. The Times Square Theatre paired the film with Buddy Rogers and Jesse Crawford in the tab stage revue *Hollywood on Broadway*, which set a house record of $94,000 that stayed in place for over a decade. The following week, Rogers boosted ticket sales at the Los Angeles Paramount.

Critical response was tepid, with the *Billboard* damning Helen with the faintest of praise: "The part could have been improved on considerably by putting another lady in the part, but it must be said to her credit that it is the best performance she has turned in to date."[5] In her defense, she faced multiple obstacles. *Roadhouse Nights* placed Helen's character in distress, not over a youngster as in her previous successes but over a man in a love-triangle plot more suited to a Joan Crawford soaper. Paramount also, likely, squandered its chance to build Helen up as the glamorous chanteuse by rushing her into production before she could lose the weight she gained for *Applause*. Frustratingly, the uncredited costume designer saw fit to squeeze Helen—in late October—into not one but two backless dresses. Period gowns in her stage vehicles offered support, but her wardrobe at Astoria accentuated her tummy.

Adding injury to the insult, during the introduction of her song, cinematographer William Steiner filmed her from every unflattering angle possible. Despite Steiner and a second-rate Jay Gorney–Yip Harburg torcher, Helen ignited the screen in song. "It Can't Go On like This" constitutes the best three minutes of the film.

The perfect method actor while singing, Helen required guidance with dialogue, which director Hobart Henley never provided. Part of the problem may have been a near epidemic of colds that ran through the studio—and through Helen.[6] Regardless, she ultimately sabotaged herself, giving the most uneven performance in her film career. In several scenes, especially in a long, wordy, intense one with Kohler, Helen, if not drunk, was befogged. She landed her marks and got out her lines but remained behind the dramatic beat. The line stumbles Mamoulian allowed into *Applause* illustrate Kitty's

"It Can't Go On like This"—the best three minutes of *Roadhouse Nights*. (Courtesy of Everett Collection)

emotional turmoil, but here, they indicate that Helen was not experienced enough to assemble her bag of acting tricks (the squeaky little-girl voice, the shaking of the head) into a new, believable character. A few effective reactions aside, rarely did she meet the histrionic challenge offered by Ruggles and Kohler, let alone Durante, who effortlessly stole the picture in his screen debut. To build up their rising star, in virtually all print ads outside of New York, Paramount placed Durante front and center and sold the film as a comedy. If Helen's image appeared in newspaper advertising at all, she remained, literally, in the background.

Helen's final connection with the 1929–1930 film season was the Vitaphone short *The Benefit*.[7] She did not appear, but she lent its star, stuttering comic Joe Frisco, a gown for a sequence in which he appeared as La Morgan, warbling "The Man I Love" from atop a piano. The Back Stage Club alumnus introduced his impersonation in the 1928 edition of *Earl Carroll's Vanities*. Helen fine-tuned his performance, advising him not to cross his legs, as many of her imitators did. If she crossed her limbs at all, she did so at the ankles.

Musical features glutted the market during the 1929–1930 season. By August 1930, the boom was over, and 100 percent talking, singing, and dancing extravaganzas fell into disfavor, replaced by a wave of gangster and horror films that better reflected the nation's mood. Helen's film career was, temporarily, over.

After Helen's acquittal, Baby Helen returned to the Morgan household. How much parenting Helen actually performed, and how much Lulu assumed, is unknown, but Helen paid to correct the waif's mastoid condition.[8] Then, just before Christmas, Thelma Halloway insisted that Helen return her baby. With no legal recourse, Helen relented, stating "a Broadway star must make a choice between art and domesticity."[9]

The loss was a blow from which Helen never recovered. In her grief, she banned all talk of Baby Helen, who joined William Zeh, Lowell Almy, and all her fathers in her book of the dead. In 1931, an otherwise congenial interview turned icy when reporter Vivian Shirley innocently inquired, "I hear you had maternal leanings once and adopted a little girl for a while. Why did you?"

Helen spat, "None of your business."[10]

Tall, broad-shouldered, but also a slob, Irving Hoffman helped Helen rebound from the loss of Baby Helen and her Paramount contract. At fourteen, the Bronx-born artistic prodigy sketched the 1924 Democratic Convention. When he entered Helen's orbit, he contributed to Walter Winchell's column, and he later wrote as the *Morning Telegraph*'s "Beau Broadway" and hosted the radio interview show *Tales of Hoffman*.[11] During the holidays, every fan who wrote Helen received an autograph along with an original Hoffman-designed Morgan greeting card. As much a Broadway character as Helen, Hoffman carried a pair of slippers in his back pocket to wear in the Stork Club when his feet hurt.

Years before, after her exodus from *Louie the 14th*, Helen heard something squeak one night in her humble digs and discovered a mouse scurrying about. When she realized it was blind, her heart melted. She caught it and kept it as a pet. "I'm not ordinarily superstitious but somehow I feel 'mousy' changed my luck. A day or two later I got a job at the Little Back Stage Club."[12] As a reminder of those dark days, Helen kept two white mice in her Ziegfeld dressing room during the run of *Show Boat* until Sammy White put the cage where Edna May Oliver dressed. The formidable character shrieked so loudly that the ruckus was heard out front. A lone mouse, Squeaks, kept Helen

Irving Hoffman's original Morgan greeting for the holidays. (Free Library of Philadelphia, Theater Collection)

company backstage at the Hammerstein, with little objection from the cast and crew.

In deference to Squeaks, Hoffman coined Helen's nickname, "Mousie," which she adopted as her telegram moniker. Some might also assign the label to Hoffman, who bowed to Helen's every whim, even walking her dogs. Arthur Loew worked in Europe that spring, so Hoffman's relationship with Helen, at least at first, may have been physical. If so, he stepped aside when Loew returned, but he remained loyal.

Writers inhabited Helen's coterie. As a cub reporter, Jimmy Cannon covered the Chez Helen Morgan raid. A few years later, he was having a drink at Frankie and Johnnie's when Helen, wearing a fur over her rehearsal clothes, popped in for a quick one. When she complimented him on a piece he had written, he bought her a drink. Helen insisted he take his money off the bar.

"I'll sing them a couple of songs. They'll start buying."

A cappella, she sang. The crowd kept the free drinks coming.

"What did I tell you?" Helen scolded. "A kid like you shouldn't be throwing his money away in saloons."[13]

Another literary ally was Louis Sobol. Helen was one of the few white celebrity patrons of the Harlem nightspots whom the Renaissance villagers called by only her first name. She even performed at one of the infamous parties held in Clinton Moore's male brothel. One night, Helen, Sobol, and three other men stumbled out of a Harlem nightspot as the sun was rising. She asked the elderly woman of color sitting on the stoop next to the speakeasy what she was doing out at such an hour. The woman replied that she was off to work. Helen collected $20 from each of her escorts, then reached into her purse, pulled out a $50, and plopped all $130 into the thunderstruck woman's lap. As they walked away, from behind, the old woman squealed, "Bless you! God bless you!"

Helen's companions chalked up the gesture as another random act of charity, but two days later, each received twenty dollars from the superstitious singer, with a note that begged their forgiveness, saying, "I want to keep those blessings all for myself."[14]

The fourth estate remained loyal, and for years Helen was the most publicized personality on Broadway. She, in turn, kept them crying when she was atop the piano and laughing when she climbed down. When her giggle failed to be infectious, she mocked irritable writers into grinning by referring to their troubles as being "only a paper mood."[15]

With increased competition from radio and the talkies, receipts for the 1928–1929 Broadway season dropped precipitously from the year before. Then the first half of the 1929–1930 season lagged behind *its* predecessor. In short, the downturn hit the legitimate stage months before Black Thursday. Helen, who rarely played the market, escaped the crash of 1929 unscathed, although Ziegfeld and Arthur Hammerstein were wiped out.

Hammerstein's brought in $42,000 a week when playing to capacity. *Sweet Adeline* did—for twelve weeks. Holiday business was disappointing, but *Sweet Adeline* did not dip beneath a comfortable $30,000 mark until the first week in February, when the cast took salary cuts to keep the show going. Many saved what they could for a rainy day that was fast approaching, but despite every good intention, Helen never had money left over on payday to put aside.

On February 10, an appendectomy temporarily forced Irene Franklin out of *Sweet Adeline*. The salary cuts offset the box office dip during her absence until the first week of March, by which time the world was feeling the effects of the crash. Franklin returned to the production on March 17, but by then the damage had been done. The bubble burst all over the Main Stem. *Sweet Adeline* shared its misery with five other productions when it shuttered on March 22, 1930.[16] For its era, *Sweet Adeline* had a moderate run, taking in a million dollars in New York. Only the last three weeks played at a loss. Otherwise, Arthur Hammerstein would have closed shop sooner.

Helen returned to the dying vaudeville circuit. At $2,500 a week, a grand more than her Hammerstein contract, she signed for a split week at the Coliseum, followed by a two-week stand at the Palace. With Martin Freed at the keys, she provided "Morganesque entertainment." Her entrance applause was the biggest hand awarded to the entire bill, but Helen failed to build on this momentum.[17]

Helen also fell ill in February, but her loyalty to the *Sweet Adeline* company, playing without Irene Franklin, compelled her to work when she should have rested. Adding to her exhaustion was her charitable work, which, after the crash, became an obsession. Guilt fueled her need to pay it forward. Why should she be dripping in furs while others went hungry? Helen could not refuse any cause, especially if it aided the members of her profession, even when it damaged her health and career. She pushed herself to the limit between her two-a-day vaudeville performances and her multiple daily benefits until she could endure no more. Starting on April 5, Irene Franklin covered Helen's second week at the Palace. Instead of resting, Helen attended the matinee, where she cheered on her friends.

Taking after her father, the sickly child became a sickly adult. She ignored the warnings from her doctors, forging ahead even when she could no longer give a credible performance. During this illness, she learned that years of Prohibition hooch had caught up with her: Helen had developed cirrhosis of the liver.[18]

In May 1929, Arthur and Dorothy Hammerstein invited Helen to cross the pond with them, but *Applause* prevented her from accepting. A year later, with months of free time on her hands, Helen left Lulu behind and joined Eleanor Tierney aboard the *France* for a European vacation.[19]

During her going-away party, a festive Helen accidentally sprayed seltzer on a woman at an adjoining table. She pulled out her checkbook and wrote a check for eighty dollars to replace the stranger's dress. The incident in no way dampened the party.

When the talkies arrived, Arthur Loew, in charge of foreign distribution, managed a division in crisis. In March 1930, he met in Rome and Paris with European film executives.

Loew was no paragon of fidelity. Sailing on the *France* to Europe, he met sixteen-year-old Colette François and promised to make her the next Jean Harlow. Allegedly, in his stateroom, Loew made her. And impregnated her. He set sail for home three days before Helen's eastbound departure, the timing of which fueled rumors that something was wrong, especially in light of her friendship with Irving Hoffman—and Martin Freed.

Shortly after Helen sailed, Freed separated from his wife, Pearl, who charged that he was so infatuated with Helen that "he forgets his home."[20] The previous Christmas, two days after Freed gave Helen an expensive gift, Pearl and her two children suffered eviction for nonpayment. Money had been scarce for months. Freed earned only $148 in royalties for his *Midnight Frolic* song "Who Cares What You Have Been?," and in the year following the closure of the *Frolic*, Helen and Freed worked in vaudeville for only a month before the team disbanded.

The highlight of Helen's European spree was an audience before Italy's King Victor and Queen Helen. She sang "Bill," "Why Was I Born?," and the Italian arias she revisited during *Sweet Adeline*. The enthusiastic reaction inspired Helen again to contemplate the operatic stage.

Helen left Rome by ship. In Taormina, she set out to visit the gardens that had captured her imagination in a D. H. Lawrence story. Other ports of call included Naples, Tunis, Gibraltar, and Casablanca. In Rabat, Morocco, she caused a sensation by throwing ten dollars in small change to the local beggars, which hampered the local traffic. Helen added to the reputation of the boorish American tourist, but the local gendarmes released her when they learned her identity.

The cruise ended at Le Havre. When Helen stepped off the gangplank, Rags, her Scottish terrier, grabbed a wharf rat and ran off to dine in peace. Helen's limited French failed to inspire the dockworkers to aid in her search, as did a 500-franc reward. She never saw Rags again.

Inspired by Berlin's burgeoning cabaret scene, Helen rented a Paris apartment while she scouted potential locations for a Gallic Chez Helen Morgan. Montmartre's nightspots bored her. She hated Zelli's. Well aware that the Fetiche was a lesbian bar, she was nonetheless flustered to learn that the handsome tuxedoed youth who turned her head was a woman.

Helen's European sojourn concluded in Monaco. When the principality rejected her letter of credit, she wired Lulu for $1,000. She won at the casinos, but she was homesick. An undoubtedly wet Helen Morgan stepped onto the dry docks of New York on July 2. Loew whisked her to Pembroke in his speedboat, where the two summered in an unaccustomedly leisurely manner.

During a riding lesson near Pembroke on August 4, the horse threw her. Helen's foot caught in the stirrup, and the horse dragged her. A fellow houseguest, boxing legend Georges Carpentier, heard her screams and grabbed the runaway horse. Shaken and bruised, she still made her scheduled CBS radio appearance that evening.

Automobiles proved no safer. Helen invited (and paid for) her aunt Elsie Dillon and sixteen-year-old cousin Fred Lang to visit. In the early hours of August 13, in Croton-on-Hudson, thirty miles north of the city, the car carrying Lulu, Elsie, and Fred crashed into a telephone pole. Cut and bruised, the sisters obtained treatment at a nearby hospital. The driver, Lewis Wilk, thrown through the windshield, died of a fractured skull. Fred escaped without injury.

Helen's most lasting European souvenir was Johnny Green's "Body and Soul," which traversed a circuitous road to success similar to that of the Gershwins' "The Man I Love." Mismatched to its original interpreter, Gertrude Lawrence, "Body and Soul" failed to click in 1929. Lawrence took it to England, where Jack Hylton's jazz band popularized it and producer Max Gordon acquired it for his upcoming Broadway revue, then called *About Town*. Helen brought the song home and included it in her act, prompting Harms Inc., which owned the American rights, to place a quarter-page ad in *Variety* announcing their ban on all performances of the song until after the revue, now renamed *Three's a Crowd*, opened in October. Without incident, Helen sang it anyway on the September 5 premiere of the Nestlé Chocolateers radio program.

Libby Holman enjoyed one of the biggest hits of her career singing "Body and Soul" in the Broadway production, but it was Helen whom Gordon fancied taking back to England for a London production of *Three's a Crowd*.[21] Things did not work out as planned, but Helen's waxing, punctuated throughout by a gong that foretells doom for the relationship, may be her finest commercial recording.

Sweet Adeline did not recoup its investment in New York.

In March 1930, Arthur Hammerstein bucked convention by not utilizing the last ten weeks of the 1929–1930 season for a post-Broadway tour.[22] Perhaps he feared the late dates for Passover and Easter, which traditionally sank box office receipts, or he simply wished to concentrate on producing film operettas. Four months later, his film career was over, and he debated whether to send Helen on the road or star her in a stage adaptation of an unproduced Hollywood property: a Friml treatment of Richard Walton Tully's *The Bird of Paradise*.[23] Mercifully, Hammerstein sent Helen on the road with *Sweet Adeline*. Renamed *Luana*, Friml's hopelessly dated operetta proved to be little more than *Golden Dawn*-goes-Hawaiian. It ran only twenty-one performances on Broadway.

Joining Helen on the road were Irene Franklin, Charles Butterworth, Jim Thornton, and Victoria Windsor, the pug dog that Franklin carried onstage with her to create a historically accurate picture of a Mauve Decade burlesque queen. The supporting cast, including Addie's three suitors, was new. The most notable replacement, as Sid Barnett, the songwriter who wins Addie's hand, was James Dunn. Like Helen, Dunn started as a movie extra. While he struggled, he drowned his sorrows in Helen's clubs. She offered encouragement and may have introduced him to Uncle Arthur. From *Sweet Adeline*, Dunn jumped to Hollywood and an Oscar-winning film career.[24]

A deepening Depression, one of the hottest Septembers on record, and fierce competition from Boston's tercentennial celebration awaited *Sweet Adeline* at the Colonial Theatre. The production reigned at the box office, but a weekly gross of $20,000 was nothing to celebrate.

While playing Detroit, Helen pointedly wished, in print, that Noël Coward would write a part for her.[25] With his contract with Helen set to expire, Arthur Hammerstein raced to her side when the company arrived in Chicago. In short order, he signed Helen for a new Kern-Hammerstein musical for the 1931–1932 season.[26]

Chicago loved Helen and *Sweet Adeline*. Lloyd Lewis gushed that the former "'Ophelia of the supper clubs' . . . is more artist than entertainer."[27] Helen received perhaps the happiest notice of her life while in the Windy City: Frank Riggin publicly acknowledged Helen as his daughter.[28]

The top Chicago attraction that November, *Sweet Adeline* could have played another month, but Arthur Hammerstein honored a prior Pittsburgh booking.

After visiting Helen for the Chicago opening of *Sweet Adeline*, Arthur Loew flew to Reno to celebrate his daughter's birthday. Mildred and the children established residency there in September in preparation for her divorcing her husband, which she did on December 7 on the grounds of extreme cruelty. According to her complaint, Loew confined "his interests and activities to matters outside of his home," but Mildred chose not to name Helen corespondent.[29] To minimize the scandal, Judge Thomas F. Moran heard the case in secrecy in his chamber and ordered all papers pertaining to the matter sealed. Exiting the court, Mildred denied rumors that she would marry comedian Phil Baker. In fact, she would not remarry for a decade, and then it would be to Paramount attorney Walter Beck, whom she would also later divorce. Burned twice, she would never again walk down the aisle.

During a weeklong hiatus after the Pittsburgh run, Helen flew to Mexico City with Loew and Hal Roach, fueling rumors of a Loew-Morgan elopement. At the end of their vacation, Loew and Roach flew on to Hollywood before starting a South American tour that lasted into the New Year. Helen returned east, still single. As she told the press, "I won't marry for a long time. I can't afford it. I support my entire family and I wouldn't ask any man to do that."[30]

After grossing over $60,000 during the first two of a three-week stand, Philadelphia's Erlanger Theatre offered Arthur Hammerstein an open-ended engagement. With a sole week, in Washington, left on the schedule, Arthur jumped at the chance. Yet, in the first week of 1931, the box office take dipped to $23,000. When the next week brought in only $17,000, *Sweet Adeline* closed on schedule anyway. If the road had been chancy in early 1930, a year later it was catastrophic. Only Chicago could boast anything approaching a theatrical life in 1931. Even with box office receipts of over $350,000 for the tour, the tally sheet for the entire eighteen-month endeavor left *Sweet Adeline* $100,000 in the red.

While painful for the Hammersteins, *Sweet Adeline* propelled Helen's 1930 income to over $117,000, a staggering Depression-era salary.[31] Yet, when she came home, Irving Hoffman was shocked to find Helen as broke as

Arthur Hammerstein. When asked where it went, she showed him the stubs of the dozens of checks she wrote to Broadway denizens fallen on hard times. From that day on, Hoffman led a posse of friends who appeared backstage every payday to lead her out of any exit other than the stage door, where a crowd habitually gathered to ask for loans. The ruse helped, but Helen found other ways to remain lady bountiful.

Arthur Hammerstein's next production, the W. C. Fields vehicle *Ballyhoo*, proved as big a disaster as *Luana*. After a two-week run, Arthur ceded the production to Walter Batchelor, who ran it as a cooperative production. The co-op originated in London in 1921 when a group of unemployed actors and writers went door to door raising the capital to mount *The Co-Optimists*. The shoestring revue became an annual event, with the 1930 edition preserved as a feature film. Imported to New York's Century Roof in 1928, *The Co-Optimists* failed to find an audience. On July 8, 1930, the venerable theatrical lodge, The Lambs Club, mounted their own co-op to keep actors working but chose the unfortunate title *Who Cares?* Too tempting a target for the critics, it folded four weeks later.

After a brief hiatus for reorganization, which included trims to the crew and orchestra, *Ballyhoo* reopened on January 8, 1931. Hammerstein wrote off his theater rent and royalties for every week the production failed to turn a profit. The principals played at reduced salaries. W. C. Fields played gratis each week the gross fell below the new break-even mark of $13,000. More a revusical than a book show, the co-op *Ballyhoo* benefited from a parade of guest star appearances, beginning with Gus Van on January 12. Bill Robinson, the blackface duo of Moran and Mack, and Eddie Cantor also donated marquee value. Cantor also recorded the title tune. On January 27, Helen sat on a piano in the orchestra pit and sang "Bill" and "Why Was I Born?"

Batchelor successfully kept the lights on and the people employed for six and a half weeks.

Helen returned to vaudeville. Bentham booked the "Greatest of Super-Headliners of Modern Song" for a five-week tour—New York, Chicago, Cincinnati, Cleveland, and St. Louis—at a career-high weekly stage salary of $3,500.[32] With Vincent Colling at the piano, Helen enjoyed her finest hour in the two-a-day vaudeville in one of the last great Palace bills. She closed the first half with a six-song set and joined fellow emcees Phil Baker and Jay C. Flippen in blackout skits between acts, sometimes sneaking in "The Man I

Love" as an encore to Baker's accordion accompaniment. At the end of the three-hour program, in black and white satin, she scored with "Body and Soul," which Gordon's office still prohibited on any other Broadway stage while *Three's a Crowd* played the Selwyn. Sidestepping the issue, Helen sang while sitting on the steps leading into the house.

On February 2, Helen treated Lulu to box seats at the Palace for her birthday. She introduced the Widder Morgan from the stage and forced her to take a bow. Helen could have held over but declined. The "tearful little earful" canceled her remaining vaudeville dates to play the Florida nightclubs, at a weekly salary of $3,000.

Wintering in South Florida became *the* thing for the Prohibition-era version of the jet set for two very good reasons: (1) the climate and (2) Cuba. The rich, bored by winter and the Volstead Act, sailed their yachts ninety miles south of the peninsula, stocked up on legal hooch, and then lay anchor off the Dade County coast in international waters, remaining close enough that they could come ashore for further entertainment. The Florida season begat lavish cabarets, hotels, and restaurants, which flourished long after Repeal.

Helen thrived in Florida.

Leaving a blizzard behind them, Helen and Colling trained south. Like most Gold Coast resorts, the Hollywood Country Club boasted a gaming parlor, and Helen dropped $500 at roulette. The club's manager, her old pal Mike Fritzel, returned the money to his canary, admonishing Helen that his wheels were for the use of his guests, not his employees.

Also in Florida was Irving Hoffman, who grew concerned one night as he watched Helen leave a rival nitery without her ermine coat. She confessed that she had given it to the wife of the cabaret owner. "Her husband would never think of giving her a fur coat and I know how she likes them."[33] The woman's mate refused to believe that Helen supplied the gift and insisted his wife was seeing another man. The dispute ended in divorce.

Having morphed beyond a cry for attention, Helen's acts of kindness became a haphazard way to atone for her sins. When sixty-year-old Belle Livingstone, the third member of the triumvirate of Manhattan's Prohibition hostesses, was jailed for violating an injunction against her 58th Street Country Club, Helen's chauffeur met Belle outside of prison on the day she completed her thirty-day sentence.[34] Belle went home in style in a bulletproof limousine designed for Belgium's King Albert.[35]

~

Everyone wintering that season paid homage to Helen, including Al Capone, who made a rare excursion from his Florida estate to visit the Hollywood Country Club.[36] After all, he was one of the club's owners.

One night, Jack Bell was out front when Helen "adopted" a young singer on the Hollywood bill who was foundering before the rambunctious crowd. Ordering the orchestra to stop playing, Helen turned to the crowd and sweetly but pointedly scolded them for being rude to someone doing her best to entertain them.

"If you want to talk, do it while I'm singing."[37]

Helen threw the crowd a kiss and walked off. The chastised crowd listened dutifully to the grateful, if unremarkable, vocalist.

On February 19, Bell saw Helen step again into the breach. Emcee Sammy Walsh introduced her to the evening's guest of honor, boxer Primo Carnera, who asked for a dance. Helen's gown had a long train, yet at one point, she felt a breeze. Carnera managed to grab the train and expose Helen's backside to everyone in the club. When the music stopped, the oaf grinned at her and asked, "Baby, what's your name?"[38]

For once in her life, Helen Morgan was speechless.

Helen moved on to Miami's version of the Club Lido on Hibiscus Island. To keep her guests at the Lido, Helen performed a different song list in her late show but still accepted requests from the crowd. She also appeared in sketches with compere and Brazilian tango artist Peppy de Albrew. Thanks to her drawing power, the one-week coda to the winter season extended to three.

Helen's winters in Florida were the happiest days of her career. Gregarious but without many truly close friends, she drew her extended family—particularly Jorge and Brownie Sanchez and Dorothy Dey—around her during these working vacations.

Dorothy Worth entered the world on October 9, 1901, in New York.[39] Her mother was English, her father, a German chef. Well-heeled, young Dorothy and her mother spent several summers in England visiting family. Dorothy's gift for spinning a yarn led to her claim that she was born in England and survived the *Titanic* sinking.[40] In later years, she claimed to be a former Ziegfeld *and* Texas Guinan girl. She married saxophonist Russell Day Plummer and corrupted his middle name to avoid confusion with Dorothy Day, the catholic social activist, when she began writing a Florida society/entertainment column for the *New York Press*. After the war, she married comedian Dean Murphy.

Helen and friends, Miami, 1931: Mrs. E. B. Martindale, Jorge Sanchez, Eleanor "Brownie" Sanchez, Joe E. Lewis, Dororthy Dey, E. B. Martindale, Helen, Courtland Martindale, and Frank Garlasco. (Free Library of Philadelphia, Theater Collection)

Both metaphorical and literal sugar daddies, the brothers Sanchez (Jorge, Julio, Marcel, and Emilio) owned a Cuban sugar plantation and a Costa Rican gold mine. Helen befriended all the Sanchez boys but was closest to Jorge and his wife, Eleanor. They wintered in Miami and owned the mansion *Casi Un Sueno* on fashionable Star Island. Eleanor (née Brown) was a Shubert showgirl. Between 1914 and 1916, "Brownie" appeared in *Dancing Around, Maid in America, The Passing Show of 1915, A World of Pleasure, Robinson Crusoe, Jr.*, and *The Show of Wonders*. She also toured in the Sophie Tucker vehicle *Louisiana Lou*.[41]

Jorge was the most profligate Sanchez. One season, his sugar harvest brought in $56,000 more than he had budgeted. To compensate, he ordered ringside seats four nights in a row in four of Manhattan's most fashionable boîtes. He treated everyone he saw nursing pedestrian quaffs such as Scotch and sodas with magnums of champagne. Anyone he could tip, he did, and extravagantly. Ninety-six hours later, his windfall was gone.

In both benevolence and extravagance, Helen found kindred spirits in the sugar family. The Sanchezes built their Camaguey, Cuba, plantation into its own functioning municipality, complete with a hospital and theater for their six thousand employees to use, free of charge. To close the 1931 winter season, the Sanchezes flew Helen and Dorothy to Cuba to enjoy legal libations before the women returned to New York.

~

Loew's work schedule kept him on the road during the theatrical season, so Helen killed time with Edmund Goulding, who was then directing Fredric March and Nancy Carroll in *Night Angel*, one of the final Paramount features produced at Astoria.[42]

Billed as "America's Greatest Star," Helen opened at New York's New Club Lido.[43] This Lido, the former Belleau, was not associated with the *old* Club Lido, which operated on the same street.[44] At the premiere, backed by Henry King and his orchestra, she sang "Love for Sale" and "The River and Me," which critics singled out as the most likely hit from her new repertoire. Texas Guinan quipped, "Morgan begins where others leave off."[45]

The New Lido's emcee, Peppy de Albrew, chose the boîte's decor: stained glass and lilies. The somber, intimate setting, more a church than a club, worked as well for him in New York as it had in Paris. He had a pet mouse, Junior. Most women shrieked at the sight of the rodent, but not "Mousie," who wanted to play whenever Junior appeared, even if it meant not going on.[46]

Helen's following was nothing if not loyal. One night, a foursome, in full evening attire, endured a Morgan delay in getting to the club. The men griped about the wasted three-dollar-a-person cover charge, but their dates pulled out a backgammon board to pass the time. On the club's last night, Mousie met her own Helen Morgan Club, a group of twelve young women who believed Helen was the world's greatest entertainer. Each wrote to her weekly to tell her so.

Thanks to her drawing power, the New Lido operated two weeks longer than scheduled. Had her schedule permitted, both Helen and the club would have continued through the summer.

On March 28, with reported liabilities of $1,649,136, Arthur Hammerstein filed for bankruptcy. He hoped to begin the new theatrical season with a clean slate, headed once again by Helen Morgan in *Camille*, this time a moderne Kern-Hammerstein musical directed by Arthur Hopkins.[47] It was not to be. Arthur's other asset, the Romberg romance *Melody*, eventually bowed in 1933, under George White's banner. Arthur Hammerstein never produced again.

Hammerstein's theater reverted to the mortgager. It remained unlucky when it reopened as the Manhattan later in 1931. Billy Rose briefly took control, and in 1936, the house played host to four productions, courtesy of the

Works Progress Administration. CBS acquired it, using it first for radio and later for television. It was not until Ed Sullivan hosted TV's greatest variety show that the house came into its own. Later, as the Ed Sullivan, it was the home to David Letterman and Stephen Colbert.

When she lost Uncle Arthur, Helen lost her link to Kern and Hammerstein—the only theater men who truly understood and could write for her.

10

Follies

While playing the Lido, Helen doubled into the Palace. The critics were appalled by her excessive number of breaths, which ruined her vocal line, and even more by her apology from the stage: her vocal exhaustion was due to her multiple benefit performances on top of her Palace and Lido chores.

She returned more successfully to film. In 1926, a year before *The Jazz Singer*, manager Lou Irwin negotiated, unsuccessfully, to feature Helen in Vitaphone sound shorts.[1] Talks resumed in early 1930, but the studio failed to concoct a suitable vehicle to shoot between Helen's European cruise and the *Sweet Adeline* tour. In April 1931, the planets aligned for the two-reel *The Gigolo Racket*. Helen earned $7,500 for perhaps a week's work. She played Helen Marlowe, star of the fictitious revue *Fast and Pleasant*. Her agent (Reed Brown Jr.) takes her to a speakeasy, which offers a startling glimpse of effeminate lounge lizards in their natural habitat. The agent points out one zaftig matron dancing with a handsome gigolo and suggests how proud she must be. Helen sniffs, "She'd better stop patting herself on the back and start on the chin."

The agent sets up a publicity stunt pairing the singer with a man (Joseph Striker) whom she believes to be a gigolo. Naturally, Helen's character falls for him. Complications ensue.

Her work is an improvement over *Roadhouse Nights*, but issues remain. She lands her few laugh lines but seems to be in a fog for the bulk of her dialogue scenes. Helen looks better than she did eighteen months earlier, particularly in a braless evening gown, but E. B. DuPar's cinematography accentuates deep lines in her throat. To convince the naysayers, Helen needed help behind the camera. East Coast studios did not have the resources necessary to build her up as a screen asset.

Vocally, she starts with the rarest of the rare: a torch song composed by a woman. Alice Boulden introduced Paul James and Kay Swift's "Nobody

Helen, with Joseph Striker and John Hamilton in the Vitaphone "Broadway Brevity," *The Gigolo Racket*. (*The Gigolo Racket*, Warner Bros. Discovery, 1931)

Breaks My Heart" late in the Broadway run of *Fine and Dandy*. Here, the vocalist actively seeks the caveman type, confident that she will emerge from the affair with her heart, if not her reputation, intact. Her second number, "I Know He's Mine," may be less assertive, but it is still optimistic as torchers go.

On display was a charm bracelet likely acquired during her Mexican trip with Arthur Loew and Hal Roach. Finally, well-wishers had an option for presents Helen would not regift: gold charms. She wore and added to the bracelet for the rest of her life.

During the 1920s, the rich and curious crossed the racial lines into Harlem to hear the music. Later they sampled queer Manhattan by patronizing the elaborate drag balls in the city's best hotels. When the Depression hit, queer

Helen and her charm bracelet. (Author's collection)

artists began playing the nightclubs. Billed as Helen Morgan Jr., drag queen Francis Dunn was one of the most successful, cohosting with the outré Gene Malin at the Club Abbey, the latest offering from the Schwartz brothers, Helen's 54th Street Club champions. The "pansy acts" nearly scuttled Manhattan's nightclub scene when police commissioner E. P. Mulrooney proposed a 1:00 a.m. curfew to combat what he considered a moral outrage.[2]

One night, Helen witnessed in the flesh one six-foot-tall, 175-pound male entertainer, possibly Dunn, taking his turn as "Camille on a Piano" in some Gotham nightspot. Helen, who fine-tuned Joe Frisco's impersonation, communicated her displeasure by leaving.[3]

On May 1, 1931, Helen and Harry Richman participated in the opening-day celebration of the Empire State Building. Both would appear in Ziegfeld's next *Follies*. Unmindful of a new world of breadlines, Ziegfeld adhered to his old formula: the brightest stars, the biggest, most costly sets, and the most revealing yet tasteful costumes. Sadly, his postcrash shows contained neither memorable books nor scores. With the dollar so tight, no production could afford to be less than exceptional. Despite strong design values and stronger openings, his new productions collapsed under their own weight.

As his financial situation worsened, Ziegfeld, noticing a dearth of annual revues in the pipeline for 1931, returned to his *Follies*. Before 1926, Ziegfeld's competition followed the master's lead. Then *Americana* made Broadway revues intimate and satirical. It was not in Ziegfeld's makeup to follow. One problem: if his book shows were old-fashioned, the 1931 *Follies*, his first since 1927, looked like something from another century.

He lured Helen with three solos, a duet with Richman, two comic sketches, and a new theatrical vehicle following the *Follies* run. She declared, "I've always wanted to play in drama and was cast for *Camille* at one time," but Ziegfeld "decided I needed to be glorified."[4] Perhaps, but Helen followed the money first and her heart second and signed a contract that offered a $1,500 weekly salary with a four-week notice clause for either party.

Ziegfeld also hired Ruth Etting. The inexplicable decision to cast the world's greatest torch singers in the same production upset the balance of the show and contributed to Helen's difficulty finding suitable vocal material. The notion of dueling divas proved irresistible to press agents, who hinted at a rivalry originating from the Chicago Montmartre days. In reality, the singers felt nothing but admiration for each other.

Advertisements for the pre-Broadway Pittsburgh run listed Helen as one of "the three-sheeted principals," a term that aptly described the state of the entire company.[5] Harry Richman noticed ninety cases of liquor aboard the private twelve-car train Ziegfeld hired to transport the show and observed that the entire company—including one stark-naked showgirl—was smashed before passing Philadelphia.

The first run-through in Pittsburgh lasted nine hours and six minutes. There were no major technical issues; Ziegfeld had enough material for three shows, the blessing and curse of having two sets of writers. He originally hired Gene Buck, Mack Gordon, and Harry Revel, but when he signed Richman, he got Barry Trivers, Jack Murray, and Ben Oakland, as well as their material from Richman's recent unrealized revue. Despite the heat, thirty-two scenes, and a nearly four-hour running time, opening night proved more than a hit: it was Pittsburgh's theatrical event of the year, and perhaps the decade.

At Ziegfeld's disposal was the ballroom atop the William Penn Hotel. Once, at 3:00 a.m., he called a rehearsal. The kitchen staff provided a mountain of food to keep the sleepy company going, and the night staff pulled double duty on the elevators to get everyone to the seventeenth floor. After an hour of strenuous labor, Ziegfeld decided that his idea did not work and sent everyone back to bed, with nary a morsel of the angry chef's food consumed.[6] Ziegfeld eventually whittled down his production to a manageable length, but his cavalier attitude toward overtime resulted in a $25,000 loss for the Pittsburgh run.

While in the William Penn, a group of hotel guests offered Helen a drink. She sat down, ordered a double brandy, and told the waiter to keep her glass filled. Her hosts blanched, but an invitation was an invitation. Helen then ordered a round for all twenty members of the party. In the end, Helen's bill far outweighed that of her hosts. It topped $300 for her two-week stay.

In Pittsburgh, the hits of the *Follies* were Hal LeRoy and Ruth Etting. LeRoy conquered by his dancing, Etting featured in the forty-five-minute playlet, *Broadway Reverie*. She played Nora Bayes in the first scene, set in Rector's in 1915. Her rendition of the old chestnut "Shine On Harvest Moon" became, troublingly, the sole hit song of the 1931 edition. The second scene was set in 1931, in a thinly disguised version of the Club Abbey. As a cigarette girl, Ruth sang "Cigarettes, Cigars," a proletariat lament modeled on her earlier hit "Ten Cents a Dance." Curiously, Gene Buck and Mark Hellinger chose not to have Helen play her drag counterpart in the playlet. The scene ended in a gangland shooting, not unlike the one that put the real Club Abbey out of business.

Helen had little to do in a show with over 150 in the cast. In the premiere performance, she appeared once in the first act, again playing mixed-race, to introduce Noël Coward's "Half-Caste Woman," a London import from *Cochran's 1931 Revue*. Ziegfeld provided an elaborate Shanghai dive and neighboring docks setting, and the uncredited no-goodnik sailor who deserted Helen as she leaned against the bar and lamented her low birth. After seeing so many imitators on stage and screen, Helen eschewed her customary piano-top perch this season.[7]

A telling sign of Ziegfeld's struggle to find suitable material for Helen was his recycling of "Bill" as a placeholder for a number to be added later. "Bill" stopped the show cold in Pittsburgh, but he was gone before the *Follies* came into New York.

In the second act, Helen joined Harry Richman in the duet "I'm All Wrapped Up in You." The number culminated in the two rolling around together on the stage. At one point, Richman slapped Helen's behind in full view of the audience. Critics were appalled. Ziegfeld replaced the number with the more tasteful "I'm with You."

Helen (briefly) dons male drag in the *Follies of 1931*. (Free Library of Philadelphia, Theater Collection)

Harry Richman sang "Don't Worry and Cheer Up" at the premiere, but by the end of the first week, Helen sang it while imitating Richman, got up in a Dietrich-esque tuxedo. She delighted in wearing men's clothes onstage, but Ziegfeld loathed obscuring what the public paid to see and reassigned the spot to Richman, who eventually sang "Help Yourself to Happiness" instead. Helen also sang Gene Buck and Dr. Hugo Riesenfeld's "Love Is All I Live For." The scene was a tableaux recreation of Sir Luke Fildes's painting *The Doctor*. Ziegfeld excised it, too, before leaving Steel Town.[8] Having failed to find even one outstanding number, Ziegfeld abandoned the idea of three Morgan solos altogether.

Helen in her favorite *Follies* costume. (Billy Rose Theatre Division, the New York Library for the Performing Arts)

Issues with material aside, Helen was "glorified" in the best Ziegfeldian manner. Applause greeted her when she made her first entrance in a skintight gold-leaf gown with red fox trim. It was Helen's favorite. Most nights, she did not change into her next costume until the last minute. Also well received was a transparent velvet dress with a silver fox collar. Whatever its faults, Ziegfeld produced a beautiful show.

Helen scored in her sketches. In the *Grand Hotel* burlesque, she played Polly Adlervitch, the Queen of the Russian Ballet, who deposited green carnations in the rooms of the hotel's male guests. Beyond this hint of homosexuality, many blanched at Mark Hellinger's blue material. During the twenties, Hellinger himself condemned others' use of the practice in his newspaper column, but by 1931, Broadway, Hollywood, and Hellinger were pouring on the sex in a desperate ploy to fill seats. *Grand Hotel* contained the evening's most questionable gag. At one point, dialect comedian Jack Pearl, as Hollywood terror Cecil B. Goldwarner, took a healthy bite of Helen's arm, smacked his lips, and exclaimed, "I'd like it even if it were pork!"[9]

"Victim of the Talkies" was perhaps the best sketch of the evening. Helpless without a Hollywood dictator, film stars and newlyweds Rommey (George Lamar) and Louella (Helen) summon Lubitsch's forty-second assistant director (Pearl) to megaphone instructions on their wedding night. In late 1932, the sketch was recycled during the West Coast tryout of the Frank Fay–Barbara Stanwyck revue *Tattle Tales* but was dropped before the show's brief Broadway run.

On July 1, this competent if undistinguished *Follies* moved into the Ziegfeld Theatre.[10] Despite the cuts made out of town, the New York premiere still ran past midnight.

Ziegfeld fought for "Half-Caste Woman" in Pittsburgh, but audiences shrugged. In New York, people hated it. *Variety* called the Coward number "a rather shoddy idea."[11] Within five days of the opening, it was gone, prompting

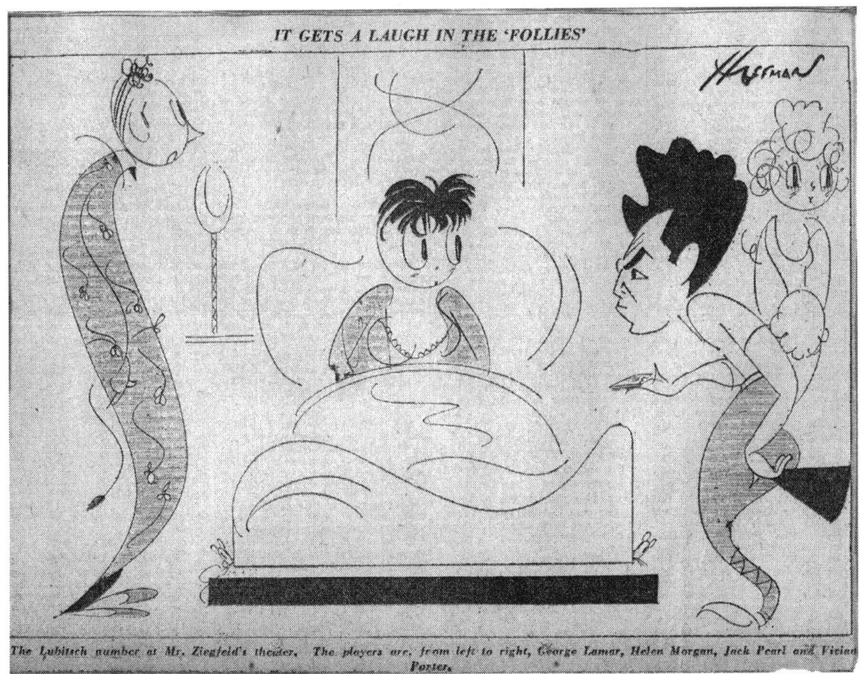

The "Victim of the Talkies" sketch in the 1931 *Follies*. (Author's collection)

many along the Main Stem to predict that Helen would depart before the month was out.[12] She stayed, and every week or so, she tried out a new song. In August, Ziegfeld and Helen gave "Love Is All I Live For" another chance. In late September, she brought in "Two Loves" (*J'ai Deux Amours*), which Josephine Baker had recently popularized in Paris.[13] Nothing clicked.

A near miss in her quest for a hit song involved crooner-songwriter Russ Columbo. Ziegfeld requested a Morgan specialty. Columbo and Leo Robin, envisioning her sitting atop her piano in chains, dashed off "Prisoner of Love."[14] Ziegfeld, perhaps in deference to Helen's current Steinway aversion, dismissed both the song and Columbo, calling him a two-bit song plugger. Recorded on October 9, 1931, "Prisoner of Love" helped launch Columbo's tragically short career.

Helen's dilemma was largely self-inflicted. During rehearsals, she refused song after song offered to her, believing that if she remained difficult, Ziegfeld would find another "Bill" for her: a song she could act. After the Broadway opening, the tables turned, and she feared she would be let go "if [she didn't] get another song and start earning [her] salary."[15] Whenever he came backstage and noted how well she had sung, she knew, despite his politeness, that he was displeased. No news from Ziegfeld was definitely good news.

Later in the run, Helen leaned against the proscenium with a stack of love letters in her hands and sang "Here Lies Love." Ruth Etting thought that the number was Helen's best but that Ziegfeld erred by ending the song with a blackout. "A blackout is for a joke. If they'd used a pin spot that gradually faded, the number would have gone over big. I know. I used it in cafés later. But I would never have dreamed of telling Mr. Ziegfeld how to stage a number."[16]

Its reputation helped make the *Follies* one of the hottest tickets in a hot town. Another contributing factor was that the Ziegfeld, after the 48th Street Theatre, was the only New York house equipped with air-conditioning. Helen exploited the new technology by organizing a Vacation Club, headquartered in her dressing room, where, when not onstage, the cast read, played backgammon, and partook in "summer beverages."[17] One member of the club was Barbara Coswell, whom Ziegfeld fired when she became too skinny for his liking. Helen intervened, advising her, "Go and cry on Flo's shoulder. Put some onion in your eyes and really weep. He never can resist tears."[18] The ploy worked.

Helen displayed her collection of first editions backstage. Her fascination peaked in 1931, when she acquired firsts by Charles Dickens, George

Moore, and D. H. Lawrence, as well as books illustrated by Rockwell Kent. The prize of her collection was an old Book of Common Prayer. "The edges seem to be of gilt when it's closed, but when you ruffle the pages a picture of Jerusalem in colour appears on the slanted edges. It seems that the method of doing this has vanished to-day, but it's lovely."[19]

There were no mice in Helen's dressing room, much to the relief of Lulu, on whom fell the burden of nursing them when they ailed and consoling her daughter when the inevitable happened. At home, Lulu also faced the unenviable task of keeping the cats away from the latest addition to the menagerie, a canary named Charley that had a "Morganesque" haircut.

Jean Howard understudied Helen in the sketches. When too wobbly to walk through her scenes, Helen called Howard into her dressing room to ensure that the costumes fit and gush about how wonderful the youngster was going to be.[20] No one understudied Helen's vocals. Etting noted that for that ever-changing solo, "Sometimes when she'd had too much to drink, they'd drape a table with cloth and place her behind it. She couldn't stand up, but she could give a perfect performance."[21]

In the late 1890s, vaudevillians Mabel Ross and Frank Fenton converted an old restaurant near Asbury Park, New Jersey, into an actor's boarding house, with occasional impromptu performances on the front porch. By 1931, the Ross Fenton Farm had become one of the most glamorous nightspots in the country. It boasted a pavilion on the lake that seated twelve hundred people and housed two casinos.

Helen played the weekend late shows on July 31 and August 1. The engagement was so successful that she was invited back two weeks later to warble from Friday through Sunday. After her *Follies* performance, police escorted her from the Ziegfeld to a hydroplane on the Hudson at Ninety-Sixth Street, which flew her to the Deal Lake resort and touched down dramatically at midnight.[22] Mistakenly believing that Helen had secured permission in advance, pilot Harry Rogers landed his seaplane on an inland lake and was arrested.[23] Helen was *not* invited back for subsequent weekends. In addition to losing a paycheck, she missed the Farm's roulette wheel, which had been lucky for her.

During the Depression, stars still earned big money on the radio, or on the vaudeville and cabaret circuits, when not plying the boards. Not so for Broadway choristers. One night in 1930, Helen Morgan, Helen Kane, Charles

Butterworth, press agent Milton Raison, and Heywood Broun brainstormed in a local speakeasy as to how they could aid the plight of unemployed stage professionals.[24] The result was Broun's Give a Job benefit. Held at midnight on April 12, 1930, the event raised $7,700 for unemployed actors. Helen, eyeing so many celebrities backstage at the Imperial, quipped that the only thing missing from the roster was Mussolini in a strongman act.

A year later, with the Depression worsening, Broun staged and hosted his own revue to keep artists working. Dorothy Parker, E. B. White, Peter Arno, Harry Hershfield, and Nunnally Johnson supplied sketches gratis. Irving Berlin and twenty other songwriters furnished the score. *Shoot the Works!* opened on the hottest night of the year, July 21, at the George M. Cohan Theatre. Imogene Coca and George Murphy were among the 150 employed. The addition of guest stars, most notably the Marx Brothers, again boosted attendance.[25] Helen did her bit on August 31 and September 1. She performed her first-act *Follies* duties, traveled via police escort to the Cohan, sang there, and returned to the Ziegfeld to finish the evening. Mounted on a bankroll of only $6,000, the production recouped in eight weeks. (Broun's angels, including Helen, expected no return on their investment.) Broun intended the show to run indefinitely, but an attack of influenza forced him out on October 3. Without him, *Shoot the Works!* shuttered that night, after eighty-nine performances.[26]

Helen returned to the world of the night. Loath as they were to have two Club Lidos on the same street, management feared that naming their cabaret after Helen would act as catnip to federal raiders. Therefore, on October 1, the club reopened, as before, as the New Club Lido. She went over big: "No one made a note when Helen Morgan sang . . . they could not . . . for she's . . . magic!"[27]

Helen's star power ultimately won out, and by mid-October, the daily papers and the New York telephone directory listed the nitery as "The Helen Morgan Club," even though the name above the door remained "The New Club Lido."[28]

When the Morgan-Loew relationship worked, it was wonderful. When it did not, everyone knew it. The couple were at very public loggerheads during Helen's time with *Shoot the Works!* The twosome reconciled backstage at the Ziegfeld during a matinee a few days later, but friction continued into the fall, when Helen cozied up with Lido orchestra leader Henry King.

Also burning for Helen was composer-accompanist Lou Alter, best remembered for writing "Manhattan Serenade," a musical cousin to "Rhapsody in Blue." He also wrote for films and the stage, including the ill-fated *Ballyhoo*. For Helen's ever-changing *Follies* solo, he provided "The Man I Used to Love," a proposed sequel to the Gershwins' "The Man I Love." Ziegfeld, again, cut it after a few performances, but Alter and Morgan connected.[29] When the New Lido opened for the fall, Alter played for her, and she featured many of his compositions. While they were never big hits like her Kern numbers, Helen remained loyal and kept Alter's songs in her repertoire for years. The best of the marriage of Morgan and Alter was "What a Life (Trying to Live without You)," which went over big at the Lido opening and was published the following day. Warners acquired the tune and used it in the feature film *The Rich Are Always with Us* and in the shorts *The Audition* and the Ruth Etting outing *Artistic Temper*.

On the day she reopened the New Lido, Helen handed Ziegfeld her four-weeks' notice.[30] The story was that one night, Helen went up during "I'm with You" and Richman covered for her in a bawdy and embarrassing manner. Days later, citing a cold, Richman dropped out of "I'm with You" yet performed everything else he did in the show.[31] In subsequent interviews, Helen harped on Richman's unprofessional antics and claimed that he once got physical with her during the blackout following the duet.

The reality was that, with the arrival of the new season and cooler weather, ticket sales at the Ziegfeld had slipped. When cutting the cast's salary by 25 percent failed to right his ship, Ziegfeld prepared a post-Broadway *Follies* tour. He likely asked his underutilized chanteuse to exit the cast as a cost-cutting move, although the fabrication of a Morgan-Richman feud seems extreme publicity to mask an old man's vanity. Ziegfeld approached Lupe Vélez to take on Helen's *Follies* duties. The "Mexican Spitfire" sneered that she was *nobody's* replacement. He commissioned Mark Hellinger to pen a vehicle for her, which initially bore the title *Laid in Mexico*.[32]

Weeks after Helen's defection, Ziegfeld met Ed Sullivan in a New York speakeasy. Pointing to the tousle-haired woman on the other side of the bar "sipping her Orangeade," he gushed, "She's the greatest artist who ever worked for me. I've seen them all, and she ranks above all for sheer artistry!"[33]

Whereas Helen was shortchanged musically, Etting, a stutterer, rarely spoke in performance. In *Whoopee*, her character was only marginally involved with the story. Occasionally she made her way to the footlights, sang songs like "Love Me or Leave Me," stopped the show, and then exited. There was no Morgan-Etting feud, but there was "Colonel" Moe Snyder. Etting's abusive husband-manager was jealous of anyone who threatened to take the spotlight away from his "little lady." Etting came down with bronchitis on or about November 7, when Helen left the production. Snyder pulled his wife out of the *Follies*. If the move was a ploy to pressure Ziegfeld to offer more money or give Helen's assignments to Etting, it failed. Instead, beginning November 21, the last day of the Broadway run, Wini Shaw covered *both* roles. She also took the production on tour. Not only did she resemble Helen but she also adopted the Morgan perch and manner while essaying Etting's original role in a short-lived revival of *Simple Simon*.

The Etting-Snyder marriage confounded the Rialto. Asked why she did not divorce him, Ruth replied, "If I leave him, he'll kill me."[34]

With an hour between her first- and second-act appearances, Helen brought a portable typewriter backstage and went to work. On August 19, she penned a column for vacationing Broadway scribe Julia Shawell. Then, on the closing day of the *Follies*, the *Morning Graphic* published her poem "Ode to a Porcelain Cat." The *New York American* praised the more ambitious "Mother and Child," although it escaped publication, as did her subsequent works, "Ode to a Duck" and "Conversation between Two Cats."[35] She sold two poems to *College Humor*. A year passed before the magazine published her work, a bit of whimsy called "Lover Camels." The magazine ultimately passed on the other, a piece of stray verse "about a China doll on the mantelpiece and a snooping bronze cat on the hearthstone."[36]

In October, US attorney Arthur H. Schwartz formally dropped his indictments on Helen, Texas Guinan, and eight of the others who pleaded not guilty to the June 1928 raids. Helen's Prohibition woes were truly over.

After her final *Follies* performance, Helen and Arthur Loew celebrated her double emancipation with a Florida vacation. A recently licensed pilot, Loew took the controls. Fog forced his plane down in Charleston, South Carolina. They continued to Miami by train. The Sanchezes entertained them on Palm Island. Later, the party flew to Havana.

The trip, like the one the year before, sparked rumors of an elopement. In Cuba, Loew set the record straight: "We are not married, nor do we plan to be married soon, nor will we be married at all. If we were married, I should be greatly pleased to say so."[37]

In December, Helen scouted locations for a potential winter season nightclub in Havana. When it failed to pan out, Helen and Lou Alter played the winter season at the Miami Lido. On opening night, the audience's enthusiasm was so intense that Helen had to beg off. She returned later in the evening to join her old and current emcee, Al B. White, in an impromptu skit.

The Lido booking forced Helen to decline an invitation to sing for President Herbert Hoover at the New York Casino on January 31. While honored, she was relieved to cancel. As her anti-Prohibition beliefs and unceasing work for those affected by the Depression suggest, her political leanings at the time were, if not pro-Democratic, anti-Republican. Among her philanthropic endeavors that winter was the annual Underprivileged Child Benefit, where she appeared with Dorothy Dalton, wife of Arthur Hammerstein. Helen played this benefit every winter she was in Florida, as much for the opportunity to reconnect with the Hammerstein clan and network for potential theatrical opportunities as for the children it aided.

She rarely held a grudge, but Helen was nobody's fool. When Arthur Loew visited her, he dropped $9,000 in one night in the Lido casino. She knew he could afford it, but at the end of the week, she seethed when her Lido paycheck bounced. She walked. Norma Terris replaced her and began her inaugural performance with her Morgan impersonation.

Helen moved to the Beach and Tennis Club.[38] The managing director, Mort Wetheimer, created this exclusive members-only Miami Beach casino/nightclub by refurbishing Shadows, the old Carl Fisher mansion. In honor of Helen's penchant for puns, Lou Alter announced his intention to write the ultimate torch song: "Mighty Lachrymose."[39]

Back in New York, Arthur Loew began to spend time with Sally O'Neil. In March, the two sailed to Europe. Born Virginia Louise Concepta Noonan in Bayonne, New Jersey, O'Neil became a popular MGM starlet in the twenties in such films as *Battling Butler* and *Sally, Irene and Mary*. Her vaudevillian roots served her well in early film musicals, but by the time she started seeing Loew, flappers and musicals were as popular as her Jersey accent. When Sally and Arthur returned to the States, her sister, Molly O'Day, announced a Loew-O'Neil engagement, which Loew, characteristically, denied. Helen rebounded by spending her time with E. R. Jones of Miami Beach. Helen acted as the mechanic (!) of his *Miss Chris Craft* when they competed in the Nineteenth Annual Biscayne Bay Regatta.

The carefree beach life began to show: Helen let her hair grow out, giving up her trademarked chrysanthemum cut. She also began to gain weight.

When the Beach and Tennis Club closed for the season, Helen treated herself to a week's vacation in Nassau. A telegram awaited her arrival:

HELEN MORGAN

DEAR HELEN YOUR MOTHER SAYS YOU ARRIVE NEW YORK 4/8 OPENING NIGHT CLUB BOSTON 4/9 FOR 2 WEEKS DO YOU PLAY THERE SUNDAY WANT YOU AS STAR ZIEGFELD RADIO SHOW SUNDAY NIGHT 8 O'CLOCK NEW YORK 4/10 WHAT ARE YOU GOING TO CHARGE ME HOW ABOUT SHOW BOAT COME HOME LOVE—Z[40]

11

Above the Title

Helen returned to Ziegfeld.

Taking Ruth Etting's "Shine on Harvest Moon" triumph as his model, Ziegfeld announced *The Follies of Long Ago*, which would feature as many stars as he could acquire. As a preamble, from April 3 to June 26, 1932, he produced the radio variety show *Ziegfeld Follies of the Air*, which ushered into America's homes his stable of personalities, including Will Rogers, Fanny Brice, and, on three occasions, Helen Morgan. During her first visit to the Ziegfeld microphone, she sang "What a Life" with the classically trained composer Lou Alter at the piano. Alter augmented those tired Tin Pan Alley piano arrangements with his own, replete with wild rococo flourishes, which Helen matched with greater vocal variation. In fine voice, she crescendos and decrescendos her final note until it comes out a moan. Alter inspired Helen to approach her material as lieder. From a technical standpoint, "What a Life" may be her best extant vocal performance.

So popular was the CBS series that Ziegfeld reimagined his *Follies of Long Ago* not as a Broadway attraction but as a series of one-night extravaganzas to play auditoria coast-to-coast. He signed radio emcee Eddie Dowling to repeat his duties on the road and Al Goodman and his orchestra to provide the music. Ziegfeld would troupe with a star roster that would include Jack Pearl, Ray Dooley, Paul Robeson—and perhaps Helen. A popularly priced *Follies* tour was a sound idea. Less so was his latest Broadway production, the Lupe Vélez vehicle, which critics damned as old-fashioned next to the satirical *Of Thee I Sing*. He countered that, if *Hot-Cha!* was dated, then so was *Show Boat*.

To prove his point, he revived his greatest success. Citing other commitments and a reluctance to repeat themselves, his veterans demurred when, in late 1930, Ziegfeld first gauged interest in a *Show Boat* revival, but eighteen months later, eight of his original principals were ripe for a sure thing: a four-week New York run followed by a national tour. Dennis King stepped in for Howard Marsh as Ravenal. The other absentee was Jules Bledsoe, whose heavy concert schedule prevented him from appearing. Paul Robeson, who triumphed in London in the role originally written for him, finally played Joe on Broadway. Helen earned the distinction of being the only cast member to perform without a contract. She earned $1,250 a week ($1,000 if the gross dipped below $30,000) and could leave at any time should something better come along. Conversely, Ziegfeld could fire her at will should she not perform to standard.[1]

As a prelude, on May 1, Helen, Paul Robeson, Jean Sargent, and Charles Carlisle sang *Show Boat* selections on the *Follies of the Air*.[2] Helen began rehearsal the following day and opened two and a half weeks later.[3] With *Hot-Cha!* ensconced in his own house, Flo leased the Earl Carroll. Before Ziegfeld and Arthur Hammerstein built their houses, in 1922, Carroll erected a monument to himself. Then, in the Depression, he razed it and built a three-thousand-seat theater on its ashes. After a single attraction, his 1931 *Vanities*, the house went into foreclosure. Ziegfeld grabbed it. To needle his longtime rival, he poured $20,000 into retrofitting Carroll's folly and renamed it the Casino.[4]

By 1932, *Show Boat* had become an American institution. So had Helen Morgan. J. Brooks Atkinson warned that readers "with no stomach for superlatives had best abandon this review immediately."[5] Robert Garland gushed, "The ten most beautiful actresses in America is Helen Morgan."[6]

Arthur Loew continued to date Sally O'Neil, who, strangely enough, started dressing like Helen, complete with fluttering kerchief. Ed Sullivan sniped that if Loew "can't have Helen Morgan, he will at least have the No. 1 road company."[7] Within days, Sally's "Morgan" look was gone. So were Helen's extra pounds. After the *Show Boat* premiere, Loew and Helen walked arm-in-arm into the opening-night party. Loew bypassed the customary opening-night gifts of flowers or liquor and presented Helen with something useful: a portable radio for her dressing room.

Gossips again heard wedding bells, which infuriated Lulu, who, while distrustful of any man who courted Helen, loathed Arthur Loew, whose dalliances, she believed, made a fool of her daughter. Helen found herself caught in the middle; she would not leave her mother, and the three could not exist together as a family.

Unlike Lulu, Helen forgave and forgot. Three months later, Sally O'Neil underwent an appendectomy. The most extravagant flower arrangement in her hospital room came from Helen Morgan.

The reaction to *Show Boat* was better than Ziegfeld dared to hope. Reeling from debt and in failing health, he postponed his tour for an open run. Helen stayed on Broadway—or, in her words, "where the girls and boys who are not on the level, meet on the square."[8]

During one matinee, Helen went to make her entrance for the pantry scene but could not get the door to the set to open. With great effort, the trouper contorted herself through the jammed doorway and onto the stage. Composing herself, she stuck to the script and gave her first line, "I had a hard time getting here," and brought down the house.[9]

Two months later, Helen, as Julie, stood in the background during Magnolia's audition scene. The guitar strings slipped, rapidly bringing down the song a half or whole step at a time until, by the end, Norma Terris had dropped a full five keys but had not missed a note. When she asked Jack Daley, "How did you like it?" the actor gave the reply Hammerstein placed in his mouth: "Lousy."[10]

Helen made a blanket offer to the chorus: save $100 during the run and receive an additional $10 from her. She offered that same 10 percent scale at $200 and $500 levels. Conversely, she insisted the company pay it forward. Chorines habitually forked over fifty cents to a dollar from each paycheck to the Actors Fund. Annie Hart, the landlady in the boardinghouse scene, had inducted Helen into the charity four years before. One day Helen overheard Hart sigh that she had wanted a chaise longue in her dressing room ever since she saw that Lillian Russell had one in hers. Helen adorned Hart's dressing room with a chaise before the week was out.[11]

Chief among Helen's philanthropic passions was the Actors' Dinner Club. This Depression charity offered thespians a bite before and after performances in a private club. More importantly, it provided unemployed actors with free meals and a place to network. The club opened in the Wesley Hall of the Union Methodist Church on December 7, 1931, and moved from space to space as better rooms became available or a commercial need required them to vacate. The club's second home, from June to October 1932, was beneath the Loew's State Theatre, at Broadway and Forty-Sixth Street. The club served over 250,000 meals before disbanding in 1935.

Helen's collection plate was ubiquitous throughout the Rialto. When she held court at the Mayfair and Pierrette Clubs, her well-trained marks dropped cash on her ringside table while dancing by. She regularly collected $200–$300 a week for the club, not counting what she gathered backstage at the Casino and her own donations. She also played their benefits. At one show, her impatience with the uncharitable raised the eyebrows of New York society. When one wealthy patron refused to donate, Helen gave him a dollar from the collection plate, stating that he obviously needed the money more than the actors did.

Loew presented Helen with a garden plot in Glen Cove, where she grew everything from radishes to watermelon. When Joan Crawford and Douglas Fairbanks Jr. visited Pembroke over the Fourth of July weekend, Helen excused herself from her guests to spend Sunday afternoon tending her vegetables. At 7:30 p.m., she trudged in, ready to slip into hostess pajamas, only to find everyone in full evening dress. Sheepishly, she dashed upstairs to dress.[12]

Loew enjoyed summertime custody of his children. Despite her frustrated desire to conceive or adopt, Helen honored his wish to keep his children at arm's length: at Pembroke, they dined separately from the adults until their fifteenth birthday. Therefore, Jane and Arthur Jr. rarely saw Helen during their summers together, but one day, Jane met Helen on the beach. Never having seen a woman with painted toenails before, Jane cried, "Oh, I like your red toes!"[13]

Helen's shellacked digits were as legendary as her dislike for stockings. Her aversion likely originated when Flo first decreed that she, like all Ziegfeld girls, must wear silk stockings onstage. Before each performance, wardrobe distributed cold hose fresh from the refrigerator. Off the stage, Helen bought a hundred stockings at a time, then, loath to wash them, discarded them after one use. In warmer weather, she effectively obviated the need for stockings by wearing open-toed shoes. For years, wags deemed the sight of Helen's toes a sure sign of spring. She was particular about her flame-red polish and brought along her own bottle when having a mani-pedi.

In June, Helen announced that she would write her autobiography. *Lusitania* survivor and war correspondent Floyd Gibbons introduced her to Eve Gray, a potential assistant and ghostwriter.[14] Nothing came of it, but Gibbons, like all of Broadway, remained fascinated by the dichotomy between the world-weary soul who suffered onstage and the childlike woman offstage who behaved like Cinderella at the ball.[15] What need had she to heed her own advice and save her money? She was one of the best-paid women in the business. She loved one of the richest men in America. In her brandy-befogged world, there was no reason to expect that midnight would ever come.

~

In June, the *Show Boat* company took a 25 percent pay cut.[16] In mid-July, another cut halved the salaries of the principals. Helen shrugged it off; half of $1,250 was what she earned in 1927. While not so philosophical, her colleagues agreed to the cuts. In appreciation, the chorus placed a notice on the Casino call-board thanking the principals for allowing the show to continue.

Money was the least of the cast's worries.

After completing the run of his radio show, an ailing Ziegfeld joined his family in Hollywood, where he entered Cedars of Lebanon Hospital with pleurisy, then suffered a heart attack. His wife, Billie Burke, left the set of RKO's *A Bill of Divorcement* in midscene and, with their daughter Patricia, raced to his bedside. They arrived two minutes after his passing, just before midnight, on July 18.

The Broadway community was stunned—the *Show Boat* family, cast adrift by the loss of its captain, most of all. During the matinee following his death, Annie Hart, who started with Ziegfeld in Chicago forty years before, sat weeping by the stage door. With the passing of Ziegfeld, Helen lost the most consistent father figure she ever knew. She retreated to her dressing room to hide her sorrow. Even outside the Casino, she mostly kept to herself.[17] She never stopped mourning him.

Helen's alcohol intake increased. Dramatically. Lou Alter often saw Helen take "a brandy or two before she made a record or went onstage . . . and that made her do the best work." Only "after the show she would overdo it . . . for performance she knew when to stop. She'd stop at two, and then she would sparkle and . . . you *lived* what she was singing."[18] Norma Terris witnessed Helen and Charles Winninger drinking before going on, even during the 1927 *Show Boat* production. Winninger believed that a dram helped him in the Trocadero scene.[19] After Ziegfeld's death, Terris saw Helen's intake increase before Morgan went on. When Norma and her husband, Dr. Jerome Wagner, hosted a weekend at their country home in Connecticut, Helen brought along a case—a *case*—of brandy and consumed every drop before heading back for the Monday performance.[20]

Billie Burke granted managerial control of her husband's assets, including the Ziegfeld Theatre and *Show Boat*, to A. C. Blumenthal but refused his request for a big New York funeral. Instead, he broadcast a one-hour radio memorial service. Helen sang "What a Life (Trying to Live without You.)." She finished with tears streaming down her face, collapsed, and was assisted to her seat and, ultimately, out of the studio.

Three weeks after Ziegfeld's death, Helen rerecorded her *Show Boat* numbers in a particularly somber manner. Recording engineer Vinnie Liebler remembered Helen consuming enough brandy that she slurred the lyrics and got offbeat. In addition to Helen, Liebler struggled with Brunswick's antiquated setup. Electric recording began in 1925, but eight years later, the Brunswick studio still used a weight-and-pulley system. When recording, a rope slowly lowered a sinker down a seven-story shaft, and the platter revolved at a consistent speed. This method worked nicely for ten-inch records but not for the twelve-inch platters Brunswick occasionally cut. As a result, the interval from the touchdown of the needle to the start of the music had to time out exactly or the weight would hit the ground and the turntable would stop cutting before the performance completed. Finally, after multiple takes, Helen's diction, pitch, and phrasing were perfect—this was the definitive performance of "Bill." Helen finished the second chorus. Then, while Alter completed his typically florid accompaniment, the weight hit the ground, ruining the take. The subsequent take Brunswick released was fine, but to Liebler, it was nowhere near the quality of that "great" one.[21]

The disc was one of four that Brunswick packaged together into Broadway's first cast album. The other discs included an Overture and Finale (specially arranged by Victor Young for the recording), Paul Robeson's "Ol' Man River," and on three sides, radio favorite James Melton. He took "You Are Love" and "Make Believe" as solos and joined with the Countess Albani on "Why Do I Love You?" Six months later, Brunswick assembled a similar souvenir album for *Blackbirds of 1928*. Like her Victor waxing of "Bill," the Brunswick *Show Boat* collection has entered the Grammy Hall of Fame.[22]

In August, Helen entertained Jorge and Brownie Sanchez aboard Loew's 130-foot yacht. The Sanchezes, in return, feted Helen with a three-day birthday bash at Ben Marden's swanky Riviera nightclub in Fort Lee, New Jersey, where she received two mouthbrooding flame fish as a gift. Helen dived headfirst into her new hobby and filled twenty-two tanks by the end of the year. Visitors to her tony new apartment overlooking Central Park endured tours of the Morgan Aquarium, as well as the odor that accompanies the life and death of fish in enclosed spaces.[23] After a few ponies of brandy, Helen was as oblivious to the stench as she was to her guests' discomfort.[24]

She paid as much as thirty-five dollars for some fish, but most came along naturally. The miracle of birth fascinated her. "You look at a tank in the morning and there are only two fish in it; you look at it that night and it's swarming with fish. It's very romantic. It makes you have faith in fish."[25] Helen procured fresh algae and pollywogs to feed her growing children. Names for her rarer specimens ranged from the lighthearted Four Marx Brothers to the more telling Brandy and Soda. When she exhibited at the Aquarium Society Show on September 3, President William G. Holbrein bestowed on her a special award for her community tank.

Helen's summer of love ended on September 15 when Arthur Loew began a trip around the world. She agonized over the prospect of a months-long separation and turned inward. Helen turned down a fancy party at the Waldorf for a more intimate soiree at the Sanchezes' New York apartment, where they gave her a pair of diamond clips, which ultimately ended up in the possession of a friend who admired them.[26] At times, Helen seemed determined to leave life as poor as she had entered it. When the Sanchezes left town in mid-October,

Arthur Loew, the love of Helen Morgan's life. (Courtesy of Everett Collection)

Helen presented Brownie with a circlet of baguette diamonds and Jorge with a rare luck piece.

Separation from Loew had another effect: by October, Helen was heavier.

On October 11, Helen performed on television. The Democratic National Committee sponsored the two-hour event, *Broadway on Parade*. Broadcast from the CBS studio on the Chrysler Building's fifty-seventh floor, the first hour went out over radio. Reviewing television for the first time, *Variety* found the second hour, viewed on a twenty-six-inch screen in an adjoining room, uninspiring and missed Helen's "lip trembling nuances" in the new medium.[27] The *Billboard* disagreed. Acknowledging Helen's extreme nervousness, it concluded that she "gave us an interesting televiz number and that her own radiant personality was not lost over the invisible sight waves."[28]

Helen first played television in April 1931, when she sang on the opening-day broadcast of W2XCR, New York's first TV station. Even Helen, Chevalier, and Gertrude Lawrence failed to sell the public on the medium in this embryonic stage.[29]

Helen also turned her attention to radio. When Chevrolet expressed interest in sponsoring a weekly series, NBC proposed two possible programs. The first featured Helen, Donald Novis, Frank Crumit as emcee, and Gus Henschen's orchestra. The second boasted Fanny Brice, the Ernö Rapée symphonic ensemble, and Willie and Eugene Howard. Chevrolet rejected both offers. The following spring, they did sign with NBC, and made history. Bypassing the variety format, they went for comedy, in the personage of Jack Benny.

Included in the Ziegfeld estate were two Kern and Hammerstein musicals. Blumenthal produced one, *Music in the Air*, and initially announced Dennis King and Helen for the leading roles. Anticipating a full season in Manhattan, Helen entered into talks to double into the El Garron. Then, Paul Robeson, Edna May Oliver, Charles Winninger, and Tess Gardella all left *Show Boat*. When Charles Ellis exited for a revival of *Liliom*, newcomer George Blackwood played Helen's Steve. With only Norma Terris, Eva Puck, and Sammy White to lead the tour, Blumenthal reshuffled. Jules Bledsoe returned for the tour. Walter Slezak and Katharine Carrington took over *Music in the Air*. King went to Hollywood, and Helen abandoned the El Garron and took to the road.

Blumenthal intended to tour *Show Boat* for a year or more, including a run through the South and another up and down the West Coast. Helen, having only played twelve cities in the Northeast and Midwest to date, committed to expanding her fan base. To sweeten the deal, Blumenthal increased her salary to $3,500 a week.

Joining Helen on the road was a new pet. The tortoiseshell cat arrived from England with the name Annabelle, but Helen called her Charley.

Dorothy Dey joined Helen in Boston, where the two screamed themselves hoarse campaigning for Franklin Roosevelt, who won a landslide victory during *Show Boat*'s next stop, Philadelphia.[30] The following day, two thousand miles away, a Category 4 hurricane ravaged Cuba. The Sanchezes' sugar plantation suffered significant damage, but it was nothing compared to the devastation when a tidal wave engulfed a nearby town. In all, three thousand Cubans lost their lives.

With both Helen and Arthur traveling, communication proved difficult.

Loew piloted his own Stinson to Hollywood, where he borrowed Hal Roach's *Spirit of Fun*, but even that larger craft could not cross the Pacific in one hop. Once their ocean liner docked in Australia, Loew ceded the controls to Captain James B. Dickson, a professional pilot with whom Loew enjoyed a friendly rivalry.[31] Dickson flew Loew and his traveling companion, Jersey City lawyer Joseph Rosthal, to China in just twenty-five hours. The next layovers were in Cairo and then Victoria Falls. On November 17, while taking off for Cape Town, Dickson failed to compensate for the short runway and crashed into a tree. The engine, thrown from the plane, landed sixty yards away from the wreck. Dickson was killed. Loew and Rosthal walked away unhurt. After receiving news of Loew's miraculous escape, the Metro brass ordered Carl Sonin, then in Johannesburg, to fly up to survey the damage and ensure that Loew's cable did not make light of his condition. Loew rented and flew a plane to Johannesburg; Rosthal and Sonin went by train.

Helen collapsed when she heard of the accident. Two days passed before she could convince herself that Loew was alive by successfully reaching him by telephone in Johannesburg—at 3:00 a.m. South African time. She reversed the $155 charge.

Loew's mother cabled her son demanding he give up airplanes. Dutifully, he sailed home, but once back at Pembroke, he returned to flying. While in the pilot's seat, he crashed two of his own planes within a year.

While popular with audiences, the cost of moving the enormous production across the country soon placed *Show Boat* $8,000 in the red. Blumenthal posted a provisional closing notice in Cincinnati. To keep the production afloat, he asked his principals to take pay cuts. Recovering from the flu, Norma Terris and Jules Bledsoe chose to leave. Eva Puck and Sammy White countered with an offer to invest $16,000 in the endeavor and run it themselves as a co-op. Blumenthal refused. Although they held run-of-the-play contracts, Puck and White graciously stepped aside to permit the production to continue. During a two-week layover in Cleveland, Blumenthal rehearsed new cast members and canceled the West Coast leg of the tour.

Helen stayed put, happy to use her marquee value to keep dozens of people employed. "Right now I don't think anyone has the right to be lazy. If people at the top everywhere would take a little less, that's the nicest kind of help

The last person to receive star billing in a Ziegfeld production. (Author's collection)

for the others."[32] On Christmas Day, Helen gave each of the 134 members of the truncated *Show Boat* cast and crew five-dollar gift certificates. In turn, they gave her an antique chair, covered with peach velvet, and a silent electric alarm clock; Helen could not sleep in the same room with all that tick-tock vying for attention. The next day, when *Show Boat* bowed at Cleveland's Hanna Theatre, she received the greatest gift of all—star billing. Helen Morgan was the only original cast member of *Show Boat* whose name appeared above the title—and the last person to star in a Ziegfeld production. More impressive, her name appeared *above* that of Florenz Ziegfeld.

Arthur and Helen's yuletide reunion in Cleveland seemed happy, but each fumed beneath the surface. The loss of Baby Helen three years before spurred Helen to doggedly vie to adopt another child. In December 1932, after being ruled an unfit mother anew, she never attempted to adopt again.[33]

Loew reserved his ire for the brass at MGM. In an accounting scheme to make the studio look more profitable on paper, Louis B. Mayer, Irving Thalberg, J. Robert Rubin, and Loew's treasurer David Bernstein eschewed their customary annual cash bonuses in lieu of options for 250,000 shares of company stock. Incensed by the clandestine dealings, Arthur tendered his resignation from Loew's when he returned to New York in January. The board persuaded Loew to rescind his notice, but he remained angry, possibly because he had not been included in the scheme this time. In 1929, William Fox obtained a $15 million loan from Western Electric and, in a hostile takeover, purchased four hundred thousand shares of Loews stock, many from Arthur, his brother David, and their mother. The stock market crash forced the overextended mogul to abandon his dream. Louis B. Mayer seethed, as did a group of minority shareholders, who sued those who profited from Fox's downfall, including Nicholas Schenck, Irving Thalberg, and Arthur Loew.

By the time it played Chicago, *Show Boat* showed its age. Critic Lloyd Lewis lamented that the lavish, supersized Kern, Hammerstein, and Ziegfeld pageant had been reduced to a big musical comedy—with the exception of Helen Morgan.[34] On opening night, she not only stopped the show cold with "Bill" but gave three encores. Ashton Stevens perhaps offered the most succinct explanation of her appeal by noting that when she sang, Helen seemed "to come right over the footlights and, in a manner of speaking—sit in your lap and tell her song to your inner ear."[35]

Helen doubled in Sam Hare's Winter Garden cabaret. Playing up the *Show Boat* connection, the sunbonneted chorines danced a spirited cakewalk. After the late show, Helen and Lou Alter continued making music: "She had a high lyric spinto voice [and] could sing a high B-flat or C very easily. For relaxation after a show we'd go through the Puccini scores and she'd sing all the arias."[36] Alter believed she might have sung some lighter opera roles if her voice had been a smidge larger. *Manon Lescaut*, in particular, inspired her, but she remained too timid to pursue her dream.[37]

Disa Jamison, now Maxwell, came up from Danville to see her childhood pal, who entertained her lavishly. Thomas Morgan also met with his stepdaughter and saw her play her greatest role. However, the late nights at the Winter Garden had taken their toll. On this matinee day, Helen arrived at the stage door minutes before the curtain.

Show Boat scaled back further.

Looking over the production in Chicago, booking agent Marvin Schenck offered a one-week booking in Chicago and another in Brooklyn. At issue: a two-week gap between the stands, which rendered the proposal economically unfeasible until Loew's offered two weeks in *their* houses. The alliance of Loew's, RKO, and Balaban and Katz gave birth to the tabloid version of *Show Boat*. The production began the final leg of its tour in this emasculated version on February 3 at the Chicago Theatre, playing five performances a day opposite the feature film *Second Hand Wife*. Reduced from eighteen scenes to twelve, the eighty-eight-minute reduction moved at a breakneck pace—until Helen sang "Bill" and stopped the show in its tracks.

On opening day in Cleveland, Arthur threw a bouquet of flowers to Helen across the footlights. Backstage, he gave her a string of pearls. On two of the three nights he was in town, they toured the city's nightlife. On the third, Helen was the guest attraction at the Carter Rainbow Room.

Joining them at their ringside table was Maurice "Buddy" Maschke Jr., son of the Ohio Republican boss. In 1911, President William Howard Taft appointed Maschke Sr. as senior customs collector.[38] As repayment, Maschke delivered Ohio's delegates for Taft at the 1912 Republican Convention despite the fact that Teddy Roosevelt won the state's primary. When other state delegations followed Maschke's lead and did likewise, Teddy ran for president under his Bull Moose Party, putting Democrat Woodrow Wilson in the White House. Eight years later, Maschke helped secure the Republican presidential nomination for another Ohioan, Warren G. Harding.

Although *Show Boat* broke the Loew's State house record, even scaled down, the huge payroll ate up most of the week's receipts. Blumenthal hired six train cars to bring the production east. He also announced that Helen would receive a reward for her loyalty in the form of an original musical in the fall. No title was given.

Taking advantage of a weeklong hiatus, Helen stayed behind for a few days with the Maschkes. Manhattan gossips hinted at a romance, which Buddy denied. "I have known Miss Morgan for about eight years, and she is nothing more than a friend. She is a friend of our whole family."[39] The family friendship began during the 1925 *Scandals* tour when Buddy was eighteen. His Harvard education coincided with Helen's reign as queen of Manhattan's nightclubs. When weekending in Gotham, he often stopped at Helen's club to pay his respects. He also visited when *Show Boat* played Detroit the previous December while preparing for the bar at Western Reserve.

Helen returned to Pembroke when she returned east.

On February 26, Helen made her New York homecoming as a one-night guest artist at the Paradise, Nick Blair's latest cabaret venture. N. T. Granlund introduced the "beloved star of the late Ziegfeld's *Show Boat*," the drum rolled, and the spotlight followed Helen as she entered. Her columnist friends wrote that, at the mention of Ziegfeld's name, she folded at the knees. Friends helped her to the wings. However, Art Arthur reported that she managed to warble a few lines of "What Have We Got to Lose" before she staggered back to her chair under her own power.[40]

Days after the Morgan party, Nick Blair was arrested. Again. This time, he padded Detective Arthur J. McCloskey's check.[41]

Helen remained the softest touch on Broadway. When her scene partner, George Blackwood, departed for a film contract, Gladstone Waldrip moved up from Jeb, the backwoodsman, to play Steve. Helen telegrammed the good news to Waldrip's mother and convinced him to adopt a more punny stage name, Stoney Wahl.[42]

One day, an old woman who sold fashion accessories in the theater district offered "Mousie" Morgan some ties backstage. Helen did not need any. The woman left Morgan's dressing room to continue her rounds. Alice Haynes, Helen's maid, caught up with her at the stage door, offering two dollars. This "Apple Annie" refused: she was no beggar. While the woman chatted with friends, Alice retreated and then returned, asking how many ties the woman had. Fifty-five, costing one dollar apiece. Alice ran back up the stairs, returned with fifty-five dollars, and relieved the peddler of her wares. Every man in the cast and crew of *Show Boat* received a tie that day, courtesy of Helen Morgan.

In addition to bearing the cost of touring *Show Boat*, Blumenthal struggled to find suitable lodgings for his integrated cast, a task that proved impossible in the segregated South. Before *Show Boat* even sailed, Blumenthal dropped stops in Richmond, Virginia, and Waco, Texas. In December, he tried to book a split week between Indianapolis and Louisville, followed by seven-day stands in both St. Louis and Kansas City, before heading to Chicago, but he could not make the logistics work. In January, Blumenthal tried for a southern swing through Louisville, Nashville, and New Orleans. Nothing. Back in New York, he entered talks to bring the tab unit to Dallas.[43] When that failed to pan out, he shuttered the production forever after it played in Brooklyn. *Show Boat* did not play the Deep South until February 21, 1949, when the 1946 revival played the Poche Theatre in New Orleans.

Back in New York, one morning Helen granted an at-home interview. Before she was seven, Helen had been a coffee addict who could drink a pot, black, all by herself.[44] As an adult, she added Hennessey's Three Star. "May as well make a coffee royal," she said. "May as well flavor the coffee. Instead of cream, I use brandy. Much better. It even makes the coffee look better." Surveying Central Park from the window of her eighth-floor apartment, Helen exclaimed, "I'm sitting on top of the world." Going for the pun, she jumped onto her piano to proclaim, "I'm sitting on top of the Wurlitzer." She sighed, "About the only things worth getting excited about are children playing in the sun and a bottle with three stars on the label and the fish in the sea."[45] The order of her favorite things was not arbitrary.

Due at the theater, she threw a coat over her pajamas, caught a taxi, and went to work.

The Metropolitan run coincided with the National Bank Holiday Franklin Roosevelt imposed to stabilize the nation's financial crisis. During that week, the recently assembled combine of Loew's, Paramount, Warner, and RKO offered Helen a paltry $750 to play a week in vaudeville.[46] She refused. Weeks before, she happily turned down an offer to tour with Lou Alter at $4,000 a week to lead the *Show Boat* tab company, at $2,500 per, because the reduction kept others working. She refused to work as a single below her market value.[47]

Instead, on March 24, Helen and Arthur Loew boarded the *Paris* to Europe. Lulu, forever giving Loew the fisheye, joined them. When the threesome returned home, US Customs accused Helen of smuggling $2,000 of French lingerie. Unfazed, she breezed past the astonished officials, blithely stating, "That's funny, because I never wear underwear."[48]

Arthur Loew made his customary disclaimer: "This report occurs now about every other month, and I presume it is about time for it to appear again. Miss Morgan and I are not married."[49] More to the point, something happened aboard ship, and, after more than four years, Helen's great love affair was over. She returned to Cleveland Heights and Buddy Maschke. The story they gave to newspaper gossips: during her previous visit, Helen had begun some dental work, and she returned to complete it. She just happened to be staying with her dear friends, the Maschkes.

Two weeks later, Helen and Buddy eloped. At 6:30 a.m. on May 15, their chauffeur-driven limousine stopped at the New Castle, Pennsylvania, house of Justice of the Peace Harrison M. Reynolds. As the courthouse did not open until nine, he offered the lovebirds breakfast. Once the paperwork was completed, Reynolds led the couple to his Union Township office, which lay just outside of town. During the nuptials, Helen learned that, in his haste, Buddy had failed to procure a ring. Ever resourceful, she twisted a hairpin into a ringlet, and the ceremony continued. For his trouble, the justice received a generous tip and, in December, one of Helen's unique Christmas cards.[50]

On the marriage license, Buddy gave his age as twenty-five, Helen as twenty-eight (she was thirty). She listed her father as Tom Morgan, deceased. She also claimed that it was her first marriage.[51]

Years later, Rouben Mamoulian recalled that, when asked why she had married the student, Helen replied, "I want to put him through college."[52]

12

"He's Just My Bud"

The day after their elopement, Buddy Maschke resumed his bar exam preparation. Helen returned to Manhattan. The Embassy Club, with the town's largest rooftop dance floor, dramatic staircase entrance, and a spectacular round bar, exemplified Manhattan at its most soigné.[1]

In addition to her hefty salary, the Embassy gave Helen all the brandy she could drink, which she did to deaden her separation anxiety. She also drank to calm her fears while in the presence of the club's owner, gangster Dutch Schultz. Bartender Edward Severi served Schultz at the Embassy multiple times during Helen's tenure—while the gangster was on the lam for income tax evasion. An occasional drinking buddy was Tammany boss James J. Hines, who ultimately was jailed for shielding Schultz.[2] A drunken Dutchman would make anybody nervous.[3]

Her neighbor, Bob Harrington, often saw Helen's driver parking her Chevrolet Cabriolet in front of their apartment building. When guiding her inside proved more trouble than it was worth, her German chauffer carried Helen to bed.[4]

After a year in *Show Boat*, she overhauled her repertoire. For "Lying in the Hay," management placed a small haystack on the dance floor. Helen, in a blue spot, lay against it and sang seductively.[5] New this season was accompanist Walter Scharf. When Helen was too primed to walk without staggering, he signaled stage management to dim the lights, led her onto the floor, and lifted her onto the piano. When her demons got to her, management lowered the lights while he helped her off the piano and escorted her to her dressing room. When she occasionally went up on a lyric, Scharf prompted her.[6] To Scharf, drink added to the little-girl-lost persona. He worked with everyone, from Frank Sinatra to Barbra Streisand. For his money, Helen Morgan had the greatest stage presence of all.[7]

Often, she jumped onto Scharf's lap and kissed him, not in a sexual way but in search of comfort. Photographs of Helen with Buddy show her to be equally clingy. George Blackwood and Stoney Wahl, her two Steve Bakers on the 1932–1933 *Show Boat* tour, claimed to have been among Helen's lovers.[8] Considering her boomerang dating of Arthur Loew and Buddy Maschke during the tab unit days, these claims ring false. She likely clung to her scene partners offstage as she did with Scharf, and such memories morphed, over time, into tales of a torrid affair.

Helen needed assurance that she made the right decision to put Arthur Loew behind her. She needed her daddy.

In May, one hundred thousand visitors viewed over four hundred tanks on display during the Spring Exhibition of the United Fish Fanciers' Society of Brooklyn. Helen wanted to enter her pair of African mouthbrooders, but Emmie was pregnant and could not be moved. Instead, she showed a tank of danio rerios she had induced to spawn—and won.[9]

Helen entered talks to appear in the first post-Ziegfeld *Follies*.[10] If she passed because of loyalty to Blumenthal, she made a big mistake: he never provided that promised stage vehicle in reward for her *Show Boat* sacrifice.

In an attempt to ease Helen's anxiety, Lulu took her daughter upstate to visit friends while Buddy sat for the Ohio bar. Afterward, Helen headed to Chicago. Mike Fritzel acquired Chez Paree, his greatest club, by betting the lessee that Franklin Roosevelt would win the 1932 Presidential election.[11] For Helen's opening, Fritzel turned off the electric fans—on the hottest night of the year. In the dead-quiet room, Helen took her spellbound audiences on an emotional journey. She *lived* her songs. If she failed to connect with a number, she did not use it.

At the time of the elopement, Helen confided with Jorge and Brownie Sanchez about Buddy but swore them to secrecy. Six weeks later, they joined her in Chicago. Once free, Buddy rushed to Helen's side, and the party started in earnest. Liquor loosened the Sanchezes' tongues. When the press hounded them, Buddy denied that the couple were even engaged. He whined, "Won't they ever stop printing that rumor?"

In addition to buying time for Buddy to study, the couple delayed announcing their union in deference to Buddy's father. Nine days after his son's elopement, Maurice Maschke Sr. resigned as chair of the Cuyahoga

County Republican Central Committee. The scandal began in 1932, when $120,000 disappeared from the local treasury. Maschke Sr. signed a note guaranteeing the shortfall, which permitted county treasurer Alex Bernstein to keep his post. Ultimately, almost half a million dollars went missing, and Maschke and four others were tried for embezzlement. The courts acquitted Maschke, but politically, he never recovered.

For two months, the press badgered Buddy's parents, seeking confirmation about their son's marriage. The elder Maschke kept to the script until July 17, when a reporter showed him a copy of the New Castle marriage license. Maschke remained stoic. "That's very strange—I supposed they're married then."[12] Mrs. Maschke phoned Chicago to tell Buddy that the story had broken.

Helen with husband number three, Maurice "Buddy" Maschke Jr. (Photofest)

At Chez Paree, for her encore, instead of singing about her "Bill," Helen sang, "He's just my Bud." Young Maschke walked up and stood by her side. He promised to support his wife's career, especially her dream of playing Camille. However, when her groom waxed poetic about her ultimate role as a homemaker, Helen hummed, loudly, "She Didn't Say Yes."

Buddy returned to Cleveland to escape the spotlight. Helen, Jorge, and Brownie continued their party.

The newlyweds reunited at a summer cottage Lulu rented on Lake George, where, on Helen's thirty-first birthday, the couple celebrated Buddy's admittance to the Ohio bar. Newsreel cameras captured Helen singing, a cappella, "What Wouldn't I Do for That Man?" while Buddy looked embarrassed.

While honeymooning, Helen worked the four-week Saratoga racing season at the Piping Rock, the Dutchman's enterprise located a mile from the track. In previous gigs, Helen, understanding the vagaries of the nightclub business, had sometimes "forgotten" to cash her paycheck and ensured that the chorines received their salaries, even if it meant paying them herself, but as a bride, she demanded the cash. Trade had been down all summer, and during her first week, she canceled an early show when she refused to sing to empty tables.[13] Her drawing power soon filled up the room, even midweek.

NBC installed a radio hookup on Thursday and Friday nights throughout her stay. On her initial broadcast, "Bill" went over big, but "I've Got to Pass Your House to Get to My House" flopped. Badly. Her performance of "I Cover the Waterfront" on a subsequent broadcast fared no better.[14] Nevertheless, NBC set up a live hookup when she opened, on September 22, at the Longue Vue Lodge, in Hastings-on-Hudson. In addition to warbling, she appeared in male drag in a skit with Abe Lyman. While directing her, Lyman said, "In this part here, you play a man—think you can do it?" She shrugged. "If Hitler can, why can't I?"[15]

Meanwhile, CBS provided Anheuser-Busch executives with a private listen to Helen, Morton Downey, and Kate Smith in a two-hour extravaganza for their sponsorship consideration. The brewer passed, but CBS signed Helen to head her own weekly half-hour series, *Broadway Melodies of Yesterday and Today*. For the premiere, she sang "Can't Help Lovin' Dat Man," "The Man I Love," "To Be or Not to Be in Love," and "Paper Moon." Happiness at home quelled the jitters that had marred earlier radio performances. She mastered the technology and, as Nick Kenny cheekily noted, made the "poor old microphone writhe in ecstasy."[16]

Helen at CBS (circa 1933). (Author's collection)

With airtime to fill, Helen turned song plugger, introducing second-tier works such as "You Have Taken My Heart" and "In Other Words, We're Through," which the Santly brothers published with Helen's portrait on the cover. A few light numbers aside, such as Lou Alter's "Steak and Potatoes" and "What Have We Got to Lose," her new repertoire remained ballad-heavy. To ensure variety, CBS augmented the show with guest artists.

Despite the two o'clock Sunday afternoon timeslot, the show cleaned up in the ratings. With just fourteen appearances under her belt, Helen still placed fourth on the *New York World-Telegram* radio editors' poll for the best female radio vocalist of 1933.[17]

~

On September 29, at Pembroke, Arthur Loew married Barbara Mae Smith, the former Mrs. Oscar Levant and 1931 *Follies* chorine. Loew insisted Barbara sign a prenuptial agreement, something he had likely demanded that Helen do during their European trip. Helen, with Lulu to support, could never have accepted those terms.

Morgan and Loew publicly congratulated each other on their 1933 marriages, but Helen, though happy with Buddy, continued holding the torch for her Arthur.

Hugh Martin was in the audience on October 27 when the curtain lowered during Helen's second number at the cavernous New York Loew's State.[18] The manager announced, "Miss Morgan is ill and cannot continue."[19] Most

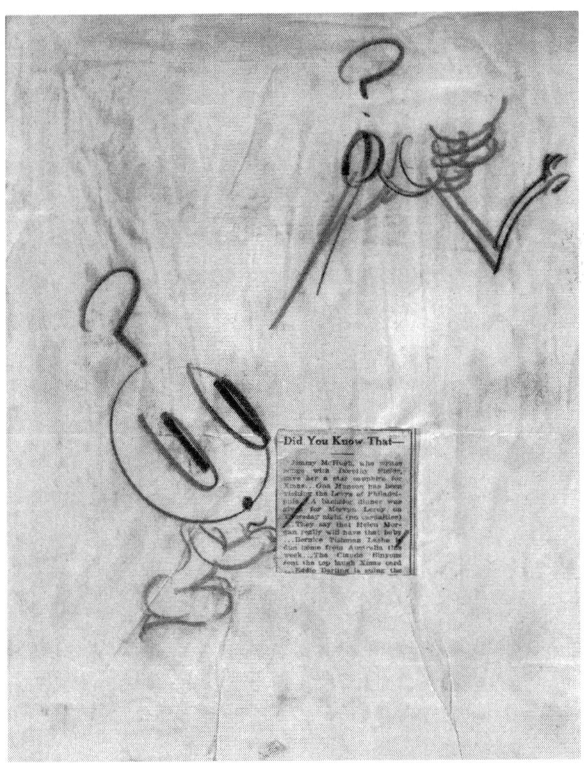

The announcement that Helen was pregnant was news to the Maschkes. (Illustration by Irving Hoffman; Free Library of Philadelphia, Theater Collection)

blamed the cancellation of her film-house vaudeville run and the following Sunday broadcast to her brandy intake, but another rumor circulated around Gotham: Helen was pregnant. Unable to bear children, Helen took the gossip with wistful good humor.[20]

On November 5, Buddy headed west to attend to family matters. That evening, Helen's world cracked. In Vancouver, Texas Guinan died of an intestinal disorder. Mousie wired Buddy to come home. He stayed but promised to commence a one-week on/off schedule between New York and Cleveland as he established himself in business, preferably in Ohio.

He forbade her to attend Guinan's funeral. Helen went anyway.

Some twelve thousand mourners filed into Campbell's Funeral Home for Tex's raucous New York send-off. After interment, in White Plains, Guinan's friends reassembled at the Gate of Heaven Cemetery. Inside the mausoleum, Helen took out a book of matches. She lit one, briefly illuminating the circle of mourners. Others followed, one by one, immersing the tomb with flickering light. "It's dark now." Helen said. "This is just when Tex would be starting to live."[21]

In November, Helen opened at New York's Simplon Club. Nick Prounis and John Johnnidis had acquired the former Henry W. Shoemaker mansion in 1927. Keeping and insuring the original artwork for $80,000, they operated the five-story, two-bar wonderland as the European Club. After the Feds closed it in the June 1928 raids, the Greeks kept their staff on full salary. After the removal of the padlock, and another renovation, they reopened as the Simplon.

One Morgan admirer was John F. Kennedy. While attending Connecticut's Choate boarding school, the future president sometimes weekended in Manhattan. One night, JFK and Ralph "Rip" Horton Jr. sent a note backstage inviting Helen to share a bottle of champagne. When she came out and saw the teenagers, she said that she was sorry but she did not drink.[22]

America's long thirst ended on December 5 with the ratification of the Twenty-First Amendment. Bandleader Don Dean flew in from Los Angeles to celebrate at the Simplon, where Helen ruled as the "Queen of Repeal."[23]

The Rialto may have gone wet, but it did not go wild. For a publicity shot of Helen taking a legal drink, Nick Prounis insisted that ginger ale be used. Many clubs did not serve liquor during those last days of Prohibition lest some final legal fracas mar the celebration. During the first few weeks of freedom, the Simplon served only wine. Business, instead of surging, dipped.

The Times Square cabarets cleaned up their act. The "pansy" acts retreated into the shadows, replaced by the likes of the squeaky-clean, French Egyptian magician Luxor Gali-Gali. Swathed in North African robes, he confounded audiences with sleight of hand accompanied by Arabic patter. His specialty was a variation of the old shell game: instead of a pea, he used live baby chicks. Helen caught his act at Moriarty's in late 1933 but fretted over the fate of his props, which she stole and drove to a friend's farm upstate so they could mature in safety.[24]

Helen stopped humming "She Didn't Say Yes" and agreed to keep house in Cleveland Heights. Eventually. She underwrote the $5,000 charge to set up Buddy as a wine merchant. He, in turn, controlled the household finances and managed the business side of her business, skills that neither Lulu nor Helen possessed. Buddy placed Helen on a hundred-dollar weekly allowance, which included clothing. When she came home from work by 2:30 a.m., he gave her a twenty-dollar bonus. When that failed, he coerced her to retire from the clubs to keep his sleep schedule. On December 31, the Simplon charged $12.50 a head to welcome in 1934 and witness Helen's final nightclub performance.[25] Within days, she again reveled in Gotham's nightlife, but now she paid for the privilege.

In November, Helen shot *Manhattan Lullaby*, a one-reel short for Educational Pictures. In what is little more than a music video, she takes a page out of her own life in "The Stork Song." In a penthouse apartment, she assembles a care package for a young mother in a tenement across town who has received a bundle of joy from a stork who, as the lyric went, "didn't look for a wedding ring."

In the first days of 1934, she shot a follow-up. *The Doctor* told the story behind the 1887 Sir Luke Fildes painting of the same name: hearing that the child of a forester (Herbert Rawlinson) and his wife (Morgan) is critically ill, Queen Victoria sent her court doctor, Sir Joseph Clark (Montagu Love), from London to save the child's life. When the child actor hired for the shoot could not stay still, producer Jack H. Skirball wrangled local urchin Dorothy Werner from a nearby Tenth Avenue tenement.[26]

Helen previously met the doctor, having briefly recreated the scene during the 1931 *Follies*. Her Dr. Hugo Riesenfeld song, "One Little Smile," appears to be a new composition and not a reworking of "Love Is All I Live For."

The Doctor ended the Morgan-Scharf collaboration. Alice Faye suggested her old coach from their days at the Embassy to Rudy Vallée. He

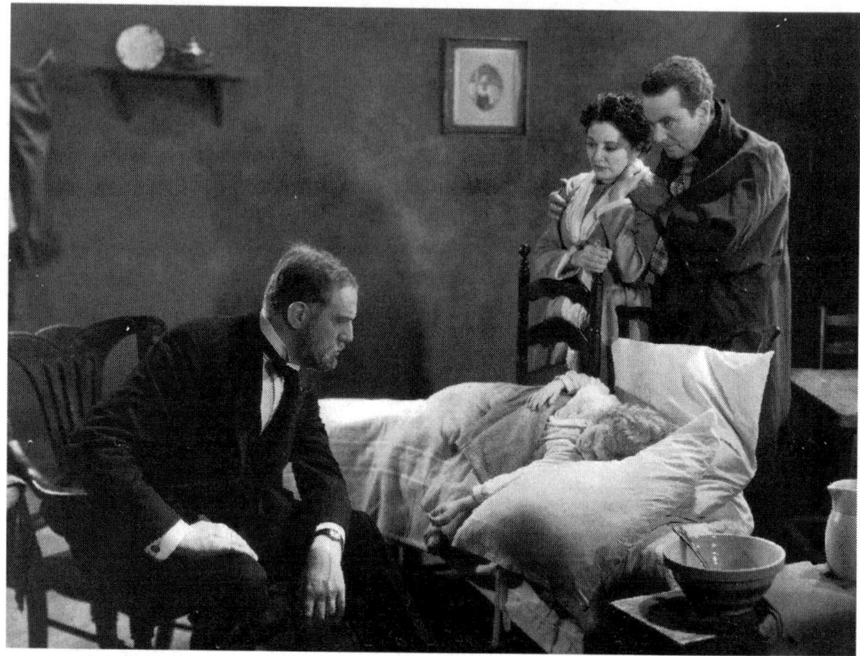

Montagu Love, Helen, Herbert Rawlinson, and Dorothy Werner in *The Doctor*. (Photofest)

offered Scharf double the industry standard to be his assistant.[27] Scharf accompanied Vallée and Faye to Hollywood, where he capped his career as a conductor, arranger, and supervisor by bringing Jule Styne's music and Barbra Streisand's voice to the screen in *Funny Girl*.

In February, Helen performed in an adaptation of Claire Kummer's one-act play, *The Choir Rehearsal*, as part of Vallée's weekly radio show. As a church singer fired for singing a scandalous song, she divided the critics. Ben Gross noted that, "always a grand singer . . . she proved herself a first rate actress."[28] Mary O'Neill disagreed: "Helen is not enough of an actress to know how to use her speaking voice, which was quite colorless."[29] To modern ears, her performance is arch and listless, like the material.

In the last days of 1933, Helen signed for her first feature in four years. *Frankie and Johnnie* tells the tale of a nineteenth-century prostitute who shot and killed her two-timing gambler lover because "he done her wrong." The contract forced her out of Vitaphone's three-reel musical, *Masks and Memories*, a Mardi Gras–themed exercise in nostalgia, designed with both Helen and

Show Boat in mind. No sooner had Lillian Roth replaced Helen at Vitaphone than director-producer Chester Erskine placed *Frankie and Johnnie* on a four-week hold while he negotiated with Universal for the loan of his Johnnie, Chester Morris. The delay cost Erskine his Nellie Bly. Recovering from the illness that forced her from the stage play *Jezebel*, Tallulah Bankhead withdrew, although one cannot imagine her accepting third billing in *anything*.[30]

Erskine's first feature for his All-Star Productions was *Midnight*, a minor melodrama notable for an early Humphrey Bogart gangster role. Erskine's second inspired the Waldorf to serve up an eponymous *Frankie and Johnnie* cocktail. New for the shoot, and the industry, was the Debrie Super Parvo camera. The most compact and quiet sound camera to date, the Debrie enabled Erskine to shoot from the tightest corners.

Erskine boasted that he could produce films more efficiently in the East. His three-and-a-half-week shoot for *Frankie and Johnnie* put the Hollywood

Biograph alum Mary Pickford clowns with the Debrie camera on the set of *Frankie and Johnnie* (note the nude statuary on the set.) (© David Shepard, Courtesy of Blackhawk Films)

average to shame, but the $290,000 price tag was no bargain. Part of the expense was renting the newly restored Bronx Biograph studio. In February, Mary Pickford visited her cinematic alma mater.[31] Missing the publicity bonanza was Erskine's replacement Nelly Bly. Lilyan Tashman, a former *Follies* clotheshorse, had battled cancer for over a year. After pushing herself during the first week of production, she required a week off to recuperate. She returned for an additional ten days, wrapping on March 8 with a 7:00 a.m.-to-midnight marathon. (Chester Morris wrapped on March 9, and Helen did so the following day.) Tashman died five days later. In another of the era's riotous funerals, ten thousand ghouls vied for glimpses of mourners Pickford, Bing Crosby, and eulogist Eddie Cantor as well as the body.[32]

From the day Arthur Hammerstein lured her with a stage revival of *Camille*, Helen desperately wanted to star in a stage drama. In the fall of 1931, Elmer Harris approached her for something called *Hell's Mothers*, and Reggie Hammerstein announced Helen and Joseph Schildkraut for *Gallery Gods*.[33] The latter, Henrietta Malkiel's adaptation of Richard Duschinsky's German backstage drama, bowed in Brooklyn in November 1931 with Dita (*La Grande Illusion*) Parlo playing the actress torn between two lovers.[34] Regardless of Parlo, advertisements promised Helen in the cast the following week in Newark, but neither Helen nor, presumably, the cash to continue showed up in time.[35] Next, Helen entered talks with producer Jimmy Cooper over a revival of *Fata Morgana*.[36] Helen would have been well suited as the bride who helps her new cousin (Douglass Montgomery) through a painful bout of puppy love. In the end, Ara Gerald played the Hungarian embodiment of Morgan le Fay, but only twenty-seven times.

The most promising project may have been *Life Begins*. Essentially *Street Scene* in a maternity ward, Mary McDougal Axelson's comedy drama told of disparate types of women and their childbearing experiences: the immigrant Italian whose child dies at birth, the hard-boiled chorus girl who has twins and is transformed by the experience, the woman with the milquetoast husband who has a healthy red-headed son with the help of a healthy red-headed doctor, the feminist determined to go it alone who insists on being addressed as "Miss," the unhappy woman who desperately wants an abortion, and so on. It is easy to see why her old accompanist-turned-producer Joe Santly thought of Helen for the central story: when complications arise, Grace Sutton, against her husband's wishes, refuses an abortion, a procedure that will guarantee her own survival, and she dies in childbirth. Grace's self-sacrificing love and her desperate need to bear children were, once again, autobiographical elements of Helen's life. Yet Joanna Roos ultimately played the tragic mother-to-be on Broadway, and Glenda Farrell, the wisecracking chorine. The play closed in a week but was later filmed by Warner Brothers.

Most tellingly, days after the *Show Boat* revival opened at the Casino, producer Guthrie McClintic invited Helen to the Beekman Place home he shared with Katharine Cornell for an informal audition, presumably for Edgar Wallace's *Criminal at Large*. The evening started splendidly, but then the brandy kicked in. Helen orated on the state of the theater and offered her increasingly socialistic views on how best to keep Depression-era artists working. After she descended from her soapbox, the evening ended, if still convivially, without a contract.[37]

After taking Helen out of *Music in the Air* for the 1932–1933 *Show Boat* tour, Peggy Fears chose her for the title role in a stage adaptation of Leyla Georgie's *The Establishment of Madame Antonia*. As the title suggests, the highly censorable property never made it into rehearsal.[38]

Each lost opportunity galled Helen. In time, the dream morphed into an obsession. Finally, on March 25, 1934, after months of negotiations, she landed her elusive stage drama.

The Homer Curran and Edwin Belasco production of Myron Fagan's *Memory* would play Los Angeles, tour the coast, and open at New York's Martin Beck Theatre in the fall. Twentieth Century offered $10,000 for the film rights, sight unseen. Helen was determined to make her name on the dramatic stage, even though she had to leave Broadway to do it. "Musical comedy is fine . . . but after all, it's in straight drama that the real actress is made, and it's in that realm that I hope to find all my future."[39]

She would still sing. Having song approval, she introduced "A Fool There Was." On March 12, Helen recorded the Stella Unger and Fred Fisher song for Victor's budget Bluebird series, which the studio rejected. Her subsequent waxing of her *Frankie and Johnnie* numbers, "Give Me a Heart to Sing To" and the title tune, ended her association with the label. From 1930 and into 1934, Victor advertised Helen as one of their best-selling artists—while dance bands covered her stage and screen material.[40] Conversely, crooners Rudy Vallée, Russ Columbo, and Bing Crosby visited the studio between 1930 and 1934, but no female vocalist waxed at length for Victor during this era. Ruth Etting and Kate Smith regularly recorded their radio material over at Columbia.

To play *Memory*, Helen broke her CBS contract.

After her final broadcast, Helen, Buddy, and *Memory* general manager Irving Strouse entrained west. The Maschkes sequestered in their compartment with ten cases of champagne and liquor until the 20th Century pulled into Chicago. The party continued until they detrained the Santa Fe Chief in California.[41]

Frankie and Johnnie's late starting date forced *Memory* to push back opening night from April 23 to April 30. A subsequent delay, while Helen skipped the first four days of rehearsal to search for elaborate Hollywood lodgings, forced the elimination of an out-of-town tryout. *Memory* would open cold in Los Angeles on May 7.

On April 22, Helen made history as the first single act to provide an evening's entertainment in the Gold Room at the Beverly Wilshire Hotel. The pathologically nervous chanteuse tore three kerchiefs to shreds, and the star-studded audience could not get enough of her. Four hundred people were turned away at the door. The *Los Angeles Times* predicted that *Memory* would prove Southern California's theatrical event of the season.

A successful playwright, director, and, for Joseph Kennedy's Pathé Pictures, screenwriter, Myron Fagan is best remembered for his polemic postwar plays *A Red Rainbow* and *Thieves' Paradise*, in which he alleged that the United Nations was designed to house a Communist One World Government. He also crusaded to unmask the alleged Hollywood "Red Conspiracy," years before Senator Joseph McCarthy's congressional witch hunts.[42] Considering his politics, it is unsurprising that Fagan clashed with Helen Morgan.

In *Memory*, Helen played a stage star who lures a successful playwright (Leon Waycoff) away from his wife (Kay Hammond) and son (Jackie Searl).[43] Fagan's vampire with a heart was named Memory by her circus-clown father because she reminded him of her mother, who died in childbirth. In the play's climax, the son begs Memory for the return of his errant father. Helen's character, again, puts the welfare of a youngster ahead of her own.

Edward Schallert rhapsodized that Helen had "that magnetic lure of personality, which caused nearly everything she did subsequently to become very fascinating . . . there might be no limits to her particular horizon in the more definite drama." Fine work from the cast aside, *Memory* remained a pedestrian backstage drama that owed much to the plot of *Zaza*. While admitting its potential, Schallert lambasted *Memory* as "fairly dull fare theatrically. It lacks much . . . both in situation and dialogue of enticing interest."[44] Excepting Helen's singing of "A Fool There Was" in the second act, the

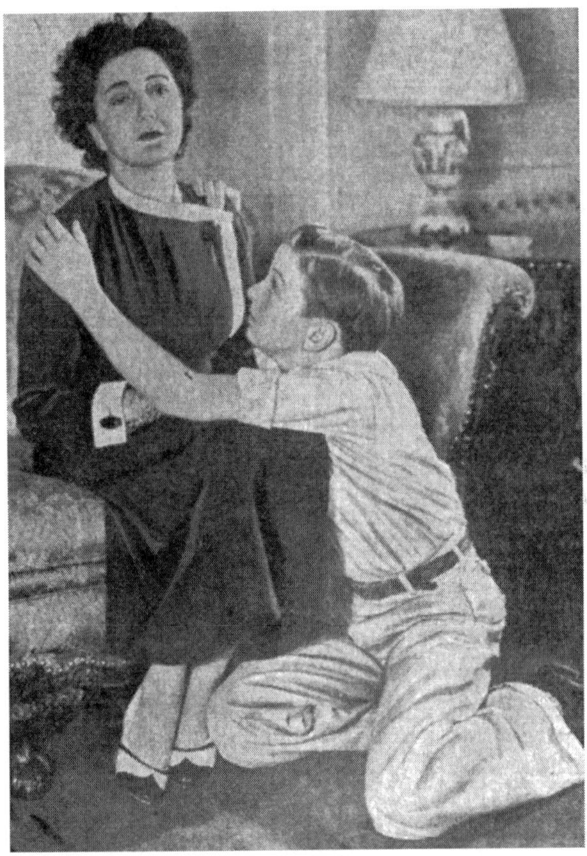

Jackie Searl pleads to Helen in *Memory*. (Free Library of Philadelphia, Theater Collection)

Hollywood Reporter suggested that one could walk in at the top of act 3 and be just as far ahead.[45] Forever supportive of his *Applause* muse, first-nighter Rouben Mamoulian shamed Marlene Dietrich back into her seat when she attempted to leave at the first interval.

Despite a healthy advance sale, a week of rain on top of the lukewarm reviews kept people away. The Biltmore management persuaded Irving Strouse not to close the production until Saturday, when the week's gross of only $8,000 proved Strouse to be correct. Strouse, along with Fagan, who exchanged words with Helen before the Tuesday performance, filed charges with Equity, claiming they canceled both dress rehearsals because she was unfit to work. They alleged that she played the first two performances so drunk she made one of her exits through the wings instead of the door.

Fagan's beef included Helen's wardrobe. Kiviette, fresh from providing the costumes for *Roberta*, provided Helen with eight gowns. When Helen refused one, she commissioned the designer to create an alternative so complicated as to require five minutes to button Helen into it—and superfluous dialogue from Fagan to cover the change.

Helen denied the accusations. "I'll admit there was a little trouble, but I didn't think any charges would be filed."[46] She countercharged that they harassed her and did not pay her salary. True, but Buddy failed to pay the $5,000 he owed the production as an investor, which was more than double her salary. (Equity paid the cast's salary for the second, unplayed week.)

Memory was the biggest mistake of Helen's career. She abandoned a lucrative radio show, and her escapades, for the first time, adversely affected a production. During *Memory*, Helen spent her nights partying, often throwing the parties herself. She went out West to prove herself a dramatic actress, but she also played *Memory* to boost Buddy's career, and its failure damaged a marriage founded on a rebound. Finding work did not worry her, but her looming legal battle did. If the Equity Arbitration Board found her guilty of insubordination and intoxication, they would suspend Helen from the union for two years, and she would be liable for monetary damages.

13

Hollywood

After the *Memory* debacle, Helen rejected an invitation from Papa Maschke to return to Cleveland to pursue film work. Earlier, when the Maschkes entrained west for *Memory*, Buddy advertised Helen's availability in the trade publications.[1] Louella Parsons baited the moguls further by suggesting that Helen would make a guest appearance in a proposed *Broadway Melody of 1934*.[2] The ruse worked. Edward Small announced that Helen would join Jack Benny and the Mills Brothers in the Reliance Production *Showboat of 1934*.[3] When Universal objected to the tie-in to their property, Small dropped Helen and the *Show Boat* angle and filmed his musical comedy murder mystery as *Transatlantic Merry-Go-Round*.

Gossips were quick to remind the Brothers Warner, then casting their film adaptation of *Sweet Adeline*, that not only Helen, but Irene Franklin and Charles Butterworth were currently in Hollywood and available to reprise their stage roles. The studio tested Helen but signed Irene Dunne, with Helen as a fallback should Dunne prove unavailable.[4]

Universal brought Helen in for an amiable, if inconclusive, chat concerning their long-gestating *Show Boat* remake. Buddy so impressed Carl Laemmle Jr. that the producer considered him for an executive position. When a lack of experience prevented a deal, Buddy vowed to obtain some by becoming a screenwriter, especially after Warners expressed interest in his work.[5]

Fox signed Helen for *Marie Galante*. The studio halted production on June 19 when Spencer Tracy went off on a bender. To offset the $125,000 lost during the shutdown, Fox halved Tracy's $2,500 weekly salary for the remainder of 1934 and fined him an additional $25,000—the highest penalty yet levied on an actor for holding up production.[6] Taking advantage of the delay, Paramount signed Helen for its tragic backstager *You Belong to Me* days before shooting began.[7]

On June 20, Helen came home tired from the studio to find Buddy entertaining, as usual. A scene followed. She excused herself, wrote him a note, packed her things, and checked into a hotel. When they met for a car ride a few days later, Buddy threatened to drive over a cliff if she refused to reconcile with him. Helen pulled the emergency brake and safely exited the vehicle.[8]

As fashioned by screenwriter Walter DeLeon, Elizabeth Alexander's backstage melodrama, *Fifty-Two Weeks for Florette* featured Helen Mack as a vaudevillian who remarries after the death of her husband/partner. Her two-timing new husband clashes with her son and ships him off to boarding school, then taunts Florette during their trapeze act. She falls to her death. When Paramount changed the name of its grouping of Gary Cooper, Carole Lombard, and Shirley Temple from *You Belong to Me* to *Now and Forever*, producer Louis D. Lighton nabbed the generic but less wonky title.

Helen and Lee Tracy clown between takes on *You Belong to Me*. (Courtesy of Everett Collection)

Helen worked three of the five weeks of shooting. Paramount and Sam Coslow dug up "When He Comes Home to Me" for her to sing. Her second Coslow song, "I Ain't Going to Carry No Torch" proved prophetic: Paramount cut it prior to release.[9] Still, Helen featured in the climactic scene where she and her estranged husband (Lee Tracy) tell the lad of his mother's accident. Clocking in at fifteen minutes, the sequence was Helen's meatiest dramatic film performance since *Applause*.

You Belong to Me was Helen's first film released under the auspices of the Production Code. After multiple scandals, in the early 1920s, religious and civic groups pressured Hollywood to clean up its act on and off the screen. In response, the moguls appointed Will Hays to head their self-censoring organization, the Motion Pictures Producers and Distributors of America (MPPDA). In practice, the studios fostered an illusion of balance between the titillation audiences craved and the morality religious leaders demanded. The ploy worked until sagging box office numbers prompted desperate filmmakers to make the Depression screen sizzle. When the Catholic Legion of Decency organized boycotts, the studios bowed to the pressure and (again) vowed to outdo any local censorship. In late 1933, the Production Code, first drafted in 1930, was strengthened—and made *enforceable*—for any film released after June 30, 1934.

You Belong to Me weathered the transition to the Code better than Helen's follow-up, *Marie Galante*. Multiple writers reduced a tale of the global tensions that would erupt into World War II into a spy-versus-spy plot: stranded in Panama, a French girl gets entangled in a plot to blow up the US fleet as the convoy maneuvers through the Canal. In preparation for the shoot, Fox obtained permission to film the actual thirty-six-hour operation in May 1934.[10]

Because of the Production Code, Marie could no longer prostitute herself to earn her return passage. Three men pursue her—one American (Crawbett; Spencer Tracy), one Japanese (Tenoki; Leslie Fenton), and one German (Brogard; Sig Ruman)—yet, incredulously, she keeps her virtue intact while working solely as an entertainer.

Originally, Helen's character, Madame Tapia, was no chanteuse. In Jacques Deval's novel, the German spy, called Staub, moves out of the city and in with Señora Isabel Tapia and her daughters Soledad and Mercedes.[11] Still burning for Marie, he weds Soledad, impregnates both sisters, loses his job as a spy, and sinks into drunkenness and madness—a censorable subplot never considered for the film. In early screenplay drafts, Tapia owned the cabaret *El*

Ligarto Loco (the Mad Alligator) but was diminished in importance in regard to both the plot and the nightclub's management in subsequent revisions. Some drafts tailored the role to Fox newcomer Alice Faye. In one scene that vanished with the Code, Marie and Tapia receive smallpox vaccinations. Tapia demands to get hers where the scar will not show; she is both a singer and a dancer. Crawbett, eyeing Tapia's abbreviated costume, advises the doctor to administer it orally.[12] During a later revision, screenwriter Reginald Berkeley envisioned a more *fatale* hostess/chanteuse, causing Ratcliff (Robert Loraine) to shudder, saying, "The formidable woman on the piano is looking at me like a boa constrictor in search of prey."[13]

Curiously absent from the *Marie Galante* writers' room was Jacques Deval, who spent the summer in Hollywood adapting his novel to the Paris stage. Apparently, neither Deval nor Fox contemplated bringing his collaborator over from Paris to work on the film. Kurt Weill, having escaped Nazi Germany, would not arrive in America for another year.[14] Instead, Jay Gorney composed three songs for the film, all presumably for Helen.[15] She sang his "Song of a Dreamer." She did not warble "It's Home," but she later recorded it and used it in her club act. The third Gorney number remains unknown. Instead, for her second vocal in the film, Helen sang the surprisingly upbeat "Serves Me Right for Treating You Wrong," supplied by Maurice Sigler, Al Goodhart, and Al and Nancy Hoffman.

Marie Galante affords Helen her best opportunity on-screen to exhibit the flair for light comedy that embodied her revue work. She trades barbs with Ned Sparks when he mocks her piano-sitting stunt. After viewing the rushes, producer Winfield R. Sheehan, prematurely, envisioned a vehicle to showcase the Sparks-Morgan chemistry.[16]

While Helen earned praise for little more than a cameo appearance, *Marie Galante* garnered lukewarm notices, which director Henry King contributed to Fox's jettisoning his, and Deval's, tragic ending for a happy one for Marie.[17]

In August, Helen and Myron Fagan aired their *Memory* grievances before an Equity arbitration board. True to form, Helen never took the stand. She sat silently while her counsel, Major John Zanft and Ralph Blum, battled Fagan and his representative, Arthur William Green. At one point, Fagan lunged after Blum. Green held him back.

Memory's general manager, Irving Strouse, described Helen's wild train trip out West and noted that, when drunk, she had "a glassy stare in her eyes and that dreamy look on her face for which she is so famous."[18] Fagan charged

An unlikely comic pairing: Helen Morgan and Ned Sparks in *Marie Galante*. (Photofest)

that Helen's fumbled line readings contributed to the languorous pacing on opening night and to the play's poor critical reception. Introducing production time sheets, he stated that Saturday night's performance, with a sober Morgan, clocked in thirty-five minutes shorter than the premiere, with, presumably, no deletions from the script.

Character witness Oscar Hammerstein II testified that during their professional association, he never saw Helen intoxicated or insubordinate.[19] Eight *Memory* cast members echoed Oscar's sentiment, adding that Fagan, a union representative, threatened to deny them future film work should they refuse to sign affidavits supporting his case against Morgan. One reluctant signer, Vera Lewis, testified that at one rehearsal, Helen "wanted to sing her song from the front of the stage, but was told that such a stunt would be 'cheap.'" Helen huffed, "If that stunt was good enough for Ziegfeld, it's good enough for Fagan."[20]

Leon Waycoff, who habitually took a shot himself before going on, swore he never detected liquor on Helen's breath. He emphatically denied that she had served liquor to him or any member of the cast, except in her home, and that he had clashed with Helen during rehearsals. When asked why the show failed, Waycoff suggested that it was "because it had been written."[21]

Bored, Helen defender Jackie Searl struck up a game of gin rummy with the stenographer.

Equity ruled Morgan not guilty of insubordination and intoxication but, because Buddy Maschke failed to pay his share of the production's bankroll, denied her salary and reimbursement for that extra gown she demanded. Four years later, Fagan unsuccessfully sued Maschke for that $5,000. Maschke, like Helen, had washed his hands of all things related to the star-crossed production.

Cleared by Equity, Helen recorded her movie songs for the Brunswick label and joined the American Society of Recording Artists.[22] In short order, she was an officer of the union, which, in 1935, aided opera singers Grace Moore, Marion Talley, and Richard Brooks in pressuring radio stations to pay royalties to recording artists when broadcasting their discs.[23]

In September, Warners offered Helen a seven-year contract, promising a flat fee of $5,000 for two days' work on Rudy Vallée's new film, with an option for a second film with a guarantee of three weeks at $4,500. If pleased by her work, Warners would extend the contract for twenty-six weeks, at a $2,000 weekly salary and with six weeks guaranteed off, allowing her to pick up nightclub and vaudeville work. At the six-month mark, Warners would further extend, or terminate, her contract.[24]

Luring Helen was the promise of a star vehicle. Warners hired Erwin Gelsey and Cedric Worth to write *Lady in Waiting*. Robert Presnell would produce. The plot concerned New York socialite Janet Stuyvesant (Helen), who, at a Junior League Buy-a-Kiss fundraiser, is torn between Tommy Carewe (written for Franchot Tone) and Dirk Spencer (for George Brent). The twist was in tailoring the love triangle to Helen's strengths. Bad-boy Tommy marries Janet, fathers her child, and places her as a singer in the nightclub circuit while he gets into underworld trouble. When she sues to divorce Tommy to marry the stalwart Dirk, the court denies either parent custody, entrusting the child to her father in the hope that the couple will reconcile. Janet/Helen suffers, primarily, for her child.[25]

Helen signed her Warners contract while she ended her cabaret "retirement" at Chez Paree. There, she reunited professionally, and perhaps romantically, with accompanist Lou Alter, who wrote a musical version of *Camille*, which he offered to Warners as a Morgan vehicle.

Although early in the season, Dolly Jarvis, one of Fritzel's Chez Paree Adorables, gushed over the three-quarter-length mink coat an admirer had given Helen. Several drinks in, Helen draped the coat over the astonished showgirl's shoulders and staggered away, ignoring the youngster's protests. The next day, Jarvis told Fritzel what had happened.

"I'm sure that today she doesn't remember giving it to me. I don't want any trouble. You'd better give it back to her," she pleaded.

Fritzel returned the $20,000 mink. Incensed, Helen brayed, "I gave that girl that coat and I want her to have it. If you don't tell her to keep that coat, I won't go on tonight."

Dolly Jarvis got the coat.[26]

Buddy moved back home to work in his father's law firm. "I was just like 20,000 other writers out there. I wrote scenarios and turned out four that are under consideration by film companies. That's as close as I came to being a success."[27] While in the Midwest, Helen visited the Maschkes, but she left unreconciled with her husband. "My place is with Buddy . . . but I want to work another year to provide for my mother who has lived a long time in New York and can't be expected to move to Cleveland."[28] Ed Sullivan suggested that Maurice Maschke Sr. may have quickened the disintegration of the marriage. Beloved as she was, it is difficult to imagine the staunch Republican leader seeing eye-to-eye with a woman who worked alongside Heywood Broun and campaigned for Franklin Roosevelt. Helen denied any familial friction.

Upon her return, Helen bought the former residence of W. C. Fields in Toluca Lake, near the studio. Greta Garbo coveted the Spanish-style house but underbid. Helen never haggled. She later regretted the purchase. The New Yorker could not sleep on the quiet lake. On the plus side, the domesticated swans came to her when she whistled. Despite her tony address, she never "went Hollywood." She eschewed glamour when not at work and often drove through Los Angeles in overalls.

By the time Helen arrived on the lot in late October, Warners had slashed the budget for the Vallée film by 20 percent. The title of the backstager waffled between *Say It with Music* and *Song of Love* before settling on the Warren and Dubin title song, *Sweet Music*. Concerning the singing rival to the film's heroine, indecisive screenwriters Warren Duff and Carl Erickson offered Warners two choices: name the rival Molly Ridgeway and never have her appear on-screen, or hire a name singer to pop in and sing a number or two.[29]

Helen croons for Rudy Vallée in *Sweet Music*. (Photofest)

Warners' choice was obvious, but three weeks before Helen filmed, the studio did not have the two numbers she would sing on-screen. In their mad pre-production dash, Warners approached Jerome Kern. He submitted "Saturday Night," but the studio chose to give Helen retreads instead.[30] The first, "I See Two Lovers" by Mort Dixon and Allie Wrubel, was a Dick Powell castoff cut from *Flirtation Walk*.[31] The second, an Irving Kahal and Sammy Fain song originally titled "Without Your Smile," was rewritten as "Winter Overnight" before Helen filmed it.[32]

Helen's second Warners assignment is notable as the only film to star Al Jolson and his wife, Ruby Keeler. Screenwriter Earl Baldwin retained only the middle of Bradford Ropes's 1934 novel when bringing *Go into Your Dance* to the screen.[33] A thinly disguised version of Ruth Etting (ultimately named Luana Wells; Helen), coaxes her husband (a promotion from the real life "Colonel" Moe Snyder, here dubbed "the Duke"; Barton MacLane) to invest in a revue to place his wife back on the stage. Our hero (Jolson) uses the money intended for an Equity retainer to bail out his sister (Glenda Farrell) and angers the gunman. Wags noted the irony of Warners deeming Helen unfit to play Addie Schmitt on film only to cast her as Etting, when Ruth herself was working in town.[34] Etting and Snyder chose not to sue.

While shooting, Helen became the darling of the soundstage when she entertained the extras between takes with an impromptu concert.[35] She also reunited with her *Midnight Frolics* accompanist Martin Freed. In 1931, Freed salvaged his career by conducting the tour of the Jolson stage vehicle *Wonder Bar*, and he stayed on the payroll until Jolie's death. Freed appeared on-screen playing for Helen as she sang "The Little Things You Used to Do."

Go into Your Dance offered Helen's most assured screen performance to date. Dressed by Orry-Kelly, she never looked better on film. She handles the rapid-fire Warners dialogue with assurance and, in her biggest departure from type in her career, plays the heavy. Her final shot in the film is noteworthy for the combination of Luana's coldness and the joyful glint in her eyes.

Late in the film, the Duke turns on the radio. Director Archie Mayo intended to cut to Helen on the nightclub stage, singing another Warren and Dubin number. Because of Harry Warren's illness in November 1934, the

Together again: Martin Freed accompanies Helen in *Go into Your Dance*. (Courtesy of Everett Collection)

songwriters never wrote her second number.[36] Mayo's easy fix: graft on a short, off-screen reprise of "Little Things." Helen lost another song.

Principal photography began on November 26. Helen was not required to be on the lot for another two weeks, but she made an impromptu visit on the night of December 4 when fire engulfed the studio machine shop.[37] It spread to other buildings, including some *Go into Your Dance* sets. Neighbors from Toluca Lake, including Bing Crosby and Dick Powell, aided the volunteer firefighters. Helen distributed coffee and water to those battling the blaze. Of the extensive damage caused by the First National Studio fire, the most heartbreaking was the loss of six film vaults.

Because of the logistical nightmare of transporting Helen's fish tanks, Lulu stayed behind in New York when Helen moved out West, the first time mother and daughter had lived apart since 1926. Because of her schedule, Helen could not spend Christmas back East, which increased both women's separation anxiety. Helen airmailed gifts and called Lulu on Christmas Eve.[38] In the morning, Helen received a special gift. Her bulldog, Peter the Second, ambled up and dropped a rabbit's foot before his mistress. She had the foot mounted and labeled, "To Helen from Peter the Second."[39]

Peter could not allay Helen's holiday depression. A few days after Christmas, she partied with Martin Freed, someone who could match her drink for drink. Jolson, more concerned than outraged, called Freed's estranged wife in New York and told her, "Pearl, you better come out here right away, or else I'm gonna have to fire Marty." Pearl recalled, "Al told me that he'd give *me* Marty's salary, but that he wouldn't give it to him because he would just drink it up. It took me a little while, but I came out to the coast with our son, Stan, and Al gave Marty's salary to me to handle until he got him back on the wagon."[40]

Hollywood talked, and the tales of Helen grew with each telling. During one inebriated misadventure, presumably in December 1934, Helen cavorted naked in a fountain with publicity agent Don Prince.[41] Perhaps she did, but the Warners call sheets do not lie. She worked her four-week shoot as scheduled. With the exception of New Year's Day, she filmed daily from December 28 to her last day, January 5.[42] Unlike Spencer Tracy, Helen never held up film production.

While awaiting her next assignment, and with Warners' permission, Helen obtained cabaret work. She flew east and met Lulu's train in Jacksonville. Arriving in Miami a week before Helen's opening night, the two camped out with Dorothy Dey.

Awaiting Helen in Florida was word from the studio: they would not take the next six-month option on her contract.[43] Warners offered no explanation. Helen had taken her punches before, but nothing like this dismissal, which left her shaking.

The Warners machine was not quick enough to stop the press releases announcing Helen for a guest spot in their *Radio Jamboree of 1935*, an exercise little more than an excuse to bring as many radio acts before the camera as possible. The threadbare story by George Bricker concerned business rivals (Hugh Herbert and Guy Kibbee), both called J. Dinwiddie Jones, who meet on a train to New York. Would-be playboy Herbert convinces Kibbee to take his place as the sponsor of a radio program in creation while he conducts an affair with a French woman (Fifi D'Orsay). Kibbee's tastes conflict with Herbert's, and, several plot contrivances and musical acts later, the executives cosponsor the program and merge their companies. Warners played with the idea for years but never produced this answer to Paramount's *The Big Broadcast*.[44]

Days before the premiere of *Sweet Music*, the studio removed "Winter Overnight," which left Helen with barely two minutes of screen time—but fourth billing.[45] History suggests that the cut hurt rather than helped the film. As Ted Sennett noted, "Except for Miss Morgan's singing, it was not an auspicious occasion."[46]

With Helen's release went *The Lady in Waiting*. Warners briefly considered retrofitting it for Bette Davis but then quashed the production.[47]

Presumably, Warners intended to develop a female equivalent to crooner Dick Powell, and Helen and Wini Shaw, who signed with Warners a few months prior to Morgan, tried out, simultaneously, for the position. While Helen was wrapping *Go into Your Dance*, Wini shot the epic "Lullaby of Broadway" production number in *Gold Diggers of 1935*. She later introduced "The Lady in Red" in *In Caliente*. Curiously, unlike Helen, Wini never recorded for Brunswick, then a Warners subsidiary. Warner Brothers may have let the wrong chanteuse go. Shaw was younger and more photogenic than Helen but was no actress. She inherited the studio's other Morgan vehicle, *Broadway Hostess*.[48] In this, her only starring feature, Wini all but disappears during the second half of the film, leaving Lyle Talbot to perform the heavy lifting. Shaw toiled in largely forgettable supporting roles for another fifteen months, then returned to short subjects. She abandoned films in 1939, around the time Dick Powell left Warners and the studio sold off Brunswick Records. The Brothers Warner hosted the amiable presence of Joan Leslie during the war but would not get a singing sweetheart of note until the late 1940s, in the personage of Doris Day.

The Deauville, Nat Evans and Tex Rickard's oval-shaped hotel at Sixty-Seventh Street and the Ocean, boasted a private beach and a nightclub/game room. It enjoyed several profitable seasons before Rickard's death. William and Lucy Cotton Thomas McGraw acquired and remodeled the complex, replete with supersize lounges, thick carpets, pools, and cabanas. They opened in December 1934, weeks before the winter season began, as the *Beautiful* Deauville. Initially, business was dismal, but it was not nearly as dismal a sight as Helen.

The McGraws sent Vincent Lopez to Dorothy Dey's to ensure Morgan pulled herself together for opening night. Over a cup of coffee, Helen assured him that it was only a case of the jitters. When the bandleader suggested she see a doctor, Helen said, "I feel like this sometimes—all keyed up and nervous about the future. But I snap out of it in time. Just seeing someone I know helps. I'm glad you thought enough to stop by, Vincent."[49]

Also greeting Morgan in Dade County were the local authorities. They took the fingerprints of everyone who worked the winter season, for, while alcohol was legal, gambling was not.[50]

The McGraws sublet the casino to Frank Zaccarino. Previously, Rickard and Evans had paid protection money, which granted them an hour's warning before a raid. Evans simply lined up the fleet of trucks he kept on hand and evacuated the gambling equipment. After the all-clear sounded, the vans returned, and the casino was operational again within minutes. Bypassing the police, Zaccarino brought in Florida state senator and fixer Henry Hayes Lewis as a partner. Agents raided throughout Helen's stay, and on February 6, they obtained proof. Lewis stood trial and easily won his acquittal.[51] The charges against the McGraws were later dropped.[52]

Placating the nervous owners, Helen again graciously offered concessions while the Beautiful Deauville operated in the red. She need not have bothered.[53] On Helen's opening night, the McGraws added extra tables, making navigation of the room difficult. Out front, Helen was more assertive. One night, she stopped in midsong, told Lopez his piano playing was lousy, took his baton, and conducted the orchestra herself from atop her piano. The audience loved it. She kept it in the act. By the conclusion of her first week, Lopez was gone and Paul Sabin was leading his own orchestra.[54] Abandoning Lopez, Lou Bring remained as Helen's musical director and followed her to

Helen, relaxing in male drag. (Free Library of Philadelphia, Theater Collection)

New York when the season ended. Helen made up with Lopez publicly by guest "conducting" at his opening at the Biscayne Kennel Club a week later.

The Ritz Brothers joined the show on February 15. The knockabout comics had accepted second billing to Helen at Chez Paree the previous September, but here they demanded first. She won the battle of billing a second time and joined the comics in a few of their rough-and-tumble routines, to the delight of the crowd.[55]

While enjoying the sun, Helen donned a man's sailor suit and an admiral's hat. She went deep-sea fishing and came back with tall tales about the sailfish that got away.[56] Later in her stay, she went after weakfish, catching fifteen. Indoors, she taught the smart set a card game she had invented, described as a cross between auction bridge and rummy.[57]

Two men vied for her heart. One, Harry Kannen, was in oil.[58] The other was Joel Goldblatt, of the Chicago department stores. Like Helen, Goldblatt put his money where his heart was, and, in 1933, he resurrected the recently shuttered *Shuffle Along* for a run at Chicago's Illinois Theatre. In deference to his conservative family, he adopted the stage name Joel Beckmeyer.[59]

When business concerns required him to return home, Joel surreptitiously entered Helen's hotel suite and gifted her two hundred hard-boiled eggs, one hundred pounds of chicken feed, and a live rooster. Delighted, Helen threw an egg-and-cocktail party at the Deauville for her friends—and the rooster.[60]

When the print of *Frankie and Johnnie* returned from the lab, days after the Code went into effect, Chester Erskine faced the onerous task of earning a certificate of approval from the Production Code Administration (PCA). Adding to his woes, deals with United Artists and Columbia to distribute the film failed to bear fruit, perhaps because the companies feared Production Code czar Joseph Breen.[61] Before the summer ended, Ben Goetz controlled the project. He recut it and retitled it *Frankie* before screening it to the PCA at the Hollywood Roosevelt Hotel on September 26.

Use of the "Frankie and Johnnie" ballad in such films as *Men without Women*, *Ladies of Leisure*, and the film version of *Life Begins* outraged local censors.[62] Chief among the bête noires was Mae West, who growled out the ditty in the 1933 film version of her stage play *Diamond Lil*, which Paramount titled *She Done Him Wrong*. Breen gunned for Mae's *Belle of the Nineties*, shot concurrently with *Frankie*.

Compounding Breen's prejudice against *Frankie* was a preproduction incident. His eastern production deputy, V. G. Hart, requested a script ahead of shooting and, after some difficulty, obtained one.[63] Alarmed by what he read, he visited the set. Erskine promised to screen the film to the PCA for approval before the July 1 cutoff date, a promise he was unable to keep.

Breen rejected *Frankie* outright.

Goetz screened it again, reel by reel, to record each objection. Offending dialogue, such as "slut" and "getting much lately" were marked for removal.[64] Equally objectionable were instances of exposed flesh and a general tenor of unpunished immorality. Breen demanded that the folk song be excised, even as background music, and especially from the funeral sequence, which included a shot of Johnnie's coffin adorned with a plaque that read "She done him wrong." Although never sung, the song ultimately was retained as background music in bizarre arrangements that almost obscure the tune. It was not used for the opening titles.

Finally, the PCA demanded that neither the source play nor its author, Jack Kirkland, receive screen credit. In 1929, Kirkland's *Frankie and Johnnie* proved so hot that producer Al H. Woods, out of town in Chicago, shuttered the play before police could raid it. Police did raid Kirkland's later, self-produced rewrite in Jamaica, Long Island. He lost his plea for a jury trial, and the Queens Court of Special Sessions found the defendants guilty but suspended their sentences. Eighteen months later, Kirkland prevailed in the state Court of Appeals when Judge Cuthbert W. Pound reversed the decision, stating, "We hold merely that the fact that 'Frankie and Johnnie' and their companions were not nice people does not in itself make the play obscene."[65]

Lou Goldberg revised the shooting script while Goetz unloaded the property onto William Saal and Select Pictures. Saal traveled to Florida to re-sign Helen to the property, now called *I Loved a Man*. He promised her a new title tune to further differentiate the project from the objectionable folk song, as well as a southern-themed follow-up vehicle, to shoot in the fall.[66]

A well-placed post *almost* prevents the risqué wallpaper from upstaging Florence Reed, Helen, Lilyan Tashman, and others in *Frankie and Johnnie*. (© David Shepard, Courtesy of Blackhawk Films)

Helen spent three days in New York reshooting with William Harrigan and their new director, Jack Auer.[67] Helen, Auer, and cinematographer Joseph Ruttenberg flew out to Hollywood on March 7 to complete the retakes at Mascot with Chester Morris, who could not travel because he had committed to start shooting *Public Hero, No 1* on the thirteenth.[68] The new cut, completed in April, did not merely fold in new footage; it excised offending scenery.[69] The decoration of the stage where Helen's Frankie sang "Give Me a Heart to Sing To" in 1934 abounded with nude statuary and risqué wallpaper, which indicated that the Mansion House was a brothel. Saal reedited Helen's solo to keep any offending visuals out of the frame. He won his certificate of approval—for *Frankie and Johnnie*—on May 2, 1935.[70] Under the RKO banner, the film previewed in Kearney, New Jersey, two weeks later.[71] Despite a positive review in the *Hollywood Reporter*, RKO sat on the film.[72]

On March 31, Helen made her New York homecoming as a Sunday-night guest artist at Leon and Eddie's nightclub. Helen made her entrance from the kitchen, by the small table at the back of the hall occupied by Hugh Martin and his mother. In her cups, Helen mistook Mrs. Ellie Martin for an old friend and cried out, "Gertie, I haven't seen you in years! How are you?"

Thinking on her feet, Ellie gushed, "So glad to see you, Helen. This is my son. You've never met my son."[73] Helen visited for ten minutes before excusing herself to begin her performance.

Two days later, Helen opened a five-week stand at the Versailles. Nicky Prounis and Arnold Rossfield acquired the Little Theatre, a former art house cinema, late in 1934. They ripped out the seats, leveled the floor to the height of the stage, and mounted photomurals on the walls to give patrons the sensation of dining on the palace grounds. Helen did not open this monument to all things French, but she was their first headliner. Management ordered extra tables and chairs to accommodate the increased patronage, but the *Times* tellingly compared her comforting presence to "a child's toy found in a corner of a bare room."[74] Absent from New York a year, Helen Morgan had become nostalgia.

Most evenings she went to the Casino de Paree for a nightcap, but one night after closing, Helen sat down the Versailles staff, paid for their drinks, and sang just for them.[75]

During Helen's year in Hollywood, Lulu had moved into a spacious flat at 1070 Park Avenue. An extra sunroom served as Helen's playhouse. It housed, among other treasures, a miniature baby grand piano and a Chinese pagoda.[76]

The Morgans shared the apartment with Helen's secretary, Frances Routa. Born in 1898 in Czechoslovakia, the beautician married real estate agent Vernon Davis a few years after landing in New York. After the marriage failed, "Franta" teamed up with Helen around the time she married Buddy. Chief among her gal Friday's duties was keeping Helen's German and French up to speed. She made the trip out to Los Angeles, where she played *Memory*'s maid, Jane.

While Helen was out West for the *Frankie and Johnnie* retakes, Louis Shurr offered her a run in London's *Café de Paree* cabaret, with a subsequent Paris and Cannes extension. In anticipation of her European tour, Helen went on a $7,000 shopping spree. She also sold her Toluca Lake home and, having qualified as a California resident, began the process of divorcing Buddy, sighing, "He's a fine boy, but he has to be in Cleveland and I have to be everywhere. You can't have a marriage on that basis."[77]

Besides, she still burned for Arthur Loew.

Colette François, the French teen Loew allegedly impregnated in 1930, and her mother sailed to New York in 1935 just before the statute of limitations in her seduction case expired. While the press reported that Justice Aaron J. Levy dismissed the $100,000 suit on the grounds that there could have been no breach of promise if the mademoiselle knew that the tycoon was married at the time their dalliance, others suggested that Loew settled the case out of court.[78] In any case, Colette upgraded her accommodations on the *Champlain* for her trip home the following day.

Loew celebrated his victory at the Versailles.[79] The sight of her Arthur sent Helen into a tailspin. Harry Kannen, her other Florida swain, reconnected with her during this emotional crisis. He promised to erect a nightclub of her own if she dried her tears. She left the Versailles on his arm.

Kannen (né Kannensohn) could afford Helen Morgan. Not only had he earned a fortune overseeing gas stations in greater New York for Standard Oil but he had mob ties, to boot.

Go into Your Dance premiered at New York's Capital Theatre on May 2, with Jolson, Keeler, and Helen in attendance. Reviews were muted, but Helen's support, and her song, "The Little Things You Used to Do," were well received. To the *Boston Globe*, Helen was "slimmer, more magnetic and far more appealing than she has ever been in a picture before."[80]

Two weeks later, Helen opened at the Club Normandie. Eddie Elkins and his orchestra made the trip over from the Versailles. Dorothy Lamour was also on the bill.[81] Management added a 9:00 p.m. dinner show, while the supper shows remained at midnight and 2:00 a.m., prompting Helen to toast, "We wine, we dine, it's fine—I pine."[82] Gotham was where Helen would stay for the present. Europe, like her film career, had been canceled at the last moment.

14

The House of Morgan

Although at liberty, Helen claimed that commitments in New York prevented her from attending her divorce trial. In California, her attorney presented her testimony in the form of an "eight-page deposition which complained that Buddy refused to permit [her] to carry out the ordinary obligation of [her] job and meet new customers, and to sing at other than specified times, with the result that one manager told [her] he would never again employ [her] as long as [she] was married." He forbade her from contacting Oscar Hammerstein II, whom she hoped would write another role for her. Whenever she talked to a man, her jealous husband put "his hand under [her] arm. It was a nice gesture—but in reality he was digging his fingernails into [her] arm and would not let go until [she] walked away with him."[1]

Maschke ran up her line of credit while throwing wild parties where his guests smoked in the same room as her fish, which proved detrimental to their well-being. Helen's gal Friday, Frances Routa, described an incident when Buddy squirted a bottle of sparkling burgundy "all over the walls and the floor. Mrs. Maschke said: 'What's the idea?' and he said: 'Go to hell, can't I have some fun?'"[2]

Also absent, Maschke submitted his written testimony, contesting neither the divorce nor Helen's allegations. When reporters knocked on the door of the Maschke manse, whoever opened it curtly stated, "All he wants to say is that he wants to be left alone. Reporters have been calling all day but he will say nothing. He hasn't said anything and he's not going to say anything. Just leave him alone."[3]

On June 19, 1935, Superior Judge Ambrose granted the divorce. The couple settled their property claims out of court.[4] Helen celebrated her freedom at Leon and Eddie's.[5]

~

That summer, while working in California, Helen befriended Margaret Chung, the first woman doctor in Chinatown. Dear to the US Armed Forces, she called thousands of military men her "sons," but, like Helen, she was most loyal to aviators. Dr. Chung presented her fellow philanthropist with a large black bag, which Helen treasured for its faint, exotic odor of incense. Helen's Asiana obsession began in the twenties when Lulu gave her a carved Chinese good-luck pendant. Before Arthur Loew and that charm bracelet, Helen wore the pendant everywhere, even to her 1929 nuisance trial. With her passion rekindled, Helen replaced her men's pajamas with Asian lounging outfits.

One night, at San Mateo's Villa Mateo, a publisher offered $30,000 for Helen's life story, which Helen offered to split with a *Variety* staff writer—if he did the writing. Ultimately, Helen failed to provide her ghost with material. Two years later, she revisited the project, titled *Only Make Believe*. Macfadden expressed interest, but she never stopped long enough to start it.

Helen in her cherished Asian lounging pajamas. (Photofest)

Helen abandoned California to sub for Lita Grey Chaplin at Saratoga's Arrowhead Inn. Good thing, too. Not so lucky was Harmon Nelson, the first Mr. Bette Davis. The man whose posterior reminded Davis of the rear end of her Oscar statuette led the Villa Mateo orchestra during Helen's tenure—and during a gambling raid the Sunday after Helen's departure.

NBC set up another radio hookup during Saratoga's racing season. Enric Madriguera led his band on a series of local and network hookups, but Helen only garnered inclusion on the final broadcast, on the last day of the races, at the unglamorous hour of 6:00 p.m.

While playing Saratoga, Helen contracted a fever she could not shake. She soldiered on during her subsequent run at Detroit's Blossom Heath roadhouse. Including encores, she took nearly forty minutes of a one-hour floorshow, even on the night when, wobbly from drink, fever, or both, she fell off her piano perch. Still ill, she returned to New York, where, on September 23, she passed out at a party and was rushed to Park East Hospital. For three weeks, she battled low blood pressure and a fever as high as 106 degrees. She later quipped that her doctors had advised Lulu to "order the lilies."[6]

Dr. Otto Brooner gave Helen the prognosis straight: she had six months to live. "They said if I gave up singing and stayed on a strict diet, I might prolong my life. If I gave up singing, I'd have to give up eating, because I've never held on to money. I decided to be as merry as I could, and go out fighting."[7] Upon her release, she threw her own welcome-home party. When Jimmy Cannon asked for a brandy and soda, she scolded, "That soda is no good for you. You drink it straight or not at all. I'm not going to let you poison yourself at my party."[8]

During an interview with columnist Michel Mok at New York's Gay Nineties Restaurant, Helen fortified herself with a sherry. Harry Kannen and Mok urged her to eat solid food, but she rejected everything they suggested; she would not offend her fellow performers with bad breath. Instead, she ordered caviar on toast, a demitasse, and a Grand Marnier. When the order arrived, she poured the liqueur into the cup and made herself a café royal.

Her attitude alarmed her loved ones. Jorge Sanchez wrote to Helen, pleading for moderation. "I would take the brandy a little easy, or none at all," he wrote. In a postscript, Brownie added, "Also be very careful about your drinking."[9] Jorge also mentioned a Walter Winchell column gossiping that Barbara Loew had moved out of Pembroke, signaling their legal separation.[10] Sanchez knew Helen still loved her Arthur.[11]

~

Recovered, Helen focused her attention on Elizabeth Collins. The former child model was now a teenager—and pregnant. Liz's father wanted no bastard grandchild, and he struck his daughter. After Liz promised not to undergo an abortion, Helen sheltered the youngster through her pregnancy. Kannen's goons dutifully took Liz for walks and guarded her against further abuse. Liz thought the world of "Uncle Harry," who, unlike Arthur Loew, treated Helen like a princess.[12]

The Saratoga effect mirrored that of 1933: CBS pursued Helen after NBC lost interest. *Let's Have Fun* offered audiences a vicarious night out, first at a Broadway musical and then at a swank supper club. In a reworking of Rodgers and Hart's *A Connecticut Yankee*, crooner Ken Murray time travels to ancient Egypt. He meets a "real" woman (Helen as Cleopatra) who proves to be too extreme a lover for our hero. Helen warbles "Please Make Me Be Good" and "I'll Have a Little of You on Toast." Rounding out the hour, Freddie Rich and His Orchestra supply dance music. At the conclusion, the cast gives an extended preview of the next episode, in which the crooner takes his time machine back to 1492. Helen, as Queen Isabella, duets with Murray on "You've Got That," a reworking of a song dropped from the film *Hollywood Party*.[13]

Recorded at Manhattan's WABC studio on October 22, the pilot played before an audience of two hundred ad men at the Waldorf-Astoria two nights later. The songs are fun, and Helen lands the few laughs the ho-hum script provides her, but potential sponsors National Biscuit Company and ginger ale manufacturer Clicquot Club passed on the series.[14] Both Morgan and Murray performed while drunk, although Helen made fewer flubs than her costar. In any event, the series was doomed from the start: even were there a sponsor willing to shell out $25,000 for each hour-long program, Rodgers and Hart could not commit to writing an original musical every week, especially once *Jumbo* reestablished the team on Broadway.[15] Helen's schedule for the next six months would prove equally heavy.

Kannen's nightclub odyssey began in 1934, when, following an aborted attempt to convert the mansion of the late Otto Kahn into a nightclub, he and Joe Moss leased the Winter Garden with the intent of converting it into a cabaret theater. Kannen's subsequent search for headliners led him to Florida—and Helen. After obtaining Helen's signature, he canceled the Winter Garden contract and acquired a lease on a new building on the southeast corner of Fifty-Fourth and Madison.

An art deco masterpiece: the House of Morgan. (Author's collection)

The work of the architectural firm of Scott and Teegen, the art deco masterpiece boasted a facade of black marble, glass brick, and limestone. Inside, Kannen's palace was a $100,000 dreamland of white leatherette, burgundy velvet, satin-finished aluminum, and chromium-plated trim. The clubroom seated over two hundred. The spacious lounge, with its round bar, held one hundred and sported mirrored walls from the floor to the ceiling. Overlooking the bar was a balcony off Helen's dressing room, from which she surveyed her domain. Six men toiled for two weeks to apply fourteen-karat gold leaf to the ceiling, at a cost of $12,000.[16] Kannen often stopped guests to point out the detailing of his classy joint, but no amount of money could mask his plebian roots. After closing time, he often stopped in at Lindy's and ate his pie with a knife.

Thanks to Kannen's open checkbook, Helen designed her own gowns and provided every player in Lou Bring's Orchestra with new eveningwear. She put the Morgan crest on the dinner plates and the club stationery. Some questioned the appropriateness of a woman displaying her crest, since that right, as opposed to one's family arms, passes down through the male line. No one was crass enough to note that, biologically, Helen was not even a Morgan.

More contentious was the title over the door, which evoked the name of J. P. and not Helen, who shrugged. "The legal name of the banking company is Morgan & Co. The House of Morgan is just the nickname for it. . . . I don't see what anyone can do."[17] NBC knew what to do. On Tuesdays and Fridays, Lou Bring broadcast from the nightclub, which the network announcers pointedly called "The Home of Helen Morgan."[18] It is unlikely that Helen sang on these broadcasts.

A thousand were denied opening-night reservations. Despite her legendary dressing room hysterics, both Helen and the club earned raves. Within days, the House of Morgan was the most popular nightspot in Manhattan—until Helen abandoned her club for a film role.

An anomaly of the era, the 1936 Universal *Show Boat* film preserves the Broadway performances of Helen, Paul Robeson, Charles Winninger, and Sammy White. Much of the casting credit for the Broadway-to-Hollywood odyssey goes to Oscar Hammerstein, who stepped in to write the screenplay after Zoë Akins failed to tame the sprawling stage libretto for the screen. On Hammerstein's recommendation, Carl Laemmle Jr. hired Broadway veteran Francis X. Mahoney for Rubberface.[19] Junior Laemmle also tested Annie Hart for the landlady, but she could not adjust her stage mannerisms for the camera.[20] May Beatty got the part.

Joseph Breen permitted the potential reteaming of Tess Gardella and Paul Robeson as Queenie and Joe but warned Universal "not to indicate any physical contact between the white woman and the Negro man for the reason that many people know Aunt Jemina (Gardella) is a white woman and might be repulsed by the sight of her being fondled by a man who is a Negro."[21] The Laemmles simplified matters by hiring Hattie McDaniel.

When the curtain first went up on *Show Boat* in 1927, the first words uttered were by the Black stevedores, who sang "N------ all work on de Mississippi / N-------s all work while de white folks play." White audiences squirmed in discomfort, as Hammerstein intended. The stevedores repeated this couplet later in this opening chorus, as did Joe as the beginning of the second verse of "Ol' Man River." The slur peppered the dialogue an additional ten times during the 1927 and 1932 Broadway productions and tours.[22]

In 1935, Universal submitted Hammerstein's screenplay to Joseph Breen who, in deference to African American audiences, championed eliminating the use of the racial epithet. Universal agreed to replace the slur in dialogue but retain it in song, "where it comes in naturally."[23] After Hammerstein acquiesced to Robeson's request to remove it from "Ol' Man River," Breen won his war on the slur throughout the production, although the replacement words of "darkies" and "Negros" remain problematic to modern audiences. Beginning with his revision for the 1946 Broadway revival, Hammerstein softened the language as he had in the film. In his last revision, made just before his death, the slur is uttered only twice, once by the villainous boat engineer Pete and the other by the racist sheriff, Vallon. Joe, Queenie, Steve, and Windy only utter euphemisms.[24]

In truth, bowdlerizing the "Ol' Man River" lyric began during the 1927 stage production, when some Stevedores chose not to sing the word in performance.[25] Jolson sang the original lyric in his 1928 recording of "Ol' Man River," while Paul Whiteman's odd arrangement, with a too-peppy vocal by Bing Crosby, bypasses the issue by omitting both verses. Bledsoe's 1929 outing for the prologue of the 1929 Universal film changed the word to "darkies," although his 1931 recording, made in the UK, includes the original lyric. Robeson omitted the second verse and its racial slur in his 1928 and 1932 recordings of the song but sang them as written on his 1930 English waxing.

From the very beginning, *Show Boat*'s interracial content raised hackles. While researching her novel, Ferber befriended Charles Hunter of the James Adams Floating Palace Theatre, who described the mixed-race couples, and their biracial children, who played showboats. Ferber watered down Hunter's description of a real-life "Steve," who, after leaving "Julie," hooked up with an even darker woman: his wife had not been Black enough for him.[26] In the autumn of 1926, Tom Leonard censored an Eveready Hour radio dramatization, presumably to soften the miscegenation subplot. Universal's 1929 film dodged the race issue entirely, as did a 1940 Lux Radio production, in which Gloria Holden's Julie left the boat not because of miscegenation but because she entered the country illegally. On two *Railroad Hour* radio outings, Julie's expulsion went unmentioned. More astounding than the thought that the miscegenation scene played on Broadway in 1927 is the fact that director James Whale managed to film the entire scene, uncut, eight years later. For the most part. Local censors in the Jim Crow South shortened the opus by almost twenty minutes—including the entire miscegenation scene.[27]

Before Whale's arrival at Universal City, Charles Winninger, who fancied himself a *Show Boat* expert by virtue of years playing Cap'n Andy (and Captain Henry on NBC's *Maxwell House Show Boat*), began editing costume designs and the script and, Laemmle complained, started "to direct."[28] In response, Whale assembled his cast of *Show Boat* veterans and established his rules: there would be no arguments that his way was not the way *Show Boat* had been done onstage.

Whale's custom of surrounding himself with British artists behind the camera did little to endear Winninger, Irene Dunne, and Allan Jones to him. They believed the foreigner failed to comprehend the best and worst of his adopted country, disqualifying him to helm Ziegfeld's all-American musical comedy. In reality, the director, with his great eye for detail, delivered the best film version of the Ferber-Kern-Hammerstein classic.

Helen was not Universal's first choice. Before testing Dorothy Lamour and Libby Holman, the studio approached Estelle Taylor. Alma Rubens beat out the former Mrs. Jack Dempsey for the role in Universal's 1929 version of *Show Boat*, but Taylor subsequently played Julie in a 1933 West Coast stage production that Helen bypassed because of her *Broadway Melodies* radio series. This post-Ziegfeld mounting brought Hattie McDaniel to the attention of the Laemmles.

Upon acknowledging that no one could play Julie like Helen, Universal warily commenced negotiations. Days before the House of Morgan opened, Helen signed an unusually harsh contract: if her behavior held up production, she would lose the role *and* would be required to pay the salary of Libby Holman, the replacement Universal kept in reserve.[29] In return, she earned $3,000 a week.

Fearing that Helen would not walk onto the lot sober, Junior Laemmle asked Hammerstein's assistant, Leighton K. Brill, to meet Helen and Lulu at the train station. Brill, who cut and restaged the 1933 *Show Boat* tab production, reported, "She looked fine and in good shape all around."[30] Allan Jones agreed: "All I can tell you is that she was sober all through the picture."[31]

Film stand-in John Latham sided with Jones. One exception: on the day Whale shot the parade sequence, Helen did not appear on set. Donald Cook suggested that Latham run down to dressing room row and get her before anyone became suspicious. Latham found her in her cups. "I mean, she was not staggering at all, but she was high."[32] He "slapped her a couple of times and said she had to get on the set—didn't she remember her contract?" He added, "I'm going to get Donald and you're going up on the set. You don't have to speak a line, just stand up in the carriage and he'll be there.'"[33] When the limousine carrying Helen and Latham arrived on the set, Cook "went over to her and said some pretty harsh things to her and accompanied her to the wagon."[34] He kept one arm around Helen's waist to keep her from

Donald Cook helps Helen avoid disaster during the filming of the *Show Boat* parade. (Photofest)

bobbing as the carriage went up and down the levee. "Between Donald and me, we kept an eagle eye on her. It was literally just that one day, and thank God it was the parade."[35]

Helen rewarded Latham for his good deed. Later, he rapped on Helen's dressing room door, saying, "Nothing would please me more if you would sing, just for me alone, 'Can't Help Lovin' Dat Man.' So she sat at the dressing room table and sang 'Can't Help Lovin' Dat Man,' followed by 'Bill,' followed by 'Sand in My Shoes,' followed by every song she ever knew."[36]

Sobriety was not Helen's sole challenge. One of the twenty-six costumes British designer Doris Zinkeisen provided Helen weighed thirty-six pounds. Its bulk left bruises on her shoulders. Not permitted to sit, as that would have damaged the bustled creation, Helen rested between takes, as best she could, face down at a slight angle, on a leaning board.

Helen arrived on the lot by six in the morning and often left at midnight. Late one night, Whale took close-ups, including one of Helen in her monster dress. He started with Helen Westley, who demurred, "No, if you don't mind,

I'd rather you shoot Miss Morgan first. She has only one close-up and I feel so fresh."[37] "Mousie" Morgan was eternally grateful.

Off the lot, Helen was less than sober, especially when she held court at Lucca's. With her long history of charity work for people of color, Helen was one of the few white members of the company Hattie McDaniel invited to a party she threw to honor Paul Robeson.

Boxing fascinated Helen. A lifelong fan, she even shadowboxed with Young Stribling in a 1931 newsreel. She met a kindred spirit in Kannen, whose dream of a boxing career ended when he broke his arm while serving in the navy during the Great War. They attended the Barney Ross–Frankie Klick fight in Miami on January 28, 1935. On June 15, she was one of the few women who saw Jim "Cinderella Man" Braddock dethrone Max Baer at the Long Island City Bowl. Ten days later, she attended the Louis-Carnera bout at Yankee Stadium. Helen rang in 1936 by attending the Hollywood bouts—with Jake Glaenzer.

Harry Kannen's hold on Helen was slipping, He rushed out West for a visit.

Whale spent the first five weeks on exterior photography. On January 13, he began the two Trocadero scenes. Since Helen would perform "Bill" realistically, with minimal orchestration, there was no reason to lip-synch. Whale shot it live. Hammerstein advised Whale to "cut it down to one verse and one chorus" and said the full song was "too long to wait for the plot to move on at this point." He warned, "Whatever you do, please don't let her sit on the piano!"[38]

As early as Lewis Milestone's 1928 crime melodrama *The Racket*, Hollywood co-opted Helen's trademark pose. So often, in fact, that Helen's signature became passé long before she arrived in the film colony. Whale placed Helen beside the upright while Harry Barris (Jake) put down his cigarette to play for her.

Disregarding Hammerstein's wishes concerning length, Whale used that second chorus to tell more of Julie's story. In earlier scenes, he keeps his distance and, aided by cinematographer John J. Mescall, makes Helen look younger than she was. In "Bill," he comes in for an extreme close-up. Helen is still bathed in that ethereal 1930s halo of light, but it shows the results of every drink, every wrong done to her. Without a word of dialogue, audiences learn what happened to Julie and Steve in the years after they left the Cotton Blossom. Helen is broken—and magnificent.

Charles C. Wilson watches, former Rhythm Boy Harry Barris accompanies, and Helen pines for her "Bill." (Photofest)

On-screen, bartenders, chorines, and even a charwoman stopped their chores, gathered around, and listened to Julie's song. A similar scene unfolded behind the klieg lights. Anybody who could get in was on the set. At the end of the take, Margaret Sullavan broke the mood when she arose from the hardwood floor shrieking in pain—with splinters in her behind.[39]

Hollywood may have regarded Helen with indifference, but when she sang "Bill," people sat up and took notice.

Helen and Lulu flew home from Hollywood. Any harm Buddy did to her fish had become a moot point. After pushing the glass top off the twenty-three tanks, her industrious cat Charley ate most of the fish. To protect the three remaining tanks, Helen made Charley (whom Helen claimed was the first ticketed feline passenger on a commercial flight) her constant traveling companion.[40]

Back East, eight weeks without Helen placed her House in financial jeopardy. June Knight, followed by Gertrude Niesen, failed to bring in business.

Sophie Tucker held over for a four-week run but cost Kannen $2,500 a week, a grand more than he paid Helen. Adding to the financial misery were mechanics' liens: one for $90 from Hubbard and Lange and an older one, for $1,980, from Regal Art Glass and Fixture Corp.[41]

For her return, the clotheshorse wore a white organdy gown with a bunch of cherries at the throat, which turned her into a walking tissue caddy. In deference to her negative body image, Helen favored period wardrobe over the sleek, satin evening gowns of the 1930s. Her wardrobe reinforced the critical opinion that she was a nostalgic product of a bygone age.

To complement the gold-leaf ceiling, she replaced her customary handkerchief with a bouquet of yellow flowers to occupy her nervous hands.[42] The press praised the *new* Helen Morgan, from her "streamlined figure" to her updated hairstyle and material.[43] One new number was "I'm in Love with the Honorable Mr. So and So." Sam Coslow wrote it while Helen was attached to the *Follies of 1934* and then put it aside until she was ready for it. She featured it in her act throughout the season. Virginia Bruce later sang it in *Society Lawyer*.[44]

Awaiting Helen at her House of Morgan was Kannen, armed with thirty dozen roses and a new chef, Henri Charpentier. Crêpe Suzette, then still a novelty, was his signature dessert. He reinstated the lunch and dinner menus removed from the lineup as a cost-saving move during the holidays.[45] Also awaiting was a second mechanic's lien, for $250, from the Steinburg Brothers Stone Company. Three more liens followed, one, from Reis and O'Donovan for $717.24, would wait nine months before being paid.[46] A series of Monday-night guest appearances, inaugurated by Edward G. Robinson, failed to shore up business.

Helen disengaged. After, and sometimes before, her performances, she patronized rival nightclubs.[47] She forgot the lyrics to her new songs. The *Billboard* forgave her, writing, "Nobody cares any more. . . . She's a good show by herself and entertains with or without words."[48] On February 18, she called out sick. Kannen removed the cover charge but did no business that night. Her absence may have been political, but Kannen himself missed several nights at the club because of illness. While he recuperated, the board of directors forged a partnership with Nick Prounis. The Versailles owner would manage, and assume half of the existing debt of, the House of Morgan.[49]

Helen took a two-week leave to follow the snowbirds, already congregated in Miami. Dorothy Dey delighted in reporting Helen's defection, reminding her readers that, when leaving the previous December to film

Show Boat, Helen had told Kannen *exactly* what she thought of his mishandling of his headwaiters, who recently quit the club. Helen personally talked Lou Bring out of rescinding his letter of resignation. At issue: Kannen treated his staff like soldiers, expecting loyalty he had not earned.[50] His temper flared before his clientele as well: reportedly, he once hit a customer over the head with a plate.[51]

Helen ended the Kannen-Bring contretemps by having Lou Bring join her at Miami Beach's Town Casino Club. She held her audience in the palm of her well-manicured hand, coaxing them to join her on the second chorus of "Make Believe." Her second night proved less successful: baseball Hall of Famer Eddie Collins, blotto, yanked her off her perch in midsong and waltzed her around the floor. When the Casino refused to provide a car and chauffeur to whisk her to and from her benefits, Helen walked. She played her second week at the nearby Hollywood Kennel Club.[52]

Fueling Helen's estrangement from Kannen was the fact that she no longer needed him. Specifically, Elizabeth Collins no longer needed Uncle Harry's protection. Liz gave birth to a girl, whom she named Helen after her benefactor. When her father learned that his wife and daughter intended to keep the baby and not offer her for adoption, he moved out of the house. A year later, Helen, who could not comprehend how anyone could reject a child, shamed him into reconciliation, claiming, "I'd give my eye teeth to have her."[53]

Receiving a better offer from Mike Fritzel, Helen quit the House of Morgan. She hardly recognized the Chez Paree. The previous summer, Fritzel and Joey Jacobson overhauled their club to the tune of $60,000, and made it the finest room in Chicago. The improvements included new kitchens, an enlarged dance floor, and artist dressing rooms. Fritzel separated the circular bar from the main café by glass, which granted patrons a view of the floorshow. Ten Raymond Katz murals, representing dancers from different countries, enhanced the main room. The "Duse of song" received a three-minute ovation when she walked out for her first show.[54]

On March 10, Kannen applied for bankruptcy protection. Unable to (again) backfill his namesake star, he closed his doors, he hoped temporarily, on March 21. He raced to Chicago to win Helen back. While there, Gilbert Kahn declared him in default of his lease, despite the partnership with Prounis. Judge Alfred C. Coxe appointed David M. Schwartz as trustee to liquidate the club. The liabilities for Hark Inc. (a contraction of Harry Kannen's name) amounted to $79,485.44 owed to 101 creditors, including one final lien for $550 from Edward A. Sears. The assets came to approximately $12,000. Kannen's primary financial liabilities were the salaries for his two alternating bands, plus star salaries and perks. Sophie Tucker ran up $72 in unpaid food bills. A black-tie dress code may have kept out the riffraff, but New York society still left over $1,000 in unpaid tabs.

Avoiding another court date, Helen, by remote deposition, claimed that she was but a hired entertainer. This prompted Samuel Newfield, counsel for the trustee, to ask Kannen, "While you took stock in Miss Morgan, she didn't take any stock in you?"[55]

A potential partner, Lucky Luciano, also failed to take stock in the enterprise. Upon learning that the House of Morgan referred to Helen, the superstitious gangster feared that Kannen's naming the club after a woman would only bring bad luck. He demanded Kannen return his $5,000 investment. Relieved, Kannen did.[56]

Later, Kannen sued Gilbert Kahn for terminating the lease after verbally agreeing to the Prounis partnership. Kannen lost the case. And the appeal.[57] Subsequent attempts to operate clubs on the site resulted in failure.

When asked why her House of Morgan failed, Helen snapped, "Bad people."[58]

15

More Scandals

Released in May 1936, *Show Boat* was a monster hit.

Helen's Julie is her best film performance. Not until Yul Brynner shot *The King and I* did a Broadway musical performance translate so faithfully, and completely, to the screen. Whale captured both her songs in full. The only other song from the stage show filmed in its entirety was "Ol' Man River."

Critics singled out Helen for high praise, second only to Robeson. *Variety* enthused that she "looks as good as she did 15 years ago" and that her performance "suggests much cinematic promise if she ever gives herself some serious attention,"[1] but her cinematic fate was sealed the following week when Republic released *Frankie and Johnnie*. Audiences paid to see Helen ply the Mississippi again, but the critical drubbing the film received confirmed Hollywood's belief that, *Show Boat* aside, Helen had little to offer in film.

Chester Erskine compromised Helen from the start, requesting that her Frankie be more nurturing than Jack Kirkland's tormented whore.[2] Once Joseph Breen removed Helen's emotionally wrought, blood-splattered shooting scene, Frankie, with her passivity, resembled a dishrag more than a woman. Not until 1965 did *Frankie and Johnnie* return, with Elvis Presley and Donna Douglas as, again, sanitized lovers.

Of the new songs William Saal used as bait to elicit her signature in 1935, only "If You Want My Heart (It Belongs to You)" is in the released film—and it has been cut in half. Saal relegated the replacement theme song, "It's You I Adore," to underscoring.[3] He recut the 1934 footage to keep "Give Me a Heart to Sing To" but could do nothing to obscure Helen's ill-fitting, strapless hoopskirt.

Minus a few 1935 close-ups to mask cuts, the first twenty-four minutes of the film consist of 1934 material.[4] As in the play, Johnnie (Chester Morris) enters the Mansion House in St. Louis with the bankroll he won aboard the riverboat *Natchez*. Veering from Kirkland, Frankie is a singer playing her last night at the saloon before marrying Curley (William Harrigan). Johnnie meets Frankie and Nellie Bly (Lilyan Tashman). Frankie warns Johnnie to leave while he still has his bankroll.

As Frankie leads Johnnie to her room, the film cuts away to the 1935 material, which eliminates Johnnie's sleeping with Frankie—and later Nellie—without benefit of clergy, as well as Frankie giving her money to a man who is not her husband. Instead, in the new footage, Frankie and Johnnie escape the Mansion House via a back exit, where they meet Andy (John Larkin). The Black coachman takes them to a wedding of freed slaves, replete with "ethnic humor" and singing. Shot to compensate for cuts elsewhere, this particularly racist moment in 1930s cinema is, today, more objectionable than any footage Breen cut. Inspired by the wedding, Frankie and Johnnie marry. In time, Tashman's not-so-vampy Nellie Bly lures away the restless Johnnie. At the thirty-nine-minute mark, when grips load a production of *Romeo and Juliet* into the St. Louis Opera House, the film returns to the heavily edited 1934 footage.

Forsaken, Frankie grabs a dainty pistol and stalks Johnnie. Because Breen decreed that she must remain morally unscathed, as released, Timothy (Walter Kingsford) shoots Johnnie before she can. Presumably. Audiences see quick close-ups of faces in the crowd before Lou (Florence Reed), the Mansion House madam, drops her handkerchief. A gunshot, then a cut to Johnnie's corpse, and the major continuity error between the 1934 and 1935 footage: the viewer assumes that Johnnie is gunned down inside the saloon, but Frankie cries over the corpse, clearly outside on the street.

While noting the film's two-year battle with the censors, the *Times* sniped, "Even without their scissoring, however, it still must have been pretty bad."[5] Probably, but had Erskine successfully released *Frankie and Johnnie* before July 1, 1934, uncensored, the film would be remembered as one of the last great pre-Code extravaganzas.

Why Erskine believed he could fashion Kirkland's play into a releasable film, no matter how much he, via Helen's presence, softened it, remains a mystery. Kirkland's first act ends with Frankie taking Johnnie upstairs, where, later, Frankie tells of Harry, the man who first "done her wrong" in Cairo, Illinois. Johnnie tells her that she was his first. Frankie becomes overwrought by the idea that she has done *him* wrong and goes out to kill herself. Hearing the peal of church bells, she repents and then asks Johnnie to marry her. He lies,

Frankie and Johnnie: the climactic confrontation we never saw. (© David Shepard, Courtesy of Blackhawk Films)

telling her that his bankroll was stolen during the night. Frankie hands him $200 and returns to the street to build a nest egg. Three weeks later, Lou and Nellie spar verbally, and Lou sneers that Nellie would probably sleep with her brother. "I did," Nellie replies. "He was the gentleman that ruined me." Johnnie begs Nellie to run off with him. When he confesses that he still has his original bankroll, she accuses him of holding out on both of them. She agrees to join him as long as she controls the money. They haggle and settle on Nellie controlling $2,500. Frankie enters, sees the two together, and shoots Johnnie dead. Nellie offers Frankie the money. Forging an uneasy truce, the two carry out their man's body to bury.

Ultimately, Kirkland had the last laugh. In December 1933, his next white-trash extravaganza landed on Broadway. When it closed in 1941, after 3,182 performances, *Tobacco Road* was the longest-running production in Broadway history.

~

In 1938, Frankie Baker, a woman of color claiming to be the historical Frankie of song and legend, sued Erskine, Helen, Morris, and the late Lilyan Tashman for $200,000.[6] This was not her first tussle with Hollywood. Her attorney, Joseph L. McLemore, dropped another suit, for $100,000, against Paramount and Mae West over their libelous use of the tune in *She Done Him Wrong*, under the belief that he had a stronger case against Helen and Republic. Baker criticized Helen specifically because, unlike Helen, Frankie was not a drinking woman. On October 15, 1899, Baker caught Albert (born Allen) Britt in the hallway of the Phoenix Hotel in St. Louis with Alice Pryar.[7] The argument continued at home, where Britt threw a kerosene lamp at the prostitute and then went after her with a knife. She shot him. He died four days later. The Four Courts acquitted her on grounds of justifiable homicide.[8]

Baker's former neighbors attested that local African American composer Jim Dooley wrote the ballad soon after Britt's death.[9] Although musicologist Sigmund Spaeth, in his *Read 'em and Weep*, claimed that the song originated in St. Louis, under oath he testified that subsequent research proved that the song took its inspiration from an 1831 murder in North Carolina and that versions of the song were sung as early as 1840. Professor Tyrrell Williams of Washington University suggested that the similarity in the details of Britt's death revived public interest in the legend. In 1912, the Leighton Brothers adapted a version, be it Dooley's or someone else's tune, into the form played today—and the first to be published.

Baker lost the case.[10]

In the wake of the Universal film, Victor rereleased Helen's 1928 *Show Boat* disc, and Warners released *The Coo-Coo Nut Grove*. The Merrie Melodies cartoon travesty of a night at the Cocoanut Grove ends with Helen atop a piano. Voiced by Wini Shaw, she wails "The Little Things You Used to Do." The short satirized not only Helen but also Hollywood's filming of her numbers, down to reaction shots of George Raft and Edward G. Robinson crying on each other's shoulders. At the end, everyone floats away on a river of tears.

With the whole country Morgan-conscious, George White signed Helen for the national tour of the twelfth edition of his *Scandals*. He had first approached her when he assembled the revue a year before, but the *Show Boat* shoot prevented her participation.

The tour broke in with a brush-up week in Atlantic City. The production moved on to Chicago, where Helen's struggle learning her lyrics may have contributed to a lukewarm assessment from Lloyd Lewis. The *Daily News*

Helen gets the Warner Bros. cartoon treatment in *The Coo-Coo Nut Grove*. (*The Coo-Coo Nut Grove*, Warner Bros. Discovery, 1936)

critic blamed the songs, not the singer. "She is beautiful as ever, but her material keeps her in the position of a moon that must be glimpsed through the clouds, and always hidden just when it begins to really shine."[11] Other critics delighted over the "new" Helen. *Variety* enthused, "She takes part in some of the skits and interludes, doing her full part and, when opportunity comes, getting down in the sawdust and qualifying as a clown."[12] A happy Helen should not have surprised anyone; this was Helen the revue artist. Audiences loved her.

The production opened with Helen warbling "Anything Can Happen" and "Life Begins at Sweet Sixteen" while seventy-five girls popped out of a giant TV screen to delight tired businessmen. If the television theme seemed familiar, it was because it mirrored the newspaper-framing device of Irving Berlin's *As Thousands Cheer*.

Despite Helen's initial reservations, "I've Got to Get Hot!" became her best-received number. Its lyric mirrored how Helen abandoned her dream to be an opera singer to earn cash singing in a girlie show. When Helen sang,

"So don't you blame me, brother / I've got a gray-haired mother / And if I shake / It's for mother's sake," the line between fiction and autobiography disappeared.[13]

White created two new spots in the second act for Helen to coax tears from her audience. The first was a scena entitled "Lost Love," wherein she held sway from her piano perch. Each time she sang a line or two from torch songs identified with her, the audience applauded. For the production's revised finale, the television set inexplicably gave the audience glimpses, a hundred years into the future, of Ponce de Leon (Willie Howard), Napoleon (Eugene Howard), Kate Smith (Edna Page), and Al Jolson (Willie Howard again). Helen, as Miss Show Boat, graced the airwaves with a medley of "Make Believe," "Can't Help Lovin' Dat Man," "Why Do I Love You?," and "Bill."

While in Chicago, Helen briefly toyed with bad-boy Woolworth heir Jimmy Donahue, about the time he signed Ruth Etting to appear in his disastrous London revue *Transatlantic Rhythm*.[14] Later, Helen reconnected with Joel Goldblatt.

Decreased railroad fees made daily jumps feasible for the first time in years. Helen urged White to book the *Scandals* in Danville, but Publix-Great States Theatres, understanding that they would need to sell out just to break even, rejected the idea. Nonetheless, one-night stands in Rockford and South Bend did turnaway business.[15]

On tour, Helen cooked, from basics, like homemade butter, to the exotic, like Russian *chahv*, a cold soup made of spinach, eggs, and cream.[16] She also taught chorines to prepare meals on an electric stove. When short on time, and when Helen agreed to eat solid food, Frances Routa ran out and got Helen a hamburger.[17]

Helen did not moonlight, and she retired early most nights. Matinee and travel days aside, she slept up to fourteen hours at a stretch until four in the afternoon. Once up, she read, awaiting long-distance telephone calls from Joel Goldblatt.[18] A contributing factor to Helen remaining sequestered was the dull nightlife. Obtaining quality brandy in the smaller towns the *Scandals* played proved so challenging that Helen switched, temporarily, to Scotch.[19]

The West Coast leg of the tour got off to a rocky start when the sleeper train pulled into San Francisco at four o'clock in the morning instead of at six. The hotel she had booked denied lodgings to Charley the fat cat and her snoring Pekinese, Cricket. Helen, Frances, and her coterie spent the morning scrambling to find first-class accommodations. At the third hotel they tried, "the room clerk looked up from his fingernail polishing long enough to direct her to the zoo."[20] The fourth time proved to be the charm. The child-woman pouted over the slight but fared better that evening: she gave three encores of "I've Got to Get Hot" before begging off the stage. The Curran run was a complete sellout, with the first three shows full before the company arrived in town.[21]

Buoyed by the strong box office, White extended the tour.

The cloister began to chafe. After purchasing more Chinese lounging outfits, Helen sent for a Los Angelean couturier to design a new wardrobe. She also splurged on a knee-length silver fox cape. "I have a short one and I was just going to have some skins added to that, but I decided to get a new one. All I have for evening is just an ermine coat and you know how it is; you get awfully tired of that."[22]

After a ten-day stand in Los Angeles, the production played one- and two-night stands through the Southwest and the Deep South. The grind got to everyone. Dogs traveling with the company targeted Charley. Cricket bit multiple Pullman porters. Helen grew equally snippy. In Tucson, during a postshow party at the Santa Rita Hotel, local politician Frank Cooper believed he deserved a kiss when he bought her a drink, but Helen cried, "Get away from me! You stink!" for all to hear.[23] In Memphis, when Bob, the rambunctious adult son of political boss Edward Hull Crump, squirted her white organdy costume with soda pop, Helen belted him in the mouth.[24]

A happier reception awaited in Austin, where University of Texas boys besieged Helen at the stage door. When programs were unavailable, she autographed shirts and hats. Hoisting her on their shoulders, the lads escorted Helen to the train depot in style. With time before her departure, she led them to a nearby Chinese restaurant, ordered the owner to set up the beers and keep them coming, and produced a flask from her purse. Even with food, the boys struggled to keep up with Helen drink for drink.[25]

A week later, Helen found herself nursing another cold. Missing one- and two-show stands would have proved economically disastrous to the company, so she sang anyway.

In December, Frances Routa, restless and homesick, handed in her resignation. Lulu joined Helen in Cincinnati. Lulu had recently purchased an eleven-room Victorian house in Flatbush, where Helen later created a three-room suite to house her collections.[26]

Between Christmas and the New Year, while the *Scandals* played Detroit, Helen doubled into the Powatan, stepping in for Nan Blackstone, who had recently been disfigured in a car accident. When a jealous matron struck a *Scandals* chorine for flirting with her husband, Helen defended her castmate. Denouncing the provincial clientele, she refused to finish the run, then left her paycheck at Blackstone's side.[27]

Failing to reach an agreement with the Howard Brothers, whose contract did not include overseas travel, George White scrapped a proposed London stand and converted the show into a tab unit.[28] Operating on a $10,000-a-week fee with a percentage split for any overage, the Howards, Helen, and most of their material remained, but White halved the size of the cast and condensed the show to fifty-seven minutes. Anticipating a twelve-week extension, the five-a-day tab *Scandals* opened at the Chicago Palace on January 15—and Helen caught another cold.

When White failed to reach a deal for a winter season swing through Florida, he announced he would cut the $10,000-a-week budget to $6,000 after the Boston stand. In response, the principals handed in their notices, and the production shuttered.

Helen, who had opened in Boston fighting another cold, left the show early. Gloria Rich finished the week.[29] Eight months on the road also took its toll on Cricket: the Pekinese took sick in September, never fully recovered, and died *en tour*. Before returning home, Helen bought Putzi, a Maltese terrier.

Helen lived with such abandon that she never understood people who prioritized life differently. Once, while hosting a get-together, the phone rang. A guest answered. Helen, busy in the kitchen, asked him to hold the wire. This was a long-distance call from Paris. Helen smiled. "But I can't answer it now. Don't you understand? I'm dyeing Easter eggs. If I leave them they'll be ruined."[30]

Playing the Broadway Loew's State, Helen abandoned her piano top for a bench placed on the theater's runway, where, needing less amplification, she simulated the intimacy of a nightclub. During the opening-day matinee, her varied vocal selections displeased the management, who demanded Helen give audiences what they expected. She did, eschewing intimacy for informality when she cajoled the crowds into singing the second choruses and threw flowers to the first row. She went over big, but the dictate so galled her that when she sailed to England the following week, she dabbed her eye with a red-and-black handkerchief and cried, "I don't think I'll ever come back. They don't appreciate me anymore."

She remained coy about her relationship with Joel Goldblatt, whom she refused to mention by name: "He's an American sailing on a later ship." When Helen hinted that she might marry abroad, Lulu blanched at the prospect of becoming a mother-in-law again. "Heaven forbid! I hope not—certainly not for ten or eleven years!"[31]

At the pier, Lulu washed dirt off Helen's neck, then handed her daughter a wad of bills, begging her to come home with some of it. After that final embrace, the Morgans wept until the gangplank was raised.

Helen's planned British invasion during the coronation of George VI unraveled as soon as the *Lafayette* landed. Her work visa clearly permitted her to work in the United Kingdom for two months, but the immigration officer who processed her at Plymouth passed her through with only a two-*week* window.[32] While eager to pick up a weekly paycheck, at $2,500, to double into the Victoria Palace and Ciro's nightclub, Helen did not realize until her arrival that the figure was for both stands combined, not each individually. To offset the lost income, she signed for a BBC radio broadcast, but producer Kurt Robitschek killed the deal. He did not want his star to give her act away two days before the opening of his Victoria Palace show, *Our Show-Boat of Laughter*.

Ten years after her last London appearance, Helen made a sensation at the Victoria, preceding each of her four selections by asking, "Would you like to hear . . .?"[33] The audience response was so tumultuous that she begged off after her encore with a rare curtain speech. The *Observer* enthused, "Her voice is sweet and cunningly modulated. She wisely disdains the microphone, does not sing too much, and gives the impression that her resources, vocal and repertorial, are infinite."[34]

Helen's response: "Voice—I haven't got a voice. I just go through the motions."[35]

Unlike her other nightclub assignments, Helen was the whole show at Ciro's. All London paid her homage, including bad boy and aviator Prince George, Duke of Kent.[36] After she finished her fourth performance of the day, the party began. Besides Goldblatt, the Sanchezes and Dorothy Dey were on hand. After her second scheduled week at the Victoria Palace and Ciro's, Helen flew to Dublin, leaving her friends, lover, and the coronation itself behind.

As she was going over her program with the manager of the Theatre Royal, he cautioned, "Whatever you do, don't sing 'Did Your Mother Come From Ireland?' because every act that comes to this theater includes that particular number." Helen, who learned the song for Dublin, sighed and pulled out her standard rep. Dublin adored her. Taken with the local tenement children and their mothers who stood in the alleyway outside her dressing room, Helen came out daily, showed them her latest gown, and gave them a song or two. Their appreciation touched her. "Sometimes London aristocrats can be so rude and thoughtless. They think nothing of interrupting a song . . . while I sang for royalty, my heart was left with the Dublin boys and girls who couldn't even get into the theatre."[37]

Returning to London, she played her rescheduled BBC debut on *The Little Show*. The next day, she sailed back to America, her British invasion over almost before it started.

Helen goes Irish. (AP Photo)

Something happened abroad. Something beyond her fight with British Immigration and, with it, talks of making a British film. Something that ended her relationship with Joel Goldblatt.

Rudy Vallée claimed that one night he dropped into Ciro's, only to see Helen, in midsong, become sick, vomit, and fall to the floor.[38] Vallée's self-aggrandizing claim that he then stepped in to cover for his fellow Yankee does not ring true. He did not land in Southampton until April 30, the last night of Helen's fortnight at Ciro's, and Vallée did not open there until the following Friday. He may have witnessed Helen vomiting, perhaps even at Ciro's, but not while she was working.[39]

When Helen arrived in New York, she cried, "My gawd, the money I owe." Much of the red ink came from a $4,000 spending spree on a tweedy Irish wardrobe. She blamed her financial woes on her stingy British employers, not her own penchant for excess. Even Flatbush disappointed her. When Lulu admitted that the tulips Helen planted before she left had already bloomed, the eyes of the child-woman filled with tears. "Oh mother," she cried, "couldn't you have coaxed them to stay for your little girl?"[40]

She had bounced back when Warners dismissed her, but this was different. Goodwill within the industry had waned. In truth, her career decline began when the stock market crashed. Projects she undertook in the 1920s had led to something bigger and better, but most of what she did in the 1930s failed to live up to what proceeded it.

Helen faced an uncertain future.

16

"Tired of Livin' and Scared of Dyin'"

Helen's star faded. Steadily.

In July 1937, making his inaugural nightclub appearance, dialect comedian Lou Holtz, and Helen, filled Chez Paree to capacity for seven weeks. The billing was telling, as was the excising of her new material, "Where are You?" and "September in the Rain," early in the run, presumably at Mike Fritzel's request.[1] After Helen limited herself solely to Kern and Hammerstein, the Holtz-Morgan team proved equally effective in a subsequent film-house vaudeville stand.[2] Audiences enthused, but her heart was clearly not in her work.[3] Illness forced her out of the Oriental three days early and into Chicago's Michael Reese Hospital, starting a vicious cycle: the more she worked, the sicker she became. The sicker she became, the more she needed to work to pay her medical expenses.[4]

In September, recovered but sans Holtz, she played the Club Eldorado, the latest Manhattan offering from her 54th Street Club champion, Lou Schwartz.[5] New Yorkers loved her, but they did not love "Lull in My Life" and "If You Were Someone Else." Later that autumn, the "Bernhardt of Song" led the floorshow at a shabby barn called the Hollywood Restaurant. One of the usually unenthusiastic showgirls gushed, "Gee, it's sure swell to be playing to an audience again, Miss Morgan."[6]

One night, Helen returned from the powder room with tears in her eyes. A companion asked what new tragedy had befallen her. Helen confessed that she had just given a hundred dollars to the attendant because the "poor thing told me she had no Frigidaire."[7]

While Helen was at the Eldorado, CBS expressed interest in having her broadcast from a Florida club during the season. When the deal evaporated,

Diminished, Helen takes second billing to comedian Lou Holtz. (Author's collection)

she joined *The Hollywood Hotel Revue*. Harry Howard secured the stage rights of the eponymous CBS radio variety series through its sponsor, Campbell's Soup, and fashioned a tab unit that played film palaces throughout the 1936–1937 season, often in Warner Brothers houses. When Harry's revue played Philadelphia, management requested he change the unit's title to avoid confusion with the upcoming Warners epic, also called *Hollywood Hotel*. He refused; called in Helen, Willie Howard, and Eugene Howard (no relation); and premiered a full evening's entertainment in Brooklyn, structured around its hotel theme. The curtain parted to reveal a telephone switchboard with the chorus girls working the cords. Shoehorned into the existing material, Helen sang five numbers in two appearances atop a Steinway. Reviews were good. Business was even better, but Howard could not continue without controlling the *Hollywood Hotel* name.[8] A lengthy showgirl production number, "World's Fairest on Parade," provided the title for his stopgap, revamped tab unit.

During a press conference while on tour, Helen's ever-growing charm bracelet proved the hit of the day. New charms included a replica of the House of Morgan and a miniature of Helen in her famous pose atop a baby grand. As she was passing around her red, white, and gold cigarette case for the boys to see, one reporter admired it. Helen gave it to him.[9]

Able to bypass the title embargo overseas, Harry Howard booked the complete *Hollywood Hotel Revue* for a twenty-week tour of New Zealand, Australia, and South Africa.[10] Howard and the William Morris Agency wrangled over Helen's contract for several months, but ultimately, she stayed home. While Sydney enjoyed the production for eight weeks, business elsewhere was disastrous. The unit never made it to South Africa.

By 1936, Arthur Loew's prenuptial agreement had proved untenable for Barbara Smith, who filed for divorce, pleading, "I am a cast-off wife without money or support. I appeal for justice while he laughs and brands me as a gold digger and money gouger."[11] Once divorced, Arthur Loew married his secretary, Melita Schmitt. A year later, recuperating from yet another plane accident, Loew wrote to his old flame, "My little family here at the house have talked of you every day—and agree with me in all my raving about Helen."[12] Indicative of both Lulu's and Helen's feelings toward him, someone tore the letter in two. Another saved it.

Lulu never stopped hating Arthur Loew. While looking for property outside of Manhattan during the 1936 *Scandals* tour, Helen suggested a property in White Plains that overlooked Long Island Sound. The house offered a view of Loew's Glen Cove estate. Lulu vetoed the choice.[13]

Helen never got over Loew. When Mildred Zukor was out front during a Morgan nightclub performance, Helen would cry on her shoulder about how much she missed her Arthur. Mildred stoically endured the spectacle though she still blamed Helen for the ending of her marriage. Years later, when her son innocently named his son Morgan, Mildred was appalled. "You named my grandson after Helen Morgan?"[14]

After his Fifth Avenue Club ran its course, Billy Rose concentrated on producing, most notably for his lavish mounting of Rodgers and Hart's circus musical *Jumbo*. In 1938, "The Bantam Barnum" replicated his colossal Dallas venue, the Casa Mañana, in Manhattan. He acquired the Casino, home to the 1932 *Show Boat* revival, where he installed a triangular thrust and an inner circular stage that elevated while turning. Out front was his Palm Beach

Bar—complete with private cabanas, sunlamps, and attendants—which he advertised as "Vitamin D with swing music."[15]

He opened his Manhattan Casa with the world's fair–inspired revue *Let's Play Fair*. When Chorus Equity objected to the firing of a chorine and demanded an increase in the chorus's salary from thirty-five dollars a week to the union minimum of forty dollars, Rose insisted that the Casa was a nightclub, not a theater. To prove his point, on April 2, 1938, he signed with the American Federation of Actors (AFA), marking the first time a New York nightspot employed an all-union cast. The AFA was an odd alternative. Six months before, during Helen's tenure at the Hollywood, the AFA also objected to a chorine who was paid five dollars less than the forty-dollar union minimum. When the Hollywood fired the lass, the union demanded a two-week severance package. Sophie Tucker, AFA president, brokered a deal, saving the cast, including Helen, the ordeal of going on strike.

AFA contract in hand, Rose fired his chorus, which included Van Johnson, with no union repercussions. Going forward, he hired only name acts. On May Day, 1,220 witnessed Rose's *Streamlined Varieties*, New York's first real vaudeville since the Palace hosted its last two-a-day five years before.[16] Helen's new numbers, "Please Be Kind" and "Joseph, Joseph," failed to please, but her comic banter with emcee Lou Holtz clicked, as did the finale, when she joined Holtz, dancer Harriett Hoctor, and Vincent Lopez in a medley of the songs that started their careers. A sentimental souvenir of the Roaring Twenties, Helen came off best in a strong bill. The Casa grossed $80,000 during the first two weeks of its new format. Rose extended the bill.

After a 1930 work injury forced an early retirement, Tom Morgan and his family moved to Chicago. He died on July 5, 1938, after a two-week illness. Helen likely never again spoke to her stepfather after he saw her in *Show Boat* in 1933, and although she was playing Chez Paree at the time, she did not attend his funeral. She did, however, send an extravagant floral arrangement to adorn her stepfather's coffin in Danville, 140 miles away.[17]

For years, Helen dreamed of retiring, buying a goat farm, and becoming a cheese maker. In 1938, she cashed in a $25,000 life insurance policy and purchased an eighty-three-acre farm in High Falls, New York, seventy-five miles upstate.[18] The land would provide Lulu with security should Helen die first. To secure the investment, fifteen years after the fact, Lulu sued Frank Payne for divorce. When Helen's attorneys failed to reach and serve Payne with the complaint at Rochester's Seneca Hotel, his last known place of residence, Judge Charles A. Williams declared Payne legally dead.[19] Unbeknownst to them, Payne had moved to Manhattan in 1924 and died of complications from diabetes on March 16, 1938.[20] The Widder Morgan was truly a widow at last.

The Morgans moved upstate on Labor Day weekend. Included with the purchase were twenty-one head of cattle and fifty white leghorn chickens. Helen planned to hire seasonal help to grow crops and to raze and replace the single-room farmhouse with a homestead capable of lodging multiple guests. As a housewarming gift, millionaire playboy and former Mr. Constance Bennett, Phil Plant, gave her two prized black-satin chickens.[21] Frank "Bring 'em Back Alive" Buck, the husband of benefactor Amy Leslie, gifted two baby goats, Sunny and Sammy. He also provided his former secretary, Gloria Swanson (not the film diva), and her sisters Olga and Lillian.[22] With the siblings on hand to keep Lulu company, Helen felt less guilt-ridden when she took to the road.

Best of all, while on the farm, Helen drank less.

On September 21, while playing a split week of vaudeville at Providence's Fays Theatre, the worst New England hurricane of the century struck Rhode Island's capital head on. During the overture for the supper show, the electricity failed. Stage management lit candles in front of the footlight reflectors to illuminate the stage. Ross Wyse Jr., the show's emcee, improvised a bit on the weather, then got the audience of 150 to join in a sing-along while the orchestra faked an accompaniment in the dark.

As the storm raged outside, Helen curled up in front of the footlights while Wyse lay in front, shining a flashlight in her face. Cheekily, she cooed, "If It Rains, Who Cares." By the end of her turn, the stage-door alley was flooded. House manager Sam Kaufman ordered everyone to wait out the storm upstairs in the balcony. Downstairs, water poured into the theater and onto the stage through the side doors. The crew scrambled to save scenery, props, and wardrobe. They failed to save the contents of Helen's dressing room: "My belongings just floated away."[23]

When the waters subsided, everyone left Fays in safety.

During a rehearsal for a return to the Casa Mañana, Holtz introduced Helen, who came out, trailing a handkerchief behind her. She sang "Bill" as beautifully as she had hundreds of times before and then turned to make her exit—and fell flat on her face. Believing that Helen had tripped on the hem of her long white gown, singer Betty Hutton rushed to her aid, but bandleader Vincent Lopez pulled her aside and whispered, "Betty, leave it alone. She's a drunk."[24]

Betty knew the horror of drink firsthand from her alcoholic mother. Ignoring Lopez, she entered Helen's dressing room to find a cornered animal, not Helen Morgan. Hugging her tightly, Betty assured her that everything would turn out fine. Helen begged Betty to keep an eye on her to help control her drinking. Hutton happily obliged.

Helen's billing slipped to fifth place behind Lou Holtz, the dance team Veloz and Yolanda, Benny Fields, and Abbott and Costello. Helen's risqué repartee with emcee Lou Holtz went over big, and critics still lauded her singing, but they balked not just at her new repertoire but also at her refusal to use her piano perch.

Busy preparing for the Christmas-night opening of his more traditional Diamond Horseshoe nightclub, Rose left well enough alone at the Casa, with the result that Helen and her colleagues worked seven weeks instead of the usual two. Four weeks into the run, when Veloz and Yolanda left, Helen graduated to second billing, before dropping to third during the last week of the stand.[25]

Rose configured his outgoing show into a tab unit, which played the Newark Shubert for the lucrative year-end week. Joining Helen were Holtz, Abbott, Costello, Hutton, and, new to the company, Ann Miller. Helen still turned heads, and, outside of the city, the reaction to her varied musical program, including "You Go to My Head," was favorable. Business was heavy all week.[26]

Despite Betty Hutton's eagle eye, which helped Helen function for two months, Rose never again employed the girl who started his nightclub career.

Rose also tired of the Casa, which, following a string of underperforming bills, he closed in May 1939. Lew Brown acquired the space, which he operated as the French Casino. The building, later converted into a Woolworth's, was razed in 1990.

During the long stand, Helen moved back into town. Her duplex, at 494 Hudson Street, boasted a balcony that encircled the living room below. When word got out that she was living in Greenwich Village, fans, almost daily, stole the handwritten placard she placed to identify her mailbox.[27] A year later, economizing further, Helen subleased the duplex and moved a few blocks away, to 74 Bank Street.[28]

~

During a belated Christmas celebration at the farm, Lulu added a thoroughbred cow to her daughter's growing menagerie of livestock.[29] Having abandoned the idea of producing goat cheese, the Morgans supplied the Stork Club with pedigreed, custom-marked Helen Morgan eggs.[30]

Helen returned to Chez Paree as a replacement booking for Lupe Vélez. Libby Holman offered competition at the Colony Club, but Helen drew in the crowds for seven weeks, although her heart was not in her work.[31] The *Billboard* warned that Helen's "indifference to the caliber of her performances [would] endanger her standing."[32] At $2,500 a week, the booking marked her final big-money contract—and her final work for Mike Fritzel. With six stands covering 214 days, Helen was second only to Harry Richman as the top-booked Chez Paree act of the 1930s.

In March, Helen joined the Campbell Playhouse's radio dramatization of the *Show Boat* novel. Margaret Sullavan was Magnolia. Edna Ferber herself read Parthy. Orson Welles narrated, played Andy, and did almost everything else. By eliminating the character of Steve Baker, Welles sidestepped the thorny issue of miscegenation. On his *Show Boat*, racial integration was enough to send Julie packing. Fumbled cues made Helen's intoxication obvious to all, but her performance, particularly of Stephen Foster's "Why No One to Love," is extremely poignant. The Campbell Playhouse marked her final network performance.

Helen struck a blow for feminism when she joined Sophie Tucker, Hildegarde, Joan Davis, Josephine Huston, Faith Bacon, Tamara, and the Frazee

Helen Morgan, second only to Harry Richman as the top-booked act at Chicago's Chez Paree during the 1930s. (Author's collection)

Sisters to become the first women to play the Friars' Club annual frolic. Helen worked the event the following year, on March 10, 1940, marking her final appearance on a Broadway stage.

In 1939, Rena Cournyn became Helen's new gal Friday. Born in 1919 in Washington, DC, to World War I veteran John J. and Hildegarde Cournyn, Rena was fatherless at age twelve and a troubled teenager soon after. In 1938, she met Helen during the *World's Fairest* DC stop. When a friend remarked that her resemblance to Helen was so uncanny that she might as well be her daughter, Rena moved to New York and leaned on her "mother's" name to find work. Helen went along with the gag, and the two, as Helen and Rena Morgan, headed out West.

Before a sold-out opening-night crowd at Marcel Lamaze's Hollywood club, Helen's encores alone constituted a typical Morgan set. She repeated "Bill" multiple times. The film colony never got enough of her signature tune. One night, the continued shouts of "My Bill!" from George Brent and others forced her to stop and, with a twinkle in her eye, warn, "That's what you'll all wind up with, you know."[33]

Helen held over a week. Had she not been expected upstate, she would have extended.

While in San Francisco, Rena was stricken with appendicitis. At Helen's request, orchestra leader Ted Lewis accompanied Rena on the flight south and into Wilshire Hospital, where noted Los Angelino surgeon Frank Nolan performed the appendectomy.[34] Helen paid the tab. When she closed in the Bay Area, Helen flew to Los Angeles and into Nolan's arms. She enjoyed his company for only a few days before flying east, but the two provided fodder for gossip columnists for over a year.[35]

Recovered and starting her own career, Rena stayed behind in Los Angeles.

A. B. Marcus and N. S. Barger's *A Night in the Moulin Rouge* was no cheap revue. Bankrolled at $150,000, the cast numbered 150 (95 percent women). Helen signed for a four- to six-month tour, with the hope of a Broadway run after the New York World's Fair (which surprisingly killed rather than buoyed Broadway attendance) closed.

Natalie Komarova handled the dances. George Komaroff wrote and conducted the nominal score. Designer and director Jean Le Seyeux, formerly of the *Folies Begère*, created a continental experience on a Parisian timetable:

open the doors at 10:00 p.m. as Rita Rio and her All-Girl Orchestra supplied dance music, start the revue at 10:30 p.m., and after the curtain descended at 1:30 a.m., end with a half hour of social dancing. In Davenport, Iowa. On a Thursday night. Exacerbating matters, on October 2, the revue premiered a full hour late. It almost never opened. A month after Germany's invasion of Poland, Buster Shaver, followed by Toby Wing, Ada Leonard, Helen, and the rest of the company, refused to sing George M. Cohan's "Over There" during the flag-waving finale. They rebelled against the inference that America would become embroiled in another European war. To end the standoff, Le Seyeux let the cast sing, "We'll stay right here 'till it's over, over there."[36]

One critic declared that the premiere performance "was as co-ordinated as King Levinsky in the 15th round."[37] There was no continuity, pace, or even structure. Toby Wing's comic striptease failed to impress. While troubled, the show was not hopeless. Grisha and Brona earned good notices for their dances, one in cellophane and, later, one as gilded Buddhas.[38] The slave-girl number clicked, as did the windmill and the "Voices in the Dark" sequences.[39] Costuming was extremely effective.

Poor lighting undermined Helen's turn, which, like others, seemed out of place among all the bare flesh. Helen had other worries. Hired solely for marquee value, she made a single eight-minute appearance before the first-act finale to sing four *Show Boat* numbers. During the "Over There" contretemps, Maureen Englin went backstage to wish her pal luck. Helen pulled out a small bottle, saying, "I would offer you a drink, but this is all they'll let me have until the end of the act."[40] The production team later prolonged her agony by moving her turn after intermission.

The following evening, the show bowed in Des Moines, also an hour late. When the curtain fell, the exhausted cast chose not to take a curtain call. Within ten days, management axed the continental schedule, with its pre- and postshow dancing, and reduced the running time from four hours to two. In late October, they scaled back the top ticket price from $3.30 to $2.75 and let Toby Wing and Rita Rio go. Wing retired. Rita Rio, born Rita Novella, moved to Hollywood, where, as Dona Drake, she brightened *The Road to Morocco*, *Louisiana Purchase*, *Let's Face It*, and other films.

Bad luck continued to plague the production. The special train used to transport the show struggled to meet its daunting schedule. Arriving in Denver two hours late, stagehands were still loading in at curtain time. While striving to titillate tired businessmen, the racy print advertisements incensed bluenoses, whose outcry forced the company to cancel a two-show stand in

Eugene, Oregon, and pressured Seattle's mayor to ban the show from the town's Civic Auditorium. Instead, it played at the privately owned Music Hall Theatre—and dropped a performance.

In San Francisco, *A Night in the Moulin Rouge* competed with the *Folies Bergère*. A midnight show on October 29 for the University of Southern California and University of California football teams helped, but the grosses told the story: *Folies Bergère* $34,200; *A Night in the Moulin Rouge*, $13,000. When a reviewer reports that a Great Dane mistook the painted fire hydrant on a drop for the real thing, something is wrong.[41]

To minimize damage, Marcus and Barger reduced the Bay Area run from sixteen days to ten. With no pickup dates, the show endured a nine-day hiatus, during which Helen visited Los Angeles and partied at the It Café with Frank Nolan. When asked to honor the patrons with a song, she gave them a free concert.[42]

Helen, again, battled a cold while the show limped through the Southwest. Then during Thanksgiving week, the production managed only a paltry $8,000 take at Chicago's Grand Opera House. Making matters worse, Helen and fellow cast members Ada Leonard, Stan Kavanagh, and the Slate Brothers faced the ire of the Theatre Authority for playing an unauthorized Chicago benefit.

Management scuttled full-week bookings for St. Louis and New Orleans and downsized into a tab unit that resumed in 1940 with Helen, thankfully, trimmed.[43] She remained diplomatic: "It had a lot of good things in it. But it started off on the wrong foot and just kept bumbling along."[44] Some audiences cheered the chance to experience Helen in the flesh, but those who paid to see strippers cared little for the overdressed Helen.[45]

Successful 1930s revues were sophisticated and satirical. *A Night in the Moulin Rouge* was neither. For months afterward, critics held it up as the gold standard of theatrical flops.[46]

Helen kept as many as thirty gowns for work. Not one cost less than $250. Some she designed herself; some she imported from Paris. "Your success has a great deal to do with the appearance you make. So I don't think I'm eccentric when I spend so much on clothes, or when I wear a gown that is at least two years advanced in style from what the average woman wears."[47] Perhaps, but her couture doggedly evoked nostalgia. For the opening of a holiday stand at Boston's Club Mayfair, she wore a "filmy white gown, shot with silver and capped with little shoulder wings, which made her look like a life-size doll, the kind whose eyes open and shut."[48]

Regardless of the label, she rarely paid more than ten dollars for a hat, but her weakness for furs continued unabated. Bored with the silver fox she purchased during the 1936 *Scandals* tour, she dropped $10,000 on a white mink, trimmed in sables, which caught her eye in a New York window.

In 1940, the work slowed to a trickle. One booking was as a last-minute substitution for Benny Fields at the Famous Door, a swing club in a Fifty-Second Street basement. Helen feared that people would find her act as dated as bathtub gin, but even in a second-rate joint, her homecoming was an event: Ethel Merman, Dorothy Lamour, Marie Wilson, Patsy Kelly, Gracie Barrie, and Iris Adrian paid their respects on opening night.[49] The intimate space proved tailor-made for her. Twice a night, when she sang "I Hadn't Anyone Since You," the jitterbugging stopped.

Beginning with Ziegfeld's death in 1932, and exacerbated by her life-threatening illness in 1935, Helen's natural joy of living came into conflict with periods of depression after she descended from her piano. By 1940, with her career in tatters, the Morgan melancholy proved hard to shake. "I guess they won't keep me for more than a couple of weeks," she said. "I guess maybe I'm not good enough for more than a couple of weeks." Thanks to the Fields contretemps, Helen extended, but not happily. "I want to finish with the nightclubs. I hate them. I want to stop singing. I hate the smoky tiny places. I hate the life. There's no excitement in it anymore. I can't get any feeling out of it and it's no good."[50]

She shared her Famous Door dressing room with Carlotta Dale, whom Helen, true to form, mothered. On opening night, while she sat next to Helen, a waiter reached to turn up Dale's champagne glass. A tiny hand stopped him.

"You are not to drink," Helen warned the youngster. "You see what's happened to me?"

Years later, Dale still regretted not having the nerve to plead, "Why don't you stop now?"[51]

At one benefit, Helen ran into Lillian Roth, to whom she announced her impending death. Roth protested, but Helen shrugged. "The doctor said the lining of my tummy is gone."[52] In 1946, Roth discovered Alcoholics Anonymous. Founded in 1935, the group did not become widely known until the publication of its eponymous book in 1939. AA helped Roth battle her addiction but never had a chance to save Helen.

In May, Norma Terris, Paul Robeson, and Helen reprised their *Show Boat* roles for the Los Angeles Civic Opera Festival. When Helen sang "Can't

Help Lovin' Dat Man" in the cavernous Philharmonic, she might as well not have opened her mouth. She redeemed herself later with "Bill." Too wobbly to climb atop the piano, she leaned against the proscenium instead and brought the proceedings to a standstill with an ovation few present ever witnessed again.[53] Regardless, when John Latham visited backstage, he found Helen sobbing, "They won't take me to San Francisco."[54]

Producer Edwin Lester fired the woman who *was* Julie.

Compounding the misery, waiting at the farm upon Helen's return was word from Danville that Lulu's father, Shadrach Lang, had died.

She popped into Manhattan for short stays to make the rounds, but even offseason club work in Florida proved elusive.[55] She jumped at a fortnight's booking for Detroit's Bowery Café. When a scheduling error reduced the stand to a single week, they offered Helen a week at the Grey Wolf Tavern in Masury, Ohio, as a consolation. She took it.

In September, Harry Howard prematurely announced Helen for a tour of Northeast and Midwest film houses in his *Hollywood Hotel* tab revue, this time anchoring a lengthy medley paying tribute to Ziegfeld.[56] Howard's contract proved so insulting that Helen returned instead to playing one-night stands. One offered her $450 and top billing to close the first act of a benefit show. Producer A. S. Cole promised to post Helen's check at least three days before the event. On September 24, when there was no check and inquiries to Cole went unanswered, the William Morris Agency called Helen to advise her to cancel the gig. She had already headed by car to Richmond, Virginia, where she was shocked to learn that the benefit was for the Ku Klux Klan. Being a professional—and broke—Helen posed for press shots, granted interviews, and appeared on local radio on the day of the show. When she asked for her salary, Cole promised to pay her backstage before the performance.

Only four hundred of the local chapter's eleven thousand members (sans sheets per Virginia law) attended the event. Helen refused to go on until she received payment, which Cole promised during the second half. She replied, "Fine. That's when I'll go on."[57] Intermission came and went, as did Cole and the money for all of the performers. It was the *Frivolities* all over again. Leonard K. Trout, of the National Theatrical Agency, provided the stranded acts their salaries and traveling expenses. Unwilling to wait, Helen returned to the farm $120 in the red for her traveling expenses but with the satisfaction of knowing that she had refused to sing for the Klan.

~

In November, Helen opened a four-week engagement in El Cerrito, California. One night, she soldiered through despite excruciating abdominal pain. The next day she collapsed in her hotel room. Some reports described her hospitalization as being for "an infection of the respiratory tract"; others wrote it was related to an "intestinal ailment."[58] Lou Hood sugarcoated the news for Lulu. "Helen just had a little bit of that old illness . . . and the doctor gave her a shot of something that he wasn't supposed to and knocked her out, so we had to take her to the hospital and give her just a little bit of oxygen—no tent like the darn papers said."[59] Lulu wasn't fooled.

Helen's condition stabilized, but only after she was "given up as dead for a period of thirty minutes."[60] To battle her megaloblastic anemia, her doctors advised her to have her spleen removed—and to take a long rest. "Can't do it," she said. "There's work to be done and money just has to be made."[61] She couldn't stop: couldn't stop drinking, couldn't stop moving, and couldn't stop making, spending, and giving away money.

While she was being discharged, Helen's check bounced. Shamed-faced, she paid in cash.

Helen returned to work at the Rancho San Pablo, where, on November 23, she witnessed a gambling raid. The men found nothing at Rancho San Pablo but did at a dozen other niteries, including the El Rio, where she worked a month later. Helen hated the life more each day.

The Morgan melancholy deepened into fatalism. She philosophized, "When you know that you are going to die, life becomes very sweet. I'm glad I lived it as fully as I have . . . I've loved one man deeply and been hurt by love. Maybe if I can go on cheating death, I may meet someone. . . . If that happens I'll really fight to live."[62]

She did, and she did. His name was Lloyd Johnson, a $160-a-month Oakland dock clerk who sold used cars on the side. They met at a racetrack. "I took one look at him and then my heart stood still. He won all his bets that day, and me too."[63] Within a month of their meeting, the couple announced that, after another year on the road, including a proposed South American tour, Helen would retire to play Mrs. Lloyd Johnson full time.

Johnson abandoned the docks. As Helen's manager, he took over the day-to-day operation of Helen Morgan Enterprises, a personalized recording outfit Helen, her accompanist, "Uncle" Lou Hood, and Charles Goodman had incorporated the previous December.[64] Helen would cut a recording—with a personalized dedication—of a favorite song (as long as it was "Bill," "Make Believe," "Can't Help Lovin' Dat Man," "Why Do I Love You?," "Why

Was I Born?," "Don't Ever Leave Me," "When I Grow Too Old to Dream," and "The Little Things You Used to Do") as a gift or souvenir.

In February, Johnson drove Helen and Lou Hood six days cross-country to Miami. Martha Raye and Peggy Fears, each appearing in competing nightclubs, visited Jack Dempsey's Pago-Pago Room between their sets to witness Helen in action. A one-week stay extended to three. A subsequent extension at the Boston Versailles forced her to postpone, and then cancel, a Sunday-night guest shot in Willie Howard's Broadway revue *Crazy with the Heat*.[65]

When Johnson took over, he saved *everything*—from grocery receipts to room service checks. In his first ten weeks on the job, Helen grossed over $8,200. Her net after hotel and traveling expenses and accompanist and booking agent fees was considerably less, but it was still a marked improvement over the shape of the Morgan ship during the previous year.[66] Johnson explained, "She needs someone to take care of her and I'm going to see to it that she wins her way back to health."[67] Helen spent her off time in bed, downing milk and eggnog. She never stopped drinking completely, but Johnson succeeded where even Lulu had failed.

Unlike Buddy Maschke, Johnson was an adult. Despite being six years Helen's junior, she called him Pop. He provided a father figure she had not had since Ziegfeld.

More bookings came in. Fueling this comeback were the wars abroad, to which she responded by adding Kern and Hammerstein's "The Last Time I Saw Paris" to her act.[68] Helen's status as an icon of a happier, bygone era manifested itself in the many autographed photos that graced military barracks in the days leading up to Pearl Harbor.[69] Another factor was Columbia records: having acquired Brunswick's post-1931 catalog, in 1941, they rereleased the 1932 *Show Boat* album, which proved all but impossible to find when Helen played Chicago's Hi-Hat Club in May.[70]

Helen earned $1,000 a week at the Hi-Hat. The booking marked her first four-figured salary in well over a year.[71] To the positive, she still controlled her audience, demanding—and receiving—absolute silence, even during the rambunctious late show. To the negative, she remained vocally and physically weak and appeared bloated.[72]

At Milwaukee's Tic Toc Club, she worked with local accompanist Wladziu Valentino Liberace. He played to Helen's satisfaction but could not finish the set without sobbing. Neither Helen nor the management reprimanded him, but, shamefaced, he vowed to control his emotions. Finally, after completing the set dry-eyed, he proudly helped Helen off the piano and led her offstage, only to have her turn on him in uncommon fury.

"What are you trying to do," she brayed, "ruin my act?"[73]

One snag complicated the couple's happiness: Johnson was still married to Catharine Mulqueeny, a former Bay Area vaudeville dancer. In December 1940, weeks before meeting Helen, Johnson separated from his wife, leaving two young boys, Mark and Ronald, behind.

While Johnson settled his house, Helen publicly cut ties with Rena, whom the press still dubbed Rena Morgan or even Helen Morgan Jr. While Rena vowed to reject engagements that billed her as Helen's daughter, she continued to use the Morgan surname professionally.[74]

Upon obtaining his divorce, on July 27, Lloyd Johnson married Helen poolside at Dempsey's, during her phenomenally successful summertime engagement.[75] Some wags wanted her entrance music to be "Bill," but she walked in, conventionally, to the strains of Wagner's Wedding March, while unconventionally clad in blue slacks. The Dempsey band did supply a musical joke by playing "The Johnson Rag" during the cutting of the cake.[76] The couple refused publicity man Ray Redman's request to have them marry perched atop a Steinway, but as a compromise, they posed with their wedding cake while sitting on a piano. Dempsey's manager, Benny Gaines, secured revenge for the newlyweds by pushing Redman into the pool.[77]

Three days later, Helen opened at Jacksonville's Roosevelt Hotel with a grueling four-a-day performance schedule, including, for the first time in her career, a one o'clock lunchtime show. The room seated six hundred yet still did turn away business. Helen moved on to Atlanta's Henry Grady Hotel. During her opening performance, they called her back for three encores.[78]

The Johnsons abandoned a nightclub tour and its potential to break the $1,500-a-week ceiling in lieu of a year of steady employment at $700 per. Helen starred in *George White's Scandals of 1941*, a tab unit the impresario culled from the floorshow of his shuttered Gay White Way Club. Breaking in at the Atlantic City Hamid's Million-Dollar Pier, Helen, suffering from laryngitis, croaked out the choruses of "Bill" and "Make Believe" and encored with "Why Do I Love You?" The audience called for more, but she declined. Her material aside, White's score and sketches were new, but this *Scandals* was but a shadow of those that preceded it. Only a dozen girls appeared in the line, and White himself emceed via an offstage microphone.

Newlyweds Lloyd Johnson and Helen Morgan. (AP Photo)

While the troupe rehearsed in Minneapolis during a four-day hiatus between bookings, Helen underwent a fluoroscopy and metabolic treatment at Chicago's Bethany Hospital. Her high-fat and protein-rich diet had failed to alleviate her severe anemia.[79]

Helen rejoined the *Scandals* over Labor Day weekend to terrific business. Inspired by Johnson, she augmented her *Show Boat* standards with "The Man I Love." She also dug up "Tea for Two." Its lyric about raising a family resonated more than ever. Although they had not met, Helen telephoned Johnson's sons, promising them a wonderful life when the touring stopped and the four became a family.[80]

The *Scandals* opened at Chicago's State-Lake on September 12 with the film *Highway West*. Despite the heat, Helen wore a cardigan over her gown to ward off the chill. Playing hooky to catch Helen, schoolgirl Betty Howard sensed that something was wrong. "I kept applauding as she hobbled off; I didn't want to see a great star 'die' on stage. It was so tragic. I went home and cried."[81]

During the third show, Helen collapsed onstage. More than three thousand get-well cards, telegrams, and letters arrived at her bedside in Henrotin Hospital. Calls from well-wishers swamped the hospital switchboard.

Lulu traveled to Chicago to be at her daughter's bedside, prepared for the worst.

On September 18, Johnson gave his wife a blood transfusion. Within a week, she received three more, one courtesy of a fan whom she treated to dinner and a show during a previous Chicago visit and another from nightclub singer Marie Austin. Helen grew stronger, even whispering to Johnson, "I'm going to lick this."[82]

The mystery and pageantry of Roman Catholicism forever fascinated Helen. Holy Name Cathedral, the site of her first wedding, organized the Catholic Actors' Guild of Chicago in 1935. In May 1941, she failed to appear at the annual guild event. After the disappointed guests left the Drake Hotel, Helen rushed in, crying, "I just couldn't make it."[83] In September, when Holy Name received the call for help, Father Emmett T. Regan hurried to Henrotin, and Helen converted. After the baptism, Regan administered Holy Communion and the last rites. Spiritually fortified, on September 25, she underwent surgery to remove her spleen, the procedure she should have undergone a year before.[84]

Initially, Helen rallied, then, twenty-four hours or so after the operation, her condition deteriorated. On September 30, her stomach began to hemorrhage, something additional transfusions failed to stabilize. Later that day, she slipped into a coma from which she never awoke. Within a week, her doctors gave up hope. On October 8, Helen received her fourteenth transfusion, but there was no change in her condition.[85] Lulu, Johnson, her uncle Robert and aunt Elsie Dillon, and a few friends, including the Swanson sisters, gathered around her bed.[86] At 11:28 p.m., the light of the torchbearer went out forever.[87]

Epilogue

Broadway's Patron Saint

Texas Guinan's death, in November 1933, anticipated the end of Prohibition. Helen, passing two months before Pearl Harbor, foretold a new, sobering era. Walter Scharf hoped never to experience anything like Helen's death again.[1] To her mourners, she should have gone on forever, shielded from life's horrors by the gentle haze of Hennessy's Three Star.

In Chicago, five thousand attended her viewing. The next day, six hundred prayed the Requiem Mass at Saint Francis Xavier Church in nearby La Grange and witnessed her interment in Holy Sepulchre Cemetery. Elsie Dillon and Vida McTigue could not console their sister. Lulu keened, "She was always laughing and now she laughs no more."[2]

On October 13, at the Theatre Authority's annual benefit, Dolly Kay, standing by the vacant table Helen reserved, sang "Bill."[3] Ten days later, the Cleveland Orchestra premiered Artur Rodzinski's "Serenade for Orchestra." Kern did not commission the twenty-two-minute suite of his *Show Boat* score with Helen in mind, but her memory haunted the performance.[4]

A month after her passing, the *Scandals* company, playing Davenport, Iowa, attended a "mind mass" for Helen while, in Manhattan, New Yorkers paid their respects at a High Mass at Saint Malachy's, the Actors' Chapel.[5] On October 8, 1942, Annie Hart attended Helen's anniversary mass at the chapel and returned for subsequent annual memorials throughout the decade.

An anonymous admirer arranged to have fresh flowers placed weekly at Helen's grave.[6] The floral tribute continued unabated for more than a year, but six years passed before well-wishers funded a rust-colored marble cross with the inscription "Our Helen Morgan" to mark her grave.[7]

~

Lulu Morgan inherited the farm in High Falls, New York. (Author's collection)

Helen did *not* die penniless. She left Lulu the High Falls farm mortgage-free.

Helen *did* die $5,000 in debt.

When Helen slipped into a coma and word spread, offers to aid Mrs. Johnson had poured in from around the country. Joe E. Lewis walked into the Chicago branch of the Theatre Authority, laid $200 on Max Halperin's desk, and said, "I knew Helen well. If you need any more, call on me."[8] The generosity comforted Lulu but embarrassed Johnson. He insisted that the gifts were not charity but a tribute to the years of assistance Helen had bestowed on others. Johnson's frustration was compounded by the fact that, a day after his wife entered Henrotin, he went to the State-Lake to grab Helen's sable scarf and silver fox coat and found her trunk empty.

George White was less generous. Theaters paid tab units a flat rate and pocketed any overage. Had White, whom the State-Lake paid in full, paid

Helen for the week and not just for the one day she played, Johnson could have settled the $527 hospital bill outright. Johnson and the American Guild of Variety Artists filed a complaint against White. Unable to backfill his star attraction, White converted his *Scandals* into a "best of" cavalcade, which theater owners nonetheless refused to book because of White's misdeeds. The *Scandals* closed in April 1942, and White filed for bankruptcy protection, listing $100,000 in liabilities and assets of $500—and a Rolls-Royce.[9]

The American Guild of Variety Artists paid off the medical bills, but Helen's estate still swam in debt. Johnson relinquished his claim, making Lulu the sole executor and beneficiary.

Within days of her death, Victor released the first Helen Morgan album, comprising eight of the twelve sides she cut for the label. Despite their popularity, Victor never remitted any royalties. Conversely, through 1950, Helen's estate earned $2,000 in residuals for the 1932 *Show Boat* album, which Columbia has kept available, almost continuously, since 1941.

In time, Buddy repaid an $850 loan from Helen to the estate, and John Wanamaker's, Marshall Field's, and other merchants settled for a payout of ten cents on the dollar. In December 1953, the estate settled. Lulu walked away with an inheritance of $113.45.[10]

During the war, Lulu leased out acreage in lieu of working the farm. With Helen's old *Show Boat* understudy Eleanor Tierney, she shared a Bronx apartment and operated a newspaper/ticket booth at 21 East Fifty-Second Street.[11] After the war, Lulu met Charles Adams, a widower from West Nyack and ten years her junior. They married on August 27, 1948, in nearby Rosendale in a Catholic ceremony.[12]

Lulu sold the Morgan homestead.

Within days of Helen's death, Paramount announced that Robert Sisk would produce a Morgan biopic in early 1942, possibly with Dorothy Lamour or Mary Martin in the lead role. Over at 20th Century Fox, Mark Hellinger pitched his own project for Alice Faye. MGM also expressed interest. The obstacle: Lulu's $100,000 asking price for Helen's life story. Fox and Paramount also lacked access to the *Show Boat* songs, which MGM acquired in 1938.[13]

Ultimately, Warners prevailed. Cash-strapped, in May 1942, Lulu accepted a check for just $5,000.[14] For the five-year length of the agreement, she granted Warner Brothers permission to dramatize the lives of both Helen and herself but forbade them from showing or referring to Helen adopting a child or giving birth. The studio purchased "Melancholy Baby" as a prospective title tune but also negotiated with Metro for the Kern-Hammerstein tunes. Following the project to Warner, Hellinger joined with Sidney Skolsky to develop an outline. Herman Mankiewicz and, later, Charles Hoffman worked on a screenplay before the project stalled.[15]

After the contract expired in 1947, others expressed interest. Bill Burton, Helen Forrest's manager, offered both singer and script for a dramatic biography either as a stage musical or for 20th Century-Fox.[16] Instead, Fox purchased *Don't Ever Leave Me*, a treatment that Irving Hoffman's brother Leonard devised and of which Lulu approved. Leonard joined attorney Greg Bautzer and Joseph Rifkin to form the Carthay Company, which put forth Dorothy Lamour as Helen and Fay Bainter as Lulu as a lure to secure financing.[17] Nope. Two years later, Howard Welsch, Chester Erskine, and A. Pam Blumenthal acquired the property for Fidelity, a Republic Pictures unit, casting Paulette Goddard as Helen.[18] The project stalled again.

Warners ignored Lulu's five-year clause and revisited the project in the 1950s, sifting through as many titles as casting options—from *The Girl on the Piano* to *Why Was I Born?* to *The Jazz Age*.[19]

While shooting *A Star Is Born*, Judy Garland was Warner Brothers' choice to play Helen. Judy first navigated Helen's oeuvre as a child, singing "Bill" atop a Steinway in her family's vaudeville act.[20] At the time of her dismissal from MGM, she was earmarked for Julie in their *Show Boat* remake.[21]

In the spring of 1956, Kim Novak seemed a go, but script delays resulted in her slipping through the studio's fingers. Others on the Warners short-list were Julie Andrews, Joan Collins, Peggy Connolly, Ava Gardner, Rita Hayworth, Audrey Hepburn, Grace Kelly, Peggy King, Peggy Lee, Julie London, Elizabeth Taylor, and Jane Wyman.[22]

After Michael Curtiz signed on as director, the search reached a fever pitch that rivaled the hunt for Scarlett O'Hara a generation before. Over its fifteen-year history, reportedly, three hundred hopefuls interviewed for the part of Helen Morgan.[23] Curtiz himself tested more than thirty women, including Patti Page, Keely Smith, Julie London, and Ann Bancroft, before returning to Ann Blyth, who, as a teen, earned an Oscar nomination in his *Mildred Pierce*.[24]

Joe Breen gunned for a swishy interior decorator character in one screenplay submission and rejected another script where, unable to have the married man she loves, Helen finds solace in the bottle and in multiple encounters with other men.[25] In response, the studio suggested its writers shoehorn a few

Morgan facts into preexisting plots—like *Carmen* (the femme fatale who destroys the man she loves), *The Judy Garland Story* (out of control offstage, Helen is truthful only when she sings), *Trilby* (Helen must escape the Svengali who made and controls her), *All About Eve* (Helen drinks to forget the people she climbed over on her way to the top), *A Streetcar Named Desire* (a broken-down Helen must confront herself), and yes, even Helen Morgan as *Camille*.[26]

The nine-week shoot commenced on January 24, 1957.[27] Apart from showing Helen singing torch songs atop pianos in speakeasies and playing Julie in *Show Boat*, the $1.4 million production ignores its subject, concentrating on a fictitious Morgan love triangle with a bootlegger (Paul Newman) and society lawyer Richard Carlson (Russell Wade). Cameos from Rudy Vallée and Walter Winchell gave the film period authenticity, as did Jimmy McHugh, who accompanied the screen Helen on his songs "I Can't Give You Anything but Love" and "The Sunny Side of the Street." *Show Boat* alum Sammy White played a speakeasy waiter. Curtiz planned cameos from Joe E. Lewis, Joe Frisco, Harry Richman, and the Duncan Sisters, but these went unfilmed.

Another thorn in Warners' side was Lloyd Johnson. In 1950, the studio dismissed his demand for screenplay approval. Then, in 1957, attorney Nathan Cohn threatened that, having acquired the film rights to Helen's life from her widower, a firm called Jamdow Enterprises would produce its own biopic.[28]

Three months before the cameras rolled, Lulu reminded Warners that their contract had expired. She demanded the return of the scrapbooks she lent the studio to research its subject.[29] She had also sold the television rights to the CBS anthology series *Playhouse 90*.[30] Warners offered the network $10,000, as well as the services of contract players Tab Hunter and Natalie Wood for a future *Playhouse 90* production, to shelve the project.[31] CBS suggested Warner Brothers renegotiate with Lulu. Ultimately, Warners rode the wake the teledrama left behind and, after briefly renaming their opus *Both Ends of the Candle*, released their project as *The Helen Morgan Story*.[32]

Polly Bergen had been in the running for the Warners biopic as early as 1952 and became the heir apparent between Garland's and Novak's attachment to the project. In 1955, she included a Morgan set while playing the Plaza's Persian Room. Lulu caught her act and congratulated Polly for working like Helen: approaching the songs as an actor. The seed planted, Bergen furnished Lulu's $10,000 asking price and sold the project, and herself, to CBS.[33]

Polly Bergen confers with Lulu in preparation for the Playhouse 90 version of *The Helen Morgan Story*. (Courtesy of Everett Collection)

A chronic nail-biter, Bergen cultivated her hands to evoke the perfection of her subject's. Further melding with Helen, she recorded an album of Morgan standards, six of which she sang live on the telecast.

Enthusiasm quickly turned to fear that Bergen would also sensationalize Helen's demons. Few of those closest to the Morgans aided Bergen and her writer, Leonard Spigelgass, with their research.[34] Lulu preemptively announced that she had not authorized the television script and was prepared to sue for libel should she find the program objectionable.[35]

This last live *Playhouse 90* production offered a largely factual, if telescoped, checklist of Helen's milestones. Large sections of the ninety-minute program concerned Baby Helen and the inability of anyone, even Lulu (Sylvia Sidney), to prevent Helen's alcoholic tailspin. Like Warner Brothers, *Playhouse 90* avoided libel by fictionalizing the men in Helen's life. Robert Lowery's Roy Paterson filled in for Arthur Loew. The Bobby Talbot of Ronnie Burns represented the youthfulness of Buddy Maschke without the unsavory aspects of their brief union. James Westerfeld played Helen's father as Frank *Piggin*. Hoagy Carmichael appeared as Helen's early champion and accompanist,

Helen was never as down-and-out as Ann Blyth in Warner Brothers' *The Helen Morgan Story*. (Courtesy of Everett Collection)

who would have saved her if only she had let him: in short, a composite of Johnson, Alter, Lou Hood, and Irving Hoffman.

Lulu lauded Bergen's performance, but Irving Hoffman complained that the program failed to paint a complete portrait of Broadway's most beloved character. Criticism that the TV program was too one-note about Helen's problems subsided after people viewed the penultimate scene in the Warner Brothers film: Blyth is strapped to a bed in a detox center, a delirium-trembling wreck, more Neely O'Hara than Helen Morgan. British censors found the sequence so distasteful that they cut it, along with shots of Paul Newman slapping Ann Blyth.

In Helen's hometown, the Chicago Theatre pulled the Warners film because of poor business. Lulu considered suing for libel, complaining that she had signed away the rights to dramatize *her* story and not that of her daughter, not to mention that Warners had produced its film under an expired contract.[36]

Polly Bergen won an Emmy Award as Best Actress for the *Playhouse 90* production.

Ann Blyth's lyric soprano graced several MGM operettas, but Warners engaged Gogi Grant to ghost *The Helen Morgan Story* vocals, perpetuating the myth of the husky torch singer.

That myth began with the second Broadway revival of *Show Boat*. The success of the 1940 Civic Opera production prompted interest in a Broadway revival, but five years passed before the dream became reality. For Julie, Oscar cast Carol Bruce from a pool of five hundred who auditioned, although he first expressed interest in the alto in 1942, and she played the role in Los Angeles in 1944. Playing the Ziegfeld, the house where the 1927 cast made history, intimidated the new cast, none more so than Bruce. In preparation, she collected clippings, stills, anecdotes—anything to do with Helen's take on Julie. After much debate, Hammerstein kept Bruce atop the upright to sing "Bill." On opening night, January 1, 1946, Bruce sensed "such an electric current. . . . The theater actually vibrated. That was my Hour of Trial—as if I were walking up to the execution block." She understood why Helen remained seated. "From that height you can only barely see the first two rows or so of people, and the height gives you a kind of feeling of aloneness that seems to help in putting over a pathetic song—it's almost as if you were sitting there reminiscing to yourself."[37]

Lightning struck twice. Bruce brought down the house.

In those pre–Tony Award days, the revival won five Donaldson Awards: Musical, Score, Book, Lyrics, and Supporting Actress, Carol Bruce.[38]

Bruce's performance changed Julie forever. In the pre-microphone days, producers cast sopranos in musical roles: their voices carried better in unamplified houses. Helen's delicate vocalism lent itself perfectly to her characterization of a fragile belle who falls victim to the sociopolitical system of the post-Reconstruction South. Bruce, and later Ava Gardner, played Julie as an earthy broad. While more faithful to Ferber's creation, these women elicited audience sympathy but never elevated Julie to the level of tragedy that Helen played so powerfully.

Lena Horne seems the obvious Julie for the post-Morgan generation. MGM cast her in the lengthy *Show Boat* section of the 1946 Jerome Kern biopic, *Till the Clouds Roll By*, where she sang "Can't Help Lovin' Dat Man" solo, the only person on camera. This common practice allowed local censors in the segregated South to clip African American performances without disturbing the rest of the film. Even outside the South, Hollywood dared not reveal that the man Horne loved was white. Consequently, when MGM remade *Show Boat* in 1951, they never considered Horne for the role. MGM faced a trickier racial quagmire: Breen rejected the 1951 screenplay because of the miscegenation scene. Only when reminded that he had approved the scene in its entirety in 1936 did Breen begrudgingly green light the remake.[39] Freed subsequently soft-pedaled race in general, and the miscegenation scene in particular. William Warfield's powerful "Ol' Man River" commented specifically on the expulsion of Julie, not the struggles of his race.

Ten years would pass before Dorothy Dandridge became the first woman of color to play Julie, on July 17, 1961, at Monterey's Wharf Theater. Lonette McKee broke the Broadway color barrier at the Uris Theater on April 24, 1983.

With its German and Japanese spies, *Marie Galante* enjoyed a wartime theatrical rerelease. Warners also reissued *Go into Your Dance* in 1947 as a tie-in to *The Jolson Story*.[40] When TV revolutionized the industry in the 1950s, Helen's sound films, minus *Applause* and the two *Show Boats*, played the small screen.[41] By the 1970s, television screenings of Helen's films had waned and, with the exception of *Applause*, rarely played revival houses or festivals.

Conversely, during the nostalgia craze that began in the late 1960s, RCA again released eight Morgan tracks on one side of an LP.[42] Two of those tracks, "Can't Help Lovin' Dat Man" and "Something to Remember You By," provided background in the 1976 proto-slasher film *Alice, Sweet Alice*. Smaller labels mined Helen's recorded output in the ensuing years.

Beginning in the late 1980s and continuing to the present day, home video, Turner Classic Movies, YouTube, and streaming services have made Helen's film and audio work available to new audiences.

Show Boat never stays in dry dock for long.

In 1978, Robert Russell Bennett and historian Miles Kreuger found much of Bennett's 1927 *Show Boat* orchestrations, discarded and unheard since World War II. (The remaining material turned up in 1982 in a Warner Brothers warehouse in Secaucus, New Jersey.) John McGlinn conducted the originals in his 1988 complete *Show Boat* recording. Some modern stage productions, particularly those by opera companies with the resources to provide a double chorus and a full orchestra, now employ Bennett's original charts.

Sadly, McGlinn failed to record a follow-up *Sweet Adeline* album, but he did offer a handful of selections on subsequent compilations. After a 1934 airing at the St. Louis Muny, *Sweet Adeline* went into mothballs, ostensibly because Kern and Hammerstein feared that only Helen could make the material work. A 1977 Goodspeed Opera House revival and concert productions by the New Amsterdam Theater Company (1985) and Encores! (1997) demonstrated that there is much to enjoy, but without Helen's pathos, the musical lacks Hammerstein's customary emotional center.

Irving Hoffman, as beloved as Helen herself, died in 1968, literally from having too big a heart.[43] The Sanchezes lived the highlife until a 1950 accident limited Brownie's mobility. Both passed in the 1960s. Dorothy Dey continued to work and play in Miami until her death in 1983.

Her career over before it began, Rena worked as a secretary, first for Mary Pickford, then for Ken Murray.[44] In 1945, she married actor and decorated Marine William Lundigan. Widowed in 1975, Rena moved to Florida, where she passed in 2006.

George White never comprehended that the Ziegfeldian revues quietly passed into history when Helen Morgan died. Tab revues in 1943, 1944, 1948, and 1949 all lost money. A disastrous 1953 floorshow at New York's Versailles prompted White to file, again, for bankruptcy protection.[45] Las Vegas productions fared no better.[46] The less said about his final *Scandals*, at the International Theater Restaurant in 1963, the better.[47] White died penniless in 1968.

Nick Blair continued in the cabaret and restaurant business until the 1960s. He retired first to Vegas and then to South Florida, where he died in 1978.

After Pearl Harbor, Arthur Loew offered his yacht for use in the war effort, and the navy used it for the duration.[48] Too old to fly for his country, Major Loew supervised the foreign distribution of American films for the Office of War Information.[49] He briefly headed the MGM studio in the 1950s. Then, after twenty years of marriage, Loew and Melita Schmitt divorced. In 1963, he married Phoenix divorcée Jacqueline Gebhard Tull. He built his new bride a more human-sized house on the grounds of Pembroke and demolished the mansion. Wife number four was by his side when he died of cancer on September 6, 1977.

William Realino Zeh learned little from his punctured romance. He did not divorce Helen until early 1922, by which time he was chasing another chorine, Sarah Jane Crawford. With his divorce not yet finalized, Sarah and he crossed the state line into Indiana and married. She left him soon afterward.[50] "Grumpy" Zeh died from complications of injuries he suffered in an auto accident in 1970, two months after the death of his fourth wife.

Lowell Almy married Catherine Fahey in Albany in 1934. In 1958, they retired near Clearwater, Florida, where he died in 1972.

Lloyd Johnson spent thirty years covering the Bay Area nightclub and restaurant scene for local papers. He dated several women in the industry, including, just two months after Helen's death, screenwriter Isabel Dawn. Only late in life did he remarry, joining forces with Lake Tahoe restaurateur Betty Chartrand. He passed in 1984.

Buddy Maschke followed Helen's example by raising money for the Greater Cleveland United Appeal, the Jewish Community Federation, the Red Cross, Mount Sinai Hospital, the Community Chest, and other charities. He served as chief executive to Moe Dalitz's Pioneer Dry Cleaning and Linen Supply and represented the mobster when, in 1940, Dalitz divorced his wife, Dorothy.[51] Maschke died in 1994, still tight-lipped about his time as Helen Morgan's husband.

In 1932, a year after the death of his second wife, Frank Riggin married Nannie Lou Norris Arms. She taught him the art of the spinning wheel and the two traveled the Midwest demonstrating both the wheel and the proficiency with which Ivory Soap (their sponsor) cleaned the wool they spun and knitted.[52] On October 23, 1947, riddled with cancer and heart disease, Frank took his own life with an overdose of phenobarbital tablets.[53]

Lulu's last, successful marriage to Charles Adams ended in 1957 with the death of her husband. In the 1960s, financial necessities forced her to move back to New York City, where she received aid from, among others, Elizabeth Collins. In 1973, unable to live on her own, Lulu entered New York's Isabella Geriatric Center, where she died on March 20, 1978, at the age of ninety-six. She lies next to her daughter in Holy Sepulchre, as was her wish.[54]

Others sang as well as she, but Helen, with no formal training, acted—no, *lived*—her songs. In her fluttering hands, Tin Pan Alley ditties became one-act plays in thirty-two bars. Every singer who acts a song as a little monologue reignites the Morgan torch. Every time a character in a musical sits on a convenient shelf and confesses a dream—Eliza Doolittle for a more "loverly" existence, Audrey for somewhere that's green—Helen lives. Torch songs no longer, they are "I want" songs. Helen's art has become part of our theatrical DNA.

Some factors that predicated her career downturn were beyond her control, key among them the loss of her two producing champions, Florenz Ziegfeld and Arthur Hammerstein. Prohibition also contributed. During the 1920s, she was in the front lines of the resistance. With Repeal, she personified a bygone era.

Some wounds were self-inflicted. Leaving her CBS radio series to play *Memory* proved a costly mistake that hastened the end of her career.

Ultimately, that burning need for acceptance, even redemption, was the fuel that lit Helen Morgan's torch and filled her glass. What made her an artist kept the intuitive actor from reaching her full potential and, eventually, destroyed her.

In the end, Helen's philanthropic turns overrode the inconsistency that marred the last six years of her career. To Irving Hoffman, Helen was destined to wind up where she started, "sleeping in hallways and hoping for free meals. While she had the money, she wanted to prevent all the people she could from sharing the experience. Her heart was controlled by only one emotion and that was generosity."[55] Her charity work was as addictive as the brandy she swilled, but it made the world a better place.

When discussing Helen with Jimmy Cannon, one Ziegfeld girl flat out called her a saint. Well, if Broadway has a patron saint, her name is Helen Morgan.

Appendix I

Stageography

Stage Productions

Frivolities of 1920

Produced by G. M. Anderson. Music and lyrics by William B. Friedlander. Book by William Anthony McGuire. Additional music by Harry Auracher and Tom Johnstone. Choreographed by Edward P. Bower and Allan K. Foster. Production supervised by G. M. Anderson and J. C. Huffman.

TOURING COMPANY PRINCIPALS: Dolly Best, Del Chain, Carlton Chase, Will Goodall, Edward Metcalfe, Eddie Nelson, Leila Ricard, Joseph Rolley[1]

The Passing Show of 1921

Music by Jean Schwartz. Dialogue and lyrics by Harold Atteridge. Additional music by Lew Pollock. Incidental music by Al Goodman. Staged by J. C. Huffman. Produced under the personal direction of J. J. Shubert.

TOURING COMPANY PRINCIPALS: Willie and Eugene Howard, May Boley, Victor Bozart, Dolly Hackett, Ina Hayward, Francis X. Mahoney, Helen and Rosalie Mellette, Emily Miles, Kathleen O'Hanlon, John Quinian, Sammy White

1921	May 30–Sep 3	Apollo	Chicago[2]
	Sep 5–10	Murat	Indianapolis
	Sep 12–24	Garrick	Detroit
	Sep 25–Oct 1	Shubert	Cincinnati
	Oct 3–8	Hanna	Cleveland
	Oct 10–15	Teck	Buffalo
	Oct 17–22	Royal Alexandra	Toronto
	Oct 25–29	Majestic	Montreal

Sally

Produced by Florenz Ziegfeld Jr. Book by Guy Bolton. Music by Jerome Kern; "Butterfly Ballet" by Victor Herbert. Lyrics by Clifford Grey.

1923–1924 TOURING COMPANY PRINCIPALS: Marilyn Miller, Leon Errol, Walter Catlett, Floyd English, Felice, Paul Frawley, Kathlene Martyn, Jacques Rabiroff, Floyd English

1923	Oct 8–20	American	St. Louis
	Oct 22–27	Hartman	Columbus, OH
	Oct 29–Nov 3	English	Indianapolis
	Nov 4–10	Grand	Cincinnati
	Nov 12–17	Royal Alexandra	Toronto
	Nov 19–24	Majestic	Buffalo
	Nov 26–Dec 1	National	Washington, DC
	Dec 3–5	Poli's New Lyric	Bridgeport, CT
	Dec 6–8	Worcester	Worcester, MA
	Dec 10–15	Shubert	New Haven, CT
	Dec 17–22	Court Square	Springfield, MA
	Dec 25–29	Parsons	Hartford, CT
	Dec 31–Jan 1, 1924	Capitol	Albany, NY

Louie the 14th

Produced by Florenz Ziegfeld Jr. American adaptation by Arthur Wimperis, from the German book by Frank and Julius Wilhelm. Lyrics by Arthur Wimperis. Music by Sigmund Romberg.

PRINCIPALS: Leon Errol, Ethel Shutta, Louis Casavant, J. W. Doyle, Harry Fender, Pauline Mason, Doris Patston, Judith Vosselli, Hugh Wakefield

1925	Feb 17–21	Ford's	Baltimore
	Feb 22–Mar 1	National	Washington, DC

George White's Scandals

7th Edition

Produced and staged by George White. Book by William K. Wells and George White. Music by Ray Henderson. Lyrics by B. G. DeSylva and Lew Brown. Costumes and curtains made in Paris by Max Weldy from designs by Erte.

PRINCIPALS: Helen Hudson, Harry Fox, Tom Patricola, Gordon Dooley, Helen Morgan, Arthur Ball, Fred Lyon, Dorothy and Margaret McCarthy, James Miller, (Flournoy) Miller and (Aubrey) Lyles, Mr. and Mrs. Norman Phillips, Norman Phillips Jr.

MORGAN AND HUDSON SCENES AND SONGS:

ACT I

Scene 3:	Drama Mixed with Revue	
	Maxwell Zunzer	Harry Fox
	Kathryn, his wife	Helen Morgan
	Irving Yates (alias Borden)	Harry Morrisey
	Mrs. Brown	Mrs. Norman Phillips
	Mr. Brown	Tom Patricola
	Temptation	Chris Crane
	Gold	Marjorie Shaw
	Flaming Passion	Marjorie Murray
	Fruit	Marion Courtney
	Cupid	James Miller
Scene 6:	"Fly Butterfly"	Helen Hudson and the Elm City Four
Scene 8:	"I Want a Lovable Baby"	Helen Morgan
	Heavy Spending Baby	Fred Lyon
	Fickle, Fickle Baby	Joe Sullivan
	Prehistoric Baby	Jim Carty
	Old-Fashioned Baby	Harry Morrissey
	Lovable Baby	Tom Patricola
Scene 14:	"Beware of the Girl with a Fan"	Helen Hudson and the Elm City Four

ACT II

Scene 6:	"Say It with a Sable"	Helen Hudson
Scene 7:	"What a World This Would Be"	Harry Fox and Helen Morgan
	First Episode: The New Cook	
	Cook	Vada Alexander
	Madame	Mrs. Norman Phillips
	Second Episode: Magic Hair Restorer	
	Barber	Tom Patricola
	Customer	James Miller

	Third Episode: The Pill of Youth	
	The Doctor	Jim Carty
	The Patient	Norman Phillips and Junior
	Fourth Episode: Too Good to Be True	
	The Husband	Gordon Dooley
	The Wife	Martha Morton
Scene 11:	Cheap Guy	Tom Patricola, Harry Fox, Martha Morton, Gordon Dooley, Helen Hudson, and Helen Morgan
	Dance by	Tom Patricola
Scene 12:	"The Actors' Prayer"	By the Principals
Scene 14:	Finale	Entire Company

1925	Jun 15–20	Apollo	Atlantic City
	Jun 22–Nov 14	Apollo	New York
	Nov 16–21	Werba's	Brooklyn
	Nov 23–Dec 5	Tremont	Boston
	Dec 7–12	Court Square	Springfield, MA
	Dec 14–19	Shubert	Newark, NJ
	Dec 21–Jan 2	Forrest	Philadelphia
1926	Jan 3–9	National	Washington, DC
	Jan 11–16	Ford's	Baltimore
	Jan 18–30	Nixon	Pittsburgh
	Jan 31–Mar 6	Illinois	Chicago
	Mar 7–13	American	St. Louis
	Mar 15–20	New Opera House	Detroit
	Mar 22–Apr 3	Ohio	Cleveland

Americana
1st Edition
Produced by Richard Herndon. Directed by Allan Dinehart. Book by J. P. McEvoy. Music and lyrics by Con Conrad and Henry Souvaine. Special material by George Gershwin, Ira Gershwin, Philip Charig, and Morrie Ryskind. Entire production designed by John Held Jr. Dances and ensembles by Larry Ceballos.

PRINCIPALS: Lew Brice, Roy Atwell, Harriett Burke, Charles Butterworth, Arline and Edgar Gardiner, Helen Morgan, Pan-American Quartet (Charles H. Downz, Joe E. Loomis, John W. Turner, Walter Hilliard)

MORGAN SONGS:

"Blowing the Blues Away" (Music by Phillip Charig, Lyric by Ira Gershwin)
Lew Brice, Betty Compton, Helen Morgan, Evelyn Bennett, Gay Nelle, and Elisabeth Morgan

"Why D'ya Roll Those Eyes?" (Music by Philip Charig, Lyric by Morrie Ryskind)
Evelyn Bennett, Betty Compton, Helen Morgan, and Lehman Byck

"Thanks Awful" (Music by Con Conrad, Lyric by Joe Young and Sam Lewis)
Helen Morgan, Lehman Byck, and Pan-American Quartet

Morgan's Interpolated Songs

"For My Sweetheart" (Gus Kahn and Walter Donaldson)
"The Two of Us" (Van Phillips, Jimmy Campbell, and Reginald Connelly)
"Nobody Wants Me" (Henry Souvaine and Morrie Ryskind)

1926 Jul 26–Jan 22, 1927 Belmont New York

American Grand Guignol
Third Bill
Four one-act plays. Staged by Georges Renavent. Settings by Cleon Throckmorton.

WE'RE ALL IN THE GUTTER—By Elfrida and Clarence Derwent
A MINUET—By Louis N. Parker
Time: The Reign of Terror Scene: The Bastille
CAST: Georges Renavent, Neleh Nagrom, Denis Gurney
DIVERTISSEMENT
Helen Morgan
Accompanied by Joe Santly
CASUALTIES—By Martin Flavin
THE MAKER OF IMAGES—By Arthur Caesar

1927 Mar 4–12 Grove Street New York

Broadway à Paris
Produced by Edmond Sayag. Direction by George Hale. *Orchestre symphonique dirigé par M. Darrieux*, Jazz Hoffman, Tango Canaro *et* Irving Aaronson *et ses Commanders*

PRINCIPALS: June, Johnny Hudgins, Helen Morgan, George Hale

Act 1, Scene 8: Helen Morgan, "*La Raquel Meller Américaine*"

1927	May 19–Jun 6	Les Ambassadeurs	Paris

Show Boat

Adapted from Edna Ferber's novel of the same name. Produced by Florenz Ziegfeld Jr. Music by Jerome Kern. Book and lyrics by Oscar Hammerstein II. Dances and ensembles arranged by Sammy Lee. Dialogue staged by Zeke Colvan.

PRINCIPALS: Jules Bledsoe, Charles Ellis, Aunt Jemima, Howard Marsh, Helen Morgan, Edna May Oliver, Eva Puck, Norma Terris, Sammy White, Charles Winninger, Francis X. Mahoney

MORGAN NUMBERS

"Can't Help Lovin' That Man" Julie, Queenie, Magnolia, Joe, Windy
"Bill" (lyric by P. G. Wodehouse) Julie

1927	Nov 15–19	National	Washington, DC
	Nov 21–26	Nixon	Pittsburgh
	Nov 28–Dec 3	Ohio	Cleveland
	Dec 5–24	Erlanger	Philadelphia
	Dec 27–May 4, 1929	Ziegfeld	New York
1929	May 6–Jun 1	Colonial	Boston

Ziegfeld Midnight Frolic

Produced by Florenz Ziegfeld Jr. Staged by Sammy Lee.

1928	Dec 29–Jan 26, 1929	New Amsterdam Roof	New York
		(Hiatus)	
1929	Feb 6–Apr 11	New Amsterdam Roof	New York

Sweet Adeline

Produced by Arthur Hammerstein. Music by Jerome Kern. Book and lyrics by Oscar Hammerstein II. Dances and ensembles arranged by Danny Dare. Book staged by Reginald Hammerstein.

PRINCIPALS: Helen Morgan, Irene Franklin, Charles Butterworth, Caryl Bergman, Violet Carlson, Robert Chisholm, Max Hoffman Jr., Len Mance, John D. Seymour, Jim Thornton, Robert C. Fischer, Jerry Jarnigan, Robert Emmett Keane, Sally Bates, Peter Bender

MORGAN NUMBERS

Folk Song—"Twas Not So Long Ago"	Addie and Ensemble
Air and Scene—"Here Am I"	Addie and Dot
Air—"Why Was I Born?"	Addie
Waltz Ballad—"The Sun About to Rise"	Sid, Jim, and Ensemble
Song and Chorus—"Some Girl Is on Our Mind"	Jim, Tom, Sid, Thornton, Addie, and Male Ensemble
Duet—"Don't Ever Leave Me"	Addie and Jim
Finaletto	Addie
Scene	Addie, Sid, and Jim
Finale	Ensemble

1929	Aug 19–24	Apollo	Atlantic City
	Aug 26–31	Shubert	Newark, NJ
	Sep 3–Mar 22, 1930	Hammerstein's	New York
1930	Sep 15–Oct 4	Colonial	Boston
	Oct 6–18	Wilson	Detroit
	Oct 19–Dec 6	Illinois	Chicago
	Dec 8–13	Nixon	Pittsburgh
	Dec 14–20	(Hiatus)	
	Dec 22–Jan 17, 1931	Erlanger	Philadelphia

Ziegfeld Follies of 1931
Produced by Florenz Ziegfeld Jr. Dialogue staged by Edward C. Liley. Dances staged by Bobby Connolly and Albertina Rasch.

PRINCIPALS: Helen Morgan, Ruth Etting, Jack Pearl, Harry Richman, Dorothy Dell, Gladys Glad, Hal LeRoy, Mitzi Mayfair, Earl Oxford, Reri, Buck and Bubbles

MORGAN SCENES AND SONGS
ACT I

Scene 3: Grand Hotel
By Mark Hellinger

Doctor Crechsen, in the lobby for years and years	John Daly Murphy
Beigle, a dying youth	Leonard Stokes
Polly Adlervitch, Queen of the Russian Ballet	Helen Morgan
Alphonso Smith, late King of Gibraltar	Milton Le Roy
Baron Al Capone, from Chicago	Harry Richman
Cecil B. Goldwater of Hollywood	Jack Pearl
Morosco, Secretary to Alphonso	Earl Oxford
Hotel Room Clerk	Cliff Hall
Doorman	Conrad Sparin
Elevator Attendant	John Gurney
Capone's Men	Jack Bruns, Frank Lang, William Royal, and Russel Johns
Bellhops	Thomas Arace and Adrian Samish
"Stooge" Bellhop	Hershel Martin
Guests	

ACT II

Scene 2:	"I'm with You" (Walter Donaldson)	Helen Morgan and Harry Richman
Scene 11:	Victim of the Talkies	
	By Murray, Trivers, and Oakland	
	Romney Renaldo	George Lamar
	Louella, His Wife	Helen Morgan
	Julius McQuiff, the Director	Jack Pearl
	Joe Eppes, His Assistant	Gene Gory
	Maid	Vivian Porter
Scene 12:	Finale: Near Central Park	Entire Company

Morgan's Interpolated Songs

"Bill" (Kern-Hammerstein II)

"Half-Caste Woman" (Noël Coward)

"I'm All Wrapped Up in You" (Ben Oakland, Barry Trivers, and J. P. Murray)

"Love Is All I Live For" (Gene Buck and Dr. Hugo Riesenfeld)
"Don't Worry and Cheer Up" (Gene Buck and Harry Richman)
"There's a Blue Note in My Love Song" (T. Shapiro)
"The Man I Used to Love" (Lou Alter)
"Two Loves: (*J'ai Deux Amours*)" (Vincent Scotto, Geo. Koger and H. Varna. English lyric by J. P. Murray and Barry Trivers)
"Here Lies Love" (Ralph Rainger and Leo Robin)

1931	Jun 15–27	Nixon	Pittsburgh
	Jul 1–Nov 7	Ziegfeld	New York

SHOW BOAT (1932 revival)
Opening-night cast the same as the 1927 production except:

Gaylord Ravenal	Dennis King
Joe	Paul Robeson

1932	May 19–Oct 22	Ziegfeld	New York
	Oct 24–Nov 5	Shubert	Boston
	Nov 7–12	Forrest	Philadelphia
	Nov 14–19	National	Washington, DC
	Nov 21–26	Ford	Baltimore
	Nov 28–Dec 3	Nixon	Pittsburgh
	Dec 4–10	Shubert	Cincinnati
	Dec 12–25	(Hiatus)	
	Dec 26–31	Hanna	Cleveland
1933	Jan 1–7	Cass	Detroit
	Jan 8–28	Auditorium	Chicago

Tab Unit

1933	Feb 3–9	Balaban and Katz	Chicago
	Feb 10–16	Loew's State	Cleveland
	Feb 17–23	(Hiatus)	
	Feb 24–Mar 2	Capitol	New York
	Mar 3–9	Loew's Metropolitan	Brooklyn

Memory
Play staged by the author, Myron C. Fagan.

PRINCIPALS: Helen Morgan, Zezan Anglan, Rafael Corio, Kay Hammond, Vera Lewis, Mia Marvin, Frances Routa, Jackie Searl, Bryant Washburn, Leon Waycoff

MORGAN'S SONG: "A Fool There Was"
(Fred Fischer and Stella Unger)

1934	May 7–12	Biltmore	Los Angeles

George White's Scandals
12th Edition
Post-Broadway touring production

Lyrics by Jack Yellen. Music by Ray Henderson. Dialogue by George White, William K. Wells, and Howard A. Shiebler. Dances by Russell Markert. Entire production conceived and directed by George White.

PRINCIPALS: Willie and Eugene Howard, Helen Morgan, Jane Cooper, George Dewey Washington, Earl Oxford, Stanley Twins, Lois Eckhart, Claire McQuillen, Edna Page, Sam, Ted, and Ray

MORGAN SCENES AND SONGS:
ACT I

Scene 1:	Tune In on the World's First Television Broadcast	Viola Paulson and Florette DuElk
	"Anything Can Happen"	Helen Morgan
	Announcer	Richard Lane
Scene 2:	"Life Begins at Sweet Sixteen"	Helen Morgan
	Peggy Joyce	Lois Eckhart
	Mamie Simple McPherson	Constance Carr
	Mrs. Vandernuts	Estelle Jayne
	Prize Fighter	James Howard
	Mae West	Edna Page
	Senator	Fred Manatt
	Bride	Claire McQuillen
	The George White Girls	

Scene 5:	"I'm the Fellow Who Loves You"	Helen Morgan, Earl Oxford, Willie and Eugene Howard, Lois Eckhart, Claire McQuillen, and the George White Girls
Scene 12:	Chrysanthemum Gardens	
	Announcer	Richard Lane
	"I've Got to Get Hot"	Helen Morgan

ACT II

Scene 3:	Lost Love	
	Maid	Lois Eckhart
	Judge Evans	Fred Manatt
	Actress	Helen Morgan
Scene 8:	"Anything Can Happen"	Helen Morgan, Earl Oxford, and the George White Girls
Scene 9:	The Year 2036	
	Announcer	Richard Lane
	(a) Ponce de Leon	Willie Howard
	Follower	Fred Manatt
	(b) Napoleon	Eugene Howard
	Josephine	Lois Eckhart
	(c) Kate Smith	Edna Page
	(d) Miss Show Boat	Helen Morgan
	(e) Al Jolson	Willie Howard
Scene 10:	Finale	Entire Company

1936	June 20–26	Garden Pier	Atlantic City
	June 28–Sep 12	Grand Opera House	Chicago
	Sep 14	Orpheum	Springfield, IL
	Sep 15	Rialto	Joliet, IL
	Sep 16	Coronado	Rockford, IL
	Sep 17	Palace	South Bend, IN
	Sep 18–19	English	Indianapolis
	Sep 20–23	Davidson	Milwaukee
	Sep 24	Parkway	Madison, WI
	Sep 25	Masonic Auditorium	Davenport, IA
	Sep 26	Shrine Auditorium	Des Moines

	Sep 27–Oct 4	Auditorium	Kansas City, MO
	Oct 5	Forum	Wichita
	Oct 6–7	City Auditorium	Denver
	Oct 8	(Travel Day)	
	Oct 9	Capitol	Salt Lake City
	Oct 10	(Travel Day)	
	Oct 11–24	Curran	San Francisco
	Oct 25	Memorial Auditorium	Sacramento
	Oct 26	Civic Auditorium	San Jose
	Oct 27	(Travel Day)	
	Oct 28–Nov 8	Biltmore	Los Angeles
	Nov 9	Orpheum	Phoenix
	Nov 10	Rialto	Tucson
	Nov 11	Plaza	El Paso, TX
	Nov 12	(Travel Day)	
	Nov 13–14	Texas	San Antonio
	Nov 15–17	Metropolitan	Houston
	Nov 18	Paramount	Austin
	Nov 19	Worth	Fort Worth
	Nov 20–21	Majestic	Dallas
	Nov 22–23	Warner	Oklahoma City
	Nov 24	Convention Hall	Tulsa, OK
	Nov 25–26	Orpheum	Memphis
	Nov 27–28	Erlanger	Atlanta
	Nov 30	Temple	Birmingham, AL
	Dec 1	Tivoli	Chattanooga
	Dec 2	Ryman Auditorium	Nashville
	Dec 3	Lyric	Knoxville
	Dec 4–5	Memorial Auditorium	Louisville, KY
	Dec 6–12	Taft	Cincinnati
	Dec 13–19	American	St. Louis
	Dec 20–24	(Hiatus)	
	Dec 25–Jan 2	Cass	Detroit
1937	Jan 4	Capitol	Flint, MI
	Jan 5	Temple	Saginaw, MI
	Jan 6	Strand	Lansing, MI
	Jan 7	Michigan	Jackson, MI
	Jan 8–9	Keith's	Grand Rapids, MI

	Jan 10	Shrine Auditorium	Fort Wayne, IN
	Jan 11	Paramount	Toledo, OH

Tab Unit

1937	Jan 15–21	RKO Palace	Chicago
	Jan 22–28	RKO Palace	Columbus, OH
	Jan 29–Feb 4	Palace	Cleveland
	Feb 5–11	Fox	Detroit
	Feb 12–14	Palace	Youngstown, OH
	Feb 15–17	(Hiatus)	
	Feb 18–24	RKO Keith	Boston

Hollywood Hotel Revue
Produced by Harry Howard. Music by Mack Davis. Lyrics by Milt Francis. Dances and ensembles by Boots McKenna.

PRINCIPALS: Willie and Eugene Howard, Helen Morgan, Marty May, Helen Honan, Robert Berry, Estelle Jayne

MORGAN SCENES:

ACT I, Scene 7: Helen Morgan

ACT II, Scene 6: Orchid Room, Hollywood Hotel

Master of Ceremonies	Marty May
Mae West	Helen Honan
George Jessel	Willie Howard
Herself	Helen Morgan
Themselves	May McKim and Boys
"Rigoletto" Quartet	Willie and Eugene Howard, Alice Carlton, and Estelle Jayne
Finale	Entire Company

MORGAN'S SONGS

"Make Believe" (Kern-Hammerstein II)
"Bill" (Kern-Hammerstein II)
"Why Was I Born?" (Kern-Hammerstein II)
"Thanks for the Memory" (Rainger-Robin)
"Can't Help Lovin' Dat Man" (Kern-Hammerstein II)

1937	Dec 27–Jan 1, 1938	Majestic	Brooklyn

World's Fairest on Parade (Tab Unit)

1938	Jan 28–Feb 3	Loew's	Montreal
	Feb 4–10	(Hiatus)	
	Feb 11–17	Loew's Capitol	Washington, DC
	Feb 18–23	(Hiatus)	
	Feb 25–Mar 3	Loew's	Richmond, VA
	Mar 4–10	Loew's	Norfolk, VA

Hollywood Hotel Revue (Tab Unit)

1938	May 27–30	Steel Pier	Atlantic City

A Night at the Moulin Rouge

Produced by N. S. Barger and A. B. Marcus. Music and lyrics by George Komaroff. Dances and ensembles staged by Natalie Komarova. Entire production conceived, designed, and staged by Jean Le Seyeux.

PRINCIPALS: Helen Morgan, Toby Wing, Stan Kavanagh, Slate Brothers, Ada Leonard, Sharon De Vries, Buster Shaver with Olive and George, Grisha and Brona, Zerby and Layton, Staples and Cerny, Rita Rio and Her All-Girl Orchestra

MORGAN SCENES and SONGS:

ACT II, Scene 2: Helen Morgan

"Bill" (Kern-Hammerstein II)
"Can't Help Lovin' Dat Man" (Kern-Hammerstein II)
"Make Believe" (Kern-Hammerstein II)
"Why Was I Born?" (Kern-Hammerstein II)

1939	Oct 2	Masonic Auditorium	Davenport, IA
	Oct 3	Shrine Auditorium	Des Moines
	Oct 4	Coliseum	Sioux Falls, IA
	Oct 5	City Auditorium	Sioux City, IA
	Oct 6–7	City Auditorium	Denver
	Oct 8	City Auditorium	Rapid City, SD
	Oct 10	Broadway	Butte, MT
	Oct 11–12	Post Street	Spokane, WA
	Oct 13–15	Music Hall	Seattle

Oct 16	City Auditorium	Portland, OR
Oct 19	Memorial Auditorium	Sacramento
Oct 20–29	Curran	San Francisco
Oct 30–Nov 7	(Hiatus)	
Nov 8–9	Municipal Auditorium	San Antonio
Nov 10–12	Music Hall	Houston
Nov 13	City Auditorium	Beaumont, TX
Nov 17–19	Fair Park Auditorium	Dallas
Nov 20	Shrine Auditorium	Oklahoma City
Nov 21	Forum	Wichita, KS
Nov 22	Shrine Mosque	Springfield, MO
Nov 23	Memorial Hall	Joplin, MO
Nov 24	Convention Hall	Tulsa, OK
Nov 26–Dec 2	Grand Opera House	Chicago

Show Boat
Produced by the Los Angeles Civic Light Opera Association: Edwin Lester. Music by Jerome Kern. Book and lyrics by Oscar Hammerstein II. Dances and ensembles arranged by Aida Broadbent. Directed by Zeke Colvan.

PRINCIPALS: John Boles, Norma Terris, Helen Morgan, Paul Robeson, Guy Kibbee, Winifred Harris, Helen Lynd, Sammy White, Bertha Powell, Victor Adams, Francis X. Mahoney

1940	May 13–18	Philharmonic Auditorium	Los Angeles[3]

George White's Scandals of 1941 (Tab Unit)
PRINCIPALS: Helen Morgan, Charles Kemper, Harris and Shore, Pat Henning, Betty Raye, Kay Penton, Martha Burnett, George Haggerty, Freda Sullivan, Barnes Twins, George White

1941	Aug 17–23	Hippodrome: Hamid's Million-Dollar Pier	Atlantic City
	Aug 24–28	(Hiatus)	
	Aug 29–Sep 4	Orpheum	Minneapolis
	Sep 5–11	Palace	Milwaukee
	Sep 12	State Lake	Chicago

Vaudeville

(William) Fairman and Morgan

1923	Sep 13–15	Maryland	Hagerstown, MD
	Sep 17–19	State	Trenton, NJ

Solo Vaudeville Appearances

1927	Jan 24–29	Palace	New York
	Jun 20–Jul 2	Coliseum	London
	Aug 1–6	Palladium	London
1930	Mar 26–28	Coliseum	New York
	Mar 29–Apr 4	Palace	New York
	Apr 12–18	Albee	Brooklyn
	Apr 19–21	86th Street	New York
	Apr 22–24	Keith's	Flushing
1931	Jan 28–30	Coliseum	New York
	Jan 31–Feb 6	Palace	New York
	Apr 25–May 1	Palace	New York
1932	Jan 8–14	Fox	Philadelphia
1933	July 7–13	RKO Palace	Chicago
	Oct 27	Loew's State	New York[4]
1934	May 24–30	Paramount	Los Angeles
	Sep 7–13	Oriental	Chicago
1937	Mar 25–31	Loew's State	New York
	Apr 19–May 1	Victoria Palace	London
	May 10–15	Theatre Royal	Dublin
	Aug 20–23	Oriental	Chicago
	Oct 20–24	State	Hartford
	Oct 28–Nov 2	Metropolitan	Boston
1938	Jan 14–17, 19–20	Fay's	Philadelphia
	Jan 18	Mount Ephraim	Mount Ephraim, NJ[5]
	May 1–21	Casa Mañana	New York
	Sep 20–22	Fay's	Providence, RI
	Nov 6–Dec 21	Casa Mañana	New York
	Dec 23	Palace	South Bend, IN
	Dec 24–29	State Lake	Chicago

	Dec 30–Jan 5	Shubert	Newark, NJ
1939	Jan 6–9	Riviera	Brooklyn
	Jan 13–16	Palace	Youngstown, OH
	Jan 17–19	Palace	Akron, OH
	Jan 27–Feb 2	Hippodrome	Baltimore
	Feb 3–4	Palace	Stamford, CT
	Feb 14	Stanley	Utica, NY
	Apr 9	Steel Pier	Atlantic City
	Apr 27–May 3	Roxy	Atlanta
	May 5–11	Flatbush	Brooklyn
	Aug 27–Sep 2	Steel Pier	Atlantic City
	Sep 24	Adams	Newark, NJ
	Dec 29–Jan 4	Minnesota	Minneapolis
1940	Sep 22	Auditorium	Lowell, MA
	Oct 13	Arena	New Haven, CT
1941	Apr 3–9	Flatbush	Brooklyn
	Apr 10–16	Windsor	Bronx
	May 16–22	State Lake	Chicago
	Jun 20–21	Riverside	Milwaukee
	Jun 25–28	Olympia	Miami

Appendix 2

Filmography

The Fighting Blade (Inspiration, 1923)

Producer: Charles H. Duell. Director: John S. Robertson. Scenario by Josephine Lovett, from the novel by Beulah Marie Dix. Photography: George Folsey. Film Editor: William Hamilton. Titles: Don Bartlett.

Production: April–June 1923, Fort Lee, NJ. Length: 8,729 ft.

Cast: Richard Barthelmess, Dorothy Mackaill, Lee Baker, Morgan Wallace, Bradley Baker, Frederick Burton, Stuart Sage, Philip Tead, Walter Horton, Allyn King, Marcia Harris.

The Heart Raider (Paramount, 1923)

Director: Wesley Ruggles. Scenario by Jack Cunningham. Story by Harry Durant and Julie Herne. Photography: Charles Schoenbaum.

Production: March–May 1923, Astoria, NY, and Palm Beach, FL. Length: 5,075 ft.

Cast: Agnes Ayres, Mahlon Hamilton, Charles Ruggles, Frazer Coulter, Marie Burke, Charles Riegel.

Six Cylinder Love (Fox, 1923)

Director: Elmer Clifton. Scenario by Carl Stearns Clancy, from the stage play by William Anthony McGuire. Photography: Alexander G. Penrod. Titles and Film Editor: Ralph Spence.

Production: June–July 1923, New York and Long Island. Length: 6,659 ft.

Cast: Ernest Truex, Florence Eldridge, Donald Meek, Maude Hill, Anne McKittrick, Marjorie Milton, Thomas Mitchell, Ralph Sipperly, Berton Churchill, Harold Mann, Frank Tweed, Grace Gordon, Helen Morgan, Miss Lunney.

Show Boat (Universal, 1929)

Producer: Carl Laemmle. Director: Harry Pollard. Scenario by Charles Kenyon, from the novel by Edna Ferber. Dialogue: Harry Pollard and Tom Reed. Photography: Gilbert Warrenton and Frank H. Booth.

Production: June–October 1928, Los Angeles. Length: 11,650 ft. (sound); 10,290 ft. (silent). Domestic Gross: $740,300 (est.).

Cast: Laura La Plante, Joseph Schildkraut, Emily Fitzroy, Otis Harlan, Elsie Bartlett, Alma Rubens, Jack McDonald, Jane La Verne, Neely Edwards, Theodore Lorch, Stepin Fetchit, Gertrude Howard.

Prologue Director: Arch Heath. Conductor: Victor Baravalle, with the original Ziegfeld Orchestra. Music: Jerome Kern. Lyrics: Oscar Hammerstein II.

Prologue Cast: Otis Harlan (Master of Ceremonies), Helen Morgan, Jules Bledsoe, Aunt Jemina.

MORGAN SONGS

"Can't Help Lovin' Dat Man"
"Bill"

Applause (Paramount, 1929)

Producer: Monta Bell. Director: Rouben Mamoulian. Screenplay by Garrett Fort, from the novel by Beth Brown. Photography: George Folsey and Joe Ruttenberg. Film Editor: Joe Bassier.

Production: June–July 1929, Astoria, NY. Length: 8,079 ft. (sound); 6,896 ft. (silent). Cost: $409,000. Domestic Gross: $244,450 (est.).

Cast: Helen Morgan, Joan Peers, Fuller Mellish Jr., Jack Cameron, Henry Wadsworth.

MORGAN SONGS

"Oceana Roll" (Lucien Denni and Roger Lewis)
"What Wouldn't I Do for That Man?" (Jay Gorney and E. Y. Harburg)
"Give Your Little Baby Lots of Lovin'" (Jos. A. Burke and Dolly Morse)

Glorifying the American Girl (Paramount, 1929)

Producer: Monta Bell. Director: Millard Webb. Screenplay: J. P. McEvoy and Millard Webb Garrett Fort. Photography: George Folsey.

Production: April–June 1929, Astoria, NY. Length: 8,071 ft. (sound); 6,786 ft. (silent). Cost: $1,043,000. Domestic Gross: $370,400 (est.).

Cast: Mary Eaton, Edward Crandall, Olive Shea, Dan Healy, Kaye Renard, Sarah Edwards, Norman Brokenshire. Guest Stars in Revue: Eddie Cantor, Helen Morgan, Rudy Vallée.

MORGAN SONGS

"What Wouldn't I Do for That Man?" (Jay Gorney and E. Y. Harburg)

Roadhouse Nights (Paramount, 1930)

Producer: Walter Wagner. Director: Hobart Henley. Screenplay by Garrett Fort, from a story by Ben Hecht. Cinematography: William O. Steiner. Film Editor: Helene Turner.

Production: October–November 1929, Astoria, NY. Length: 7,207 ft. (69 minutes). Cost: $287,980.77. Domestic Gross: $403,600 (est.).

Cast: Helen Morgan, Charles Ruggles, Fred Kohler, Jimmy Durante, Eddie Jackson, Lou Clayton, Fuller Mellish Jr., Leo Donnelly, Tammany Young, Joe King.

MORGAN SONGS

"It Can't Go On Like This" (Jay Gorney and E. Y. Harburg)

The Gigolo Racket (Vitaphone, 1931)

Producer: Samuel Sax. Director: Roy Mack. Story: Burnet Hershey. Added Dialogue: Stanley Rauh. Cinematography: Edwin B. DuPar.

Production: April–May 1931, Brooklyn, NY. Length: 2 reels (21 min.) Vitaphone 1255–56.

Cast: Helen Morgan, Joseph Striker, Reed Brown Jr., John Hamilton, Winifred Harris, Barton MacLane, Alphonse Martell.

MORGAN SONGS

"Nobody Breaks My Heart" (Kay Swift and Paul James)

"I Know He's Mine" (Bud Green, Sam Stept, and Herman Ruby)

Manhattan Lullaby (Educational, 1933)

Producer: Jack White. Director: William Watson. Music: Walter Scharf. Orchestra: Henry King.

Production: November 1933, New York. Length: 1 reel (9 min.).

Cast: Helen Morgan

MORGAN SONGS

"The Stork Song" (James F. Hanley)

The Doctor (Educational, 1934)

Producer: Al Christie. Executive Producer: Jack H. Skirball. Director: Johnnie Walker.

Production: January 1934, New York. Length: 1 reel (8 min.).

Cast: Helen Morgan, Herbert Rawlinson, Dorothy Werner, Montagu Love.

MORGAN SONGS

"One Little Smile" (Dr. Hugo Riesenfeld and Gene Buck)

Frankie and Johnnie (All-Star/Republic, 1934/1935/1936)

Producer: William Saal. Director: Chester Erskine (retakes by John H. Auer). Screenplay: Moss Hart. Added Dialogue: Lou Goldberg. Original Play: James Kirkland. Cinematographer: Joseph Ruttenberg. Editor: William Thompson.

Production: February–March 1934, Bronx. Retakes: March 1935, New York and Los Angeles. Length: 1934: 6,700 ft. (69 min.); 1936: 66 min.

Cast: Helen Morgan, Chester Morris, Lilyan Tashman (uncredited), Florence Reed, Walter Kingsford, William Harrigan, John Larkin, Cora Witherspoon, Montagu Love.

MORGAN SONGS

"Give Me a Heart to Sing To" (Victor Young and Ned Washington)

"If You Want My Heart" (J. Russel Robinson and Bill Livingston)

You Belong to Me (Paramount, 1934)

Producer: Louis D. Lighton. Director: Alfred Werker. Screenplay: Walter DeLeon. Adaptation: Grover Jones and William Slavens McNutt. Story: Elizabeth Alexander.

Cinematographer: Leo Tover, ASC.

Production: June–July 1934, Hollywood. Length: 67 min.

Cast: Lee Tracy, Helen Mack, Helen Morgan, David Jack Holt, Arthur Pierson, Lynne Overman, Dean Jagger.

MORGAN SONGS

"When He Comes Home to Me" (Sam Coslow and Leo Robin)

"I Ain't Gonna Carry No Torch" (Sam Coslow; cut before release)

Marie Galante (Fox, 1934)

Producer: Winfield Sheehan. Director: Henry King. Screenplay by Reginald Berkeley, from the novel by Jacques Deval.

Production: June–September 1934, Century City, CA. Length: 88 min. Domestic Gross: $700,000 (est.).

Cast: Spencer Tracy, Ketti Gallian, Ned Sparks, Siegfried Ruman, Helen Morgan, Stepin Fetchit, Robert Lorraine, Leslie Fenton, Arthur Byron.

MORGAN SONGS

"Song of a Dreamer" (Jay Gorney and Don Hartman)

"Serves Me Right for Treating You Wrong" (Maurice Sigler, Al Goodhart, and Al Hoffman)

Sweet Music (Warner Bros., 1935)

Producer: Samuel Bischoff. Director: Alfred E. Green. Screenplay: Jerry Wald, Carl Eriskon, and Warren Duff. Cinematographer: James Van Trees. Editor: Herbert Leonard.

Production: October–November 1934, Burbank, CA. Length: 100 min. Domestic Gross: $2,000,000 (est.).

Cast: Rudy Vallée, Ann Dvorak, Ned Sparks, Helen Morgan, Robert Armstrong, Allen Jenkins, Alice White, Al Shean, Phillip Reed, William Davidson, Henry O'Neill, Russell Hicks, Clay Clement, Addison Richards, Rudy Vallée's Connecticut Yankees, and the Frank and Milt Britton Band.

MORGAN SONGS

"I See Two Lovers" (Allie Wrubel and Mort Dixon)

"Winter Overnight" (Sammy Fain and Irving Kahal; cut before release)

Go into Your Dance (Warner Bros., 1935)

Producer: Sam Bischoff. Director: Archie Mayo. Screenplay by Earl Baldwin, from the novel by Bradford Ropes.

Production: November 1934–February 1935, Burbank, CA. Length: 95 min. Domestic Gross: $2,600,000 (est.).

Cast: Al Jolson, Ruby Keeler, Glenda Farrell, Helen Morgan, Barton MacLane, Patsy Kelly, Sharon Lynne, Akim Tamiroff, Benny Rubin, Phil Regan, Gordon Westcott, William Davidson, Joyce Compton, Joseph Cregan, Joyzelle Joyner

MORGAN'S SONG

"The Little Things You Used to Do" (Harry Warren and Al Dubin)

Show Boat (Universal 1936)

Producer: Carl Laemmle Jr. Director: James Whale. Screenplay by Oscar Hammerstein II, from the novel by Edna Ferber. Music: Jerome Kern. Lyrics: Oscar Hammerstein II. Cinematographers: John J. Mescall and John P. Fulton. Film Editors: Ted Kent and Bernard W. Burton.

Production: December 1935–March 1936, Los Angeles. Length: 110 min. Domestic Gross: $5,000,000 (est.).

Cast: Irene Dunne, Allan Jones, Charles Winninger, Paul Robeson, Helen Morgan, Helen Westley, Queenie Smith, Sammy White, Donald Cook, Hattie McDaniel, Francis X. Mahoney, Marilyn Knowlden, Sunnie O'Dea, Arthur Hohl, Charles Middleton, J. Farrell MacDonald, Clarence Muse.

MORGAN SONGS

"Can't Help Lovin' Dat Man"
"Bill"

Between April and August 1923, Helen Morgan may have played bit parts in several films, including **Wife in Name Only** (Pyramid), **Lawful Larceny** (Paramount), and **Zaza** (Paramount), but these appearances have not been confirmed.

Appendix 3

Radiography

All broadcasts from New York unless otherwise noted.

Starring Radio Series

Broadway Melodies (CBS)

Time Slot:	Sundays, 2:00–2:30 p.m. (EST)
Sponsor:	Bi-Si-Dol antacids
Announcer:	Andre Baruch
Conductor:	Albert Bartlett (September 24–October 15) Jerry Freeman (October 22–March 25)
Broadcast from:	New York City September 24, 1933–March 25, 1934 Total Broadcasts: 26[1]

Guest Appearances on Network Radio

Sonatron Program (CBS)	March 24, 1929
Majestic Theatre of the Air (CBS)	September 15, 1929 September 29, 1929
Paramount-Publix Hour (CBS)	October 5, 1929
The Fleishman Hour (NBC Red)	February 27, 1930 November 26, 1931 March 9, 1933 February 8, 1934 November 15, 1934 (from Hollywood)

RKO Hour (NBC Red)	April 1, 1930
	January 30, 1931
	May 1, 1931
Winchell/Sacs on Broadway (CBS)	August 4, 1930
	December 8, 1931
Nestlé Chocolateers (NBC Blue)	September 5, 1930
Maxwell House Show Boat (NBC Red)	June 4, 1931
	March 11, 1937
Vitality Personalities (CBS)	December 2, 1931
Broadway's Greatest Thrills (CBS)	January 19, 1932
	June 19, 1932
Ziegfeld Follies of the Air (CBS)	April 10, 1932
	May 1, 1932
	June 12, 1932
Goodyear Program (NBC Red)	May 4, 1932
Gem Highlights (CBS)	June 12, 1932
Linit Bath Club Revue (CBS)	October 23, 1932
Meet the Artist (CBS)	October 7, 1933
Parade of Champions (CBS)	November 14, 1933
	November 16, 1933
	December 25, 1933
Chrysler Show (CBS)	January 7, 1934
Musical Cruise (NBC Blue)	February 28, 1934
Voice of America (CBS)	March 22, 1934
Bits from Broadway Hits (CBS)	March 24, 1934
Hall of Fame (NBC Red)	July 15, 1934 (from Hollywood)
Welcome Valley (NBC Blue)	September 3, 1935
Paul Whiteman's Musical Varieties (NBC Blue)	February 16, 1936
First Nighter with Dick Himber (CBS)	April 17, 1936
Jamboree Musicale (NBC Red)	July 18, 1936 (from Chicago)
The Little Show (BBC)	May 18, 1937 (London)
Melodies from the Sky (Mutual—Chicago)	July 21, 1937 (from Chicago)
Campbell Playhouse (CBS)	March 31, 1939

Nonnetwork Radio Appearances

"Chicago Prima Donna" (WHN-NY)	April 7, 9 & 23, 1925
(WHN-NY)	July 7, 1925
(WMCA-NY)	August 13, 1925
"Stars of George White's Scandals" (WEEI-Boston)	December 3, 1925
(WMCA-NY)	April 24 & 30, 1926
(WHN-NY)	August 10, 1926
(WPAP-Palisades, NJ)	August 23, 1926
(WMCA-NY)	November 11, 1926
Cartoonists of America Dinner (WMCA-NY)	March 18, 1927
All-Sports Dinner (WGBS-NY)	May 22, 1928
Radio Station Grand Opening (WMCA-NY)	December 23, 1928
Israel Orphan Asylum Benefit (WMCA-NY)	March 22, 1930
"Newspaper Hour" (WOR-NY)	March 23, 1930
Grand Opening Warner's Hollywood Theatre (WGBS-NY)	April 22, 1930
"The Nutty Club" (WBBM-Chicago)	November 16, 1930
Press Photographers' Ball (WEAF-NY)	January 23, 1931
"Tales of (Irving) Hoffman" (WGBS-NY)	May 9, 1931
"Voice of Broadway" (WOR-NY)	October 11, 1931
Peacock Ball Benefit (WJZ-NY)	November 6, 1931
"Osborne Orchestra" (WOR-NY)	January 20, 1932
Ziegfeld Memorial Concert (WMCA-NY)	July 29, 1932
Actor's Dinner Club Event (WMCA-NY)	August 22, 1932
Bide Dudley's Party (WMCA-NY)	August 23, 1932
Dedication of Station (WEVD-NY)	September 28, 1932
Democratic Committee Entertainment (WOR-NY)	October 17, 1932
Show Boat program with Terris, Puck, and White (WWSW-Pitt)	November 30, 1932
Palace Theatre Varieties (WMAQ-Chicago)	July 5, 1932
77th Annual Charity Ball (WJZ-NY)	December 7, 1933
Magazine of the Air (WOR-NY)	January 10, 1934
Yeshiva College All-Star Show (WMCA)	April 15, 1935
Daughters of Israel Home Benefit (WMCA)	December 1, 1935
George White's Scandals (WGN Chicago)	July 10, 1936

Helen, a pioneer performer on television. (Photofest)

Nightclub Live Feeds[2]
(Network and Local Broadcasts)

NIGHTCLUB	STATION	DATES
Chez Helen Morgan, NYC (Les Stevens Orchestra)	WHN-NY	October 4, 18, 21, 25, & 28 and November 1 & 4, 1927[3]
Piping Rock, Saratoga, NY (Bob Grant and His Embassy Club Dance Orchestra)	NBC Red	**August 3, 4, 10, 11, 17, 18, 24, 25 & 31, 1933**
Piping Rock, Saratoga, NY (Bob Grant and His Embassy Club Dance Orchestra)	WGY (Schenectady, NY)	**August 5, 8, 9, 12, 14, 15, 16, 19, 22, 23 & 26, 1933**
Longue Vue Lodge, Hastings-on-Hudson, NY (Will Osborne Orchestra)	NBC Red	**September 22, 1933**

NIGHTCLUB	STATION	DATES
Arrowhead Inn, Saratoga, NY (Enric Madriguera and his Continental Orchestra)	WGY/NBC Red	August 9–12, 15–18, 22–25, & 29–**31**, 1935
The House of Morgan, NYC (Lou Bring and His Orchestra)	NBC Blue	November 7, 15, 22 & 29 and December 6, 13, 20 & 27, 1935
The House of Morgan, NYC (Lou Bring and His Orchestra)	NBC Red	November 19 and December 3, 10 & 17, 1935

Television

Opening Day Event	W2XCR	New York	April 26, 1931[4]
"Tales of (Irving) Hoffman"	W2XCR	New York	May 9, 1931
Democratic National Committee	W2XAB	New York	October 11, 1932
World's Fair Demonstration	NBC	New York	May 12, 1939

Appendix 4

Discography

Commercial Recordings

ca. July 1927, London

acc. by Leslie A. "Hutch" Hutchinson

"Me and My Shadow" (duet with Hutchinson) (Dave Dreyer, Billy Rose, Al Jolson)	Brunswick 104
"When I Discover My Man" (Jerome Kern, Alice Duer Miller—*The Charm School*)	Brunswick 104
"You Remind Me of a Naughty Springtime Cuckoo" (Leslie Sarony, Jimmy Campbell, Reginald Connelly)	Brunswick 110

ca. July 1927, London

acc. by Leslie A. "Hutch" Hutchinson and Orchestra

"Just Like a Butterfly (That's Caught in the Rain)" (Mort Dixon, Harry Woods)	Brunswick 110

ca. July 1927, London

acc. by Leslie A. "Hutch" Hutchinson

"A Tree in the Park" (Richard Rodgers, Lorenz Hart—from *Peggy-Ann*)	Brunswick 111
"Where's That Rainbow?" (Richard Rodgers, Lorenz Hart—from *Peggy-Ann*)	Brunswick 111

R-166 "Possibly" Brunswick 113
(James Dyrenforth, Carroll Gibbons)

ca. July 1927, London

With Orchestra

R-181 "Lazy Weather" Brunswick 113
(Peter De Rose, Jo Trent)
"Nothing But" Brunswick 122
(Henry Busse, Ben Bronfin, Ferde Grofé, Sam Ward)
"Wanting You" Brunswick 122
(Maurice Abrahams, Mickey Kippel, Bernie Grossman, Arthur Sizemore)

ca. July–August 1927, London

acc. by Leslie A. "Hutch" Hutchinson and Orchestra

"Do-Do-Do" Brunswick 129
(George and Ira Gershwin—from *Oh, Kay!*)

ca. August 1927, London

acc. by Leslie A. "Hutch" Hutchinson

"Maybe" (with Check Endor and Paul Reese) Brunswick 129
(George and Ira Gershwin—from *Oh, Kay!*)

February 14, 1928, New York

With Victor Orchestra under the direction of Victor Baravalle

BVE-42442-1 "Can't Help Lovin' Dat Man" Victor 23238
(Jerome Kern, Oscar Hammerstein II—from *Show Boat*)
BVE-42443-2 "Bill" Victor 23238
(Jerome Kern, Oscar Hammerstein II—from *Show Boat*)

March 6, 1929, New York

With Victor Orchestra under the direction of Leonard Joy

BVE-50917-3 "Who Cares What You Have Been?" Victor 21930
(Martin Freed, L. Wolfe Gilbert—from *Ziegfeld Midnight Frolic*)

BVE-50918-2 "Mean to Me" Victor 21930
(Roy Turk, Fred E. Ahlert)

September 24, 1929, New York

With Victor Orchestra under the direction of Leonard Joy

BVE-56711-1 "What Wouldn't I Do for That Man" UNISSUED
BVE-56711-2 (Jay Gorney, E.Y. Harburg—from *Applause*
BVE-56711-3 and *Glorifying the American Girl*)

BVE-56712-1 "More Than You Know" UNISSUED
BVE-56712-2 (Vincent Youmans, Edward Eliscu, Billy
BVE-56712-3 Rose—from *Great Day*)

October 8, 1929, New York

With Victor Orchestra under the direction of Leonard Joy

BVE-56711-5 "What Wouldn't I Do for That Man" Victor 22149
(Jay Gorney, E.Y. Harburg—from *Applause* and *Glorifying the American Girl*)

BVE-56712-4 "More Than You Know" Victor 22149
(Vincent Youmans, Edward Eliscu, Billy Rose—from *Great Day*)

October 16, 1929, New York

With Victor Orchestra under the direction of Leonard Joy

BVE-56191-2 "Why Was I Born?" Victor 22199
(Jerome Kern, Oscar Hammerstein II—from *Sweet Adeline*)

BVE-56142-4 "Don't Ever Leave Me!" Victor 22199
(Jerome Kern, Oscar Hammerstein II—from *Sweet Adeline*)

September 5, 1930, New York

With Victor Orchestra under the direction of Leonard Joy

BVE-63625-1 BVE-63625-2 BVE-63625-3	"Body and Soul" (John Green, Robert Sour, Edward Heyman, Frank Eyton—from *Three's a Crowd*)	UNISSUED
BVE-63626-1 BVE-63626-2 BVE-63626-3	"Something to Remember You By" (Howard Dietz, Arthur Schwartz—from *Three's a Crowd*)	UNISSUED

September 12, 1930, New York

With Victor Orchestra under the direction of Leonard Joy

BVE-63625-5	"Body and Soul" (John Green, Robert Sour, Edward Heyman, Frank Eyton—from *Three's a Crowd*)	Victor 22532
BVE-63626-4	"Something to Remember You By" (Howard Dietz, Arthur Schwartz—from *Three's a Crowd*)	Victor 22532

August 9, 1932, New York

With Brunswick Orchestra under the direction of Victor Young acc. by Louis Alter

BX12161-A	"Bill" (Jerome Kern, Oscar Hammerstein II—from *Show Boat*)	Brunswick 20115-12
BX12162-A	"Can't Help Lovin' Dat Man" (Jerome Kern, Oscar Hammerstein II—from *Show Boat*)	Brunswick 20115-12

March 12, 1934, New York

With Hotel Taft Orchestra under the direction of George Hall

BS-81880-1	"A Fool There Was" (Fred Fisher, Stella Unger—from *Memory*)	UNISSUED

March 21, 1934, New York

With Victor Orchestra under the direction of Nat Shilkret

BS-81969-1	"Frankie and Johnnie" (Leighton Brothers, Ren Shields—from *Frankie and Johnnie*)	Victor 24650
BS-81968-1	"Give Me a Heart to Sing To" (Victor Young, Ned Washington—from *Frankie and Johnnie*)	Victor 24650

September 1934, Los Angeles

With Brunswick Orchestra

CP 1127	"When He Comes Home to Me" (Sam Coslow, Leo Robin—from *You Belong to Me*)	Brunswick 6984
CP 1129	"(I've Got) Sand in My Shoes" (Louis Alter, Arthur Swanstrom—from *Convention Girl*)	Brunswick 6984

September 1934, Los Angeles

With Brunswick Orchestra

CP 1126A	"It's Home" (Jay Gorney, Jack Yellen—from *Marie Galante*)	Brunswick 7329
CP 1128A	"Song of a Dreamer" (Jay Gorney, Don Hartman—from *Marie Galante*)	Brunswick 7329

December 5, 1934, Los Angeles

With Brunswick Orchestra under the direction of Jimmie Grier

LA-274B	"Winter Overnight" (Sammy Fain, Irving Kahal—from *Sweet Music*)	Brunswick 7391

December 5, 1934, Los Angeles

With Brunswick Orchestra under the direction of Constantin Bakaleinikoff

	"I See Two Lovers" (Allie Wrubel, Mort Dixon—from *Sweet Music*)	UNISSUED

January 9, 1935, Los Angeles

With Brunswick Orchestra under the direction of Constantin Bakaleinikoff

LA-275D	"I See Two Lovers" (Allie Wrubel, Mort Dixon—from *Sweet Music*)	Brunswick 7391

January 9, 1935, Los Angeles

With Brunswick Orchestra under the direction of Constantin Bakaleinikoff

LA-309A	"The Little Things You Used to Do" (Harry Warren, Al Dubin—from *Go into Your Dance*)	Brunswick 7424
LA-310A	"I Was Taken by Storm" (Louis Alter, Edward Heyman—from *Dizzy Dames*)	Brunswick 7424

Appendix 5

Principal Cabaret Appearances

Moulin Rouge Café	Chicago	June 4–13, 1924
Villa Venice	Chicago	June 14–September 13, 1924
New Café Montmartre	Chicago	September 17, 1924–January 24, 1925
Back Stage Club	New York	March 12–May 2, 1925
54th Street Club	New York	April 26–June 8, 1926
Silver Slipper	Atlantic City	July 2–9, 1926
Tommy Guinan's Playground	New York	September 9–November 3, 1926
Helen Morgan's 54th Street Club	New York	November 15, 1926–May 4, 1927
Café Anglais	London	June 13–July 9, 1927
Ross Fenton Farm	Deal Lake, NJ	September 17–18, 1927
Chez Helen Morgan	New York	September 17–November 12, 1927 December 29–30, 1927
The Helen Morgan Club	New York	January 11–June 2, 1928
Helen Morgan's Summer Home	New York	June 4–August 4, 1928
Hollywood Country Club	Miami	February 10–March 1, 1931
Club Lido	Miami	March 3–21, 1931
New Club Lido	New York	April 7–May 28, 1931
Ross Fenton Farm	Deal Lake, NJ	August 1–2, 1931 August 14–16, 1931
New Club Lido	New York	October 1–November 8, 1931 November 14–28, 1931
Club Lido	Miami	January 29–February 18, 1932
Beach and Tennis Club	Miami	February 19–March 26, 1932
Mayfair	Boston	April 9–22, 1932

Chez Maurice	Montreal	April 28–30, 1932
Mounds Club	Cleveland	December 12–24, 1932
Sam Hare's Winter Garden	Chicago	January 8–29, 1933
Embassy	New York	May 18–June 20, 1933
Chez Paree	Chicago	June 27–August 1, 1933
Piping Rock	Saratoga, NY	August 3–September 2, 1933
Longue Vue Lodge	Hastings-on-Hudson, NY	September 22–October 12, 1933
Simplon	New York	November 9, 1933–January 1, 1934
Chez Paree	Chicago	September 16–October 6, 1934
Beautiful Deauville	Miami	January 21–February 24, 1935
Versailles	New York	April 2–May 8, 1935
Normandie	New York	May 15–30, 1935
Villa Mateo	San Mateo, CA	July 31–August 6, 1935
Arrowhead Inn	Saratoga, NY	August 8–31, 1935
Blossom Heath	Detroit	September 5–18, 1935
House of Morgan	New York	November 7–30, 1935 January 24–March 2, 1936
Town Casino Club	Miami	March 6–11, 1936
Hollywood Kennel Club	Hollywood, FL	March 12–16, 1936
Chez Paree	Chicago	March 20–April 9, 1936
Pierre's New Log Cabin	Louisville KY	April 29–May 3, 1936
Blossom Heath	Detroit	May 14–27, 1936
Ciro's	London	April 19–30, 1937
Chez Paree	Chicago	July 2–August 19, 1937
Eldorado	New York	September 18–October 14, 1937
Hollywood	New York	November 11–December 3, 1937
Merry-Go-Round	New York	December 4–11, 1937
Chez Paree	Chicago	June 3–July 21, 1938
Grand Hotel	Highmount, NY	July 22–24, 1938
Riviera	Fort Lee, NJ	July 28–August 17, 1938
Bath & Turf Club	Atlantic City	August 19–25, 1938
Mayfair Farms	Pennsauken, NJ	September 10–15, 1938
Rancho San Pablo	El Cerrito, CA	October 5–18, 1938
Lookout House	Covington, KY	October 21–November 3, 1938
Chez Paree	Chicago	February 10–March 30, 1939
Jack Lynch's	Philadelphia	April 6–19, 1939
Chez Paree	Omaha	May 13–26, 1939

Principal Cabaret Appearances

Café LaMaze	Los Angeles	June 7–July 4, 1939
Club Moderne	San Francisco	July 6–August 16, 1939
Mayfair	Boston	December 18–23, 1939
Chez Maurice	Montreal	February 12–25, 1940
Famous Door	New York	February 27–March 19, 1940
Grey Wolf Tavern	Masury, OH	June 26–July 2, 1940
Bowery	Detroit	July 8–14, 1940
Rancho San Pablo	El Cerrito, CA	November 6–9, 1940[1]
		November 20–December 3, 1940
Club Moderne	San Francisco	December 12–25, 1940
Club El Rio	El Cerrito, CA	January 9–22, 1941
Hotel Dempsey-Vanderbilt	Miami	February 20–March 12, 1941
Versailles	Boston	March 17–30, 1941
Hi-Hat	Chicago	May 2–15, 1941
Tic Toc	Milwaukee	June 6–19, 1941
Hotel Dempsey-Vanderbilt	Miami	July 1–23, 1941
Roosevelt Hotel	Jacksonville	July 30–August 5, 194
Henry Grady Hotel	Atlanta	August 7–13, 1941

Appendix 6

Confirmed Benefit Performances

Date	Event	Venue	City
June 30, 1925	Benefit for Mae Kemp	Lafayette	Harlem
June 22, 1926	Mother of George W. Walker	Alhambra Theatre	Harlem
October 3, 1926	Actors' Theater	Hotel Astor	New York
October 28, 1926	NY American Christmas and Relief Fund	Belmont Theatre	New York
October 28, 1926	NY American Christmas and Relief Fund	Knickerbocker Theatre	New York
October 31, 1926	NY American Christmas and Relief Fund	Cosmopolitan Theatre	New York
November 5, 1926	NY American Christmas and Relief Fund	Rialto Theatre	New York
December 19, 1926	NY American Christmas and Relief Fund	Werba's Theatre	Brooklyn
December 19, 1926	NY American Christmas and Relief Fund	Roseland Dance Hall	New York
December 20, 1926	NY American Christmas and Relief Fund	Apollo Theatre	New York
January 27, 1927	Graphic's Lonely Hearts' Ball	Central Opera House	New York
January 30, 1927	Jr. Matron's Aux Orphan Children	Times Square Theater	New York
March 13, 1927	Jewish Comm. Centre of Jackson Heights	Lyric Theatre	New York
March 18, 1927	Cartoonists of America	Hotel Astor	New York
May 27, 1927	Families of Dead French WWI Fliers	Theatre de Champs-Elysées	Paris
October 30, 1927	Naer Tormid Society of the NYFD	Hotel Astor	New York
February 19, 1928	14th Annual Catholic Actors' Guild of American Benefit	Manhattan Opera House	New York

(Continued)

Continued

Date	Event	Venue	City
March 23, 1928	New York Newspaper Women's Club	Ritz-Carlton	New York
March 25, 1928	Hannah Lachman Society	Ziegfeld Theatre	New York
May 17, 1928	American Women's Association	*Ile de France*	(docked in) New York
May 22, 1928	NY Graphic All-Sports Dinner	Hotel Astor	New York
June 3, 1928	Burlesque Club Annual Jamboree	Columbia Theatre	Brooklyn
June [7?], 1928	Anchor Club Cabaret and Dance	Mecca Temple	New York
October 25, 1928	Honoring newspaper column conductors	Russian Kretchma	New York
November 8, 1928	Hope Farm (Duchess County) Children's Shelter/Vocational Training	Plaza Grill	New York
November 14, 1928	Musicale and teas for Children's Shelter of Manhattan	Mrs. Phillip Glemby, 339 W. 113th St.	New York
November 18, 1928	Theatrical Mutual Association, NY Lodge #1	Hudson Theatre	New York
December 2, 1928	4th Annual Authors' League Fund	Hotel Roosevelt	New York
December 9, 1928	Jewish Consumptive Relief Association	Century Theatre	New York
March 22, 1929	Scholarship for the Blind	Hotel Pennsylvania	New York
April 7, 1929	Eddie Cantor's Boys' Camp	Ziegfeld Theatre	New York
April 7, 1929	Grand Street Boys' Association	Century Theatre	New York
April 7, 1929	Jewish Consumptive Relief Society	Casino Theatre	New York
April 7, 1929	Testimonial Dinner	Brooklyn Elks	Brooklyn
April 14, 1929	Harlem Children's Fresh Air Fund	Al Jolson Theatre	New York
April 26, 1929	Marshall Stillman Movement	Star Casino	New York
May 17, 1929	Press Club Annual Frolic and Ball	New Ocean House	Swampscott, MA
July 14, 1929	Hostess of the picnic of the International Photographers of the M P Industries Local 644, IATSE	Glenwood Landing	Long Island
October 27, 1929	Naer Tormid Society of the NYFD annual entertainment and reception	Hotel Astor	New York
November 26, 1929	5th Annual Reunion of Summer Residents—proceeds for Sacred Heart Church, Cairo, NY, and St. Edmund's Chapel, Acra, NY	Brooklyn Elks Lodge	Brooklyn

Confirmed Benefit Performances

Date	Event	Venue	City
December 1, 1929	St. Benedict's Day Nursery	Casino Theatre	New York
December 8, 1929	NAACP	Forrest Theatre	New York
January 13, 1930	Hebrew National Orphan Dinner	Hotel Astor	New York
January 25, 1930	Newspapermen's Club of New York	Hotel Astor	New York
January 28, 1930[1]	Actors' Fund	Hammerstein's Theatre	New York
January 31, 1930	Press Photographers' Ball	Hotel New Yorker	New York
February 20, 1930	Frank Lee Donoghue Testimonial	Hotel New Yorker	New York
February 22, 1930	IATSE Ball Benefit Relief Fund	Madison Square Garden	New York
February 28, 1930	Newspaper Club Ball	Ritz-Carlton	New York
March 22, 1930	Israel Orphan Asylum	Madison Square Garden	New York
March 28, 1930	New York Newspaper Women's Club	Delmonico's	New York
March 30, 1930	"L'assistance Franco-Americaine aux Orphelins Francais" (tubercular French orphans)	Mecca Temple	New York
March 30, 1930	Ladies' Auxiliary of the Grand Street Boys' Association	Ziegfeld Theatre	New York
April 4, 1930	25th Anniversary, Women's Club of East Orange	Orthopedic Hospital	East Orange, NJ
April 4, 1930	Crippled Children's Country Home	Country Home	Westfield, NJ
April 4, 1930	Briarcliff Holiday House Association of Miss Dow's School	Park Lane Hotel	New York
April 6, 1930	All-Star Gala Testimonial and Review for Mrs. Ida Gropper	Booth Theatre	New York
April 6, 1930	"A Night under the Big Top"—benefiting clothing fund for poor schoolchildren	Hotel Commodore	New York
April 12, 1930	Heywood Broun's Give a Job Benefit	Imperial Theatre	New York
April 20, 1930	Jewish Community Center and Social Service Fund of Saranac Lake, NY	Carnegie Hall	New York
July 1, 1930	Grand Cabaret—benefiting Seamen's Fund for the French Line	Salon Louis IV	SS *France* (at sea)
November 2, 1930	American Theatrical Hospital	Erlanger Theatre	Chicago
November 8, 1930	Good Fellows Bazaar (jobless benefit)	Hardy's Restaurant	Chicago

(*Continued*)

Continued

Date	Event	Venue	City
November 10, 1930	American Legion's Armistice Ball	Palmer House	Chicago
December 9, 1930	Post-Gazette's Union Trust Cent-a-Claus	Union Trust Building	Pittsburgh
January 23, 1931	NY Press Photographers' Association	Hotel New Yorker	New York
February 24, 1931	Fort Lauderdale Elks	Sunset Theatre	Fort Lauderdale
February 25, 1931	Kiwanis Underprivileged Children	Paramount Theatre	Palm Beach, FL
March 2, 1931	Mayor Reeder's Fund for Work Unemployed	Olympia Theatre	Miami
March 3, 1931	Mayor Reeder's Unemployment Committee	Hialeah Racetrack	Miami
April 17, 1931	Briarcliff Holiday House Association	Park Lane Hotel	New York
April 26, 1931	National Variety Artists' Pageant	Metropolitan Opera	New York
April 30, 1931	Eve Graphic All-Sports Dinner	Hotel Astor	New York
May 5, 1931	Saints Peter and Paul, Hoboken	Lambs	New York
September 6, 1931	Third Ward Republican Club Welfare Fund	Apollo Theatre	Atlantic City
November 1, 1931	Friars' Ball and Carnival	Madison Square Garden	New York
November 6, 1931	Peacock Ball—Association for Improving the Condition of the Poor	Waldorf-Astoria	New York
November 8, 1931	NY American and Evening Journal Christmas and Relief Fund	New Amsterdam	New York
November 15, 1931	NY American and Evening Journal Christmas and Relief Fund	Imperial Theatre	New York
November 15, 1931	Riverside Synagogue	Selwyn Theatre	New York
November 20, 1931	Tea Dance and Fashion Show—benefiting the Hospital for the Relief of the Ruptured and Crippled	Park Lane Hotel	New York
November 21, 1931	NY Sun Club	Essex House	New York
November 22, 1931	Wall Street Synagogue	Hotel Pennsylvania	New York
November 29, 1931	Great Meadow Prison	Great Meadow Prison	Comstock, NY

Confirmed Benefit Performances

Date	Event	Venue	City
November 29, 1931	Daily Mirror City Hospital Radio Fund	Selwyn Theatre	New York
December 27, 1931	Sing Sing Prison	Sing Sing	Ossining, NY
February 2, 1932	St. Francis Hospital	Biscayne Kennel Club	Miami
February 5, 1932	Junior League Annual Charity Ball—for Children's Home	Biltmore Country Club	Miami
February 11, 1932	Val C. Cleary Unemployment Fund	Flamingo Park	Miami
February 23, 1932	Charity Event	Hialeah Park	Miami
February 25, 1932	7th Annual Kiwanis Event—free clinics for the unemployed	Paramount Theatre	Miami
March 14, 1932	Miami Little Theatre	Kennel Club Racetrack	Miami Beach
March 19, 1932	University of Miami	Tropical Park	Miami
May 13, 1932	Block Aid Community Org.'s Emergency Unemployment Relief Committee	Petrushka Club	New York
May 19, 1932	NY Graphic's Annual Sports Dinner	Hotel Astor	New York
June 6, 1932	Unemployment Relief Day	Belmont Racetrack	Elmont, NY
June 12, 1932	Emergency Food Relief	Fort Hamilton	Brooklyn
June 12, 1932	First Annual Contract Bridge Party—benefiting Actors' Fund	Waldorf-Astoria	New York
June 14, 1932	Hebrew Kindergarten and Infants' Home	Casa Del Mar	Long Beach, NY
August 14, 1932	Building Fund for the University of American Theatre (Amagansett)	Guild Hall	East Hampton, NY
August 21, 1932	2nd Concert—benefiting Amagansett	Guild Hall	E. Hampton, NY
September 5, 1932	Actors' Dinner Club	Atlantic Beach Club	Atlantic Beach, NY
September 7, 1932	Old Time Mardi Gras	Livingston Ave. Elks Club	Brooklyn
September 8, 1932	Newspaper Club's Unemployment Relief Fund	Arrowhead Inn	New York
September 10, 1932	"Marinescope" pageant for needy children of Nassau County	Sands Point Bath Club	Port Wash-ington, NY
September 16, 1932	Freeport Police Benevolent Association	Grove Theatre	Freeport, NY
October 9, 1932	Actors' Dinner Club	Casino Theatre	New York

(Continued)

Continued

Date	Event	Venue	City
October 16, 1932	Eva Tanguay benefit	Casino Theatre	New York
October 22, 1932	"Parade of the Stars" fashion show—benefiting the Actors' Dinner Club	Waldorf-Astoria	New York
January 3, 1933	Idle Local 2 Theatrical Stage Employees Union	Grand Opera House	Chicago
March 19, 1933	"Irish Night"	St. Teresa's RC Church	Brooklyn
June 5, 1933	Unemployed Newspaper Men and Women	Belmont Racetrack	Elmont, NY
June 5, 1933	Patrolmen's Association	Lynbrook Theatre	Brooklyn
June 18, 1933	NY Guild for the Jewish Blind	NY Home for the Jewish Blind	Yonkers
June 19, 1933	St. Elizabeth Hospital Benefit Vaudeville	Ritz Theatre	Elizabeth, NJ
July 23, 1933	St. Aloysius Church and School	Great Neck Playhouse	Great Neck
August 24, 1933	Annual Saratoga Springs Police Benevolent Associations	Convention Hall	Saratoga Springs, NY
November 5, 1933	Stage Relief Fund	New Amsterdam	New York
November 12, 1933	Brooklyn Federation of Jewish Charities	Hotel St. George	Brooklyn
November 12, 1933	17th Annual National Vaudeville Artists Benefit	Manhattan Opera House	New York
November 19, 1933	NY Evening Journal and American Christmas Fund	Imperial Theatre	New York
November 21, 1933	5th Annual Dinner of the Typochondriacs	Towers Hotel	New York
November 25, 1933	Actors' Dinner Club	Sherry's Restaurant	New York
December 2, 1933	Beth-El Hospital	Waldorf-Astoria	New York
December 3, 1933	NY Evening Journal and American Christmas Fund	Winter Garden Theatre	New York
December 7, 1933	Annual Charity Ball for NY Nursery and Child's Hospital	Ritz-Carlton	New York
December 16, 1933	Dinner/Dance for City Court Justice Louis Goldstein—benefiting YMHA and YWHA	Unity Club	Brooklyn
December 16, 1933	Midnight Frolic–associated charities of North Queens	Jackson Theatre	Jackson Heights
December 16, 1933	"Reunion in Tel Aviv" Hannukah celebration	Madison Square Garden	New York

Confirmed Benefit Performances

Date	Event	Venue	City
December 17, 1933	11th Annual Banquet and Dance—benefiting Brooklyn Women's Hospital	Park Manor	Brooklyn
February 2, 1934	Press Photographers' Association of New York	Hotel Commodore	New York
February 8, 1934	10th Annual Benefit Dinner—Beth-El Hospital	Waldorf-Astoria	New York
February 16, 1934	Scottsboro Boys Defense Fund	Savoy Hotel	New York
February 21, 1934	Independent Theater Owners	Waldorf-Astoria	New York
March 2, 1934	Helen Morgan Club (benefiting various welfare charities)	Hotel Astor	New York
March 11, 1934	Ed Sullivan Show for Sing Sing prisoners	Sing Sing	Ossining, NY
April 26, 1934	Benefit for new B'nai B'rith clubhouse	Lodge 487, B'nai B'rith	Los Angeles
January 30, 1935	President Roosevelt's Birthday Party—Warm Springs benefit	Roney Plaza Hotel	Miami Beach
February 8, 1935	Junior League Children's Home benefit	Columbus Hotel	Miami
February 13, 1935	10th Annual Kiwanis Event—free clinics for the unemployed	Paramount Theatre	Palm Beach, FL
March 31, 1935	Variety Club	Stanley Theatre	Pittsburgh
April 6, 1935	Brooklyn Hebrew Orphan Society	Waldorf-Astoria	New York
April 7, 1935	Hebrew Orphans and Sheltering Home of Lincoln Ave	Mosque Theatre	Newark, NJ
April 14, 1935	Yeshiva College Dinner	Waldorf-Astoria	New York
April 26, 1935	Bushwick Hospital	Towers Hotel	Brooklyn
April 28, 1935	Eddie Cantor's Boys' Camp	Alvin Theatre	New York
May 18, 1935	NVA and NY State Masonic Clubs	Madison Square Garden	New York
May 19, 1935	Testimonial benefit to Jack Inglis	Ambassador Theatre	New York
July 29, 1935	Boxing event to benefit Most Holy Redeemer Church	Freeport Stadium	Brooklyn
August 21, 1935	St. Clement's Bazaar	St. Clement's	Saratoga Springs, NY
August 23, 1935	Saratoga Springs Police Ball	Convention Hall	Saratoga Springs, NY
August 30, 1935	Annual Military Ball of the 39th Annual National Encampment of Jewish War Veterans	Convention Hall	Saratoga Springs, NY
September 18, 1935	Musical Tea for the League of Catholic Women	Walbri Hall	Bloomfield Hills, MI

(Continued)

Continued

Date	Event	Venue	City
November 24, 1935	8th Annual Dinner—Federation for the Support of Jewish Philanthropic Societies	Waldorf-Astoria	New York
December 1, 1935	Daughters of Israel Home benefit	Hotel Commodore	New York
December 12, 1935	LA Examiner's Christmas Benefit	Shrine Auditorium	Los Angeles
January 24, 1936	Press Photographers' Ball	Hotel Commodore	New York
March 17, 1936	Junior League Charity Ball	Surf Club	Miami
April 19, 1936	Hebrew Orphans and Sheltering Home of Lincoln Ave.	Mosque Theatre	Newark, NJ
July 2, 1936	Marcey Center and Madonna Center	Coliseum	Chicago
August 22, 1936	Chicago Defender's Annual Bud Billiken Parade and Children's Picnic	Washington Park	Chicago
March 20, 1937	Benefit preview screening of *The King and the Chorus Girl*—benefiting flood victims	7th Regiment Armory	New York
April 13, 1937	Seamen's Fund		*Lafayette* (at sea)
May 6, 1937	"Midnight with the Stars"—benefiting the Cinematograph Trade Benevolent Fund	Empire Theatre	London
June 21, 1937	6th Annual Night of Sports—benefiting Leonard S. Morange Post's welfare & civic work, also the League for Service and Bronxville Boy and Girl Scouts	Chambers Field	Bronxville, NY
August 14, 1937	Chicago Defender's Annual Bud Billiken Parade and Children's Picnic	Washington Park	Chicago
August 15, 1937	Will Rogers Memorial Hospital		Chicago
October 21, 1937	Union Drawn Steel Athletic Association	State Theatre	Hartford, CT
October 31, 1937	1937–1938 Associated Jewish Philanthropies	Hotel Somerset	Boston
November 15, 1937	Medical Division of Local 802 (Musicians' Union)	Hotel Astor	New York
November 17, 1937	United Palestine Appeal "Night of Stars"	Madison Square Garden	New York

Confirmed Benefit Performances

Date	Event	Venue	City
November 25, 1937	NY Journal American and Hollywood Restaurant Thanksgiving Dinner	Hollywood Restaurant	New York
December 21, 1937	Chorus Equity—Christmas Ball and Entertainment	Manhattan Opera House	New York
December 23, 1941	Automotive Boosters Club #13 Christmas Party for Underprivileged Children	Empire Hotel	New York
February 12, 1938	Thrift Shop Ball—benefiting Children's Country Home, Children's Hospital, Child Welfare, and Columbus Hospital	Sulgrave Club	Washington, DC
February 28, 1938	Circus Saints and Sinners Costume Ball—benefiting W. W. Workman Tent	Roof Garden of the Hotel John Marshall	Richmond, VA
March 18, 1938	Brooklyn Police Athletic League	Brooklyn Academy of Music	Brooklyn
March 27, 1938	34th Annual Entertainment of the Jewish Consumptive Relief Society	Hotel Astor	New York
April 3, 1938	Jewish Theatrical Guild	Imperial Theatre	New York
April 20, 1938	Adult Education Fund	Pelham Memorial High School	Pelham, NY
April 30, 1938	3rd Annual Ziegfeld Club Dance	Hotel Plaza	New York
May 7, 1938	Charity Bazaar for Beth David Hospital	Hotel Pennsylvania	New York
May 12, 1938	Nursing Sisters of the Sick Poor	Columbus Club	Brooklyn
May 20, 1938	Brooklyn Police Athletic League	Brooklyn Academy of Music	Brooklyn
May 22, 1938	All-Star Show-Dance-Frolic Benefit for Hebrew Orphans	Armory	Newark, NJ
July 16, 1938	"Westchester Youth Aliyah Fete"—to relocate refugee Jewish children from Austria, Poland, and Germany to Palestine	Harry Warner's Estate	Mount Vernon, NY
July 20, 1938	William McKinley Camp, No. 6, Spanish-American War Veterans	Edward Hines Jr. Memorial Hospital	Chicago
November 13, 1938	United Palestine Appeal	Madison Square Garden	New York
November 17, 1938	National Showmen's Association—hospitalization and funeral fund for tent performers	Hotel Commodore	New York

(*Continued*)

Continued

Date	Event	Venue	City
December 16, 1938	New Amsterdam News Christmas Basket Fund	Apollo	Harlem
December 18, 1938	Temple Ezrath Israel (the Actors' Synagogue)	Alvin Theatre	New York
December 21, 1938	Aliyah Fund to settle German Jewish children in Palestine	Sow Bar	Forrest Hills, NY
January 22, 1939	57th Annual Actors' Fund Concert	Winter Garden	New York
January 30, 1939	President's Ball—campaign against infantile paralysis	Fifth Regiment Armory	Baltimore
February 18, 1939	Press Photographers' Ball	Hotel Commodore	New York
March 10, 1939	Prince Street Boys' Association	Mosque Theatre	Newark, NJ
April 2, 1939	15th Annual Camp Sussex Frolic—benefiting diabetic children	Waldorf-Astoria	New York
April 9. 1939	30th Annual Friar's Frolics	Alvin Theatre	New York
April 22, 1939	4th Annual Ziegfeld Club Ball and Midnight Frolic—benefiting ill and needy Ziegfeld girls	Waldorf-Astoria Starlight Roof	New York
December 22, 1939	3rd Annual Christmas Party	Cambridge Tuberculosis Sanatorium	Cambridge, MA
February 25, 1940	Le Regiment de Maisonneuve and Les Fusiliers de Mont-Royal	Chez Maurice	Montreal
March 10, 1940	31st Annual Friar's Frolics	Winter Garden	New York
March 13, 1940	Annual Entertainment for Patients	Montefiore Hospital	Bronx
April 18, 1940	Queen's Finnish Relief Committee	Carlton Theatre	Jamaica, NY
April 26, 1940	Newspaper Guild of New York Parade of 1940	Manhattan Center	New York
September 29, 1940	Daniel Frohman Testimonial—Actors Fund Benefit	Ben Marden's Riviera	Fort Lee, NJ
February 24, 1941	"Night of Stars" for the Jewish Welfare Bureau	Olympia Theatre	Miami
February 26, 1941	Miami Beach Elks Charity Fund	Plaza Theatre	Miami Beach
February 27, 1941	Chicago Infantile Paralysis Fund	Beachcomber Restaurant	Miami
March 3, 1941	Actor Benefit	Club Wit's End	Miami
March 12, 1941	Coral Gables Police Benevolent Society	Coral Gables Country Club	Coral Gables, FL

Confirmed Benefit Performances

Date	Event	Venue	City
March 21, 1941	Greek War Relief	Metropolitan Theatre	Boston
March 30, 1941	Menorah Institute	Colonial Theatre	Boston
May 17, 1941	CYO Youth Benefit Ball		Chicago
May 18, 1941	Rest Haven Convalescent Home	Rest Haven Convalescent Home	Chicago
July 17, 1941	USO	Hotel Dempsey-Vanderbilt	Miami
July 29, 1941	Benefit for critically ill Chick Endor	Coral Club	Miami
August 31, 1939	Musicians' Protective Association Welfare Fund	Hotel Chelsea	Atlantic City, NJ

Notes

Abbreviations

Archives

AMPAS/MHL—Margaret Herrick Library, Academy of Motion Picture Arts and Sciences
BRTD/NYPL—Billy Rose Theatre Division, New York Public Library
FOX/USC—Fox Studio Archive, School of Cinematic Arts, University of Southern California
IAM/MK—Institute of the American Musical, Miles Kreuger, President
LJS—Lloyd Johnson Scrapbook, author's collection
LTP/BYU—L. Tom Perry Special Collection, Brigham Young University
MS/FLP—Helen Morgan Scrapbook, Free Library of Philadelphia
OHA/LOC—Oscar Hammerstein II Archive, Library of Congress
U/USC—Universal Studio Archive, School of Cinematic Arts, University of Southern California
WBA/USC—Warner Bros. Archives, School of Cinematic Arts, University of Southern California

Periodicals

BB—Billboard: 1920–1946*BDE—Brooklyn Daily Eagle*: 1923–1941, 1946, 1951
BG—Boston Globe: 1924–1942
CDN—Chicago Daily News: 1921–1939
CT—Chicago Tribune: 1898, 1909, 1915–1941, 1948, 1956–1957, 1967–1970, 1983
CPD—Cleveland Plain Dealer: 1930–1941
LAT—Los Angeles Times: 1929–1965
MDN—Miami Daily News: 1935–1941
MH—Miami Herald: 1935, 1983
MT—Miami Tribune: 1935–1937
NYA—New York American: 1929–1936
NYDM—New York Daily Mirror: 1925–1937
NYDN—New York Daily News: 1926–1942, 1951, 1957, 1976
NYEG—New York Evening Graphic: 1927–1932
NYEJ—New York Evening Journal: 1929–1935

NYEP—New York Evening Post: 1926–1943, 1956
NYMT—New York Morning Telegraph: 1926–1937
NYS—New York Sun: 1925–1940
NYT—New York Times: 1898, 1923–1950, 1957, 1968, 2001
NYWT—New York World-Telegram: 1933–1941
OT—Oakland Tribune: 1928–1953
PP—Pittsburgh Press: 1924–1938
SFE—San Francisco Examiner: 1929–1958
TFD—Film Daily: 1923, 1929–1934, 1947
THR—Hollywood Reporter: 1934–1935, 1956–1957
Variety: 1912, 1918–1942, 1950, 1956–1957, 1977
WaPo—Washington Post: 1928–1957

Prologue: Songs from the Heart

1. Malcolm Johnson, "Cafe Life in New York," *NYS*, March 7, 1940.
2. Olga Swanson to Jack Warner, June 10, 1957, WBA/USC.

1. "Only Make Believe"

1. Birth certificates were not required in Iowa in 1882, but Lulu listed Bloomfield as her natal city on her US passport, #366352. "New York, U.S., Arriving Passenger and Crew Lists (including Castle Garden and Ellis Island), 1820–1957," *Ile de France*, September 6, 1927, sheet 13. https://www.ancestry.com.

2. Frank Allen Riggin and Lulu Lang, "Marriage Certificate No. 13809" (Office of the County Clerk, Danville, IL, 1899).

3. Frank Allen Riggin, "Death Certificate No. 4003949" (Indiana State Board of Health, 1947).

4. Frank A. Riggin, "Examination Preliminary to Muster-Out of U. S. Service or Discharge" (Spanish-American War Military Pension File No. 1295167, October 22, 1898).

5. Riggin infant, "Record of Birth" (Fountain-Warren Indiana County Health Department, book 44, June 21, 1901), 24; "Record of Death" (book 421, June 21, 1901), 28.

6. Michel Mok, "Helen of Flatbush: The New House of Morgan," *New York Post*, August 8, 1938.

7. Earl Wilson, "It Happened Last Night," *NYEP*, October 10, 1943.

8. Polly Bergen (via assistant Eva Schegulla), email, July 20, 2001.

9. Frank A. Riggin v. Lula Riggin, "For Complaint" (155 Fountain Cir. Ind. Sept. 16, 1902).

10. All extant documentation through 1923 (school records, census reports, newspaper articles) clearly state that Helen was born in 1902. Beginning in 1927 (passports, census, marriage licenses, etc.), Helen claimed that she was born in 1904. The fiction that she was born in 1900 apparently arose from Burns Mantle, ed., *The Best Plays of 1928–1929* (New York: Dodd, Mead, 1929), 521.

11. *Fountain-Warren (IN) Democrat*, February 26, 1903.

12. Riggin, "Pension File 1295167."

13. "Lewis G. Riggin Passes Away," *Attica (IN) Daily Tribune*, May 18, 1917.

14. William Wilkins and Lulu Riggin, "Marriage Certificate No. 16863" (Office of the County Clerk, Danville, IL, 1903).

15. Specifically, 2910 Lake Park Avenue. "Loses His Heart," *Covington (IN) Republican*, October 17, 1902.

16. Lulu Wilkins v. William Wilkins, "Certificate of Evidence Gen. No. 285316 Term No. 25557" (Cook Cir. Ill. Feb. 13, Sept. 24, 1908).

17. Gary Wilkins, biography of his grandfather William Wilkins, author's collection.

18. "Acquired Art from Contact with Life," *Cincinnati Times-Star*, December 7, 1932.

19. "When Helen Morgan Went Blind!," *Hollywood*, July 1936, 44–45.

20. Alice L. Tildesley, "Philosophy of a Torch Singer," *Baltimore Sun*, March 10, 1935.

21. Sidney Skolsky, "When Broadwayites Were Kids," *Buffalo Courier-Express*, January 25, 1931; Hazel Flynn, "Danville Days Recalled by Miss Morgan," *Chicago Evening American*, n.d., MS/FLP, book 3, 6B.

22. Thomas Morgan and Lulu Wilkins, "Marriage Certificate No. 1004" (Office of the County Clerk, Berrien, MI, 1909).

23. Not until six months after the shooting did the court issue a bench warrant for Louis's arrest and set bail at $500. "A Neighborly Affair," *Louisville Courier-Journal*, June 28, 1882; "The Dockets—Official Report," *Louisville Courier-Journal*, December 7, 1882.

24. 1082 West Lake Street. *Chicago City Directory* (Chicago: Chicago Directory Company, 1909), 1732.

25. Danny later became a doctor. Louis Sobol, *Down Memory Lane with Helen Morgan* (New York: Palace Theatre Program, 1931), 4.

26. Grant School forms, Class a2, September 9, 1910, and 2b, May 15, 1912: Helen Morgan, date of birth August 2, 1902, address 104 Washington, and father Thomas Morgan. MS/FLP, book 1, 1B.

27. "Helen Morgan Tells All!," *Grand Rapids Herald*, January 9, 1937.

28. Gene Coughlin, "Tragedies of the Stage," *American Weekly*, September 4, 1949, 7.

29. The house on Washington was around the corner from where Helen was born. Becky Mabbry, "First 'Torch Singer' Called Danville Home but Never Sang There," *Champagne (IL) News-Gazette*, December 1, 1995.

30. Leila E. Bracy, "Could Cook When She Was Eight," *Detroit Free Press*, October 11, 1930.

31. Grace Kingsley, "World's Champion Torch Singer Goes Domestic in Hollywood," Screen and Radio Weekly, *Detroit Free Press*, February 3, 1935, 4.

32. Evan Olson, letter, March 29, 1992.

33. Tildesley, "Philosophy of a Torch Singer."

34. Lulu Morgan v. Thomas Morgan, "Bill for Divorce" (Vermilion Cir. Ill. Jan. 1915).

35. "Morgan under Arrest at Danville," *Munster (IN) Times*, September 27, 1913.

36. "Morgan Is Guilty, According to Jury," *Danville (IL) Commercial News*, November 28, 1913; other articles from September to December 1913.

37. The Morgans lived at 631 South Sohl Street, less than a mile from the Illinois border. 1920 US Census (Lake County, Indiana, Hammond City, Enumeration District 63, Sheet 6A, Dwelling 183, Family 142) and 1930 (Enumeration District 45-131, Sheet 5A, Dwelling 631, Family 95), https://www.ancestry.com.

38. "Officer Strong Nabs Man," *Times* (Munster, IN), December 29, 1917.

39. Linda Badger, Record Section, Prisoner Review Board, State of Illinois, letter, August 22, 1994.

40. "Conroy Springs a Surprise, Clears Man," *Times* (Munster, IN), June 7, 1922.

41. "Helen Morgan Tells All!"

42. Harry T. Brundidge, "Helen Morgan, Madcap of Stage and Radio, Tells of Happy-Go-Lucky Life," *St. Louis Star*, April 4, 1930.

43. Arsonia Café, 1654 Madison Street. Arthur Sheekman, "Ahead of the Times," *Chicago Daily Times*, September 5, 1929.

44. Helen claimed that she attended twenty-six schools during her nomadic childhood. The actual number was likely six or seven. "Helen Morgan Tells All!"

45. Edward G. Kroeter and Lulu Morgan, "Marriage Certificate No. 719884" (Office of the County Clerk, Chicago, IL, 1916).

46. Nanette Kutner, "She Started Out to Be a Dancer," *Dance Magazine*, July 1930, 21, 60.

47. Beverly Maxwell, telephone interview, April 24, 1991.

48. Kutner, "She Started Out to Be a Dancer."

49. "Local and Personal Mention," *Attica (IN) Daily Tribune*, December 5, 1918.

50. *Fountain-Warren (IN) Democrat*, December 13, 1917.

51. *Marshall Field Glass* (store employee publication, summer 1936), WBA/USC.

52. Booking agent: H. Allen Smith, "Interviewer Takes Helen Morgan's Place on Piano," *NYWT*, September 18, 1937. Dancing master: Beatrice May Miller, "Helen Morgan: The Enigma," *Cabaret Stories*, December 1928, 22–23.

53. *Happy Days* (January 13–March 15, 1919), bowed as the first Beck revue. The next production, *Spring Joys*, ran from March to April, followed on May 7 by Bill Robinson in *Starlights*. In early July, *The Revue of Revues* (later renamed *Skylarks*) ran during Helen's brief marriage. William Zeh caught Helen in the chorus of the fall production, *Spotlights*, in mid-October. *Snowflurries* played into March 1920. It is unlikely that Morgan stayed through the summer of 1920. Her name does not appear in programs for *Happy Days* in Kenneth Irwin and Charles O. Lloyd, *Ruth Etting: America's Forgotten Sweetheart* (Lanham, MD: Scarecrow, 2010), 56—nor in *Skylarks* or *The Passing Parade* (Summer 1921), either. Author's collection.

54. William Howland Kenney, *Chicago Jazz: A Cultural History, 1904–1930* (New York: Oxford University Press, 1993), 81.

55. "Wet Cabaret and Special Bars Both Die," *CT*, May 7, 1918.

56. The exception to the rule: on this marriage license, Helen claimed to have been born in 1900, making her eighteen going on nineteen, not sixteen going on seventeen. William Realino Zeh and Helen Riggin, "Marriage Certificate No. 833660" (Office of the County Clerk, Chicago, IL, 1919).

57. Dorothy Dey, "Night and Day," *NYMT*, January 1, 1935.

58. "Wants an Accounting," *Evening Star* (Washington, DC), July 30, 1908.

59. "Mayor Blocks New Move for Wilson Avenue Saloon," *CT*, April 23, 1915.

60. "Women Protest Madonna with Short Skirts," *CT*, February 23, 1921.

61. William Zeh v. Helen Zeh, "Bill for Divorce, B-79940" (Cook Cir. Ill. Jan. 1922).

62. "Helen Morgan's Voice Stilled by Death at 37," *Music and Rhythm*, November 1941, 11.

63. The strangulation incident occurred in Minnie A. Page's boarding house at 2201 Washington. Mamie Ward's house was at 1303 Washington. Lulu Kroeter v. Edward Kroeter, "Bill for Divorce, B-71684" (Cook Cir. Ill. Feb. 17, 1921).

64. June Provines, "Front Views and Profiles," *CT*, August 7, 1936.

65. Production manager Frank Hill remembered scrambling to pad out his chorus before the Broadway opening, but more likely, he backfilled the line en route to the West Coast or late in the run when the production played one- and two-night stands in western tank towns. Wood Soanes, "Curtain Calls," *OT*, October 15, 1936.

66. "First of Aubrey's New Comedy Series Will Be Called *The Decorator*," *Moving Picture World*, July 17, 1920, 368.

67. The local sheriff seized the physical production on behalf of the union, storing it in the Kansas City Convention Hall until May 1921, when Equity sold the collection, valued at $160,000, for $7,000. "To Sell Show," *Billboard*, May 21, 1921, 38.

68. Helen Morgan is mentioned by name. "*Frivolities* Ordered Stopped in K. C. by Equity's Man," *Variety*, December 24, 1920, 10.

69. "150 in Cast of *Night at the Moulin Rouge*," *Sioux Falls Argus-Leader*, October 1, 1939.

70. "Rainbo Garden, 2 Others Raided, by Major's Men," *CT*, August 10, 1920.

71. "Little of Everything," *CDN*, various Saturday editions, April–August 1921.

72. While Kutner suggests that it was a one-off, Rian James claims that Helen was part of the company from the start and that Smith came aboard later. Rian James, "Names Make News!," *BDE*, December 20, 1931.

73. Robert Baral, *Revue: A Nostalgic Reprise of the Great Broadway Period* (New York: Fleet, 1962), 113.

74. "$75,000 Loss," *BB*, November 5, 1921, 34.

75. Dorothy Dey, "Night and Day," *NYMT*, November 16, 1937.

76. Frank P. Payne and Lulu Morgan, "Marriage Certificate No. 1054" (Office of the County Clerk, St. Joseph, MI, 1921).

77. "Personals," *Clyde (NY) Herald*, April 26, 1922.

2. "Insufficient Sweetie"

1. Art Arthur, "With Art Arthur," *BDE*, April 19, 1935.

2. "Introducing 'Kayser' Italian Silk Underwear in Canada," Perrin Kayser Company pamphlet, MS/FLP, box 2, folder 1.

3. "Fashion's Best on Living Models," *Montreal Daily Star*, January 4, 1923.

4. The Columbus, Ohio, competitor won the 1922 and 1923 contests. The pageant revised its rules to prevent winners from competing again.

5. Another pre-1927 documentation of 1902 as the year of Morgan's birth: "Two Beauties Call upon Mayor Hylan," *NYT*, January 21, 1923.

6. "Theatre Audience Cheers 2 Beauties," *NYT*, January 23, 1923.

7. "Farewell Reception for Visiting Beauties," *New York Herald*, January 23, 1923.

8. Specifically, International News #9. "Resume of News Weeklies," *Motion Picture News*, February 10, 1923, 713.

9. O. O. McIntyre, "O. O. McIntyre," *Chattanooga (TN) News*, March 24, 1937.

10. Upon learning they would be judged on beauty alone and not athleticism, several Miss Montreal—and Miss Canada—contestants rebelled against the teas and photo ops that preempted athletic events, but only the Montreal Amateur Athletic Association pulled their Miss Montreal candidate, Grace Newmark, from the competition.

11. "Fifteen Selected as Candidates," *Montreal Gazette*, January 27, 1923.

12. "Fifteen Girls Now in Contest," *Montreal Daily News*, January 27, 1923.

13. On February 2, judges chose the candidate sponsored by *La Presse*, Gabrielle Rivet, to be Miss Montreal. Katherine Campbell never returned, as scheduled, on February 11, when judges crowned Winifred C. Blair of Saint John, New Brunswick, as Miss Canada.

14. "La Decision Des Juges Du Concours Sera Connue Ce Soir, Ou Demain Soir," *La Presse*, February 2, 1923 (trans. Josh Borden).

15. "N.V.A. Notes," *Variety*, March 2, 1923, 14.

16. "Paramount Announces 'Super 39,'" *Exhibitors Herald*, January 6, 1923, 65, 73–76.

17. "Screen Face Contest," *Louisville Courier-Journal*, June 4, 1923.

18. "To Decide Winner in Movie Contest at Arcadia Hall," *Chat* (Brooklyn), March 24, 1923.

19. Regina Crewe, "Croon Princess of Song," *NYA*, August 12, 1934.

20. Paramount features produced in the East from March to August 1923, and in which Helen may have appeared, include *The Ne'er-Do-Well*, *Fog Bound*, *The Exciters*, *Homeward Bound*, *Zaza*, *The Spanish Dancer*, and *His Children's Children*. Morgan also worked for other studios during this period.

21. "Paramount Trims Schedule to 52 Productions Annually," *Exhibitors Herald*, May 26, 1923, 39.

22. William Anthony McGuire, *Six Cylinder Love*, condensed in *The Best Plays of 1921–22* (New York: Dodd, Mead, 1922), 163–98.

23. Vivian Shirley, "Vivian Shirley Learns Road to Fame Isn't Always Easiest to Tread, but Goal Is Worthy," *Philadelphia Public Ledger*, March 2, 1931.

24. "Maryland Vaudeville Exceptionally Good: Opportunity Night Tonight," *Hagerstown Morning Herald*, September 14, 1923.

25. "'Is Divorce a Failure?' Registers Hit at State," *Trenton Evening Times*, September 18, 1923.

26. Warren G. Harris, *The Other Marilyn: A Biography of Marilyn Miller* (New York: Arbor House, 1985), 70–119.

27. The comedy *Lightnin'* (August 26, 1919, Gaiety) and the musical *Irene* (November 18, 1919, Vanderbilt) ran longer than *Sally*. "*Sally* over $2,000,000 Gross Mark, U. S. Boxoffice Record," *Variety*, April 14, 1922, 1, 3.

28. Jan Hall, daughter-in-law to Edward T. Hall and Joan Gardner, email, February 7, 2005.

29. "Miss Mount Royal Wed; Quits *Sally*," *Albany Times-Union*, January 2, 1924.

30. Address: 39 Glendale Avenue in the Brighton neighborhood. "Lowell Almy Weds Miss Helen Morgan," *BG*, January 4, 1924.

31. Helen Almy v. Lowell F. Almy, "Bill for Divorce, No. 40500" (Cook Cir. Ill. July 1924).

32. "'Turned Down' by Ziegfeld," *BG*, May 12, 1929.

33. Moulin Rouge, 416 South Wabash, Chicago. United States of America v. Albert Bouche, Leo Kamerman, Philip Craft, William Comstock, John R. Thompson, Flora Bouche, and Nick Sebastian, "Decree," 2743 (N.D. Ill. June 12, 1923).

34. "Bomb Wrecks Loop Cabaret," *CT*, June 17, 1924.

35. "Helen Morgan in Coloroto," *NYDN*, July 25, 1937.

36. "Villa Venice Is a Home of Real Delight," *Chicago Herald and Examiner*, July 13, 1924.

37. Tamiris, "Tamiris in Her Own Voice: Draft of an Autobiography," *Studies in Dance History*, Fall/Winter 1989–1990, 21–22.

38. "Fighting Parson Loses Tilt with Goddess Chance," *CT*, October 24, 1924.

39. Ken Michaels, "Dean Martin Plays to de Common Folk," *CT Sunday Magazine*, November 26, 1967, 87.

40. The Green Mill is the rarest of the rare: a Prohibition-era club that is still in existence. Green Mill Jazz Club (website), accessed October 28, 2022, http://greenmilljazz.com.

41. "Montmartre, Chi, Reopens 'Palace of Hallucinations,'" *Variety*, October 8, 1924, 39.

42. Advertisements, *Chicago Daily Journal*, December 6, 1924, January 10, 1925.

43. Amy Leslie, "Where Clever Young Beauties Come From," *CDN*, January 10, 1925; Leslie, "Brush Up on Classics for Sophie Tucker," *CDN*, January 31, 1925.

44. Marjorie Farnsworth, *The Ziegfeld Follies* (New York: Putnam, 1956), 118–19.

3. Scandalized

1. Jimmy Durante and Jack Kofoed, *Night Clubs* (New York: Alfred A. Knopf, 1931), 65.

2. Harry Richman, *A Hell of a Life* (New York: Duell, Sloan and Pearce, 1966), 175.

3. "Webster Guest 'Find' of Parkway Guest" (Chicago: Webster Hotel, ca. 1926). Helen also wrote atop a photo of Leslie in her scrapbook, "I owe everything to Miss Leslie." MS/FLP, book 1, 6B, 13A.

4. "Songwriters Opening New Cabaret, the Backstage," *BB*, March 2, 1925, 20.

5. Herbert G. Goldman, *Fanny Brice: The Original Funny Girl* (New York: Oxford University Press, 1992), 133.

6. Jack Burton, *The Blue Book of Tin Pan Alley* (Watkins Glen, NY: Century House, 1950), 360–63.

7. Hal Eaton, "Going to Town," *Long Island Daily Press*, September 7, 1944.

8. John and the Missus, "Back Stage Club Is an Early Morning 'Wow,'" *NYDM*, April 3, 1925.

9. Ibid.

10. Radio listing, *Brooklyn Standard Union*, April 7, 1925.

11. Earl Conrad, *Billy Rose: Manhattan Primitive* (Cleveland: World Publishing, 1968), 69–71.

12. Ibid.

13. "Broadway Slang Capital of World," *Baltimore Sun*, November 20, 1927. Damon Runyon credited Lyman with coining the term in the earliest mention of "torch song" in print. "Runyon Says," *Asheville (NC) Citizen-Times*, October 31, 1926.

14. Al Clark, "A Piano-Sitter Quits," *PP Magazine*, July 5, 1931.

15. John and the Missus, "Back Stage Club Is an Early Morning 'Wow.'"

16. Earl Wilson, "It Happened Last Night," *NYEP*, October 10, 1943.

17. Gene Fowler, *Schnozzola: The Story of Jimmy Durante* (New York: Viking, 1951), 140.

18. George Eels, *Ginger, Loretta and Irene Who?* (New York: Putnam, 1976), 156.

19. Stanley Green, *The World of Musical Comedy*, 4th ed. (New York: Da Capo, 1980), 132–34.

20. "With Night Clubs behind Her, Helen Morgan Would Forget 'Em," *Atlantic City News*, August 23, 1929.

21. B. G. DeSylva, Lew Brown, and Ray Henderson, *I Want a Lovable Baby* (New York: Harms, 1925), 4; B. G. DeSylva, Lew Brown, and Ray Henderson, *What a World This Would Be,* (New York: Harms, 1925), 2–3.

22. Amy Leslie, "Helen Morgan, Young Singer and Beauty, on Her Way to Stage Career," *Chicago News*, July 31, 1925.

23. Robert Coleman, "*Scandals* Gorgeous," *NYDM*, June 24, 1925.

24. Sime Silverman, "*Scandals*," *Variety*, July 1, 1925, 21. Also "Inside Stuff," *Variety*, July 8, 1925, 20, 40.

25. Based on *Variety* estimates, averaging over $25,000 weekly throughout the twenty-one-week Broadway run. "Shows in N. Y. and Comment," *Variety*, July 1, 1925, 20, and subsequent issues.

26. Advertisement, *NYS*, August 19, 1925.

27. "Seventh Edition of *Scandals* Found Pleasing at the Shubert," *Newark (NJ) Evening News*, December 15, 1925.

28. Leonard Hall, "Georgie's Seventh," *Washington Daily News*, January 4, 1926.

29. Ed Sullivan, "Now and Then," *NYDN*, June 18, 1933.

30. Herbert G. Goldman, *Jolson: The Legend Comes to Life* (New York: Oxford University Press, 1988), 139–40.

31. Amy Leslie, "White's *Scandals* Is Lively, Lovely Show," *Chicago News*, February 1, 1926.

32. Story related by Riggin's wife, Anna, to Attica mayor Harold Long, related to local researcher Donna Prather, related to the author, letter dated July 20, 1993.

33. "'Turned Down' by Ziegfeld," *BG*, May 12, 1929.

34. Irving Hoffman, "Helen Morgan, of Danville, Would Like to Play 'Camille,'" *BDE*, February 1, 1931.

35. *NYMT*, May 12, 1926, MS/FLP, book 1, 12A.

36. "Night Life Throngs See Fire That Destroys 54th St. Club," *NYEP*, June 9, 1926.

37. "William Collier Out of *Americana* Revue," *BB*, July 10, 1926, 25.

38. One unnamed Jersey reviewer singled out "Thanks Awful" as the show's best number but did not mention who sang it. The playbill offered little help crediting the cast's contributions. "At the Theatres," *Long Branch (NJ) Daily Record*, July 13, 1926.

39. Richard G. Massock, "About New York," *Yonkers Herald*, April 29, 1929.

40. Robert Coleman, "*Americana*'s Bow," *NYDM*, July 27, 1926.

41. "Melody Mart Notes," *BB*, August 7, 1926, 21.

42. Advertisement, *Stage* (London), September 2, 1926, 4.

43. Leonard Sillman, *Here Lies Leonard Sillman: Straightened Out at Last* (New York: Citadel, 1959), 86.

44. J. P. McEvoy later claimed that Helen sat on the lip of the stage because the house was so tiny there was no room to bring in the chorus behind her for the subsequent number. Mark Barron, "McEvoy Reformed by His Fling in 'Cinematic Art,'" *CPD*, January 8, 1939.

45. A planned fall run never came to fruition, presumably because so many key cast members signed on to other projects. "Revive *Americana* for Chicago," *BB*, June 25, 1927, 23.

4. The Queen of Modern Song

1. Advertisement, *Variety*, October 27, 1926, 100.

2. Nicholas Blair, "Death Certificate No. 70-030722" (Florida State Board of Health, 1978).

3. Mark Hellinger, "All in a Day," *NYDM*, January 21, 1930.

4. Nils Thor Granlund, *Blondes, Brunettes, and Bullets*, with Sid Feder and Ralph Hancock (New York: David McKay, 1957), 156.

5. Tommy Guinan's Playground, 201 W. Fifty-Second Street, near Seventh Avenue.

6. Lewis Yablonsky, *George Raft* (New York: McGraw-Hill, 1974), 46.

7. "Helen Morgan Greeting Broadway Tonight at the Opening of Her New Night Club," *NYMT*, November 12, 1926.

8. Lester R. Allen, "No Money Left in Night Club Life," *Boston Post*, May 9, 1929.

9. "Variety's Broadway Guide," *Variety*, January 25, 1927, 33.

10. William McBrien, *Cole Porter: A Biography* (New York: Alfred A. Knopf, 1988), 178.

11. Schuyler Livingston Parson, *Untold Friendships* (Boston: Houghton Mifflin, 1955), 134.

12. Jon Sansoni, "The Real Helen Morgan Story!," *Inside Story* 4, no. 6 (1958): 70.

13. "Reasons Advanced for Holdup in Biarritz," *Variety*, October 27, 1926, 100.

14. Edward Behr, *Prohibition: Thirteen Years That Changed America* (New York: Arcade, 1996), 221–23.

15. Assistant US Attorney Lowell Wadmond witnessed the sale of whiskey at the 54th Street Club on November 23 and 26, prompting the December visit by the Feds. United States of America v. Fifty-Fourth St. Club Inc., L. Schwartz, Pres., Helen Morgan,

L. Schwartz, Helen Morgan's 54th St. Club, Charles E. Miller, and John Doe, "Bill of Complaint, no. E39-310" (S.D.N.Y. 1926).

16. Paul Sweinhart, "Keith-Albee Palace Track," *Zits*, January 29, 1927, 6166.

17. "Rubberin' 'Round," *Variety*, January 26, 1927, 37.

18. "New York Theatres," *Passaic (NJ) Daily Herald*, February 8, 1927.

19. During the 1926–1927 season, Helen and Lulu lived at 161 W. Fifty-Fourth Street, near the 54th Street Club. US passport, #366352. "New York, U.S., Arriving Passenger and Crew Lists (including Castle Garden and Ellis Island), 1820–1957," *Ile de France*, September 6, 1927, sheet 13. https://www.ancestry.com.

20. Percy Hammond, "The Theaters," *New York Tribune*, March 5, 1927.

21. Walter Winchell, "Opening Nights: Helen of Joy," *NYEG*, March 7, 1927.

22. Gary Chapman, *The Delectable Dollies: The Dolly Sisters, Icons of the Jazz Age* (Gloucestershire: Sutton, 2006), 178–79.

23. "Sail For Paris," *NYDN*, May 4, 1927.

24. The advertisement listed George Hale, Helen Wherle, Jonny Hudgins, and bandleader Irving Aaronson; Helen's name was conspicuously absent. *Le Figaro*, May 19, 1927.

25. Jacques Calmy, "Paris after Dark," unidentified newspaper clipping, May 20, 1927, MS-FLP, Book I, p. 13B.

26. Helen clearly appears, eighth on the bill of sixteen (eleven acts in the first half, five in the second) in the undated program posted in her scrapbook. MS/FLP, Book I, p. 12B.

27. "Helen Morgan Finds World Sadder," *Boston Sunday Advertiser*, September 21, 1930.

28. *Bricktop*, with James Haskins (New York: Atheneum, 1983), 123.

29. She earned $500 a week in Paris. John McClain, "On the Sun Deck," *NYS*, February 24, 1933.

30. The snowball photo was doctored for an article describing the wedded bliss of Helen and Lowell Almy and Joan Gardner and Edwin T. Hall. "Ha! A Modern Miracle Happens at Last," *PP* Sunday Magazine, *American Weekly*, February 3, 1924, 16.

31. "Will Wales Take a New World Bride?," Sunday Magazine, *Baltimore Sun*, September 30, 1923, 2.

32. Rian James, "Names Make News!," *Brooklyn Eagle Magazine*, September 20, 1931, 18.

33. "Nora Bayes Can't Follow Will Fyffe," *Variety*, June 22, 1927, 3.

34. "Helen Lowell in *A la Carte*," *BB*, April 23, 1927, 27.

35. "The Gramophone Review," *Melody Maker*, September 1927, 881.

36. Maureen Englin, "I Remember Helen Morgan," *Rock Island (IL) Argus*, September 18, 1971.

5. The All-American Musical Comedy

1. Advertisement, *NYDN*, December 25, 1927.

2. An inside joke: the boys set scenes at the 1893 Chicago World's Fair and the Trocadero, where Ziegfeld began his legendary career.

3. All *Show Boat* scholarship begins and ends with Miles Kreuger. All subsequent information brought to the table is little more than dotting the i's and crossing the t's. Miles Kreuger, *"Show Boat": The Story of a Classic American Musical*, rev. ed. (New York: Da Capo, 1990), 18–20.

4. Unidentified article, *NYMT*, April 24, 1927, MS/FLP, book 1, 16B.

5. *Variety* stated that *Show Boat* went into rehearsal right after Labor Day. ("Shows in Rehearsal," *Variety*, September 7, 1927, 51.) At the time, actors received no pay for rehearsals, and a nine-week schedule, even for a show of this size, seems excessive. Most likely, Ziegfeld spent September casting the chorus and overseeing set and costume preparation, and rehearsals began in earnest on October 17. "Theatrical Notes," *NYT*, October 15, 1927.

6. Oscar Hammerstein II, "Memories of First *Show Boat* Launching," *NYT*, June 23, 1957.

7. In late October, Helen got her Steve. Initially a drops painter for the Provincetown Players, Charles Ellis acted in the original mountings of several Eugene O'Neill works, notably as Eben Cabot in *Desire under the Elms*. *Show Boat* proved a rare foray into musical comedy.

8. Hugh Fordin, *Getting to Know Him* (New York: Random House, 1977), 84–85.

9. Katherine Leigh Axtell, "Maiden Voyage: The Genesis and Reception of *Show Boat*, 1926–1932" (PhD diss., University of Rochester, 2009), 171.

10. "Many Broadwayites Helped Christen New Night Club," unidentified newspaper, September 28, 1927, MS/FLP, book 1, 15B.

11. Jerome Charyn, *Gangsters and Gold Diggers: Old New York, the Jazz Age, and the Birth of Broadway* (New York: Four Walls Eight Windows, 2003), 97–110.

12. Robert Sylvester, *No Cover Charge: A Backward Look at the Night Clubs* (New York: Dial, 1956), 203–4.

13. Jon Sansoni, "The Real Helen Morgan Story!," *Inside Story* 4, no. 6 (1958): 72.

14. Warren G. Harris, *Cary Grant: A Touch of Elegance* (New York: Doubleday, 1987), 37–41.

15. Dale Kramer, *Heywood Broun: A Biographical Portrait* (New York: A. A. Wyn, 1949), 185–86.

16. Michael Mok, "'Marry? Never Again!' Is Helen Morgan's Refrain. But It's a Torch Song in Spite of Her Gaiety," *NYEP*, October 24, 1935.

17. Robert Russell Bennett, *The Broadway Sound: The Autobiography and Selected Essays of Robert Russell Bennett*, ed. George J. Ferencz (Rochester, NY: University of Rochester Press, 1999), 104.

18. E. B. (Zeke) Colvan, *Face the Footlights!* (New York: Whittlesey House, 1940), 82.

19. Ira Gershwin, *Lyrics on Several Occasions* (New York: Viking, 1959), 4–7.

20. Unsuitable for the first try at *Strike Up the Band* in 1927, Ira reworked the song for *Rosalie*, only to cut it again after Helen's triumph at Chez Helen Morgan: the song needed no show to spotlight it.

21. Abel Green, "Plays on Broadway," *Variety*, January 4, 1928, 26–27.

22. William G. Hyland, *The Song Is Ended: Songwriters and American Music, 1900–1950* (New York: Oxford University Press, 1995), 40.

23. "*Scandals* Torch Singer Sees 'Legit' on Way Back," *Lansing (MI) State Journal*, January 6, 1937.

24. Michael Freedland, *Jerome Kern* (New York: Stein and Day, 1978), 89.

25. A script from the rehearsal period notes that Helen has been cast as Julie but does *not* include the lyrics to "Bill." After Julie says, "I'm ready, Jake, whenever you are," the stage direction reads, "Jake pounds out the introduction to Julie's song on the piano. Julie sings a popular sentimental ballad characteristic of the time." Jerome Kern and Oscar Hammerstein II, *Show Boat*, undated libretto ca. September 1927, BRTD/NYPL.

26. Hugh Martin, telephone interview, February 23, 1992.

27. Kreuger, "*Show Boat*," 57.

28. Kreuger, "*Show Boat*," 51.

29. Bennett, *Broadway Sound*, 101–102.

30. As published, F major.

31. Because of its late addition to the score, Hans Spialek, and not Bennett, orchestrated "Bill."

32. Edna Ferber, *A Peculiar Treasure* (Garden City, NY: Country Life Press, 1939), 317–18.

33. Ethan Mordden, *Make Believe: The Broadway Musical in the 1920s* (New York: Oxford University Press, 1997), 220.

34. Todd Decker, "*Show Boat*": *Performing Race in an American Musical* (New York: Oxford University Press, 2013), 116.

35. Kern and Hammerstein, *Show Boat*.

36. Charles Higham, *Ziegfeld* (Chicago: Henry Regnery, 1972), 184–85.

37. Robert Coleman, "Premier at the Ziegfeld," *NYDM*, December 28, 1927.

38. Gordon M. Leland, "The New Plays on Broadway," *BB*, January 7, 1928, 10.

39. Maurice Campbell, "Morgan Raid? Pooh! Say Real Eve Revelers," to *NYDN*, December 31, 1927.

40. William Howland Kenney, *Chicago Jazz: A Cultural History, 1904–1930* (New York: Oxford University Press, 1993), 151.

41. Moulin Rouge: United States of America v. William R. Rothstein et al., 5956 (N.D. Ill. 1926). Friar's Inn: United States of America v Mike Fritzel et al., 5958 (N.D. Ill. 1926).

42. Rotogravure, *NYDN*, December 31, 1927.

43. "Broadway Slang Capital of World," *Baltimore Sun*, November 20, 1927.

44. "New York Night Clubs Worried over Tonight," *BG*, December 31, 1927.

45. "New York Night Club Raided," *London Times*, December 31, 1927.

46. "$50,000 Club Wrecked by Dry Raiders," *New York Telegram*, December 31, 1927.

47. Skolsky's appears to be the earliest of many versions of the rosary story. Sidney Skolsky, "Behind the News," *NYDN*, April 3, 1931.

48. N. T. Granlund, "Joys and Glooms of Broadway," *Variety*, January 11, 1928, 43.

49. "$50,000 Club Wrecked by Dry Raiders."

50. "N. Y. Raid Angers Night Club Owners," *Baltimore Sun*, December 31, 1927.

51. "Says Dry Law Is Enforceable," *NYS*, January 11, 1928.

52. "$50,000 Club Wrecked by Dry Raiders."

53. Arrested with Morgan were Arthur Gordoni, emcee; John Golden, entertainer; Barney Brown and Louis Green, waiter captains; John Leonard, cashier; and Herman Bloom, Eddie Brown, Jake Corbett, and Karl Messer, waiters.

6. "I Want a Lovable Baby"

1. Leonard W. Joy, liner notes for *Helen Morgan*, Victor album P-102, 1941.

2. Exceptions: Tess Gardella included both Julie's and Queenie's verses on her "Can't Help Lovin' Dat Man" recording. Helen, Bledsoe, and Gardella sang their numbers for the 1929 Universal film prologue. After the Broadway run, Jules Bledsoe recorded "Ol' Man River." Helen, Charles Winninger, and Sammy White reprised their stage roles in the 1936 film.

3. Abel Green, "Disk Reviews," *Variety*, March 28, 1928, 55.

4. Recording Academy, "Grammy Hall of Fame Award," accessed November 7, 2022, https://www.grammy.com/awards/hall-of-fame-award.

5. "By Joe Williams," *Buffalo News*, February 27, 1945.

6. George Jessel, *The World I Lived In*, with John Austin (Chicago: Henry Regnery, 1975), 60–62.

7. Elizabeth Collins, telephone interview, January 25, 1992.

8. "Through Eddie Cantor's Eyes," *Long Island Star-Journal*, January 4, 1955.

9. Glenn Shirley, *Hello, Sucker!* (Austin, TX: Eakin, 1989), 66.

10. Also raided were the Beaux-Arts (Fortieth and Sixth); Mimic (132 W. Forty-Second); Silver Slipper (Forty-Eighth and Broadway); Charm Club (135 W. Fifty-First); Furnace Club (131 W. Fifty-Second); Jungle Club (201 W. Fifty-Second); Frivolity (Broadway near Fifty-Second); the European Club (26 W. Fifty-Third); Chateau Madrid (231 W. Fifty-Fourth—the old Helen Morgan's 54th Street Club); the Little Club (216 W. Forty-Fourth); U. S. I. Restaurant (108 W. Forty-Fifth); Footlight Club (121 W. Forty-Ninth); Owl Club (161 W. Forty-Ninth); Marguery Rendez Vous (121 W. Fifty-First); Loretta McDermott Club (135 W. Fifty-Second); and Tommy Guinan's venture, Chez Florence (117 W. Forty-Eighth). Over two hundred people faced charges.

11. "Why ONE 'Padlock Queen' Laughed While the OTHER Wept," *Philadelphia Inquirer Magazine*, October 7, 1928, 5.

12. "Dry Force Mobilized by Doran for Drive to 'Mop Up' New York," *NYT*, July 1, 1928.

13. Dorothy M. Brown, *Mabel Walker Willebrandt: A Study of Power, Loyalty and Law* (Knoxville: University of Tennessee Press, 1984), 50.

14. Stanley Walker, *The Night Club Era* (New York: Frederick A. Stokes, 1933), 64.

15. "Countess Spy Led Raid, Helen Morgan Aid Says," *NYDN*, February 11, 1928.

16. Maurice Campbell, "Credit Given Willebrandt in Club Raids," *WaPo*, September 24, 1930.

17. "Dry Force Mobilized by Doran."

18. "3 Genteel Guests Just Dry Raiders," *NYEP*, July 12, 1928.

19. "108 Indicted in War on the Night Clubs," *NYT*, July 31, 1928.

20. "Ziegfeld Bars Helen Morgan's Night Club Role," *Binghamton (NY) Press*, August 6, 1928.

21. "Miss Morgan Ends Night Club Career," *NYT*, August 6, 1928.

22. Collins, telephone interview.

23. Ziegfeld planned a second *Show Boat* company, to break in on Broadway concurrent with the original production prior to a national tour. Libby Holman would play Julie. When Actors' Equity suspended Ziegfeld's Joe of choice, Paul Robeson, for breaking a contract, Ziegfeld scrapped the idea.

24. Goldie Stanton Clough's notebook lists Helen's original weekly salary for *Show Boat* at $600. While the entry is undated, she also lists the raise to $700. Clough notebook, courtesy of Miles Kreuger and the Institute of the American Musical. A salary list from the week ending January 26, 1929, shows Helen at $700. Richard Ziegfeld and Paulette Ziegfeld, *The Ziegfeld Touch: The Life and Times of Florenz Ziegfeld, Jr.* (New York: Harry N. Abrams, 1993), 146.

25. *Whoopee* made it to the stage, as did a new *Follies* (produced as a *Frolic*). When William Anthony McGuire staged a one-man work slowdown to protest Ziegfeld's royalty lethargy, Ziegfeld retaliated by canceling the productions of McGuire's musicals *Six Cylinder Love* and *East Is West/Ming Toy*. *Joan of Arc* also went unrealized, as did Ziegfeld's intention to produce more plays. "Inside Stuff—Legit," *Variety*, January 1, 1930, 48.

26. Marc Miller, *The New Amsterdam Theatregoer* (company mailing, May 1985).

27. "Helen Morgan a Talkie Hit," *BB*, September 7, 1929, 28.

28. "Order Arrest of 'N.T.G.' and Helen Morgan," *Yonkers Statesman*, August 6, 1928.

29. "Broadway Dry War Jams Court Session," *NYT*, August 7, 1928.

30. Adler provided counsel to Helen, N. T. Granlund, Texas Guinan, the Silver Slipper, and the Jungle, Charm, and Frivolity Clubs. "Helen Answers Rum Bid to Court, Granlund Absent," *BDE*, August 7, 1928.

31. Helen's codefendants were Nick Blair, Herman Brooks, city alderman Murray W. Stand, Charles Hansen, Louis Holzer, Jake Green, Nathan Gordon, Louis Zalud, Samuel Harris, Herman Brooks, and Albert Berryman, headwaiter at the Frivolity. Willebrandt's agents gained entrance to the Summer Home on June 11, 1928, using a Frivolity Club business card, signed by Berryman, which stated that the three were OK. United States of America v. Helen Morgan, no. C 57-681 (S.D.N.Y., 1929).

32. "Doran Predicts Legal Battle on Club Padlocking," *BDE*, September 12, 1928.

33. Blair operated the space at 151 W. Fifty-Fourth Street after the Chez Helen Morgan raid in December 1927 and before his move to the Summer House in June 1928.

34. "The Most Important Thing in Life," *Picturegoer Summer Annual*, 1935, 47–48.

35. "Bad Luck and Vision," *Variety*, April 25, 1928, 57.

36. "Chatter in New York," *Variety*, January 2, 1929, 31.

37. "Through Eddie Cantor's Eyes."

38. Sid Silverman, "Ziegfeld Roof," *Variety*, January 9, 1929, 64.

39. "Through Eddie Cantor's Eyes."

40. Unidentified clipping, MS/FLP, book 1, 24A.

41. Ward Morehouse, "Roving the Rialto," *NYS*, November 24, 1926.

42. "Helen Morgan Is Ill, Perhaps of Lost Love," *NYEJ*, January 17, 1929.

43. Arthur M. Loew, "First World War Service File, no. 181-76-07," 1918.

44. "Alleged *Show Boat* Stage Rights Prevent Play's Film from Employing Sounds," *Variety*, May 16, 1928, 5.

45. With the Fox equipment on loan, in nine days, Heath also shot *The Melody of Love*, the third all-talking picture and the first in Movietone.

46. James Curtis, *James Whale: A New World of Gods and Monsters*, rev. ed. (Boston: Faber and Faber, 1998), 263.

47. Jay Carmody, "Miss Morgan Reveals Talents for Being Interviewed," *Evening Star* (Washington, DC), February 10, 1938.

48. Donato Cedrone, letter to the author, February 7, 1992.

49. "'Turned Down' by Ziegfeld," *BG*, May 12, 1929.

50. "Helen Morgan and First Billion Dollar Audience to See Palm Beach Premiere of *Show Boat*," *Universal Weekly*, March 23, 1929, 12.

51. Miles Kreuger, *"Show Boat": The Story of a Classic American Musical*, rev. ed. (New York: Da Capo, 1990), 84.

52. Robert E. Sherwood, "Movie Album," *Tampa Bay Times*, April 20, 1929.

53. R. C., "Broadway Film Reviews," *BB*, April 27, 1929, 25.

54. "New U. Shorts," *BB*, August 10, 1929, 20.

55. Alvin J. Kayton, "In the Theatres on Broadway," *Brooklyn Daily Star*, January 29, 1929.

56. Martin sometimes spelled his surname Fried, but during the 1929–1930 season, when he accompanied Helen, he spelled it Freed, which, for the sake of consistency, will be used throughout.

57. *Midnight Frolic* playbill, weeks of February 6 and 25, 1929, BRTD/NYPL.

58. Lillian Roth, *Beyond My Worth* (New York: Frederick Fell, 1958), 104–5.

59. Meryle Secrest, *Stephen Sondheim: A Life* (New York: Alfred A. Knopf, 1998), 138.

60. Courtney Terrett, "Broadway's Two Poor Little Rich Girls Rake In Cash despite Activities of Uncle Sam's Liquor Sleuths," *New York Telegram*, August 3, 1928. However, Sidney Skolsky claimed that the mother retrieved this first baby two months later. Skolsky, "Times Square Tintypes," *NYS*, January 14, 1929.

61. Thelma claimed that she married Leonard in Milwaukee on Christmas Day, 1926, but later admitted that the child was born out of wedlock. She went home to her widowed mother in Newark, New Jersey. The three are enumerated in the 1930 census, but they left Newark shortly afterward. "Helen Bathes the Baby with Real Mother There," *NYDN*, March 23, 1929; US Census Bureau, "Essex County, New Jersey, Newark, Enumeration District 7-11563, Sheet 4B, Dwelling 39, Family 135," 1930 Census, https://www.ancestry.com.

7. Trials

1. Mabel Walker Willebrandt, *The Inside of Prohibition* (Indianapolis: Bobbs-Merrill, 1929), 250–62.

2. John O'Donnell, "Drys Brag of Rum Bouts with Helen Morgan," *NYDN*, April 17, 1929.

3. "Helen Morgan Demure as She Goes on Trial," *Brooklyn Standard Union*, April 16, 1929.

4. "Helen Morgan Shuns Notice at Her Trial," *NYT*, April 17, 1929.

5. "Helen Morgan to Testify Soon," unidentified article ca. April 18, 1929, MS/FLP, book 1, 33A.

6. O'Donnell, "Drys Brag of Rum Bouts."

7. "Reports Tell How Drys Lavished U. S. Cash on Broadway Night Clubs," *Binghamton (NY) Press*, August 2, 1928.

8. O'Donnell, "Drys Brag of Rum Bouts."

9. "Helen Morgan Joined Dry's Rum Spree, He Tells Court," *NYA*, April 17, 1929.

10. "Helen Morgan Shuns Notice."

11. O'Donnell, "Drys Brag of Rum Bouts."

12. "Helen Morgan Got Drunk and Served Him $15 a Pint Brandy, Dry Agent Swears," *BDE*, April 16, 1929.

13. "Helen Now Packs 'Em In Even as Tex Guinan Did," *Baltimore Evening Sun*, April 16, 1929.

14. "Helen Morgan to Testify Soon."

15. O'Donnell, "Drys Brag of Rum Bouts."

16. Congressman Fiorello La Guardia to J. Arthur Adler, April 10, 1930, MS/FLP, box 2, folder 1.

17. United States of America v. Helen Morgan, Nicholas Blair, Charles Hansen, Louis Holzer, Jake Green, Nathan Gordon, Louis Zalud, Samuel Harris, Buck "Doe," Murray "Doe," and Herman Brooks, "Affidavit, no. C 57-681" (S.D.N.Y. April 17, 1929).

18. "Helen Morgan Case Up for Trial Today," *NYT*, April 15, 1929.

19. "Helen Morgan Free; In Tears at Verdict," *NYT*, April 19, 1929.

20. Mark Hellinger added that Chez Helen Morgan was the only Rialto club doing turn away business. "About Broadway," *NYDN*, December 4, 1927.

21. "Helen Morgan Free; In Tears at Verdict."

22. Ibid.

23. "Night Club Helen Acquitted, She Kisses the Jury," *St. Louis Star*, April 19, 1929.

24. "Helen Morgan Free; In Tears at Verdict."

25. "Helen Morgan in Tears When Jury Frees Her," *Wilkes-Barre (PA) Evening News*, April 19, 1929.

26. John O'Donnell, "Helen Morgan Cleared," *NYDN*, April 19, 1929.

27. Tom Pettey, "Helen Morgan Freed on Rum Charge," *CT*, April 19, 1929.

28. "Future of Dry Law in New York Appears Dubious," *CT*, April 20, 1929.

29. The waiters were Charles Hansen, Louis Holzer, Jacob Green, Nathan Gordon, and Samuel Harris.

30. United States of America v. Herman Brooks et al., "Nolle Prosequi, no. C 57-681" (S.D.N.Y., October 1, 1931).

31. United States of America v. Hyman Berger, nos. C 93-482, C 93-554, and C 57-681 (S.D.N.Y., July 23, 1933).

32. Mark Hellinger, "All in a Day," *NYDM*, January 21, 1930.

33. United States of America v. Nicholas Blair, no. C 83-814 (S.D.N.Y., April 14, 1932).

34. United States of America v Murray Stand, "Nolle Prosequi, no. C 57-681" (S.D.N.Y., December 10, 1931).

35. "Guinan Escapes Prison," *NYT*, February 26, 1930.

36. Pettey, "Helen Morgan Freed on Rum Charge."

37. Maurice Campbell, "Campbell Declares Official Insincerity and Politics Hinder Success of Dry Law," *WaPo*, September 8, 1930, and eighteen subsequent articles through September 26, 1930.

38. Felix Deyo, "World of Music," *Brooklyn Standard Union*, February 23, 1929.

39. At 572 performances, *Show Boat* became the eighteenth longest-running Broadway show and number six on the long-running musicals list behind *Irene* (670), *A Trip to Chinatown* (657), *The Student Prince* (608), *Adonis* (603), and *Blossom Time* (576). *The Best Plays of 1928–29* (New York: Dodd, Mead, 1929), 514.

40. After Eleanor Tierney, Morgan's understudy, left the production because of injuries sustained in a taxi accident, Margaret Carlisle played Julie for the final three weeks in Boston and during the subsequent fall tour.

41. "Paris Chatter," *Variety*, May 15, 1929, 66.

42. "Loews Separate to Test Love and 'Retain Respect,'" *SFE*, May 22, 1929.

43. "Texas Guinan Club Shut for 10 Months," *NYT*, June 8, 1929.

44. "Hostesses Let Off; Drys Are Indignant," *NYT*, June 12, 1929.

8. Applause for and with Miss Helen Morgan

1. Beth Brown, *Applause* (New York: Grossett and Dunlap, 1928).

2. "Helen Morgan at $5,000 as Lead of *Applause*," *Variety*, May 22, 1929, 57.

3. "Mae West in *Applause?*," *Variety*, April 10, 1929, 5.

4. John Kobal, *Gotta Sing, Gotta Dance: A Pictorial History of Film Musicals* (London: Hamlyn, 1970), 66–67.

5. David Luhrssen, *Mamoulian: Life on Stage and Screen* (Lexington: University Press of Kentucky, 2013), 44.

6. Richard Koszarski, *Hollywood on the Hudson: Film and Television in New York from Griffith to Sarnoff* (New Brunswick, NJ: Rutgers University Press, 2008), 196.

7. Louella Parsons, "Helen Morgan of Night Club Fame to Sing in New Talkie," *SFE*, May 27, 1929.

8. Louis Sobol, "Your Broadway and Mine," *NYEG*, February 7, 1930.

9. Kobal, *Gotta Sing, Gotta Dance*, 67.

10. Douglas Fox, "Paramount Making Two Audiens at Once at Eastern Studio," *Exhibitors Herald-World*, June 22, 1929, 124.

11. "No Cutting Is Required in Negative Produced by New Paramount Director," *Exhibitors Herald-World*, August 24, 1929, 39.

12. Gregory Koseluk, *Eddie Cantor: A Life in Show Business* (Jefferson, NC: McFarland, 1995), 153.

13. Richard Barrios, *A Song in the Dark: The Birth of the Musical Film*, 2nd ed. (New York: Oxford University Press, 2010), 197.

14. Brian Taves, *Robert Florey: The French Expressionist* (Metuchen, NJ: Scarecrow, 1987), 106.

15. No press releases from Paramount or the Hammerstein offices report Helen taking time away from *Sweet Adeline* to film this number during the three-week window between the wrapping of *Applause* and the announcement that retakes on *Glorifying the American Girl* were completed.

16. The Breen Office scuttled a proposed 1938 reissue not because of naughty words or the revealing costumes but because of the film's depiction of Jewish stereotypes, deemed inflammatory on the eve of World War II. *Glorifying the American Girl*, MPAA file, AMPAS/MHL.

17. Florenz Ziegfeld, telegram to Adolph Zukor, August 9, 1929, *Glorifying the American Girl* file, Zukor Collection, AMPAS/MHL.

18. Florenz Ziegfeld to Adolph Zukor, October 9, 1929, *Glorifying the American Girl* file, Zukor Collection, AMPAS/MHL.

19. Edna Ferber to Oscar Hammerstein, October 8, 1943, in *The Letters of Oscar Hammerstein II*, ed. Mark Eden Horowitz (New York: Oxford University Press, 2022), 302.

20. Although it states that Helen worked as a singing waitress at "Addie's, a beer-garden," in her youth, the most likely scenario is Helen's haunting of Mike Fritzel's Arsonia Café as a child. Marc Miller, *The New Amsterdam Theatregoer* (company mailing, May 1985).

21. Violet Carlson, interview with the author and Miles Kreuger, September 2, 1992.

22. "Concerning That Hit Up 53d St. Way," *NYT*, September 15, 1929.

23. "Ziegfeld Calls 'Canned' Score Half-Canned Idea," *NYDN*, April 7, 1929.

24. "Heading for Broadway," *NYT*, August 25, 1929.

25. Oscar Hammerstein II, *Sweet Adeline* libretto, OHA/LOC.

26. Todd S. Purdum, *Something Wonderful: Rodgers and Hammerstein's Broadway Revolution* (New York: Henry Holt, 2018), 34.

27. *Sweet Adeline* program, Atlantic City Nixon's Apollo Theatre, week of August 19, 1929.

28. Sime Silverman, "Plays on Broadway," *Variety*, September 11, 1929, 62.

29. Robert Littell, "At the Play," *Buffalo News*, September 14, 1929.

30. Robert Benchley, "The Theatre," *New Yorker*, September 14, 1929, 34.

31. Gilbert Seldes, "What Songs the Sirens Sang," *New Yorker*, October 12, 1929, 50.

32. Helen Morgan to Gilbert Seldes, ca. 1929–1930, courtesy of Marian Seldes.

33. "'Actresses Not Only Read Many Good Books, but Usually Understand Them,' Says Sally Bates," *Crimson*, February 27, 1931, https://www.thecrimson.com/article/1931/2/27/actresses-not-only-read-many-good/.

34. Morgan to Seldes.

35. "Helen Morgan to Do *Camille*," *BB*, October 5, 1929, 4.

36. Walter Winchell, "On Broadway," *Glens Falls (NY) Post-Star*, January 6, 1930.

37. "With Night Clubs behind Her, Helen Morgan Would Forget 'Em," *Atlantic City News*, August 23, 1929.

38. *On the High C's*, *The Spy*, and *After the Ball—Applause* program, Criterion Theatre, opening night, IAM/MK.

39. "When He Comes Home to Me," NY Censor Board License T13830, NY State Archives, October 8, 1929.

40. "Casey Pan Able to 'Swing High' with Pathe Opus," *Motion Picture News*, July 19, 1930, 38.

41. Mordaunt Hall, "The Screen," *NYT*, October 8, 1929.

42. HDS, "New Films Caught in New York," *BB*, October 19, 1929, 24.

43. Erskine Johnson, "In Hollywood," *Lubbock (TX) Evening Journal*, February 26, 1951.

44. Al Wilkie, "Highlights of *Applause*," reprinted in Mark Spergel, *Reinventing Reality: The Art and Life of Rouben Mamoulian* (Metuchen, NJ: Scarecrow, 1993), 97.

45. Koszarski, *Hollywood on the Hudson*, 200.

46. *Applause*, MPAA file, AMPAS/MHL.

47. Mark A. Vieira, *Sin in Soft Focus: Pre-Code Hollywood* (New York: Harry N. Abrams, 1999), 16.

48. *Applause*, NY Censor Board file, License T13835-T13856, NY State Archives, October 8, 1929.

49. Spergel, *Reinventing Reality*, 100.

50. As did Worcester, Massachusetts. *Applause*, MPAA file, AMPAS/MHL.

51. Advertisement, *Sioux Falls (SD) Argus-Leader*, January 8, 1930.

52. State censors held up a proposed run at Toledo's Princess Theater in January 1930. "Toledo," *BB*, January 25, 1930, 43.

53. *Glorifying the American Girl*: sound (8,505 feet) / silent (8,445 feet). *Applause*: sound (8,079 feet) / silent (6,896 feet). "Quick Reference Chart," *New York Herald-World*, January 4, 1930, 56.

54. "Film Notes," *BB*, October 26, 1929, 22.

55. Charles Higham, *Marlene: The Life of Marlene Dietrich* (New York: W. W. Norton, 1977), 170–71.

56. *Applause*, MPAA file, AMPAS/MHL.

57. William K. Everson's championing of *Applause* in the 1960s was critical in its reevaluation, but New York's Film Society was the first to reassess it, in an April 23, 1933, screening. "Society Reviving *Applause* and *Paths to Paradise*," *TFD*, April 13, 1933, 6.

9. America's Greatest Star

1. William MacAdams, *Ben Hecht: The Man behind the Legend* (New York: Charles Scribner's Sons, 1990), 117.

2. Douglas Fox, "Paramount, RCA and Warners Lead Eastern Studio Activity," *Exhibitors Herald-World*, November 9, 1929, 51.

3. Malcolm H. Oettinger, "Million-Dollar Blues," *Picture Play*, February 1930, 74, 114.

4. Chester B. Bahn, "Huston Will Be 'Lincoln' for Griffith," *Syracuse (NY) Herald*, December 16, 1929.

5. J. F. Lundy, "Roadhouse Nights," *BB*, March 1, 1930, 23.

6. Ruth Chatterton, finishing *Laughing Lady*, also fell to the bug. "Along the Rialto," *TFD*, November 4, 1929, 6.

7. Film elements of *The Benefit* are currently lost, but the soundtrack exists, courtesy of Ron Hutchinson's Vitaphone Project, accessed November 16, 2022, https://soundcloud.com/vitaphone/joe-frisco-benefit-excerpt.

8. Jack Bell, "O'er the Sports Desk," *MDN*, February 17, 1935.

9. Alfred Albelli, "Helen Morgan Gives Up Borrowed Baby for Art," *NYDN*, December 25, 1929.

10. Vivian Shirley, "Vivian Shirley Learns Road to Fame Isn't Always Easiest to Tread, but Goal Is Worthy," *Philadelphia Public Ledger*, March 2, 1931.

11. Neal Gabler, *Winchell: Gossip, Power and the Culture of Celebrity* (New York: Alfred A. Knopf, 1994), 437.

12. John Lawson, "Helen Morgan Talks of Mice and Showmen," *CDN*, February 3, 1933.

13. Jimmy Cannon, *Nobody Asked Me, But . . .: The World of Jimmy Cannon*, ed. Jack Cannon and Tom Cannon (New York: Holt, Rinehart and Winston, 1978), 288.

14. Louis Sobol, *The Longest Street* (New York: Crown, 1968), 53–54.

15. Phil Baker, "Radio Dial Log," *BDE*, September 14, 1936.

16. The others were *Mei Lang Fang*, *Bitter Sweet*, *Top Speed*, *Everything's Jake!*, and *Many a Slip*. Coincidentally, March 22, 1930, also marked the birth of Stephen Sondheim.

17. Elias E. Sugarman, "Vaudeville Reviews," *BB*, April 5, 1930, 16.

18. Helen battled cirrhosis for ten years before her death. Helen Morgan, "Death Certificate No. 27331" (Illinois State Board of Health, October 8, 1941).

19. Lulu Morgan to Arthur Lukens, June 18, 1930, MS/FLP, box 1, folder 3.

20. "News from the Dailies," *Variety*, October 20, 1931, 48.

21. "Gordon to See Evergreen," *NYT*, November 17, 1930.

22. William F. McDermott, "Euclid and Broadway," *Cleveland Plain Dealer*, March 27, 1930.

23. "Talkies Have Reached Their Peak, Says Arthur," *NYDN*, June 15, 1930.

24. Dunn won for *A Tree Grows in Brooklyn* in 1946.

25. Mary Madison, "Helen Morgan: Whose Singing Won the Gods," *Playgoer*, October 12, 1930, 30.

26. Gail Borden, "Young Bob Clark Tooted on Flute," *Chicago Daily Times*, October 24, 1930, 30.

27. Lloyd Lewis, "Helen Morgan Proves Artist in *Sweet Adeline*," *CDN*, October 20, 1930.

28. "Frank Riggin Says Helen Morgan Is His Daughter," *Greencastle (IN) Daily Banner*, November 27, 1930.

29. Mildred Z. Loew v. Arthur M. Loew, "Bill for Divorce, no. 33537" (Nev. 2d. Dist. December 8, 1930).

30. Harriet Mencken, "Turning the Dial," *Screen Book*, January 1931, 53.

31. Irving Hoffman, "Helen Morgan the Magnificent," *Life*, February 1932, 35.

32. "$3,500 For Helen Morgan," *Variety*, January 28, 1931, 48.

33. Hoffman, "Helen Morgan the Magnificent."

34. "Belle Livingstone Finishes Jail Term," *NYT*, March 8, 1931.

35. "Speakeasy Queen of 20s Dead at 92," *WaPo*, February 8, 1957.

36. Edward Doherty, "Capone: King of Crime," *NYDN*, February 20, 1931.

37. Bell, "O'er the Sports Desk."

38. Sidney Skolsky, "Behind the News," *NYDN*, March 13, 1931.

39. Dorothy Worth Dey, "Social Security Application," Form SSII, January 16, 1937, accessed via Ancestry.com.

40. "Ex-Herald Columnist Dorothy Murphy; Rode Titanic, Interviewed the Famous," *MH*, September 17, 1983.

41. Sophie Tucker, *Some of These Days* (Garden City, NY: Garden City Publishing, 1946), 112.

42. Vernon Duke, *Passport to Paris* (New York: Little, Brown, 1955), 241.

43. New Club Lido, 240 W. Fifty-Second Street (West of Broadway). Flyer advertisement, MS-FLP, book 2, 66B.

44. Walter Winchell, "Walter Winchell on Broadway," *Tampa Daily Times*, April 8, 1931.

45. Frank X. Lynch, "The Supper Clubs," *NYEP*, April 11, 1931.

46. Douglas Byng, *As You Were* (London: Gerald Duckworth, 1970), 135–36.

47. Oscar Hammerstein to Jerome Kern, March 26, 1931, in *The Letters of Oscar Hammerstein II*, ed. Mark Eden Horowitz (New York: Oxford University Press, 2022), 45.

10. Follies

1. "Miss Morgan Spurns Miami Offer," *NYMT*, November 2, 1926.

2. George Chauncey, *Gay New York: Gender, Urban Culture and the Making of the Gay Male World, 1890–1940* (New York: Basic Books, 1994), 315, 332.

3. "Broadway Chatter," *Variety*, April 9, 1930, 58.

4. Al Clark, "A Piano-Sitter Quits," *PP Magazine*, July 5, 1931.

5. Harvey Gaul, "Opening Here of *Follies* a Big Event," *PP*, May 30, 1931.

6. A. R. D'Albert, *Bed, Bath and Bedlam* (New York: Vantage, 1959), 200–203.

7. Stirling Bowen, "The Theatre," *Wall Street Journal*, July 3, 1931.

8. Opening night Pittsburgh program, Ruth Etting collection, University of Nebraska, Lincoln. Also, Pittsburgh program broadside, undated, author's collection.

9. Percy Hammond, "*Follies* Used to Shock Him, Hammond Says," *Schenectady (NY) Gazette*, July 11, 1931.

10. J. Brooks Atkinson, "The Play," *NYT*, July 2, 1931.

11. Isma (Ibee) Pulaski, "Plays on Broadway," *Variety*, July 7, 1931, 54.

12. Karl Krug, "The Show Shops," *PP*, July 8, 1931.

13. Bide Dudley, "The Stage," *New York Telegram*, September 26, 1931.

14. Jim Stincic, of WUAB Cleveland, letter to the author, February 24, 1994.

15. Helen Morgan, writing for Julia Shawell's Getting Personal column, *NYEG*, August 19, 1931.

16. George Eells, *Ginger, Loretta and Irene Who?* (New York: Putnam, 1976), 155–56.

17. Walter Winchell, "On Broadway," *NYDM*, July 23, 1931.

18. Julia Bristol, "A Pretty Girl Is Like a Melody," *Tampa Times All Florida*, November 4, 1961, 12.

19. Alice L. Tildesley, "Philosophy of a Torch Singer," *Baltimore Sun*, March 10, 1935.

20. Jean Howard, telephone interview, July 17, 1992.

21. Eells, 156.

22. "Pilot Seized for Landing on Lake," *Asbury Park Evening Press*, August 15, 1931.

23. "Helen Got There, but Taxi Flier Lands in Court," *NYDN*, August 16, 1931.

24. A militant socialist, Broun lost the 1930 congressional election for New York's Seventeenth ("Silk Stocking") District. Edna Ferber, Robert Benchley, Fred Astaire, and other Broadway luminaries served on the campaign committee for the wet candidate. Helen did as well but, being on tour during his campaign, did little work for him.

25. Hector Arce, *Groucho* (New York: Putnam, 1979), 195.

26. "Broun's Revue Closed," *NYT*, October 6, 1931.

27. May Christie, "In Mayfair," *NYEJ*, October 19, 1931.

28. Phone number CO5-2806. New York Telephone directory, winter of 1931–32, *Zan-13682J 1931–1932, NYPL.

29. Sidney Skolsky, "Bright Light People," *NYDN*, August 2, 1931.

30. "Theatre Notes," *NYDN*, October 3, 1931.

31. Irving Hoffman, "The Town in Review," *NYMT*, October 16, 1931.

32. Joe Bishop, *The Mark Hellinger Story: A Biography of Broadway and Hollywood* (New York: Appleton-Century-Crofts 1952), 183.

33. "Ed Sullivan Sees Broadway," *NYEG*, November 28, 1931.

34. Marjorie Farnsworth, *The Ziegfeld Follies* (New York: Putnam, 1956), 146.

35. "Singing Helen Morgan Turns Poetess, but Remains True to Her First Love," *NYA*, November 7, 1931.

36. Bernard Sobel, *Broadway Heartbeat: Memoirs of a Press Agent* (New York: Hermitage House, 1953), 127.

37. "Helen Morgan Loew's Bride? No, He Insists," *NYDN*, November 12, 1931.

38. Beach and Tennis Club at Lincoln Road and the Ocean, Miami Beach: Nick Blair had a hand in its operation. Jimmy Durante and Jack Kofoed, *Night Clubs* (New York: Alfred A. Knopf, 1931), 184.

39. Irving Hoffman, "The Town in Review," *NYMT*, March 5, 1932.

40. Florenz Ziegfeld to Helen Morgan, March 30, 1932, MS/FLP, book 2, 89.

11. Above the Title

1. Only Robeson, at $1,500 a week, had a higher salary. Goldie Stanton Clough's notebook, IAM/MK.

2. Program: "Cotton Blossom" & "Make Believe"—Ensemble; "Ol' Man River"—Robeson; "Can't Help Lovin' Dat Man"—Morgan; "Why Do I Love You?"—Sargent

and Carlisle; "Bill"—Morgan; "You Are Love"—Carlisle; "Ol' Man River"—Robeson. The same cast returned six weeks later for an encore performance. "Radio Programs," *Brooklyn Daily Times*, May 1, 1932.

3. "Rehearsals Begin for *Show Boat*," *NYEG*, May 3, 1932.

4. Katherine Leigh Axtell, "Maiden Voyage: The Genesis and Reception of *Show Boat*, 1926–1932" (PhD diss., University of Rochester, 2009), 319.

5. J. Brooks Atkinson, "The Play," *NYT*, May 20, 1932.

6. Robert Garland, "Cast and Miscast," *NYWT*, May 19, 1932.

7. "Ed Sullivan Sees Broadway," *NYEG*, April 18, 1932.

8. Irving Hoffman, "The Town in Review," *NYMT*, May 14, 1932.

9. Irving Hoffman, "The Town in Review," *NYMT*, June 15, 1932.

10. Irving Hoffman, "The Town in Review," *NYMT*, August 1, 1932.

11. "Morgan Plays Lady Bountiful," *NYEG*, June 28, 1932.

12. "If Helen Morgan Had a Daughter," *BG*, October 30, 1932.

13. Jane Loew, *Out of the Limelight* (self-pub., 2007), 44.

14. Floyd Gibbons to Morgan, July 7, 1932, MS/FLP, book 3, inside front cover.

15. O. O. McIntyre, "New York Day by Day," *NYA*, July 29, 1932.

16. Throughout July and August 1932, seven productions played the Main Stem. For the week of August 22–27, 1932, only *Another Language*, *Bridal Wise*, a revival of *That's Gratitude*, and the musicals *The Cat and The Fiddle*, *Of Thee I Sing*, and *Show Boat* played Broadway. Summer 1933 was just as bad, but the nadir of the Depression occurred from July 30 to August 18, 1934, when only five shows—*Sailor, Beware!*; *She Loves Me Not*; *Tobacco Road*; *Are You Decent*; and the musical *As Thousands Cheer*—played in the district.

17. Louis Sobol, "The Voice of Broadway," *NYEJ*, September 14, 1932.

18. Lou Alter, sound recording, 1972, Frank Driggs Collection, FD-CASS-10, Marr Sound Archives, University of Missouri–Kansas City.

19. Robert Wahls, "Footlights," *NYDN*, July 4, 1976.

20. Norma Terris recollection, courtesy of Miles Kreuger.

21. Vinnie Liebler recollection, courtesy of Miles Kreuger.

22. Recording Academy, "Grammy Hall of Fame Award," accessed November 7, 2022, https://www.grammy.com/awards/hall-of-fame-award.

23. 6 W. Seventy-Seventh Street at Central Park West. "Park Av. Suites Rented," *NYT*, September 14, 1932.

24. Bernard Sobel, *Broadway Heartbeat: Memoirs of a Press Agent* (New York: Hermitage House, 1953), 127.

25. Marcia Winn, "Helen Morgan's Golden Career Ends Penniless," *CT*, October 10, 1941.

26. Louis Sobol, "The Voice of Broadway," *NYEJ*, September 16 and 19, 1932.

27. Odec, "Television Reviews," *Variety*, October 18, 1932.

28. Benn Hall, "Television," *BB,* October 22, 1932.

29. "Throng Surges to Opening of First Television Station," *Brooklyn Daily Times*, April 27, 1931.

30. Dorothy Dey, "Dots by Dey," *New York Press*, November 16, 1932.

31. Some sources spell the name Dixon. To be consistent, Dickson will be used throughout.

32. Helen C. Bower, "A Real Trouper, Helen Puts 'the Show' above Own Gain," *Detroit Free Press*, January 4, 1933.

33. "Helen Seeking Another Girl after Losing 2," *Pittsburgh Sunday Sun-Telegraph*, December 4, 1932.

34. Lloyd Lewis, "Helen Morgan Rides Piano to Save the *Show Boat*," *Chicago Daily News*, January 9, 1933.

35. Ashton Stevens, "Helen Morgan Worth Waiting For in *Show Boat*," *Chicago American*, January 9, 1933.

36. Alter, sound recording.

37. "Helen Morgan Bares Secret; World Hears," *Chicago Herald Examiner*, January 25, 1933.

38. Philip W. Porter, *Cleveland: Confused City on a Seesaw* (Columbus: Ohio State University Press, 1976), 48.

39. "To Wed La Morgan? Maschke Says: 'We're Just Friends,'" *Cleveland Free Press*, February 21, 1933.

40. "Art Arthur," *NYDM*, February 26, 1933.

41. "Night Club Prices under Police Here," *NYT*, February 28, 1933.

42. Unidentified newspaper clipping, ca. February 1933, MS/FLP, book 2, 44B.

43. "Cab Calloway's Band Is Booked for Dates Here," *Dallas Morning News*, March 3, 1933.

44. "Helen Morgan Sang for Mother While Perched on Ironing Board as Girl and Sits on Pianos Now," *Danville Commercial News*, July 16, 1933.

45. Joseph Mitchell, "Helen Morgan Got Two Fish as a Birthday Present and Then, Before She Knew It, She Had 22 Tanks Full," *NYWT*, March 15, 1933.

46. "Attempt to Slash Acts' Pay Seems Headed for the Rocks," *BB*, March 25, 1933, 6, 9.

47. John Lawson, "Helen Morgan Keeps *Show Boat* Afloat," *Chicago Daily News*, February 7, 1933.

48. "Cal York's Monthly Broadcast from Hollywood," *Photoplay*, August 1933, 88.

49. "Helen Morgan Returns," *NYT*, May 3, 1933.

50. "Death of Helen Morgan Recalls Marriage Here," *New Castle (PA) News*, October 9, 1941.

51. Maurice Maschke Jr. and Helen Morgan, "Marriage Certificate No. 32323" (Office of the County Clerk, Lawrence, PA, 1933).

52. Robert Sylvester, "Dream Street," *NYDN*, October 5, 1957.

12. "He's Just My Bud"

1. Embassy Club, 151 E. Fifty-Seventh. Margaret Case Harriman, *Blessed Are the Debonair* (New York: Rinehart, 1956), 235.

2. Paul Sann, *Kill the Dutchman! The Story of Dutch Schultz* (New Rochelle, NY: Arlington House, 1971), 202.

3. Herbert Asbury, *The Great Illusion: An Informal History of Prohibition* (Garden City, NY: Doubleday, 1950), 202.

4. Bob Harrington, letter to the author, December 8, 1991.

5. H. Allen Smith, *To Hell in a Handbasket* (Garden City, NY: Doubleday, 1962), 277.

6. Walter Scharf and Michael Freedland, *Composed and Conducted by Walter Scharf* (Totowa, NJ: Valentine, Mitchell, 1988), 15–19.

7. Walter Scharf, telephone interview, November 11, 1992.

8. Wahl recounted his relationship with Helen to Miles Kreuger. Blackwood's recollections are prevalent in Gilbert Maxwell, *Helen Morgan: Her Life and Legend* (New York: Hawthorn, 1974), 107–58.

9. "Prize Awards at Brooklyn Show," *NYA*, June 3, 1933.

10. Nominally produced by Billie Burke, it was actually a Shubert production. Herbert G. Goldman, *Fanny Brice: The Original Funny Girl* (New York: Oxford University Press, 1992), 155.

11. "Mike Fritzel Dies; Famed as Club Operator," *Chicago Sun Times*, September 29, 1956.

12. "Helen Morgan Wed to Maschke, Jr.," *CPD*, July 18, 1933.

13. Joe Mahar, "Sports," *Albany Times-Union*, August 9, 1933.

14. "As I Hear It," *Albany Evening News*, August 4 and 19, 1933.

15. Unidentified clipping, MS/FLP, book 2, 44B.

16. Nick Kenny, "La Morgan Conquers Hard-Boiled Mike," *NYDM*, November 27, 1933.

17. Ruth Etting topped the list for the second year in a row with 200 votes. Runners-up were Kate Smith (133), Ethel Waters (63), and Morgan (33). Kenneth Irwin and Charles O. Lloyd, *Ruth Etting: America's Forgotten Sweetheart* (Lanham, MD: Scarecrow, 2010), 155.

18. Arthur Tracy subbed for the rest of the week. "Theatrical Notes," *NYT*, October 30, 1933.

19. Hugh Martin, telephone interview, February 23, 1992.

20. The Morgan scrapbook contains an unidentified clipping surrounded by original Hoffman cartoons of a puzzled baby and stork. MS/FLP, book 3, 13A.

21. Louise Berliner, *Texas Guinan, Queen of the Night Clubs* (Austin: University of Texas Press, 1993), 194.

22. Joan and Clay Blair Jr., *The Search for JFK* (New York: Berkley, 1976), 33–34.

23. "Flies to Drink with Helen," *Des Moines Tribune*, December 6, 1933.

24. Herbert K. Cruickshank, "Mad, Glad Morgan," *Picture Play*, February 1935, 52, 75.

25. "Gotham Plans Brisk Parties for New Year," *MDN*, December 29, 1933.

26. "Along the Rialto," *TFD*, January 18, 1934, 6.

27. Jane Lenz Elder, *Alice Faye: A Life beyond the Silver Screen* (Jackson: University Press of Mississippi, 2002), 48–49.

28. Ben Gross, "Listening In," *NYDN*, February 9, 1934.

29. Mary O'Neill, "As I Hear It," *Albany Evening News*, February 9, 1934.

30. "Delayed by Illness," *Motion Picture Daily*, January 3, 1934, 8.

31. "Glamor of Filmland Returns to Bronx with Reopening of Biograph Studio," *Bronx Home News*, February 25, 1934.

32. Eve Golden, *Golden Images: 41 Essays on Silent Film Stars* (Jefferson, NC: McFarland, 2001), 180.

33. *Hell's Mothers*: Louis Sobol, "The Voice of Broadway," *NYEJ*, October 16, 1931. *Gallery Gods*: "Helen Morgan in Drama," *CT*, October 25, 1931.

34. Arthur Pollock, "The Theaters," *BDE*, December 1, 1931.

35. "Deborah League to Hold Theater Party When 'The Gallery God' Comes Here Dec. 7," *Newark (NJ) Jewish Chronicle*, November 27, 1931.

36. "Helen Morgan for Cooper," *Billboard*, October 31, 1931, 14.

37. Bernard Sobel, *Broadway Heartbeat: Memoirs of a Press Agent* (New York: Hermitage House, 1953), 127. Also Irving Hoffman, "The Town in Review," *NYMT*, May 25, 1932.

38. Noel Thornton, "Drama Will Test Censor's Attitude toward Broadway," *Buffalo News*, August 27, 1932; Regina Crewe, "Gotham Gossip of Films," *Boston Sunday Advertiser*, October 30, 1932.

39. Florence Lawrence, "Helen Morgan Ambitious," *Los Angeles Examiner*, May 6, 1934.

40. Victor covers include (1) "Here Am I," Leo Reisman & His Orchestra, 22187-B, rec. 9/20/1929; (2) "Twas Not So Long Ago," Nat Shilkret & His Orchestra, 22188-B, rec. 10/17/1929; (3) "I'm with You," 22816-A, Ted Black & His Orchestra, rec. 9/11/1931; (4) "Half-Caste Woman," 22819-A, Noel Coward, rec. September 1931; and (5) "What a Life," 22950-A, Coon-Sanders Orchestra, rec. 3/9/1932.

41. Bernard Sobel, "Helen Morgan an Artist with Wide Interests," *NYDM*, March 27, 1934.

42. Myron Fagan, *The Illuminati and the Counsel on Foreign Relations*, 1967, transcript, Jesus-Is-Savior, accessed December 28, 2022, https://www.jesus-is-savior.com/BTP/Myron_Fagan/illuminati_and_cfr.htm.

43. Because of the change of dates, Kay Hammond replaced Erin O'Brien-Moore. John Scott, "Wini Shaw Signed for Musical Show," *LAT*, April 17, 1934.

44. Edwin Schallert, "Pathos Achieved in Play," *LAT*, May 9, 1934.

45. "The New Plays," *THR*, May 9, 1934, 6.

46. "Helen Morgan to Face Charges before Equity," *Los Angeles Evening Post-Record*, May 14, 1934.

13. Hollywood

1. Advertisement, *TFD*, March 24, 1934, 2, and subsequent editions.

2. Louella O. Parsons, "James Cagney Is Making 'Hey, Sailor,' Picture on Battleship at Long Beach," *SFE*, April 4, 1934.

3. "Helen Morgan, Mills Bros. Go in 'Showboat,'" *Daily Variety*, May 21, 1934, 1.

4. "Warners Clears Title for *Sweet Adeline*," *THR*, May 3, 1934, 6.

5. Glenn C. Pullen, "Footlights and Bright Lights," *CPD*, May 23, 1934.

6. "Spencer Tracy Draws Severe Penalty," *Variety*, September 11, 1934, 3.

7. "Para. Signs Helen Morgan," *TFD*, June 15, 1934, 4.

8. "Helen Morgan Feared Mate Would Kill Her," *NYDN*, June 15, 1935.

9. "Coslow and Robin Set Record for Song Speed," *THR*, June 19, 1934, 5.

10. George Shaffer, "Anna Sten Dogs Cause Reprisal by Ann Sothern," *NYDN*, August 13, 1934.

11. Jacques Deval, *That Girl*, trans. Lawrence S. Morris (New York: Viking, 1932), originally published as *Marie Galante* (Paris: Albin Michel, 1931).

12. Sonya Levion and Samuel Hoffstein earmarked roles for Spencer Tracy, Ned Sparks, and Stepin Fetchit (who made the film) and Faye (who did not). *Marie Galante* draft, March 5, 1934, Fox/USC.

13. *Marie Galante* draft, June 20, 1934, Fox/USC.

14. John Mucci and Richard Felnagle, "Marie: Still Waiting . . ." *Kurt Weill Foundation for Music Newsletter*, Spring 1991, 14–16.

15. "Gorney Finishes Score," *THR*, July 31, 1934, 11.

16. No such script was ever produced. Regina Crewe, "Croon Princess of Song," *NYA*, August 12, 1934.

17. Henry King, based on interviews by David Shepard and Ted Perry, edited by Frank Thompson. *Henry King: Director; From Silents to 'Scope* (Los Angeles: Directors Guild of America, 1995), 88–91.

18. "Morgan Trial a Hit," *Variety*, August 28, 1934, 47.

19. "Equity Acquits Helen Morgan of Being Tipsy," *NYWT*, August 23, 1934.

20. "Helen Morgan Cleared by Arbitration Board," *BG*, August 23, 1934.

21. "Morgan Trial a Hit."

22. Card 357, June 1, 1934, MS/FLP, book 3, 27B.

23. Alan McElwain, "Opera Stars Ask Pay for Records," *Berkeley (CA) Daily Gazette*, April 2, 1935.

24. Morgan personnel file, WBA/USC.

25. *Lady in Waiting* file, L-48, 2706A, WBA/USC.

26. Tony Martin, Cyd Charisse, and Dick Kleiner, *The Two of Us* (New York: Mason/Charter, 1976), 50.

27. "So Local Boy (Bud Maschke) Comes Back to Make Good," unidentified Cleveland paper, September 1934, MS/FLP, book 3, 38B.

28. Sidney Andorn, "News of Clevelanders in Chicago," *Cleveland Press*, September 10, 1934.

29. Reduced from the original $500,000 budget, Warners' negative cost was $388,698. Final revised script, September 11, 1934, *Sweet Music* file, WBA/USC.

30. Henry Spitzer to Hal Wallis, September 12, 1934, *Sweet Music* file, WBA/USC.

31. Both Eddy Duchin and Russ Columbo (in his final session) recorded the tune in August 1934.

32. Edwin H. Morris to Hal Wallis, September 9, 1934, and additional music notes, October 10, 1934, *Sweet Music* file, WBA/USC.

33. Bradford Ropes, *Go into Your Dance* (New York: Alfred H. King, 1934).

34. Sidney Skolsky, "Hollywood," *NYDN*, August 27, 1934.

35. Dan Thomas, "Hit Elevates Director among High-Powered Few," *Los Angeles Evening Post-Record*, January 29, 1935.

36. Sam Bischoff to Koenig, November 23, 1934, *Go into Your Dance* file, WBA/USC.

37. "Films Go On Despite Fire," *LAT*, December 6, 1934.

38. Helen Morgan to Lulu Morgan, December 18, 1934, MS/FLP, box 2, folder 1.

39. "Likes Pup's Present," *Los Angeles Evening Post-Record*, December 31, 1934.

40. Herbert G. Goldman, *Jolson: The Legend Comes to Life* (New York: Oxford University Press, 1988), 220.

41. Charles Higham, *Bette: The Life of Bette Davis* (New York: MacMillan, 1981), vii.

42. Also budgeted at $500,000, the film hit a final estimated cost of $425,000. Daily memos, *Go into Your Dance* file, WBA/USC.

43. R. J. Obringer to Mr. Warner, January 23, 1935, Helen Morgan file, WBA/USC. In an earlier letter on January 7, Obringer supported Helen's request to pick up club work during what was assumed to be a period between films.

44. Other guest stars included Rudy Vallée, Dick Powell, and Phil Regan. Edwin Schallert, "Marlene Dietrich Will Play Empress Josephine if Napoleon Search Successful," *LAT*, February 6, 1935; *Radio Jamboree of 1935* file, WBA-USC.

45. Warners never altered the press kit to reflect the cut. "9 Catchy Airs Featured with Vallee Movie," *Kilgore (TX) News Herald*, November 21, 1935.

46. Ted Sennett, *Warner Brothers Presents* (New Rochelle, NY: Arlington House, 1972), 109.

47. "One for Bette Davis," *THR*, January 29, 1935, 8.

48. "Worth to Warners on Helen Morgan Story," *THR*, October 18, 1934, 11.

49. Vincent Lopez, *Lopez Speaking* (New York: Citadel, 1960), 283–86.

50. "Gang Killings Blast Miami's Biggest Gambling 'Boom,'" *Fort Lauderdale (FL) News*, March 15, 1935.

51. "Lewis Acquitted," *MT*, February 20, 1935.

52. "Pine Whitewashes Deauville Crowd," *MT*, March 19, 1935.

53. Reni, "Staying Up with the Stars," *MDN*, January 22, 1935.

54. Dorothy Dey, "Night and Day," *MT*, January 29 and 31, 1935. Also Erebus, "Fun after Dark," *MT*, February 3, 1935.

55. "Ritz Brothers Open in Deauville Event," unidentified clipping, February 1935, MS/FLP, book 3, 48A.

56. Erl Roman, "Angler Notes," *MH*, January 21, 1935.

57. Jimmy Starr, "Gaby Deslys' Life to Be Filmed; but Who'll Play Her," *San Francisco Call-Bulletin*, February 12, 1935.

58. Dey, "Night and Day."

59. Advertisement, *CT*, April 27, 1933, and subsequent issues.

60. "Helen Morgan Entertains at Beautiful Deauville," *MH*, February 13, 1935.

61. United Artists: "Sapolio for *Frankie and Johnny*," *Variety*, January 29, 1935, 3. Columbia: "Erskine Busy on Deal," *Motion Picture Daily*, April 24, 1934, 9.

62. Peter Stanfield, *Body and Soul: Jazz and Blues in American Film, 1927–63* (Urbana: University of Illinois Press, 2005), 55, 58.

63. V. G. Hart to Will Hays, March 20, 1934, *Frankie and Johnnie*, MPAA file, AMPAS/MHL.

64. Joseph I. Breen to Ben Goetz, October 8, 1934, *Frankie and Johnnie*, MPAA file, AMPAS/MHL.

65. "*Frankie and Johnnie* Wins in High Court," *NYT*, March 4, 1932.

66. "Helen Morgan to Make Film Built around Weeks Hall's Home," *New Orleans Item*, March 5, 1935.

67. Regina Crewe, "Helen Morgan in Town from Points South," *NYA*, March 6, 1935.

68. "New York Unit Sent Here by Plane for Scenes with Morris," *THR*, March 6, 1935, 4.

69. William Saal to the PCA, April 4, 1935, *Frankie and Johnnie*, MPAA file, AMPAS/MHL.

70. Joseph I. Breen to Select Productions, May 2, 1935, *Frankie and Johnnie*, MPAA file, AMPAS/MHL.

71. "*Frankie and Johnnie* Gets Eastern Preview," *THR*, May 18, 1935, 1.

72. "*Frankie and Johnnie* Okay: Should Do Plenty at the B.O.," *THR*, May 20, 1935, 3.

73. Leon & Eddie's: 33 W. Fifty-Second Street. Hugh Martin, telephone interview, February 23, 1992.

74. "Night Club Notes," *NYT*, April 6, 1935.

75. Versailles, 151 E. Fiftieth Street. Paul Harrison, "In New York," *Tulsa Tribune*, April 29, 1935.

76. "Helen Morgan Enjoys Work of Homemaking," unidentified newspaper, ca. May 1935, MS/FLP, book 3, 60B.

77. "Helen Morgan Sues to Divorce Maschke," *NYT*, April 5, 1935.

78. "Collette Suit Thrown Out by Judge; 'Sorry,'" *NYDN*, April 6, 1935.

79. Walter Winchell, "On Broadway," *Minneapolis Star Tribune*, April 16, 1935.

80. "New Films Reviewed," *BG*, April 20, 1935.

81. Club Normandie, 112 Central Park South by Sixth Avenue. "Helen Morgan Is Star at Normandie," *NYWT*, May 14, 1935.

82. W. S. Farnsworth, "Sidewalks of New York," *NYEJ*, n.d., MS/FLP, book 3, 56A.

14. The House of Morgan

1. "Helen Morgan Free," *SFE*, June 20, 1935.

2. "Poor Fish Help Maschke Divorce," *CPD*, June 20, 1935.

3. "Maschke, Jr. Is Silent on Suit," *CPD*, June 16, 1935.

4. Helen Maschke v. Maurice Maschke, "Interlocutory Judgment of Divorce, D130896" (Los Angeles Superior Cal. June 19, 1935).

5. Leonard Lyons, "The Lyons Den," *NYEP*, July 1, 1935.

6. Michael Mok, "'Marry? Never Again!' Is Helen Morgan's Refrain. But It's a Torch Song in Spite of Her Gaiety," *NYEP*, October 24, 1935.

7. Mary X. Sullivan, "Helen Morgan Tossed Gags in Battle to Beat Death," *Boston Advertiser*, October 12, 1941.

8. Jimmy Cannon, *Nobody Asked Me, But . . .: The World of Jimmy Cannon*, ed. Jack Cannon and Tom Cannon (New York: Holt, Rinehart and Winston, 1978), 289.

9. Jorge Sanchez to Helen Morgan, October 21, 1935, MS/FLP, box II, folder 1.

10. Walter Winchell, "On Broadway," *MT*, October 30, 1935.

11. The Loews separated on September 9, 1935. "Loew Sued for Alimony," *LAT*, October 25, 1935.

12. Elizabeth Collins, telephone interview, January 25, 1992.

13. Frederick Nolan, *Lorenz Hart: A Poet on Broadway* (New York: Oxford University Press, 1994), 208–209.

14. "A Novel Audition," *Broadcasting*, November 1, 1935, 10.

15. "Broadway," *THR*, November 4, 1935, 2.

16. The club stood at 49 East Fifty-Fourth Street. "The House of Morgan," *American Architect*, February 1936, 41–44.

17. Claude A. La Belle, "Star of Song Walks Room as She Learns New Piece," *San Francisco News*, July 29, 1935.

18. John Chapman, "Mainly about Manhattan," *NYDN*, November 9, 1935.

19. Oscar Hammerstein II to Carl Laemmle Jr., October 1, 1935, in *The Letters of Oscar Hammerstein II*, ed. Mark Eden Horowitz (New York: Oxford University Press, 2022), 98.

20. Carl Laemmle Jr. to Oscar Hammerstein II, December 2, 1935, OHA/LOC.

21. Joseph I. Breen to Harry Zehner, October 17, 1935, *Show Boat*, MPAA file, AMPAS/MHL.

22. Jerome Kern and Oscar Hammerstein II, *Show Boat*, as printed in *American Musicals 1927–1949* (New York: Library of America, 2014), 5–37.

23. Joseph I. Breen to Harry Zehner, November 15, 1935, and Zehner to Breen, December 14, 1935, *Show Boat*, MPAA file, AMPAS/MHL.

24. Jerome Kern and Oscar Hammerstein II, *Show Boat*, as rented by the Rodgers and Hammerstein Theatre Library (New York: Library of America, 1962), 6–34.

25. Todd Decker, *Show Boat: Performing Race in an American Musical* (New York: Oxford University Press, 2013), 102.

26. Ibid., 14.

27. A. R. D., "Theater Gossip," *St. Petersburg (FL) Evening Independent*, August 19, 1936.

28. Carl Laemmle Jr. to Oscar Hammerstein II, December 2, 1935, LOC/OHC.

29. Laemmle telegrammed Hammerstein on November 6: "Have you seen Morgan we probably will use her however have taken test of Libby Holman." Carl Laemmle Jr. to Oscar Hammerstein II, November 6, 1935, LOC/OHC.

30. Oscar Hammerstein II to Carl Laemmle Jr., December 4, 1935, LOC/OHC.

31. Allan Jones, telephone interview, 1991.

32. John Latham, telephone interview, May 17, 1992.

33. James Curtis, *James Whale: A New World of Gods and Monsters*, rev. ed. (Boston: Faber and Faber, 1998), 274.

34. Latham, telephone interview.

35. Curtis, *James Whale*, 274.

36. Latham, telephone interview.

37. Irving Hoffman, "Morgan the Magnificent, Croon Princess of Song," *NYA*, February 2, 1936.

38. Oscar Hammerstein II to James Whale, November 18, 1935, LOC/OHC.

39. Hedda Hopper also visited the "Bill" set. Latham, telephone interview.

40. "Blues Singer's Cat Ruins Her Career in Sea Fish," *Detroit News*, September 4, 1935.

41. "Business Records," *NYT*, November 16 & December 19, 1935.

42. L. L. Stevenson, "Daily Lights of New York," *Binghamton (NY) Press*, March 7, 1936.

43. George Ross, "Tips on Tables," *NYWT*, February 1, 1936.

44. Sam Coslow, *Cocktails for Two: The Many Lives of Giant Songwriter Sam Coslow* (New Rochelle, NY: Arlington House, 1977), 222.

45. Advertisement, *New York World-Telegram*, January 23, 1936.

46. "Business Records," *NYT*, January 30, March 2, March 13, & March 17, 1936.

47. Bernard Sobel, *Broadway Heartbeat: Memoirs of a Press Agent* (New York: Hermitage House, 1953), 127.

48. George Spelvin, "Broadway Beat," *BB*, March 7, 1936, 24.

49. Walter Winchell, "On Broadway," *Glens Falls (NY) Post-Star*, March 21, 1936.

50. Dorothy Dey, "Night and Day," *MT*, December 12, 1935.

51. Walter Winchell, "On Broadway," *MT*, May 3, 1936.

52. Erebus, "Fun after Dark," *MT*, March 8 and 11, 1936.

53. Collins, telephone interview.

54. Gay Knight, "Engaging Show Takes Floor with Three Stars at Chez Paree," *Chicago Herald and Examiner*, March 23, 1936.

55. "Pinned His Faith on Helen Morgan," *NYS*, October 16, 1936.

56. "Luciano Had Slice of Helen Morgan's Club," *NYDN*, October 31, 1936.

57. Harry Kannen, Murray Geller, and Henry Kannensohn v. Gilbert W. Kahn and Oheka Corporation, "Points of Plaintiffs-Respondents" (N.Y. App. Div. April 1, 1938).

58. Paul Holt, "Ace Blues Singer Is Here," *London Daily Express*, April 16, 1937.

15. More Scandals

1. Abel Green, "*Show Boat*," *Variety*, May 20, 1936, 12.

2. James Kirkland, *Frankie and Johnnie*, NCOF+, BRTD/NYPL.

3. *Frankie and Johnnie*, cue sheet 11,569, LTP/BYU.

4. John H. Auer and William Saal, *Frankie*, screenplay, with additional material by Lewis Graham, BRTD/NYPL.

5. "*Frankie and Johnnie* at the Globe," *NYT*, May 25, 1936.

6. "Frankie Who Says She Shot Johnny Sues for $200,000," *St. Louis Star and Times*, October 14, 1939.

7. "Amid the Suffering," *St. Louis Post-Dispatch*, October 19, 1899.

8. For all things Frankie Baker, see "Frankie Shot Johnny," *BluesLetter*, July 2013, https://stlouisbluessociety.org/blogs/the-st-louis-blues-society-bluesletter/posts/bluesletter-number-61-july-2013-online-edition.

9. "Folklore Expert Testifies Woman Is 'Frankie' of Ballad Fame," *St. Louis Globe-Democrat*, February 18, 1942.

10. "Frankie Baker Loses in Suit for $200,000," *St. Louis Star and Times*, February 24, 1942.

11. Lloyd Lewis, "Handsome Women," *CDN*, June 29, 1936.

12. Loop, "Out of Town," *Variety*, July 8, 1936, 46.

13. Jack Yellen and Ray Henderson, *I've Got to Get Hot*, (New York: Harms, 1935,) 5.

14. Kenneth Irwin and Charles O. Lloyd, *Ruth Etting: America's Forgotten Sweetheart* (Lanham, MD: Scarecrow, 2010), 176–81.

15. "Beauty Chorus Wins Audience at *Scandals*," *Rockford Register-Republic*, September 17, 1936; Byron Troyer, "Palace Rocks to Applause at Presentation," *South Bend News-Times*, September 18, 1936.

16. June Provines, "Front Views and Profiles," *CT*, August 7, 1936.

17. Eleanor Nangle, "Through the Looking Glass," *CT*, July 19, 1936.

18. Lily May Caldwell, "Helen Can Sing without Sitting on a Piano but Doesn't Like To," *Birmingham News*, November 30, 1936.

19. Rider Richmond, "Times Better, Says Singer," *Des Moines Register*, September 27, 1936.

20. "Mad, Mad, MAD!," *SFE*, October 12, 1936.

21. John Hobart, "Scandal's a Hit," *San Francisco Chronicle*, October 12, 1936.

22. Betty Turner, "A Chat with Helen Morgan," *San Francisco Chronicle*, October 20, 1936.

23. Roy P. Drachman, *Just Memories* (self-pub., 1979), 132.

24. "Names Make News," *Time*, December 14, 1936, https://content.time.com/time/subscriber/article/0,33009,757166,00.html.

25. Jack L. Hart, "When Helen Morgan Tosses a Party, It's a Real One," *Austin (TX) American*, November 20, 1936.

26. The Morgans closed on the house, valued at $50,000 and located at 466 E. Eighteenth, on November 1, 1936. "Helen Morgan Buys Home in Flatbush," *BDE*, October 14, 1936.

27. Ed Sullivan, "Broadway," *NYDN*, January 4 & 18, 1937.

28. "News of the Stage," *NYT*, January 5, 1937.

29. "Republic Discovers New Faces," *PP*, October 13, 1937.

30. George Tucker, "About New York," *OT*, April 7, 1937.

31. "Weepy Helen Morgan Sails, Sobbing of Exile and Love," *NYEP*, April 7, 1937.

32. Helen Morgan passport 384629 (work visa 5014, April 6, 1937), LJS.

33. R. E., "Helen Morgan Back after 10 Years," *London Daily Express*, April 20, 1937.

34. H. H., "Our Show Boat," *London Observer*, April 25, 1937.

35. R. E., "Helen Morgan Back after 10 Years."

36. Dorothy Day, “Londoners Sour on Top Hat Mardi Gras,” *MT*, May 12, 1937.

37. Marjorie Adams, “Helen Morgan Sang for Group in Dublin Alley,” *BG*, October 28, 1937.

38. Rudy Vallée, *Let the Chips Fall* (Harrisburg, PA: Stackpole, 1975), 151.

39. Dorothy Kilgallen, “London Has Been Virtually Taken Over by Yankees,” *St. Louis Star and Times*, May 6, 1937.

40. “Helen Morgan Back Home Bitter over British Wages,” *NYEP*, May 26, 1937.

16. "Tired of Livin' and Scared of Dyin'"

1. Clark Rodenbach, “Favorites, New-Old,” *CDN*, July 3, 1937.

2. Clark Rodenbach, “Melodious Melancholy from Helen Morgan,” *CDN*, August 23, 1937.

3. Gold, “Chez Paree, Chi,” *Variety*, August 14, 1937, 58; Sam Honigberg, “Oriental, Chicago,” *BB*, August 28, 1937, 20.

4. “Helen Morgan Taken Ill; in Hospital,” *CDN*, August 24, 1937.

5. 157 W. Fifty-Sixth Street, formally the Club Richman. Abel Green, “Café El Dorado, N. Y.,” *Variety*, September 22, 1937, 48.

6. Dorothy Dey, “Night and Day,” *NYMT*, November 16, 1937.

7. Walter Winchell, “On Broadway,” *NYDM*, November 30, 1937—the first of many tellings of this story.

8. “‘H’wood Hotel’ Unit Sues WB over Title,” *Variety*, January 19, 1938, 4.

9. Nelson B. Bell, “A Celebrated Singing Star Comes to Town, Is Feted, Displays Some Unique Trinkets, and Makes a Present,” *WaPo*, February 10, 1938.

10. “News of the Theater,” *New York Herald-Tribune*, July 5, 1938.

11. Diana Altman, *Hollywood East: Louis B. Mayer and the Origins of the Studio System* (New York: Birch Lane, 1992), 261.

12. Arthur Loew, undated letter, ca. 1937–1928, MS/FLP, box 2, folder 1.

13. Elizabeth Collins, telephone interview, January 25, 1992.

14. Arthur Loew Jr., telephone interview, November 18, 1993.

15. Stephen Nelson, *Only a Paper Moon: The Theatre of Billy Rose* (Ann Arbor, MI: UMI Research Press, 1987), 81.

16. Robert Sylvester, “All-Star Vaudeville Is Revived by Rose in Cabaret Setting,” *NYDN*, May 2, 1938.

17. Fay Feidler, “Death Stills Famous Voice of Helen Morgan, Who Sang in Danville Choir as Girl,” *Danville Commercial-News*, October 9, 1941.

18. Thomas Kelland, “Helen Morgan Left Friends, No Money,” *NYWT*, October 10, 1941.

19. Lulu M. Payne v. Frank P Payne, “Bill for Divorce, No. 37S14629” (Cook Cnty. Ill. Superior 1938).

20. Frank P. Payne, “Death Certificate No. 5997” (New York State Board of Health, March 16, 1938).

21. Jack Pierce, “Helen Morgan Buys Property at High Falls,” *Ulster County (NY) Press*, September 9, 1938.

22. "Gives Blood to Helen Morgan," *Chicago Herald American*, September 20, 1941.

23. "Helen Morgan Refugee from Flood Here in Need of Shoes," *San Francisco Chronicle*, October 5, 1938.

24. Betty Hutton, *Backstage You Can Have: My Own Story*, with Carol Bruno and Michael Mayer (self-pub., 2009), 110–11.

25. Multiple *NYDN* advertisements: Fifth billing, November 4–December 3, 1938; second, December 4–17, 1938; third, December 18–20, 1938.

26. "*Varieties* Draw," *Newark (NJ) Evening News*, December 31, 1938.

27. Dale Harrison, "Dale Harrison's New York," *OT*, February 9, 1939.

28. A year later, Helen economized further, subleasing the duplex and taking up residence a few blocks away at 74 Bank Street. "Leases 14 Rooms in East Side House," *NYT*, March 21, 1940.

29. Clark Rodenbach, "One Hen Won't Work," *CDN*, December 27, 1938.

30. Maybelle Manning, "Talk of the Tower," *MDN*, July 8, 1941.

31. C. J. Bulliet, "Trio of Geniuses," *CDN*, February 11, 1939.

32. Sam Honigberg, "Chez Paree, Chicago," *BB*, February 18, 1939, 19.

33. Harrison Carroll, "Behind the Scenes in Hollywood," *Vineland (NJ) Daily Journal*, July 5, 1939.

34. "Pretty Sick Girl," *Los Angeles Citizen-News*, August 16, 1939.

35. Specifically, Louella Parson, "Two Studios Share Ida Lupino Contract," *Philadelphia Inquirer*, September 20, 1940; and "Walter Winchell . . . on Broadway," *Cincinnati Enquirer*, September 9 and November 15, 1940.

36. "Revise of Words for 'Over There' Saves Production," *Waterloo Courier*, October 3, 1939.

37. Weber, "*Moulin Rouge* Break-In Rough, but Show Has Real Possibilities," *BB*, October 14, 1939, 5, 60.

38. Allen Hoschar, "Ragged Night at Moulin Rouge," *Des Moines Register*, October 4, 1939.

39. RHS, "Superb Dancing in Forum Show," *Wichita Eagle*, November 22, 1939.

40. Maureen Englin, "I Remember Helen Morgan," *Rock Island (IL) Argus*, September 18, 1971.

41. Wood Soanes, "Paris 'Trip' Offered by New Show," *OT*, October 24, 1939.

42. "Hollywood Chat," *Hayward (CA) Daily Review*, November 1, 1939.

43. The unit folded on March 7, 1940. "*Moulin Rouge* Folds in Atlanta," *BB*, March 23, 1940, 17.

44. Elliott Arnold, "Helen Morgan's Sick of 'Her Bill,'" *NYWT*, March 9, 1940.

45. "Helen Morgan Doesn't Dazzle North Robinson like Broadway," *Daily Oklahoman*, November 21, 1939.

46. Cecil Smith, "Chicago to See Comedy before New York Does," *CT*, January 28, 1940.

47. Helen Morgan, "I'm Through with Music Forever," *Music and Rhythm*, August 1941, 18.

48. Mary X. Sullivan, "She Had Only 6 Months to Live," *Green Magazine, Boston Sunday Advertiser*, December 24, 1939, 3.

49. Dorothy Kilgallen, "The Voice of Broadway," *Mansfield (OH) News-Journal*, March 5, 1940.

50. Arnold, "Helen Morgan's Sick of 'Her Bill.'"

51. Carlotta Dale, interview, *First Ladies of Radio: Helen Morgan, Program #11*, CD-199, Redmond Nostalgia, Redmond, WA.

52. Lillian Roth, *Beyond My Worth* (New York: Frederick Fell, 1958), 105–6.

53. John Kinloch, "*Show Boat* Tugs into Philharmonic under Full Steam," *California Eagle* (Los Angeles), May 16, 1940.

54. John Latham, telephone interview, May 17, 1992.

55. "Night Club Notes," *MDN*, July 19, 1940.

56. Ardus Smith, "Seven More Stage Shows Booked by 20th Century," *Buffalo News*, September 25, 1940.

57. "Helen Morgan Not Paid Off by K.K.K.," *Variety*, October 2, 1940, 1, 63.

58. "Respiratory tract": "Torch Singer Seriously Ill in Hospital," *Buffalo News*, November 11, 1940. "Intestinal ailment": "Helen Morgan Critically Ill in California," *BDE*, November 11, 1940.

59. Lou Bring, Helen Morgan home recording, October 15, 1940, IAM/MK.

60. "Helen Better," *Variety*, November 20, 1940, 2.

61. Gene Coughlin, "Tragedies of the Stage," *American Weekly*, September 4, 1949.

62. Mary X. Sullivan, "Helen Morgan Tossed Gags in Battle to Beat Death," *Boston Advertiser*, October 12, 1941.

63. "Helen Morgan to Wed West Coast Motor Car Man in August," *BG*, March 20, 1941.

64. Helen Morgan Enterprises, "Articles of Incorporation" (Secretary of State, Sacramento, CA, December 6, 1940).

65. Also in *Crazy with the Heat* were Gracie Barrie and Helen Hudson, each making their final Broadway appearances. "'My Fair Ladies' Here Tomorrow," *NYT*, March 22, 1941; "'Fiddler's House' Offered Tonight," *NYT*, March 27, 1941.

66. Multiple receipts and notes, LJS.

67. Sullivan, "Helen Morgan Tossed Gags."

68. George Holard, "Boston after Dark," *Boston Evening American*, March 18, 1941.

69. Servicemen requests: PFC Jim Cozzola, Co G, 132nd Infantry; Bill Evanchuck, 35 Field Artillery, Battery F (Brooklyn) July 30, 1941; and Private Anthony C Pennucci, 4th Platoon Company D, 29th Infantry, August 12, 1941. LJS.

70. Bob Dillner to Helen Morgan, May 18, 1941, LJS.

71. Louis Falkenstein and Helen Morgan, Hi-Hat Club contract, April 18, 1941, LJS.

72. "Helen Morgan Feared Near Death in Chicago," *Syracuse (NY) Herald-American*, September 21, 1941.

73. Charles Champlin, "Smiling Liberace Has Last Laugh," *LAT*, July 7, 1965.

74. "Broadway," *Variety*, August 7, 1940, 45.

75. Lloyd Johnson v. Catharine Johnson, "Final Decree, No. 69931-D" (Dade Cir. Fla. July 24, 1941).

76. "Helen Morgan Marries as Miami Beach Mob Stands By," *Tampa Tribune*, July 28, 1941.

77. "Pushes His P. A. Into Pool—Just for a Laugh," *BB*, August 9, 1941, 24.

78. Dudley Glass, "Helen Morgan at Paradise Room," *Atlanta Constitution*, August 9, 1941.

79. Bethany Hospital receipt, LJS.

80. Mark Johnson, telephone interview, April 20, 1994.

81. Philip K. Scheuer, "A Town Called Hollywood," *LAT*, March 10, 1957.

82. "Fight for Life," *Detroit Evening Times*, September 22, 1941.

83. Edward Vincent Daily, *The Pastor's Cat and Other People* (Milwaukee: Bruce, 1955), 44–45.

84. "Helen Morgan Has Serious Operation," *LAT*, September 26, 1941.

85. "Public Funeral Arranged for Helen Morgan," *Pittsburgh Sun-Telegraph*, October 9, 1941.

86. Olga Swanson to Jack Warner, June 10, 1957, *Helen Morgan Story* file, WBA/USC.

87. Helen Morgan, "Death Certificate No. 27331" (Illinois State Board of Health, October 8, 1941).

Epilogue: Broadway's Patron Saint

1. Walter Scharf, telephone interview, November 11, 1992.

2. "High and Low Pay Respects at Last Rites for Helen Morgan," *Detroit Free Press*, October 12, 1941.

3. "Last Rites Held for Helen Morgan," *MDN*, October 11, 1941.

4. Donald Rosenberg, *The Cleveland Orchestra Story: Second to None* (Cleveland: Gray, 2000), 68.

5. "*Scandals* Company Attends Mass Here for Helen Morgan," *Davenport (IA) Daily Times*, November 8, 1941.

6. "Chicago Briefs," *Chicago Sun*, December 14, 1942.

7. "High Falls," *Kingston (NY) Daily Freeman*, April 24, 1948.

8. Marcia Winn, "Helen Morgan's Golden Career Ends Penniless," *CT*, October 10, 1941.

9. "George White Says He's Broke," *LAT*, June 10, 1942.

10. Helen E. Johnson, née Morgan, "Decree—Judicial Settlement No. 1821" (Office of the Surrogate Court, County of Ulster, NY, October 22, 1952).

11. Earl Wilson, "It Happened Last Night," *NYEP*, October 10, 1943.

12. Charles Adams and Lulu Morgan, "Marriage Certificate No. 43658" (Office of the County Clerk, Kingston, NY, 1948).

13. Miles Kreuger, *"Show Boat": The Story of a Classic American Musical*, rev. ed. (New York: Da Capo, 1990), 155.

14. Warner Brothers and Lulu Morgan contract, May 22, 1942, *Helen Morgan Story* file, WBA/USC.

15. Mark Hellinger to James Geller, May 28 & August 24, 1942, *Helen Morgan Story* file, WBA/USC.

16. Erskine Johnson, "In Hollywood," *Ironwood (MT) Daily Globe*, April 28, 1944.

17. "More Indies Here," *Independent Exhibitors Film Bulletin*, March 1, 1948, 14.

18. "5-Film Program for New Fidelity Pictures," *Variety*, March 8, 1950, 4.

19. *The Girl on the Piano*: Ted Sherdeman to Steve Trilling, November 25, 1952, WBA/USC. *Why Was I Born?*: Finlay McDermid to Richard Whorf, May 18, 1955, WBA/USC. *The Jazz Age*: "'Helen Morgan' Retitled," *THR*, December 31, 1956, 7.

20. David Shipman, *Judy Garland: The Secret Life of an American Legend* (New York: Hyperion, 1993), 38.

21. John Fricke, *Judy: A Legendary Film Career* (Philadelphia: Running Press, 2010), 213.

22. Short list of possible casting choices, *Helen Morgan Story* file, WBA/USC.

23. James Bacon, "Ann Blyth Given Helen Morgan Role," *Charlotte Observer*, September 15, 1957.

24. Alan K. Rode, *Michael Curtiz: A Life in Film* (Lexington: University Press of Kentucky, 2017), 510–11.

25. Letters dated September 19, 1952, and April 17, 1956, *Helen Morgan Story*, MPAA file, AMPAS/MHL.

26. Milton Sperling, directive dated October 21, 1954, *Helen Morgan Story* file, WBA/USC.

27. Roy Obringer to H. E. Holman, March 8, 1957, *Helen Morgan Story* file, WBA/USC.

28. Nathan Cohn to Warner Brothers Studio, May 10, 1957, *Helen Morgan Story* file, WBA/USC.

29. Lulu Morgan to Warner Brothers, November 12, 1956, *Helen Morgan Story* file, WBA/USC.

30. R. J. Obringer to Jack Warner, February 8, 1957, *Helen Morgan Story* file, WBA/USC.

31. Jack Warner to Roy Obringer, February 4, 1957, *Helen Morgan Story* file, WBA/USC.

32. Name change to *Both Ends of the Candle*: Jack Warner, memo to all departments, May 24, 1957, *Helen Morgan Story* file, WBA/USC. Name change to *The Helen Morgan Story*: Jack Warner, memo to all departments, June 19, 1957, *Helen Morgan Story* file, WBA/USC. Warners released the film as *Both Ends of the Candle* abroad.

33. Pete Rahn, "Polly Made Hard Battle for 'Helen Morgan' Story," *St. Louis Globe-Democrat*, May 12, 1957.

34. Charles Mercer, "Helen Morgan's Life Story TV'd Tonight," *Los Angeles Examiner*, May 16, 1957.

35. Dorothy Kilgallen, "Polly Bergen, Network Face Lawsuit," *WaPo*, August 9, 1957.

36. Dale Foster, "Career of City's Helen Morgan to Be Featured on *Playhouse 90* Nationwide TV Thursday," *Danville Commercial-News*, May 14, 1957.

37. Irving Drutman, "Specter of Helen Morgan Haunts Carol Bruce in *Show Boat* Role," *New York Tribune*, January 20, 1946.

38. Bruce also competed in the leading actress category. The *Billboard*, which sponsored the Donaldsons, published the results in order of votes received but did not include the vote count. For Best Actress, Bruce came in third, after Mitzi Green

(*Million Dollar Baby*) and the winner, Betty Garrett (*Call Me Mister*). Jan Clayton, who played Magnolia, came in sixth. "... And the Runners-Up," *BB*, July 27, 1946, 49.

39. Hugh Fordin, *MGM's Greatest Musicals: The Arthur Freed Unit* (New York: Da Capo, 1996), 334.

40. *Marie Galante* reissue: "*Marie Galante* Revived at News," *Philadelphia Inquirer*, June 1, 1942. *The Doctor* reissue: "New and Recent Releases," *BB*, January 30, 1943, 28. *Go into Your Dance* reissue: "Down Lane of Memories," *Pittsburgh Post-Gazette*, June 13, 1947.

41. TV syndication debuts as early as *Glorifying the American Girl*, WKRC-Cincinnati, *Cincinnati Enquirer*, May 27, 1961; *Roadhouse Nights*, WKRC-Cincinnati, *Cincinnati Enquirer*, March 30, 1962; *Frankie and Johnnie*, WABD New York, *BDE*, February 7, 1951; *You Belong to Me*, WBIR Knoxville, *Knoxville (TN) Journal*, July 19, 1958; *Marie Galante*, WHTM Harrisburg, *Carlisle (PA) Evening Sentinel*, February 2, 1961; *Sweet Music*, KPTV Salem Oregon, *Salem (OR) Statesman Journal*, July 2, 1957; *Go into Your Dance*, KTVU San Francisco, *SFE*, October 26, 1958.

42. On the flip side were seven Fanny Brice cuts, three of which Barbra Streisand sang in the 1968 *Funny Girl* film.

43. Earl Wilson, "Irv Hoffman Revered for His Kindness," *Detroit Free Press*, December 13, 1968.

44. Pickford: Erskine Johnson, "In Hollywood," *Helena (MT) Independent-Record*, April 18, 1945. Murray: "Helen Morgan's Daughter Given Secretary Job," *LAT*, May 1, 1945.

45. "Producer George White Files in Bankruptcy," *Fresno (CA) Bee*, December 29, 1953.

46. George White, "Mosby In Hollywood," *Nevada State Journal* (Reno), December 27, 1956.

47. Dorothy Kilgallen, "Scandals May Fold Soon," *Cincinnati Enquirer*, October 21, 1963.

48. "400 Small Boats Lent for War Jobs," *NYT*, February 15, 1942.

49. Helen Zigmond, "Our Film Folk Go to War," *Canadian Jewish Chronicle*, September 11, 1942, 80. Also, "Of Local Origin," *NYT*, June 20. 1944.

50. William Zeh v. Sarah Zeh, "Decree for Divorce, B-131657" (Cook Cir. Ill. January 1926).

51. Michael Newton, *Mr. Mob: The Life and Crimes of Moe Dalitz* (Jefferson, NC: McFarland, 2007), 99.

52. Hud Robbins, "Daughter of Danville's Brightest Star in Theatrical World Gains Own Fame at Attica with Old Spinning Wheel," *Danville Commercial-News*, July 17, 1938.

53. Frank Allen Riggin, "Death Certificate No. 30788" (Indiana State Board of Health, 1947).

54. Lulu Morgan Adams, "Death Certificate No. 156-78-104838" (New York State Board of Health, March 20, 1978).

55. Thomas Kelland, "Helen Morgan Left Friends, No Money," *NYWT*, October 10, 1941.

Appendix 1

1. Chorus Equity did not require that choristers be listed in playbills until the 1924–1925 season. Helen Morgan may have played the entire run but more likely hired on as a replacement in June or during the grueling schedule of one- and two-night stands in October and November. Morgan was in the cast when it closed in Kansas City on December 18, 1920, with the cast listed above.

2. Helen Morgan's start date in this production remains unclear. Most likely, she hired on late in the Chicago run. In any event, the Shuberts trimmed the cast during the Montreal stand.

3. Production played the week of May 20–25 at San Francisco's Curran, with Ava Josette taking over as Julie.

4. Booked for the week, she withdrew after the first day because of illness.

5. Sunday pickup performance due to Pennsylvania blue laws.

Appendix 3

1. Morgan missed the October 29, 1933, and February 18, 1934, broadcasts because of illness. Tess Gardella replaced her.

2. Nightclub broadcasts usually highlighted the orchestras. Confirmed Morgan broadcasts are in bold.

3. The series did not continue while Morgan was on the road with Sh*ow Boat*.

4. First day broadcast from New York's first television station.

Appendix 5

1. Hiatus due to illness.

Appendix 6

1. Extra matinee performance of *Sweet Adeline* to benefit the Actors' Fund.

Index

Page number in italics refer to illustrations.

Screen Classics

Screen Classics is a series of critical biographies, film histories, and analytical studies focusing on neglected filmmakers and important screen artists and subjects, from the era of silent cinema through the golden age of Hollywood to the international generation of today. Books in the Screen Classics series are intended for scholars and general readers alike. The contributing authors are established figures in their respective fields. This series also serves the purpose of advancing scholarship on film personalities and themes with ties to Kentucky.

Series Editor

Patrick McGilligan

Books in the Series

Olivia de Havilland: Lady Triumphant
Victoria Amador
Mae Murray: The Girl with the Bee-Stung Lips
Michael G. Ankerich
Harry Dean Stanton: Hollywood's Zen Rebel
Joseph B. Atkins
Hedy Lamarr: The Most Beautiful Woman in Film
Ruth Barton
Rex Ingram: Visionary Director of the Silent Screen
Ruth Barton
Conversations with Classic Film Stars: Interviews from Hollywood's Golden Era
James Bawden and Ron Miller
Conversations with Legendary Television Stars: Interviews from the First Fifty Years
James Bawden and Ron Miller
They Made the Movies: Conversations with Great Filmmakers
James Bawden and Ron Miller
You Ain't Heard Nothin' Yet: Interviews with Stars from Hollywood's Golden Era
James Bawden and Ron Miller
Charles Boyer: The French Lover
John Baxter
Von Sternberg
John Baxter
Hitchcock's Partner in Suspense: The Life of Screenwriter Charles Bennett
Charles Bennett, edited by John Charles Bennett
Hitchcock and the Censors
John Billheimer

A Uniquely American Epic: Intimacy and Action, Tenderness and Violence in Sam Peckinpah's The Wild Bunch
Edited by Michael Bliss
My Life in Focus: A Photographer's Journey with Elizabeth Taylor and the Hollywood Jet Set
Gianni Bozzacchi with Joey Tayler
Hollywood Divided: The 1950 Screen Directors Guild Meeting and the Impact of the Blacklist
Kevin Brianton
He's Got Rhythm: The Life and Career of Gene Kelly
Cynthia Brideson and Sara Brideson
Ziegfeld and His Follies: A Biography of Broadway's Greatest Producer
Cynthia Brideson and Sara Brideson
Eleanor Powell: Born to Dance
Paula Broussard and Lisa Royère
The Marxist and the Movies: A Biography of Paul Jarrico
Larry Ceplair
Dalton Trumbo: Blacklisted Hollywood Radical
Larry Ceplair and Christopher Trumbo
Warren Oates: A Wild Life
Susan Compo
Helen Morgan: The Original Torch Singer and Ziegfeld's Last Star
Christopher S. Connelly
Improvising Out Loud: My Life Teaching Hollywood How to Act
Jeff Corey with Emily Corey
Crane: Sex, Celebrity, and My Father's Unsolved Murder
Robert Crane and Christopher Fryer
Jack Nicholson: The Early Years
Robert Crane and Christopher Fryer
Anne Bancroft: A Life
Douglass K. Daniel
Being Hal Ashby: Life of a Hollywood Rebel
Nick Dawson
Bruce Dern: A Memoir
Bruce Dern with Christopher Fryer and Robert Crane
Intrepid Laughter: Preston Sturges and the Movies
Andrew Dickos
The Woman Who Dared: The Life and Times of Pearl White, Queen of the Serials
William M. Drew
Miriam Hopkins: Life and Films of a Hollywood Rebel
Allan R. Ellenberger
Vitagraph: America's First Great Motion Picture Studio
Andrew A. Erish
Jayne Mansfield: The Girl Couldn't Help It
Eve Golden
John Gilbert: The Last of the Silent Film Stars
Eve Golden
Strictly Dynamite: The Sensational Life of Lupe Velez
Eve Golden
Stuntwomen: The Untold Hollywood Story
Mollie Gregory
Jean Gabin: The Actor Who Was France
Joseph Harriss
Yves Montand: The Passionate Voice
Joseph Harriss

Otto Preminger: The Man Who Would Be King, updated edition
Foster Hirsch
Saul Bass: Anatomy of Film Design
Jan-Christopher Horak
Lawrence Tierney: Hollywood's Real-Life Tough Guy
Burt Kearns
Hitchcock Lost and Found: The Forgotten Films
Alain Kerzoncuf and Charles Barr
Pola Negri: Hollywood's First Femme Fatale
Mariusz Kotowski
Ernest Lehman: The Sweet Smell of Success
Jon Krampner
Sidney J. Furie: Life and Films
Daniel Kremer
Albert Capellani: Pioneer of the Silent Screen
Christine Leteux
A Front Row Seat: An Intimate Look at Broadway, Hollywood, and the Age of Glamour
Nancy Olson Livingston
Ridley Scott: A Biography
Vincent LoBrutto
Mamoulian: Life on Stage and Screen
David Luhrssen
Maureen O'Hara: The Biography
Aubrey Malone
My Life as a Mankiewicz: An Insider's Journey through Hollywood
Tom Mankiewicz and Robert Crane
Hawks on Hawks
Joseph McBride
John Ford
Joseph McBride and Michael Wilmington
Showman of the Screen: Joseph E. Levine and His Revolutions in Film Promotion
A. T. McKenna
William Wyler: The Life and Films of Hollywood's Most Celebrated Director
Gabriel Miller
Raoul Walsh: The True Adventures of Hollywood's Legendary Director
Marilyn Ann Moss
Veit Harlan: The Life and Work of a Nazi Filmmaker
Frank Noack
Harry Langdon: King of Silent Comedy
Gabriella Oldham and Mabel Langdon
Mavericks: Interviews with the World's Iconoclast Filmmakers
Gerald Peary
Charles Walters: The Director Who Made Hollywood Dance
Brent Phillips
Some Like It Wilder: The Life and Controversial Films of Billy Wilder
Gene D. Phillips
Ann Dvorak: Hollywood's Forgotten Rebel
Christina Rice
Mean . . . Moody . . . Magnificent! Jane Russell and the Marketing of a Hollywood Legend
Christina Rice
Fay Wray and Robert Riskin: A Hollywood Memoir
Victoria Riskin

Lewis Milestone: Life and Films
Harlow Robinson
Michael Curtiz: A Life in Film
Alan K. Rode
Ryan's Daughter: *The Making of an Irish Epic*
Paul Benedict Rowan
Arthur Penn: American Director
Nat Segaloff
Film's First Family: The Untold Story of the Costellos
Terry Chester Shulman
Claude Rains: An Actor's Voice
David J. Skal with Jessica Rains
Barbara La Marr: The Girl Who Was Too Beautiful for Hollywood
Sherri Snyder
Lionel Barrymore: Character and Endurance in Hollywood's Golden Age
Kathleen Spaltro
Buzz: The Life and Art of Busby Berkeley
Jeffrey Spivak
Victor Fleming: An American Movie Master
Michael Sragow
Aline MacMahon: Hollywood, the Blacklist, and the Birth of Method Acting
John Stangeland
My Place in the Sun: Life in the Golden Age of Hollywood and Washington
George Stevens, Jr.
Hollywood Presents Jules Verne: The Father of Science Fiction on Screen
Brian Taves
Thomas Ince: Hollywood's Independent Pioneer
Brian Taves
Picturing Peter Bogdanovich: My Conversations with the New Hollywood Director
Peter Tonguette
Jessica Lange: An Adventurer's Heart
Anthony Uzarowski
Carl Theodor Dreyer and Ordet: My Summer with the Danish Filmmaker
Jan Wahl
Wild Bill Wellman: Hollywood Rebel
William Wellman Jr.
Harvard, Hollywood, Hitmen, and Holy Men: A Memoir
Paul W. Williams
The Warner Brothers
Chris Yogerst
Clarence Brown: Hollywood's Forgotten Master
Gwenda Young
The Queen of Technicolor: Maria Montez in Hollywood
Tom Zimmerman